**SAGE** was founded in 1965 by Sara Miller McCune to support the dissemination of usable knowledge by publishing innovative and high-quality research and teaching content. Today, we publish over 900 journals, including those of more than 400 learned societies, more than 800 new books per year, and a growing range of library products including archives, data, case studies, reports, and video. SAGE remains majority-owned by our founder, and after Sara's lifetime will become owned by a charitable trust that secures our continued independence.

Los Angeles | London | New Delhi | Singapore | Washington DC | Melbourne

# COMPARATIVE DEVELOPMENT *of* India & China

# COMPARATIVE DEVELOPMENT of India & China

## Economic, Technological, Sectoral and Socio-cultural Insights

EDITED BY
Neena Sondhi
Ramakrushna Panigrahi
Miao Pang
Rajashri Chatterjee

SAGE | spectrum

Los Angeles | London | New Delhi
Singapore | Washington DC | Melbourne

*First published in 2021 by*

SAGE | spectrum

**SAGE Publications India Pvt Ltd**
B1/I-1 Mohan Cooperative Industrial Area
Mathura Road, New Delhi 110 044, India
*www.sagepub.in*

**SAGE Publications Inc**
2455 Teller Road
Thousand Oaks, California 91320, USA

**SAGE Publications Ltd**
1 Oliver's Yard, 55 City Road
London EC1Y 1SP, United Kingdom

**SAGE Publications Asia-Pacific Pte Ltd**
18 Cross Street #10-10/11/12
China Square Central
Singapore 048423

**International Management Institute Kolkata**, 2/4 C Judges Court Road, Alipore, Kolkata 700027, India

**International Management Institute Delhi**, B-10, Qutab Institutional Area, Tara Crescent, New Delhi - 110016, India

**International Management Institute Bhubaneswar**, IDCO Plot No. 1, Gothapatna, PO: Malipada, Dist.: Khurda, Bhubaneswar - 751003, India

**Sichuan Academy of Social Sciences**, West Yihuan Road 155#, Qingyang District, Chengdu, Sichuan Province, P.R. China 610072

Published by Vivek Mehra for SAGE Publications India Pvt Ltd. Typeset in 10.5/13 pt Adobe Caslon Pro by AG Infographics, Delhi.

**Library of Congress Control Number: 2020951171**

**ISBN:** 978-93-5388-606-6 (HB)

# Contents

## Part III: Socio-cultural Insights

# Preface

India and China, these two great nations with a rich heritage of culture, wealth and resources have defined the nature of the Asian continent since time immemorial. However, bold and turnaround policies and economic reforms in the latter half of the 20th century have phenomenally changed the economic and socio-cultural landscape of the two countries. The two players opened up their respective economies and liberalized market regulations, which led to a tectonic shift in the countries' agriculture-based economies to manufacturing and service-based economies. Further, both the countries, with a large population base, were fuelled by the added benefit of cheap labour. Thus, the 21st century was marked by two Asian emerging economies, which once upon a time stood at the periphery of the world order. These two nations have been near indestructible, even in the face of the global meltdown of 2008.

Not only are these economies forces to reckon with in the global marketplace today but are also futuristic enough to realize the need to increase and improve relations with each other. As a function of this, one observes an increase in bilateral trade between the two nations. This is currently more apparent in the chemicals, machinery and transport equipment sectors. However, when one compares their individual strategic focus areas in building trade relations with each other as well as on a global platform, one observes a variation. While China mostly looks at composite offerings in terms of finished goods, India does so in terms of both unfinished and manufactured goods as well as agricultural exports. Hence, it is evident that China has encashed on its huge manufacturing hubs to rapidly emerge as a superpower and is forecasted to reach the number one position by the next decade. India is not far behind, with its focus on creating stronger manufacturing hubs as well as working towards improving trade relations with both developed and developing countries. Other interesting commonalities that work in their favour are the huge populace and increased disposable income, as well as rapid adoption of technology, which has made these two countries the favoured markets of global brands and firms alike. Thus, the two Asian giants have caught the attention of practitioners and researchers alike both as economic superpowers and consumer markets. Interestingly, while one observes divergence in terms of political mindset, there are significant areas of similarity when one considers the regional and cultural diversity. Both nations have a rich cultural past and are bound by cultural exchanges as a function of the silk route.

This edited volume titled *Comparative Development of India and China: Economic, Technological, Sectoral and Socio-cultural Insights* presents some emerging perspectives and studies that look at three key areas in the context of India and China. The first section on 'economic insights' raises concerns on topics that have global relevance such as impact of economic development and reforms on environmental concerns. The section discusses steps taken in the two countries for poverty alleviation and welfare of migrant workers. Since, both nations are marked by rapid industrial growth, this section looks at ethical and privacy concerns in organizations and looks at best practices that can be deployed by firms operating in the two geographies. The section has also highlighted the lessons learnt by China and India from past experiences, which have assisted them in shaping their trajectory for regeneration. The next section on 'sectoral insights' deals at length with the comparison of the manufacturing and services sectors in India and investigates the possibility of a global value chain analysis with respect to the manufacturing and services sectors in the two nations. Further, this section has chapters that provide insights into the banking, insurance, retail and film industries and their functioning in the two countries. The last section takes the reader from economic and sectoral issues to 'socio-cultural insights' and draws parallels and points of parity between the two nations on several areas such as ancient methods of holistic healing and development and propagation of the Buddhist culture.

The 26 chapters are diverse in approach and perspectives. From a discussion on the Belt and Road Initiative to presenting a comparative analysis of the manufacturing and service sectors in the two countries to the synergistic belief in Buddhism, the breadth and depth of issues are sure to provide an expansive reading opportunity to the reader. The contextual and extremely significant issues that will impact the economic and socio-cultural landscape of India and China will intrigue and help identify areas of further research for the academicians and at the same time establish avenues that need some strategic thinking on part of the practitioners.

# Acknowledgements

This edited volume titled *Comparative Development of India and China: Economic, Technological, Sectoral and Socio-cultural Insights* would not have been possible without the contribution of all the academicians, scholars and researchers from the International Management Institute (IMI) New Delhi, Kolkata and Bhubaneshwar, India and the Sichuan Academy of Social Sciences (SASS), Chengdu, China. The chapters of the present volume are diverse yet, together, provide the reader a holistic understanding of the two Asian giants—India and China.

We would like to thank the driving force behind this volume—Professor Arindam Banik, Director, IMI Kolkata for his continued guidance and support in helping us put together the publication. Our sincere thanks also go out to Professor Xiang Baoyun, President, SASS and Professor Guo Xiaoming, SASS. Our sincere gratitude to Dr Himadri Das, Director General, IMI New Delhi and Professor Ramesh Behl, Director, IMI Bhubaneshwar for their encouragement and support in the endeavour. We would also like to take this opportunity to thank Ms. Amrita Datta in appreciation of the editorial assistance provided by her. Last but not least, we express our gratitude to all our family members and well-wishers who unfailingly believe in us and support us in all our ventures.

# Introduction

China and India have witnessed rapid economic growth since 1980. China, however, has reformed and developed at a much faster rate than India; the socio-economic, technological and military transformations have been remarkable for the country. In the year 1978, that is, the period when China's opening-up policy was launched, the per capita GDP of China and India had been almost similar. Whereas in 2019, China's per capita income is around 4.6 times that of India (*Outlook*, 2019). Thus, there are several key lessons to be learnt by India from China. In the past few decades China placed high importance on human development in terms of health and education while these sectors are still a concern for India and the country is far behind China in health care and education. Again, in spite of the advantages offered by a huge demographic dividend, India's inability to develop a labour-intensive manufacturing sector has been quite detrimental to its economic growth. China on the other hand emerged as the manufacturing hub of the world, creating employment for its population and raising their standard of living.

China, too, has certain lessons to learn from successful Indian experiences and endeavours. According to Zhao Gancheng, Director, Center for Asia-Pacific Studies at the Shanghai Institute for International Studies, the way India manifests and promotes its 'soft power' (*Times of India*, 2018) is more acceptable worldwide. Indians have also outpaced their Chinese counterparts in the job market in the US due to various reasons.

Looking at the remarkable advancement of the two nations since 1980, the concept of the Asian Century has been put forth. The rise and supremacy of Asia on the global front is predicted to happen in the near future with China and India inevitably playing crucial roles in the growth. In this backdrop it is imperative to examine the various facets of Sino-Indian economics, trade and cultural exchange and relations and their bilateral ties, in order to gauge its impact in the international scenario. This book earnestly tries to interweave all these aspects as well as attempts to fill up the gaps in India–China literature.

There is a long saga of close association between the two nations and their peaceful coexistence with a brief spell of hostility in the 20th century with border conflicts jeopardizing friendly exchanges. Nonetheless, since the late 1980s relations started improving with both nations trying to revisit the legacy of their strong economic ties and redevelop the same. Though tensions still continue to exist over the disputed boundary, China and India regularly engage in meaningful discourse to avoid any escalation of trivial issues and resolve misperceptions. In addition to the economic ties, the two ancient civilizations of the world have shared a strong cultural bond. The socio-cultural section of this volume thus highlights this connection by delving deep into the countries' history as well as the present relationship. The Buddhist missionaries have definitely played a pivotal role in strengthening the Sino-Indian bond through the ages. While Kashyapa Matanga, Dharmaraksha and Zhikong travelled from India to China to disseminate Lord Buddha's teachings, Fa Hien and Xuanzang travelled from China to India to learn from the Buddhist scriptures and convey Buddhist wisdom and culture to China. In this process Indian culture got integrated into the east Asian culture. The Chinese monks have also left a permanent impression in India through their records, which helped to comprehend ancient Indian civilization and history to a substantial extent.

Both from the socio-cultural and economic points of view the Silk Road again deserves a special mention. These routes have assisted in creating and developing a resilient alliance between China and India that is hard to find between any other nations in the world. Currently China is trying to revamp the historic Silk Road with President Xi Jinping's Belt and Road Initiative (BRI). The BRI, which comprises the Silk Road Economic Belt and the 21st Century Maritime Silk Road, is a massive infrastructure project taken up to link Asia with Africa and Europe. While a section of people, who perceive China's rise in the global scenario to be a threat, consider this initiative to be frightening, others argue that the extension of trade routes will be advantageous for various nations in terms of speeding up their economic progress. Since its conception in the year 2013, BRI is evolving continuously over the years. However, India, with her concerns on China's undue influence in Asia and beyond, as well as the fear of being laden with debt, has stayed away from the arrangement and not voiced its interest in the same. Nevertheless, a 2019 report by Moody's Analytics highlighted that the initiative offers opportunity to access infrastructure funding to several nations and if BRI investments are judiciously made, productivity and employment are expected to rise leading to the economic growth of many nations (Moody's Analytics 2019).

In the context of various aspects discussed so far pertaining to China and India and the relationship between them, this volume seeks to weave several economic insights, technological insights, socio-cultural insights as well as produce some sectoral studies pertaining to the two neighbouring giants. The chapters in this book try to bring into light the extent of the neighbours economic and socio-cultural ties in the past, present and future, the current scenario of China and India in the various socio-cultural, economic and technological domains as well as comparative analyses based on China and India.

This volume is a sincere attempt of a number of Indian and Chinese researchers to come together to present a big picture of various economic, technological and socio-cultural aspects, advancements and challenges in the context of China and India. It also comprehensively sheds light on the Sino-Indian cooperation in such domains in the past as well as in the present.

According to Oxford University Professor Ian Goldin, growth of emerging markets is pulling up the global economy, with China and other rapidly growing Asian markets leading this growth (CNBC, 2019). It may be noted here that as the trade tussle between China and the United States now intensifies, it creates opportunities for India to develop its manufacturing landscape. However, this trade war between two powerful economies will surely lead to an unfavourable impact on the growth of the world economy.

At the regional level as well as from the global perspective, peaceful coexistence and common development of China and India is extremely important. Chinese Emissary Luo Zhaohui, in a seminar held in New Delhi in 2018, mentioned that Sino-Indian relations could be promoted with the '5 Cs', namely, communication, cooperation, contacts, coordination and control; the two countries should work together to face the global challenges to foster global economic integration (Xinhuanet, 2018). Nobel Laureate Rabindra Tagore, a fervent advocate of strengthening Sino-Indian collaboration visited China twice in the 1920s. He had repeatedly stressed on mutually beneficial communication between these two, great ancient civilizations for their comprehensive development and ascendency in the global platform. Few months before his death in 1941, Tagore recalled his visit to China and wrote a poem. Few lines from the same are reproduced below:

> Once I went to the land of China,
> Those whom I had not met
> Put the mark of friendship on my forehead
> Calling me their own

Thus, keeping in view the ascent of Asia in the world and the significance of Sino-Indian relations in achieving the same, this book is an earnest attempt to bring together several insights pertaining to the two giant neighbours.

## References

CNBC. 2019. 'Asia could be the driving force of the world economy as the 'center of gravity' shifts, says Oxford professor.' https://www.cnbc.com/2019/09/10/china-emerging-asia-sustaining-global-economy-says-oxford-professor.html

Moody's Analytics. 2019. 'The Belt and Road Initiative—Six Years On.' https://www.moodysanalytics.com/-/media/article/2019/belt-and-road-initiative.pdf

*Outlook*. 2019. https://www.outlookindia.com/newsscroll/what-can-india-learn-from-chinas-70-years-of-economic-growth-column/1634864

*Times of India*. 2018. 'What China can learn from India, according to Chinese state media.' https://timesofindia.indiatimes.com/india/what-china-can-learn-from-india-according-to-chinese-state-media/articleshow/63265415.cms

Xinhuanet. 2018. 'Chinese envoy to India proposes '5 Cs' to promote Sino-Indian ties.' http://www.xinhuanet.com/english/2018-06/19/c_137263210.htm

# Part I

# Economic and Technological Insights

Over the last three decades, phenomenal economic growth registered by India and China has ensured their rightful prominence in the global economic order. Their economic and technological attainments are also instrumental in changing geopolitical alignments enabled by their rapidly increasing economic and military capabilities. With more than a third of the world's population between them, these two nations have been playing a significant role in a new world order backed by their enormous demographic dividends. Apart from being the fastest growing nations in the world, China and India are ranked number one and number three respectively, among the top economies in the world in terms of the GDP/PPP. Between them, they have a huge market for final output as well as factors of production, thereby assuming a very crucial role in the advancement of world economy in the present century.

The chapters in this section on 'Economic and Technological Insights' of the book cover a wide range of topics. They probe into the dynamics of economic progress enjoyed by India and China over the last three decades and examine the sustainability of such progress in the decades to come in the light of rising concerns on environmental issues and climate change. The first chapter of the book puts forth the lessons that China and India learned from their past experiences pertaining to their decline in the 19th century from their glorious stature on the global platform. Those lessons shaped the initiatives taken to revive their economy since the late-20th century. The chapter thus seeks to shed light on this, focussing on certain social and economic dynamics in the context of China and India. The second chapter deals with the economic development models followed by these two countries since they undertook economic reforms, which have put them on centre-stage with the tag of fastest growing economies in the world. This study also outlines many similarities and differences between these two countries and maps their journey of economic progress over last three decades. The chapter also raises concerns about sustainability of such economic progress with a rapidly declining global ecological environment with evident traces of a state of climate emergency. The next chapter deals with the BCIM Economic Corridor project and outlines the benefits of the project, which has the potential to boost economic activities. The study argues for Sino-Indian cooperation for completion of the project and outlines the importance of greater Sino-Indian exchanges in all the fields to boost economic progress.

Poverty has been a bane for both the countries since the beginning of the 20th century. Higher economic growth experienced in China during the last three decades has addressed the issue of poverty in an effective manner whereas India has a long way to go to eradicate absolute poverty. The chapter on poverty alleviation provides a comparative analysis of poverty reduction patterns in both India and China, and argues that each country can learn the best practices from each other to effectively address the issues to ensure better reduction in poverty. The next chapter analyses migrant workers' welfare in both the countries and provides recommendations to solve the difficulties of migrant workers in their workplaces. The sixth chapter studies the pension systems in India and China to analyse the similarities and differences and finds that provisions of social security for the elderly must be addressed from an institutional point of view. Since average age is on a rise in both the countries with an enhanced life expectancy at birth (LEB), a dignified life during sunset years must be ensured through state intervention and both the countries can learn from each other's experiences to effectively address this important issue on social security.

Chapter 7 of the book provides a Sino-Indian comparison of total factor productivity (TFP) in the manufacturing sector based on Malmquist Decomposition Index. The study finds that China should pay attention to the improvement of technological progress and human capital while India should focus on technical efficiency. Chapter 8 of the book deals with the adaptability of labour force, which is transferred from the agricultural sector to the manufacturing sector. The study provides insight on the intensification of manufacturing intelligence, which has a huge impact on the employment of workers transferred from the agricultural sector in both the countries. The study finds that both the countries must find new avenues to employ the surplus workers from agriculture in sectors like tourism so that they can contribute to the economic progress of their respective nations. Chapter 9 deliberates on management control frameworks for modern day organizations and compares them based on 10 parameters to allow the countries to choose the best framework for effective management of organizations. Chapter 10 deals with ethics and privacy concerns in a digital age and finds that a robust digital ecosystem is the need for the customers to overcome the dilemma of privacy paradox. Chapter 11 on the other hand deals with the impact of Indian festivals on Chinese imports. The study finds that despite negative political rhetoric, Chinese imports to India are on a rise over the years during major festivals seasons. The study also finds that the political rhetoric and anti-China sentiments in the Indian media have no economic foundations, which is evident from higher levels of imports from China during festival seasons over the years. Hence in totality, this section outlines contemporary economic and technological issues of China and India with comparative analysis of various sectors highlighting the economic and technological attainments of these two countries.

CHAPTER 1

# Learning from the Asian Experiences

## *A Commentary Based on China and India*

**Rajashri Chatterjee and Arindam Banik**

## Introduction

From the first century till the 18th century, China and India, two influential neighbours in the world history, showcased enormous opulence in terms of their respective share of world GDP. Asia's predominance, more specifically China and India's supremacy on the global economic platform was therefore held for long and the other regions of the world looked at these two nations with deep veneration.

With improved agricultural knowhow China observed a sharp increase in its share of global GDP in the early 19th century as compared to its share a century ago. The nation's population in the early 19th century had been around 2.8 times the figure in 1700 (Maddison, 2006). In the late 18th century, however, several socio-economic disorders had put the nation in deep trouble. On the other hand, India's predominance started waning in the 18th century itself.

The reasons behind this decline have been attributed to various reasons by the intellectuals, apart from the fall of the Mughal Empire and political fragmentation in the country, which facilitated the mounting authority of the British over India. A dramatic transition of the economic opulence in terms of the major share of world GDP from these two Asian world powers to the West occurred during the late 19th century. Nonetheless, the signs of such imminent transformation had steadily become distinct since the 18th century itself. The several reasons behind this transition, therefore, provide meaningful historic lessons especially in the context of Asia trying to make a comeback as the leading power in the world with China and India coming to the limelight with their economic recovery and speedy growth since the late 20th century.

In this backdrop it is clear that the Asian experiences, especially the Chinese and the Indian experiences over the past three centuries carry important lessons for these two nations as well as for various other economies across the world involved in shaping the new world order. It is also noteworthy that China and India have displayed several similarities as well as divergences in their experiences in various social and economic domains. An emphasis on such areas is therefore imperative to comprehend the rise and the sustainability of the Asian century. Section II of this chapter thus focuses on certain social and economic dynamics of China and India in the past specifically the period from the 18th century till just before the late 20th century to gather important lessons pertaining to the reasons for their development and decline. Section III shifts the focus to the late 20th century period as the two nations embarked on a trajectory to emerge as leading economies of the world. The progress of China and India in various domains since the 1990s, when both the economies had adopted reforms for economic liberalization, have been presented. China's evolution since then is especially noteworthy as it displayed unprecedented development in various domains. In the backdrop of the discourse held in Section I, II and III, Section IV discusses various lessons learnt from the experiences of China and India in the context of the resurgence of the Asian Century. Section V finally wraps up the chapter with some conclusive remarks.

## Economic and Social Dynamics of China and India in the Past: 18th Century to the Late-20th Century

China and India had been the largest economies in the world till the 18th century and the rest of the world had held the Asian giants in reverential esteem for their prosperity, wisdom and culture. In 1700, China, India and Europe were almost comparable in terms of their share of world GDP. While China and India occupied about 22 per cent and 24 per cent share of world GDP respectively, western and eastern Europe together occupied around a 25 per cent share (Maddison, 2006). However, many argue that in absence of major productivity shifts due to technological advancements, it was China and India's massive population at that point of time which shaped their GDP. Nonetheless, these places possessed an abundant array of resources and capital that had attracted the Europeans to arrive at these places with commercial interests. In the 17th century, India possessed a huge trade surplus with Europe mostly due to its thriving textile sector. The nation also exported various agricultural goods to various parts of the world in lieu of treasures like silver and gold. The Indian subcontinent saw increase in production, income, prosperity and population throughout the 17th century and it was a leading manufacturer in the early 18th century. Frank (1996) found that during the period between the 15th and the 17th century, China and India had been the principal regions for industrial production. West and South-east Asia were also of more economic importance than Europe at the time. He inferred that common global economic development since the 15th century had been too advantageous for Asia in particular. But since the late 18th century, the Asian regions, one after the other, witnessed several problems like socio-economic schisms, political confusions, gradual loss of competitive advantages, reversal in bullion flows, pressure on resources due to population spurt, etc. Production and income declined over time and Asia eventually became a source for cheap labour. The researcher further argues that at this stage in history, the western world took advantage of the pan-Asian crises and was able to climb on the shoulders of the previously prominent Asian economies through administrative expertise, favourable policies and innovation.

In the early 19th century, China and India occupied 33 per cent and 16 per cent shares of the world GDP, respectively. The population of China in 1820 had been 2.8 times the figure in 1700. However, if per capita GDP is considered, there wasn't any decline for China in 1820 as compared to the figure in 1700 which can be attributed to improvement in agriculture through better utilization of various techniques in the 18th century. India's population on the other hand increased by 26 per cent in 1820 as compared to the figure in 1700; the per capita GDP dropped by 3 per cent during this period (Maddison, 2006). In the 19th century itself, China again faced several socio-economic disorders such as the White Lotus Rebellion (1796–1805), Daoguang Depression (1820–1850), the Opium War disaster (1839–1842) and the Taiping Rebellion (1850–1864). Moreover, from the 1840s to the 1940s, aggression by certain European nations, Japan and Russia as well as China's civil war put the country into deep trouble leading to substantial losses. When compared to early 19th century, China's per capita GDP had dropped to quite some extent in the early 20th century, share of world GDP became one-fourth of the figure in early 19th century and annual average compound growth of per capita GDP was negative during the period 1820–1913 (Maddison, 2006). In spite of Maddison's (2006) estimates of India's declining share of world GDP through the 19th century, Morris (1963) interestingly held that India's economic scenario in this century can be characterized by improvement in economic activity under the British *raj* due to improvement in political stability, standardization and efficacy in administration, infrastructural development, commercial rationalization, expansion in agricultural output on average and development of modern industries. But whatever progress took place could not bring in the structural alterations that are essential to create a platform for an industrial revolution. Nonetheless, whatever changes took place may be thought of as the factors leading to rise in per capita GDP during 1820–1913 according to the statistics presented by Maddison (2006).

Since the late 19th century, a histrionic transition was witnessed in the global platform with the economic opulence in terms of share of world GDP shifting towards the West. The western world eclipsed Asian supremacy. The Industrial Revolution expanded the imperial reach of the western European powers to various sections of the world, which helped them access and accumulate resources and exploit the colonial labour force as well (Banik and Barai, 2017). According to Pomeranz (2000) the reasons for the *great divergence* were predominantly the fortuitous episode pertaining to the discovery of the Americas that became a greater source of primary resources for Europe than any other Asian nation and the advantage from the perspective of easy availability of coal which reinforced massive industrialization in Europe.

Trade openness has been claimed to be a crucial element of a nation's economic headway. As we focus on the foreign trade dynamics in the context of China and India since the mid-18th till the mid-20th century (Table 1.1), numerous areas attract one's attention and it is observed that both the countries could not ultimately benefit from foreign trade during this period under review. When the two countries are compared, it is seen that both have moved through various cycles. In the 18th century, while China took a restrictive stance, India suffered as the East India Company (EIC) tried to impose monopolistic trade between Britain and India. In the 19th century, China was forced to relax its policies due to western pressure to open up its ports to the world. Scholars claim that it could be well expected that this opening up would have been unfavourable to Chinese interests. There was growth in the varieties of merchandise imported and exported during the treaty port era (i.e., 1842–1940s). Nonetheless, China had a deficit in commodity trade through this period (Keller et al., 2011). For India, the whole period from mid-18th to mid-20th centuries can be characterized by a consistently favourable balance of trade. But the nationalist writers treated the entire amount of the export surplus as a net drain from the country emphasizing its impoverishing effects (Chaudhuri, 1983). The advantageous circumstances in the second half of the 19th century could have developed the nation to a substantial extent if India had brought revolutionary changes in technology, production and various other economic domains, making an effort to move out from the imperial grip.

From the perspective of human development, Escosura (2015) put forth that while India progressed steadily in this parameter since

Table 1.1 *Foreign Trade Regime in China and India: Mid-18th to Mid-20th Century*

| *Timeline* | *China* | *India* |
|---|---|---|
| Second half of the 18th century | • Restricted to a single port<br>• Usually permitted under a 'tributary system' | • EIC imposed monopolistic trade between Britain and India |
| 19th century | • The Treaty of Nanjing (1842) brought an end to the tributary system, compelled China to relax its foreign trade regime<br>• The treaty brought in an era of the 'treaty port system'<br>• Numerous other treaty ports came up subsequently | • Charter Act of 1813 ended EIC's exclusive monopoly over Indian trade, which led to the opening of the Indian market and rapid increase in exports and imports<br>• Structural changes in the commodity composition<br>• Second half of the century brought construction of railway lines and the Suez Canal, which offered huge opportunities for phenomenal increase in India's foreign trade; Globally, it was a period focusing on multilateralism and free trade |
| First half of 20th century | • Treaty port era continued till 1948<br>• China could penetrate several new markets | • Multilateralism in trade came to a halt in 1914<br>• India suffered under the Great Depression of 1929, political disorders, various controls inflicted during the wars or post-war leading to foreign trade being absolutely volatile |

*Source:* Keller et al. (2011) and Chaudhuri (1983)

the late-19th century despite claims of colonial negligence towards investment in such spheres, China too witnessed much advancement during the first half of the 20th century. Over seven decades since 1870, China's performance, however, had been seen to be marginally better than India. Interestingly, Escosura (2015) argued that human development did not match per capita GDP trend for the nations during the first half of the 20th century due to the fact that while health and education practices became increasingly globalized during this period, per capita GDP suffered a decline due to the disintegration of the commodity and factor markets.

During the Maoist era in China (1950s to 1970s), although per capita GDP almost doubled, development efforts suffered major setbacks due to calamitous experimentations in the socio-economic domains and wars with certain Asian economies. Furthermore, the country was also not able to take advantage of the flourishing world economy for being fundamentally a closed economy with foreign trade aiming at self-sufficiency (Maddison, 2006, 2007). For India, the nation grew steadily between 1950 and 1980 without any lengthy stagnation or deterioration due to the fact that the government ensured macroeconomic stability and policy credibility. India's per capita GDP rose sharply during the period. The period between 1950 and 1975 in India was characterized by tighter controls in the foreign trade regime and focus on autarchy while the period 1976–1990 witnessed some relaxation in policies (Panagariya, 2004). From the perspective of human development, India and China were almost at par in 1950. In fact, India was slightly better than China at that time (Escosura, 2015). Subsequently both the nations have progressed, but China pulled ahead of India to quite some extent.

## Economic and Social Dynamics of China and India: Late-twentieth Century Onwards

The resurrection of China and India was again witnessed since the late-20th century. China's ascent since 1980 has been amazing with the government opening the economy to huge foreign investment and adopting privatization and other significant reforms or measures.

Since the 1980s, India, too, has increasingly considered a private sector orientation and embarked on a high growth trajectory since economic liberalization in the 1990s. This section of the chapter especially aims to compare the developmental trajectories of the two nations in various domains since the late-20th century, which definitely carry important lessons for the future.

## Human Development

In terms of human development, the two nations were almost at par in 1950 with India's performance being slightly better. Post-1950 China moved ahead. The Human Development Index (HDI) values portray that China has been consistently outperforming India since 1990 (Table 1.2). The table also depicts the extent to which China has remained ahead of India on the education front (in terms of the education index) as well as on the health front in terms of life expectancy at birth. China's investment in education has been on the rise continuously. During 2005–2014, it increased at a rate of 19 per cent on average and government appropriations comprising of budgetary and non-budgetary funds have been the major source of finance for the education system (OECD, 2016). The country's total expenditure on health as a share of GDP rose from 3.5 per cent in 1995 to 5.6 per cent in 2014 (WHO, 2020). India's total expenditure on health as a share of GDP increased from 4.02 per cent in 1995 to 4.7 per cent in 2014. From the point of view of education, public expenditure on education as a percentage of GDP has remained unchanged in 2014–2015 as compared to 1999–2000 at 4 per cent (Indiastat, 2019). In terms of eradication of poverty, India and China have been both immensely successful. According to the World Bank, India has halved its poverty rate since 1990s (*Economic Times*, 2019). China, on the other hand, aims at eliminating absolute poverty in 2020. Such rapid pace of poverty reduction is unparalleled in the history of mankind.

## Foreign Trade

China and India initiated programmes for economic liberalization in the late 1970s and early 1990s respectively. India chose to embark on a series of structural reforms for a more open economy in 1991 amidst

Table 1.2 *Human Development Dynamics of China and India: 1990–2018*

| | *China* | | | | | | | *India* | | | | | | |
|---|---|---|---|---|---|---|---|---|---|---|---|---|---|---|
| | *1990* | *1995* | *2000* | *2005* | *2010* | *2015* | *2018* | *1990* | *1995* | *2000* | *2005* | *2010* | *2015* | *2018* |
| HDI | 0.501 | 0.549 | 0.591 | 0.643 | 0.702 | 0.742 | 0.758 | 0.431 | 0.463 | 0.497 | 0.539 | 0.581 | 0.627 | 0.647 |
| Education Index[1] | 0.405 | 0.442 | 0.481 | 0.535 | 0.602 | 0.642 | 0.649 | 0.311 | 0.344 | 0.379 | 0.429 | 0.478 | 0.54 | 0.558 |
| Life Expectancy at Birth | 69.1 | 69.9 | 71.4 | 73 | 74.4 | 75.9 | 76.7 | 57.9 | 60.3 | 62.5 | 64.5 | 66.7 | 68.6 | 69.4 |

*Source:* UNDP Human Development Data (1990-2018)

severe balance of payment crises. Again, the Great Leap Forward initiated by Mao Zedong that led to the massive famine of 1959–1961 as well as the damage inflicted by the cultural revolution compelled China to rethink economic reforms under the able guidance of Deng Xiaoping. Obviously, what happened prior to 1978 had taught China important lessons about the slipups that should not be repeated. India joined the World Trade Organization (WTO) in 1995 and China joined six years later in 2001. The economic liberalization and accession to WTO have been argued to have played an important role in the ascent of these two nations to prosperity in the current century.

The trade-to-GDP figures for China and India since 1990 have been shown in Figure 1.1. For India, with liberalization, trade as percentage of GDP has risen consistently. The degree of openness peaked in 2008 after which it suffered some setback in the aftermath of the global financial crisis. Though it recovered soon, it has displayed a fluctuating trend in the recent past. China's trade-to-GDP figure has been higher than India since the 1980s, especially after it opened up to the global community and overseas investment. Trade as percentage of its GDP peaked around mid-2000s just after its accession to the WTO. This indicator has however overall displayed a decreasing trend in the recent past specifically since 2011 and the value each year has been less than that of India.

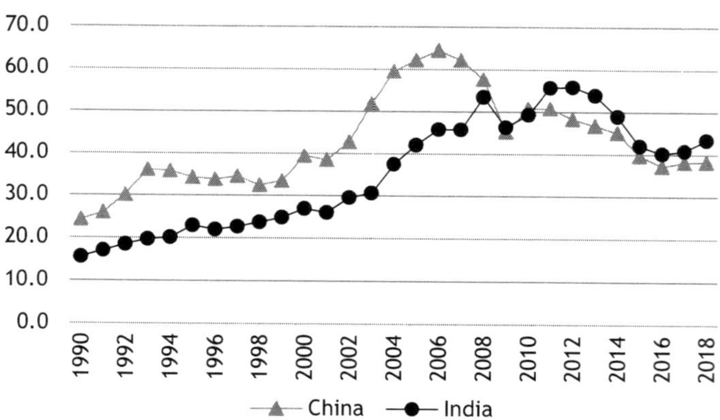


Figure 1.1 *Trade Openness: China and India: 1990–2018*

*Source:* World Development Indicators, The World Bank, 2019

One serious cause of concern however is that since India's opening up, trade deficit has increased manifold. The reasons have been attributed to decline in the growth of the manufacturing sector, increase in imports of certain products like oil, machinery, electronic goods, etc., slowdown in developed economies, sovereign debt crisis, worldwide crisis, etc. (*Economic Times*, 2014). As India's trade deficit widens the government has taken several steps to increase exports to reduce the impact of the discrepancy. China, on the other hand, is maintaining consistent trade surpluses since the 1990s and various arguments have been put forth, starting from structural aspects to exchange rate manipulations, to explain the causes for the same.

## Economic Growth

Figure 1.2 displays that the standard of living measured by per capita GDP (2011 PPP $) has seen a sharp increase since 1990 for China. Though India also observed a rising trend, it has been difficult to catch up with China in its rise in this respect. While China's per capita GDP was lower than India in 1990, in 2018 it is about 2.35 times of India's per capita value.

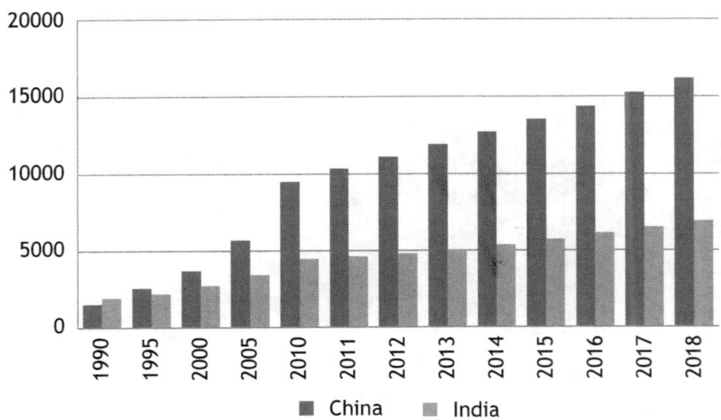


Figure 1.2 *GDP per capita (2011 PPP $): China and India: 1990–2018*

*Source:* UNDP Human Development Data (1990-2018)

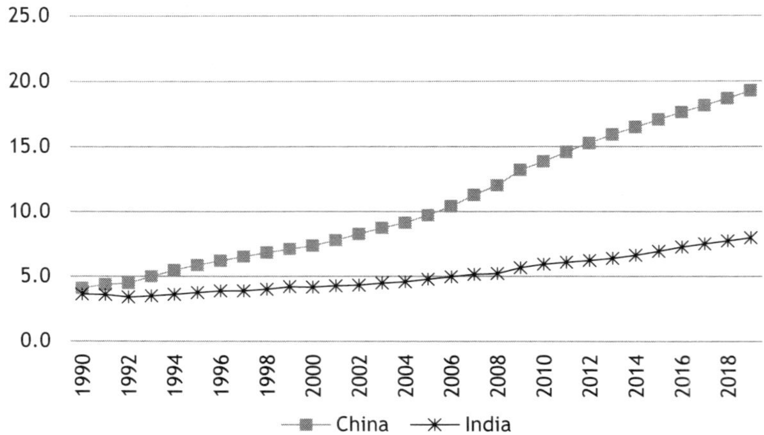


Figure 1.3 *GDP based on PPP, Share of World (% of world): 1990–2018*

*Source:* IMF, 2019

Further, China's share of world GDP was almost at par with India in 1990 (Figure 1.3). Nonetheless, subsequently this share showed a sharp increasing trend reaching to 2.4 times of India's share in 2018. The increase in India's share has been steady over the years. It is argued by the economists that much of China's economic growth has been due to rapid growth in productivity and substantial capital investment. It is again noteworthy that while China's annual average GDP growth rate has been around 9.6 per cent over the period from 1991–2018, annual growth rate in India averaged around 6 per cent during the same period (World Bank, 2019).

## Competitiveness

China has been much ahead of India in terms of competitiveness (Table 1.3) according to the Global Competitiveness Report 2019 that focuses on various factors that drive economic growth, productivity and human development in the nations. India needs to place serious attention on improving its position on various parameters. For the Asian Century to materialize propelled by China and India's

Table 1.3 *Competitiveness of China and India: 2019*

| *Pillars*[a] | *China: Rank* | *India: Rank* |
|---|---|---|
| Institutions | 58 | 59 |
| Infrastructure | 36 | 70 |
| ICT adoption | 18 | 120 |
| Macroeconomic stability | 39 | 43 |
| Health & primary education | 40 | 110 |
| Skills | 64 | 107 |
| Product market | 54 | 101 |
| Labour market | 72 | 103 |
| Financial system | 29 | 40 |
| Market size | 1 | 3 |
| Business dynamism | 36 | 69 |
| Innovation capability | 24 | 35 |
| **Global Competitiveness** | **28** | **68** |

*Source:* World Economic Forum (2019a)
*Note:* [a] Rank among 141 world economies.

supremacy, the two nations, particularly India, need to reinforce their development efforts and bring in further reforms wherever necessary.

So, as we focused on China and India's resurrection on the global platform since the late-20th century, it could be seen that both have progressed substantially in various social and economic dynamics. China's progress, in particular, has been spectacular. Rising China has therefore been perceived as a threat by several nations as it underscores an imminent change in the global order. The major reasons for the resurgence of the two nations include systemic reforms and favourable economic policies, absence of any foreign intrusion, peaceful integration with the global economy, opening up to foreign investment, favourable demography, privatization, deregulation of industries, investment in infrastructure (particularly huge in case of China), technological diffusion and obviously, the steps taken for human development. Furthermore, high domestic savings as well as high productivity of capital assisted in China's phenomenal growth in the recent past. The favourable milieu that was created by the two economies since the late-20th century for improvement and ascent in the global economy was undeniably dictated by the lessons they learnt through their past experiences. In this process of development of the two giant economies, Asia emerged as a region having major share of global trade, capital, resources and demographic dividend; an Asian Century is thus predicted. However, there is some setback in the growth momentum of the two neighbours at present and so, several domains call for an assessment in the light of the past experiences.

## Lessons from the Asian Experiences in the Context of Resurgence of the Asian Century

The discourse revealed some interesting lessons from the past in the context of the growing prominence of China and India in the world at present and the reappearance of the Asian Century. First, China and India's sovereignty in the global economy in the past faded away due to several reasons, which are as follows—(a) Technological obsolescence and the nations being incapable of bringing any revolutionary changes in technology and production. On the other hand, Industrial Revolution occurred in the West because of their enterprising outlook, resourcefulness, better governance and easy availability of coal; (b) Inability to open up to the global economy in a beneficial way; (c) Political disintegration or upheavals within the nations which enabled other realms to enhance their influence on these nations; (d) The West could climb up the global economic ladder and eventually exert strong influence on these Asian economies due to its superior administrative competence in particular, when these economies were gradually falling prey to various crises; (e) Loss of comparative advantages; (f) Civil wars, conflicts with other regions; and (g) Adopting destructive or inopportune policies. Hence, in order to emerge or sustain as superpowers in all domains, China and India need to focus on various such areas of concern to avoid any crisis and degeneration at present and in future.

China had been restrictive in the foreign trade domain for a long time in the past. Chinese leaders then had always feared foreign invasions that could disrupt the stability of the nation. Relaxation of policies to open up initially took place under Western pressure in the 19th century. The economic liberalisation of China at the time had not been beneficial for the country, as could be well anticipated, and it seemed as if the nation was increasingly giving in to the imperialist forces. India, too, suffered under the monopolistic trade regime enforced by EIC in the 18th century. Subsequently, since the 19th century despite an unhindered foreign trade regime and fortuitous advantageous circumstances, India could not make proper use of the huge export surplus it derived from overseas trade, yet again, due to the domination of imperialist forces.

In terms of human development, China and India, in spite of being extremely rich in culture and wisdom, could not outstrip the Western world in the past. Divergence in the standards of living between the two nations and Europe existed before the Industrial Revolution and only widened over time. It may be reasoned here that the nations had not been able to reach to the level of human development as attained by the Western economies presumably because of the burden of a large population, lack of political autonomy, internal conflicts, absence of concrete policies and inability to harness their potential in bringing technological and socio-economic changes.

As China and India lost their prominence after a long and glorious stint as world leaders in economic terms, the two neighbours definitely learnt from their varied experiences. They cannot afford to give in to the slipups that forced them to lose their prominence in the past.

Coming to the present, in the 21st century, China and India have emerged as the fastest growing nations of the world. This chapter has therefore highlighted the progress of China and India in various domains since the late-20th century. China's renaissance and transformation in particular has been breath-taking since its opening up in late 1970s. However, there are several areas that need serious contemplation for sustained growth and development and the rise of the Asian Century.

As China and India undertook reforms for opening up and integrated with the global economy, they witnessed enormous growth, which has also been established by various empirical studies.

Marelli and Signorelli (2011), in their study, evaluated the miracle of China and India's enormous growth in the three decades since 1980 in the light of the growing trade openness to figure out the linkage between economic growth and their integration in the world economy. They inferred that there is a positive impact of openness on economic growth in the context of these two economies. They also underscored that this robust growth for the two neighbours has assisted them to combat the initial impact of the global financial crisis and has helped the global economy at large to recover from the recession. Gries and Redlin (2012) took into account a balanced panel data set comprising 158 nations including China and India. The period considered was 1970–2009. The researchers found evidence of a positive significant causality from openness to GDP per capita (i.e. growth) and vice versa, in the long run signifying international integration to be advantageous for growth in the long run. Lal (2017) adopted a multivariate causal framework to investigate the short and long run association between FDI, trade openness and GDP in the context of three nations, namely, India, China and Mexico. The study covered a period from 1980 to 2011 and concluded that there are distinct benefits as an economy opens up in terms of foreign trade and investments. Interestingly, the study puts forth that as an economy integrates itself into the global platform, FDI inflows are majorly *efficiency seeking*, which directly impact economic growth and trade openness. Thus, empirical studies have held that openness of the nations is crucial for their development. This is also true with respect to the past experiences that underscore the demerits of isolationism. It is clear that India and China could have been able to reap huge benefits from overseas trade in the past, particularly in the 19th century, if imperialist forces or foreign interventionism were not there or had there been enough preconditions and expertise necessary to bring in revolutionary changes to pull ahead with the help of the growth stimulus provided in that century.

In the context of foreign trade as we again move to the present times, the US–China trade war needs a special mention. With huge Chinese export losses due to the conflict, it is helping other players in the US market to become more competitive. This may be an opportune moment for the other regional economies like India, as they can gain from trade diversion. But Asia's forte, eminence and supremacy should be based on common development, cooperation, shared vision and rejuvenation at the regional and sub-regional level. A win-win situation among the Asian countries is sought for the rise of Asia as the supreme power. The Asian Century is not possible with the degeneration of any prominent Asian market.

China and India are different in their administration—the former is autocratic while the latter, democratic. They have also taken diverse trajectories towards prosperity. While China has become the global manufacturing hub, India's growth has been propelled by the service sector to a substantial extent. For the Asian Century to fortify, both China and India's contribution to the world economy needs to be substantial in all respects. They are the global leaders in terms of market size. If we look at India, factors like massive young English–speaking population and relatively lower remuneration in India have enabled the country to become so successful in the service sector. The two nations, therefore, cannot permit any such circumstances that are detrimental to their development efforts at this expansion stage. China has been the global leader in terms of manufacturing with USD 3080 billion value added in 2016, while India occupied the sixth rank with just USD 336 billion value added and has still much to achieve in this sector (Levinson, 2018). India's status in this respect is quite different from what it was during the Mughal regime when it was a manufacturing powerhouse. Though, India has emerged as a technology powerhouse in recent times, challenges remain in employing the unskilled mass and covering up huge deficit in merchandise trade. China again at present is facing several challenges in the backdrop of the Fourth Industrial Revolution (or Industry 4.0) in terms of adopting Industry 4.0 technologies, productivity improvement, its demographic profile, competitiveness in terms of quality, etc. All these call for serious assessment and prompt actions. Lot of uncertainties evolve in a dynamic world and there is a need for the economies to search for the best recompenses from those uncertainties in order to develop or they will wane in the everchanging competitive scenario.

Next, inefficient administrative policies and internal or external concerns and strife had earlier led to the waning of the two nations. Yet again, the speedy ascent of China and India has suddenly suffered a setback due to certain current crises. China's annual GDP growth rate is on the decline since 2011. Similarly, India's GDP growth rate for 2019–2020 is estimated to be around five per cent. Stressed assets, ballooning debt and debt service becoming increasingly risky, crony capitalism, domestic issues, fragilities of various industrial sectors, credit crisis, diminishing returns on investment (for China in particular) are restraining the rapid development of these giants and remedial actions are immediately sought. Additionally, slowing down of the economy of the world at large has also contributed to the setback to some extent. Amidst the ageing population and dwindling working age populace and the rising wages, China is facing major impediments to its growth. The trade war, too, has taken a toll on its economic growth. India is also unable to leverage the advantage offered by its demographic dividend successfully, which is imperative to boost the labour-intensive manufacturing sector. The nation falls behind numerous economies in infrastructure development, Information and Communication Technology (ICT) adoption, human development in terms health, education and skillsets and it still has a long way to go. Investments have also soured in the nation. Demonetization hit the unorganized sector severely at a juncture when the country was taking serious strides in development. Thus, the assumption that China and India will continue the miraculous growth story indefinitely may be erroneous without proper actions taken to address the growing concerns. The nations are thereby trying to take measures to combat various looming crises that may restrain their development progress. Much overhaul is still needed for the current century to be driven by these Asian centres. Asian nations have displayed enormous potential in the past four decades. Serious efforts and cooperation are sought from all these nations to move ahead briskly to bring growth prospects back on track for the new world order to emerge with the drivers of global growth centred in Asia.

## Concluding Remarks

This chapter brought into light the reasons behind China and India's decline from their glorious past and their amazing resurrection in the late-20th century. China's growth since the *opening up* of its economy in late 1970s has been spectacular in particular. The aim of this chapter has been to put forth the lessons they learnt from their past experiences, which have assisted in shaping their revival process. Though China and India are suffering from certain predicaments in recent times, which is restraining their growth momentum, both the nations hold enormous potential to exhibit the growth miracle giving rise to the Asian Century. The countries are not troubled by foreign imperialist forces at present. The national leaders are now able to bring in revolutionary transitions with apposite policies, strong governance as well as soft power. The two nations are trying to build a concrete and robust roadmap from their respective stances to sustain as the drivers of economic growth in the current century. The current downturn and various apprehensions thereof should not therefore smash the hope for Asia's looming predominance in the 21st century. By 2040, Asia is expected to generate more than half of the world GDP and 40 per cent of global consumption (World Economic Forum, 2019b). A new global order is anticipated. Obviously both China and India are expected to be the key drivers of this development process. Therefore, Asia cannot afford to take any inappropriate stance in any domain, viz. economic, political, social or cultural, at this stage that may lead to degeneration or growth moderation of any kind and intensity.

## References


Banik, A., and M. K. Barai. 2017. 'Introduction.' In *Towards A Common Future: Understanding Growth, Sustainability in the Asia-Pacific Region,* edited by Arindam Banik, Munim Kumar Barai and Yasushi Suzuki, Palgrave pp. 3–18. Macmillan.

Chaudhuri, K. N. 1983. 'Foreign Trade and Balance of Payments (1757–1947).' In *The Cambridge Economic History of India,* edited by Dharma Kumar and Meghnad Desai, pp. 804–877. Cambridge University Press.

*Economic Times.* 2014. 'India's Trade Deficit Jumps 22 Times Since 1990-91.' *The Economic Times.* https://economictimes.indiatimes.com/news/economy/indicators/indias-trade-deficit-jumps-22-times-since-1990-91/articleshow/45640529.cms?from=mdr

*Economic Times.* 2019. 'India Halved Its Poverty Rate Since 1990s: World Bank.' *The Economic Times.* https://economictimes.indiatimes.com/news/economy/indicators/india-halved-its-poverty-rate-since-1990s-world-bank/articleshow/71608220.cms?from=mdr

Escosura, L. 2015. 'World Human Development: 1870–2007.' *The Review of Income and Wealth* 61, No. 2, 220–247.

Frank, A. G. 1996. 'India in the World Economy, 1400–1750.' *Economic and Political Weekly* 50–64.

Gries, T., and M. Redlin. 2012. 'Trade Openness and Economic Growth: A Panel Causality Analysis.' https://www.researchgate.net/publication/260321248_Trade_Openness_and_Economic_Growth_A_Panel_Causality_Analysis/link/5407fd030cf2c48563b8920b/download

IMF. 2019. IMF Data Mapper. https://www.imf.org/external/datamapper/datasets

Indiastat. 2019. Expenditure on Education as Percentage of Total Budget and Gross Domestic Product/State Domestic Product (GDP/SDP). https://www.indiastat.com/economy-data/8/plans/8017/expenditure-on-education-as-percentage-of-total-budget-and-gross-domestic-product-state-domestic-product-gdp-sdp/369168/stats.aspx

Keller, W., B. Li, and C. H. Shiue. 2011. 'China's Foreign Trade: Perspectives from the Past 150 Years.' *The World Economy* 34, 853–892.

Lal, A. K. 2017. 'Foreign Direct Investment, Trade Openness and GDP in China, India and Mexico.' *The Singapore Economic Review* 62, No.5, 1059–1076.

Levinson, M. 2018. 'U.S. Manufacturing in International Perspective, Congressional Research Service.' https://fas.org/sgp/crs/misc/R42135.pdf

Maddison, A. 2006. *The World Economy: Historical Statistics*, Development Centre Studies, Development Centre of the Organisation for Economic Co-operation and Development.

Maddison, A. 2007. Chinese Economic Performance in the Long Run: 960–2030 AD. http://piketty.pse.ens.fr/files/Maddison07.pdf

Marelli, E., and M. Signorelli. 2011. 'China and India: Openness, Trade and Effects on Economic Growth.' *The European Journal of Comparative Economics* 8, No.1, 129–154.

Morris, M. D. 1963. 'Towards a Reinterpretation of Nineteenth-Century Indian Economic History.' *The Journal of Economic History* 23, No. 4, 606–618.

Organisation for Economic Co-operation and Development (OECD). 2016. Education in China: A Snapshot. https://www.oecd.org/china/Education-in-China-a-snapshot.pdf

Panagariya, A. 2004. 'India's Trade Reform.' *India Policy Forum*, pp. 1–68.

Pomeranz, K. 2000. *The Great Divergence: China, Europe, and the Making of the Modern World Economy*. Princeton: Princeton University Press.

The World Bank. 2019. World Development Indicators. http://datatopics.worldbank.org/world-development-indicators/

UNDP. 2018. Human Development Data (1990–2018). http://hdr.undp.org/en/data

WHO. 2020. Global Health Observatory Data. https://www.who.int/data/gho/data/indicators/indicator-details/GHO/total-expenditure-on-health-as-a-percentage-of-gross-domestic-product

World Economic Forum. 2019a. The Global Competitiveness Report 2019. http://www3.weforum.org/docs/WEF_TheGlobalCompetitivenessReport2019.pdf

World Economic Forum. 2019b. 'We've Entered the Asian Century and There Is No Turning Back.' https://www.weforum.org/agenda/2019/10/has-world-entered-asian-century-what-does-it-mean/

CHAPTER 2

# Indo–Chinese Economic Development Models in Post Reforms Era

Ramakrushna Panigrahi

## Introduction

In recent times, India and China have taken the center-stage in global geo-politics due to their economic might attained through high growth rates during the last few decades. The exceptional economic history of these two countries, with a rich cultural background has been phenomenal in the economic history of human civilization. However, during the colonial era, both the countries had lost their past glory; India, due to the British rule and China under the feudal autocratic rule of Qing dynasty. After India's independence and China's establishment as a republic, since early 1950s, both these countries have experimented with various models in their quest for faster economic growth and development. Though these two countries have almost no notable commonalities in terms of history, culture, religion, language and political institutions, their rapid growth led by economic reforms and ensuing performance in the last three decades have generated a large amount of interest in a comparative research. A significant portion of these research interests and attention focuses on their performance during the last few decades and attempts to articulate the influence of economic reforms on growth. This study attempts to do a comparative analysis of Sino–Indian economic development models pursued by these two countries, which brought them to global prominence, and the challenges they face in sustaining their attainments in an increasingly globalized economic environment in the coming decades.

## An Overview of Economic Development Models

The economic development models pursued by India and China during the last three decades have yielded desired outcomes in terms of social and economic attainments. In neoclassical models, the emphasis has been on achieving higher growth of national income, rising levels of which are instrumental in all-round societal prosperity reflected in better quality of life. Economic growth models' focus is on an increase in aggregate output, which is quantifiable without any ambiguity in measuring attainments. The theories of development focus on attainments in human capabilities through growth and redistribution of income and all-round development of the population that represents a prosperous society.

Ricardo (1817) has pioneered the classical theory of economic stagnation through law of diminishing returns to explain economic development. The classical theories laid emphasis on capital which was crucial for production. Marx (1867) has undermined the sustenance of capitalism for production due to potential workplace revolt and championed the ideals of socialism. Baran (1957) has countered the Marxian speculation possibilities of homegrown variety of capitalistic revolution in the least developed countries (LDCs). Rostow (1960) articulates the stages of economic growth. Nurkse (1953) has emphasized on the synchronized application of capital to a wide range of industries to achieve higher economic growth. On the contrary, Hirschman (1998) advocated for deliberate unbalancing of the economy, which he believed could lead to higher growth.

Furtado (1964) explains that underdevelopment is a result of subjection to colonial rule and imperial domination of foreign powers that forces international division of labour where LDCs specialize in manufacturing primary products while depending on developed countries for technological progress. Prescott (1988) stresses on the importance of savings and capital formation for economic development that results in convergence of per capita income between rich and poor countries. Romer (1986) emphasized on the role of technology in economic growth. Bass (2008) and Nurkse (1953) explain that the circle of demand and supply is related to poverty, where low incomes lead to lower savings that in turn lead to lower levels of investment and income. Robert Solow (1956) and many other economists have conceptualized the *economy* that produces economic output using resources such as land, labour and natural resources using contemporary technology that is available in the economy to explain economic development.

The neoclassical growth models have advocated for capital investment for employment and raising factor productivity through technological innovation to achieve higher economic growth. The theories of economic growth do not account for issues in sustainability and the association of a rising GDP with a decline in environment and quality of life. The neoclassical economics' orientation on short-run optimal resource allocation often ignores long-term aspects of economic prosperity. The distinction between growth and development assumes significance (Acemoglu et al., 2002; De Soto, 2000; Moyo, 2009).

Economic development entails a fundamental transformation of an economy so that people work more productively, and economy shifts toward higher value activities (Schumpeter, 2011). Sen (2005) emphasizes on autonomy and substantive freedoms, which allow individuals to fully participate in economic life. The literature on economic growth and well-being no longer focuses on income parameters alone and thus represents social welfare in a more comprehensive manner[1].

Despite their inherent shortcomings, the neoclassical growth models have helped many countries achieve higher levels of attainments, which followed the macroeconomic policy prescriptions of growth models. Further, the new classical economic models are based on the premise of minimal government intervention to facilitate market economy to achieve optimal levels of resource allocation to enhance productivity and total output. These models emphasize on free market equilibria and free trade, which are crucial to make the production process competitive and attain higher levels of economic growth.

Both China and India mostly followed neoclassical models, which resulted in their spectacular growth during post reforms era. There are quite a few studies that articulate China's evolvement from a centrally planned economic system to an emerging market economy (Zhang, 2014; Wei, 2007; Paulino, 2010). The dominance of political ideology over economic policies, following the establishment of People's Republic of China in 1949, till 1978, witnessed a slow growing Chinese economy that faced acute poverty and economic deprivation during this period. The recurrent economic uncertainties during that period, characterized by poverty and an authoritarian regime that laid too much emphasis on income re-distribution, made the resurgence of a new political leadership possible, which effected the ideological shift during the reform process. The focus was on creation of an equal society, which was based on forgoing the emphasis on an interest group and state supervised redistribution measures. This allowed the government to adopt economic reforms and growth-oriented policies. Yao (2008) explains that the growth consensus along with the introduction of a *dual-track price system* in 1978 that aimed at liberalizing price controls led to the coexistence of both planned and market prices for identical goods in the economy. The privatization of state-owned enterprises, started in mid-1980s and was accomplished by the new millennium, following a bottom-up system (Cao et al., 1999, Guo et al., 2003), which was crucial for economic reforms. Though the 'growth consensus' followed by China has a lot of similarities to the policy prescriptions of the Washington Consensus (Williamson, 2004), it resembles a heterodox economic model to structural reforms, which does not concur with standard economic conventions. The Chinese growth and development model is articulated as Beijing Consensus (Ramo, 2004) where economic reforms prescribed in Washington Consensus have been pursued under an authoritarian regime in which government intervention and regulations are planned and are swift to achieve the reforms objectives.

After independence, India's development strategy was based on economic modernization through industrialization (Singh, 2008).

The influence of western economic models on India's postcolonial political economy is evident. Despite slow progress in economic attainment levels, the quality of human capital was instrumental for an advanced service sector. In essence, it is evident from the literature that China and India have broadly followed the neoclassical model of economic development to provide necessary economic and social infrastructure to create capabilities for their workforce and attainments in development parameters, as envisaged in the Washington Consensus, which put much emphasis on economic reforms. However, these two countries share a few similarities and a lot many differences during their high growth era, which are discussed in the following section.

## Similarities and Differences

Both China and India shared similar rates of growth, GDP, unemployment, acute poverty and per capita income, FDI inflows and many infrastructural indicators till 1980s. However, the buoyant transformation that China has experienced post reforms looks very different from the gradual developments seen in India, where reforms started a decade later. China has traditionally championed the cause of absolute central planning but during post reforms transformed itself into a mixed economy with many aspects of a command system. India had not gone for any radical transformation like China as it had been a mixed economy and espoused western development models from the very beginning with government intervention limited to few redistributive aspects. However, since the days of economic reforms, these two economies share a few similarities along with the many glaring differences.

The most unique similarity is apparent with GDP figures for the two countries in the year 1980, which were same for both—USD 189.6 billion (Table 2.1). Similarities can also be seen in the recording of highest growth rates in post reform years and sustenance of the same. Similarities also lie in having same level of road and railway infrastructure. The rapid growth of China was made possible by high savings, high investments and high external competitiveness. Like China, India's growth story relied heavily on the same. While

China's external competitiveness was in manufacturing, India had done well in the service sector. Both India and China, due to their large size, had a long tradition of decentralized administrative system and with the much more open markets, scope had been given to decentralized experimentation. Both the countries concentrated on productive investments to create hospitable economic environments to attract FDI. In mid-1990s, China prepared for its eventual WTO entry that involved a fairly radical dismantling of much of its protectionist apparatus, much similar to India. The Chinese government has pursued a prudent fiscal policy similar to India. In its quest for external competitiveness, SEZs were devoted solely to export production and many instruments initially used by China to improve its trade performance were similar to policies in India. Both countries provided a host of incentives toward export promotion. Broadly, similar macroeconomic stances were followed by both these countries as their macroeconomic policies were in pursuit of higher growth.

The differences between these countries are much more than the similarities. The most important difference emerges in the political paradigm and administrative execution. A proper macroeconomic policy framework needs an efficient bureaucracy that is not prey to political interests or tainted by corruption. While China had the advantage of executing its reform policies to near perfection due to an authoritarian regime and centralized planning, India's administrative execution was fraught with powerful opposing forces halting the reforms process. The difference is also in the levels of corruption and political nepotism in awarding government contracts affecting outcomes of public sponsored investments in India.

Another major difference can be attributed to China's development strategy being more open to external trade policy compared to India. This is true not only for FDI, but also for trade, which resulted in a rapid rise in the Chinese trade/GDP ratio as compared to India.

China's external competitiveness was promoted by the vast sector of small Township and Village Enterprises (TVEs), which were nominally in the public hands, but were overwhelmingly managed by private and foreign firms. Using the trading skills of the Chinese diaspora in Hong Kong and Taiwan and the cheap labour and other facilities available in many coastal provinces, foreign enterprises invested massively in China. While India followed the same strategy, the TVEs equivalents were neither competitive nor profitable and became a huge burden on India's exchequer.

Though the Indian government welcomed FDI, many big-ticket investment projects faced hostility from an unreasonably over-active civil society that stalled such investments by labelling them anti-poor and foul. India, being a democracy, had to bow to such anti-corporate public sentiments very often, though they made little social and economic sense.

The most glaring difference emerges in the area of income distribution. While the Chinese had laid so much emphasis on redistribution and equality, India had no such stated objectives; rather it championed the cause of capitalism and free market, though electoral politics forced the government to follow policies that resulted in redistribution of income mostly through transfer payments without distorting market equilibrium.

However, much of the redistribution programs failed to reach the target due to corruption and nepotism. The socialistic objectives remained at policy level in India while Chinese implementation has been more effective[2]. There are a few differences in non-economic parameters that have profound influence on economic development experienced by these two countries. While China's population is broadly homogeneous, India has a diverse population with many different languages, social cultures, food habits and tastes and preferences. The *Varna* system of India further adds to the heterogeneity of the workforce. Also, the *Varna* system had a lot of influence on educational attainment in India, as the system was hostile to written documentation since education was monopolized by a single caste, *Brahmins*. Since *Brahmins* constitute less than 5 per cent of the population, close to 95 per cent of Indians remained illiterate till recent centuries. China did not have such historical drawbacks in knowledge dissemination and as a result has reaped huge demographic dividends from its better educated and skilled homogenous workforce. During the last few decades, the demographic growth has been very subdued in China due to the one child policy and very strict implementation of it; whereas India's fall in the birth rate is more to do with rising awareness and health care access. These differences have contributed to the economic performance of the countries in the past and will prove crucial in sustaining high growth rates in 21st century.

## Key Drivers of Growth and Development

China and India have amazed the world by their impressive economic performance. The key drivers of growth and development have been the policy reforms articulated in the Washington Consensus. As evident, the fiscal discipline measures have helped both the countries in curtailing public debt. Allocation of more resources toward primary health care, education and infrastructure has added to attainment of development parameters while creating a conducive environment for economic investments. The tax reforms have boosted domestic consumption, which has been crucial to growth. The financial and trade liberalization have helped both the countries boost their trade shares with a robust inclusive financial system.

The reforms measures to liberalize FDI inflows helped both China and India attract huge FDI that was also crucial in building massive reserves. Whereas India maintains a competitive exchange rate regime, many economists argue that China's fixed rate regime has helped in removing uncertainties of capital movements making transnational dealings easier with Chinese companies, which has been a key driver of growth. China has followed an aggressive stance on privatization of its state enterprises that saw close to 100,000 firms with RMB 11.4 trillion worth of assets getting privatized between 1995 and 2005. These firms were comprised of two thirds of China's SOEs and state assets, making it the largest privatization (Jie, 2008) in the world, thereby making these firms more efficient. Similar privatization of public sector in India has helped in raising efficiency and making them more competitive. The reforms on deregulation in India are more visible in recent years, while Chinese deregulation has been swift though not devoid of significant control by the Chinese government. The legal security on property rights in India has been unambiguous[3]. The 'Property Law of the People's Republic of China' passed in 2007 is a giant leap forward in codifying property rights to provide ownership of assets to private individuals. These factors have largely been the key drivers of economic growth that transformed these two countries from desperate to economic superpowers.

## Sino-Indian Economic Development: 1980–2014

Prior to 1980, both India and China faced extreme deprivation and acute poverty. In the year 1980, both China and India had a GDP of USD 189.6 billion[4] each, with India having a higher per capita income due to lesser population. The poverty levels were so high that India's 55.6 per cent of population lived below USD 1 a day with no access to social security and minimal basic amenities. Corresponding figure for China was much higher at 64.6 per cent. However, after economic reforms were implemented in 1990, China surpassed India's GDP by USD 32 billion, though in per capita terms, it still fell short of India. Table 2.1 tracks the macroeconomic development parameters of both these countries from 1980 to 2014.

It is evident that after 1990s, even though India opened up its economy and registered significantly higher GDP growth, it was no match for China's performance. Persistent higher growth rates in the Chinese economy could achieve a GDP of USD 10.36 trillion in the year 2014, which is more than five times of India's USD 2.066 trillion. Also, per capita income of China at USD 7,594 is far ahead of India's USD 1,595. However, in terms of purchasing power parity (PPP), Indian economy is better poised at USD 7.5 trillion against China's USD 17.56 trillion. Similarly, India's PPP$ per capita income of USD 5,855 compares better with China's USD 12,879 as per the official exchange rate per capita.

Apart from income, China has been far ahead of India in other development parameters. In health, with a life expectancy at birth (LEB) of 77 years, it is far ahead of India, which could achieve only 68 years. Similarly, in education, China with a 95 per cent literacy rate is way ahead of India's 69 per cent. China's superior health and education parameters reflect in its higher HDI values since 1980. Despite India's higher per capita income levels till mid-1990s, China's HDI values and HDI rank was far superior due to health and educational attainment. China's increased per capita income in recent years along

Table 2.1 *Economic Development of India and China (1980 to 2017)*

| | *India* | | | | *China* | | | |
|---|---|---|---|---|---|---|---|---|
| *Indicators of Development* | *1980* | *1990* | *2005* | *2017* | *1980* | *1990* | *2005* | *2017* |
| Population (Million) | 687 | 849 | 1,095 | 1,339.1 | 981 | 1,135 | 1,305 | 1,386.4 |
| GDP at current prices (billion USD) | 189.6 | 326 | 834 | 2,597.49 | 189.6 | 358 | 2,268 | 12,237.7 |
| GDP per capita (Current) | 275 | 383 | 761 | 1,939.6 | 193 | 315 | 1,737 | 8,827.0 |
| GDP at PPP (billion USD) | 389 | 999 | 3,217 | 9,448.6 | 296 | 1,082 | 6,442 | 23,300.7 |
| GDP per-capita PPP (USD) | 566 | 1,177 | 2,938 | 7,055.6 | 302 | 954 | 4937 | 16,806.7 |
| Literacy rate (%) | 41 | 48 | 63 | 74 | 66 | 78 | NA | 96 |
| LEB in years | 55 | 59 | 66 | 69 | 69 | 71 | 75 | 76 |
| HDI Value | 0.345 | 0.410 | 0.507 | 0.640 | 0.407 | 0.495 | 0.637 | 0.752 |

*Source:* World Development Indicators (2017)

with health and education parameters moved its HDI ranking to much higher than India.

During post reforms period, China had a better macroeconomic environment to grow faster than India. For instance, the gross capital formation (GCF), which is the cornerstone of a neoclassical growth model, for China is 35.4 per cent that is almost double of India's 18.7 per cent. At the same time, China saved 35 per cent of its GDP, whereas India's saving rate was less than half at 15.5 per cent. This low GCF combined with higher fiscal deficits in India with severe capital movement restrictions meant that it was not possible to invest in economic infrastructure, which was crucial for economic growth. However, the gross domestic savings improved with rising income levels and so did the GCF. But India lagged far behind China with a GCF of 31 per cent compared to China's impressive 48 per cent, which was principally instrumental for its higher growth during the last few decades. Table 2.2 chronicles the macroeconomic environment of these two economies since 1980.

It is evident that apart from savings and GCF, on the merchandise trade front, China remained ahead of India all along. India's merchandise trade has grown from 12.4 per cent in 1980 to an impressive 37.6 per cent in 2014. During the same time, China has grown from 20.1 per cent to 41.5 per cent. While India consistently ran into trade deficits all these years, China had trade surpluses in most of these years fuelling an export led growth for its economy. The drastic fall of average tariff rates since 1980 has been instrumental in increased share in international trade. For example, the average tariff rate, which was a whopping 99.4 per cent, fell to less than 10 per cent in India despite its widening trade deficits. Since China had introduced reforms a decade earlier, average tariff rate in China remained around 39 per cent till 1990s, which eased off to less than 10 per cent, supported by its huge trade surplus.

The FDI movements to these countries have also increased due to removal of restrictions. India's net FDI inflows as a percentage of GDP rose from 0.04 per cent in 1980 to 1.7 per cent in 2014. During the same period, China's inflows went up from 0.03 per cent to 3.7 per cent as it became a manufacturing hub and an investment destination for many countries.

Table 2.2 *Macroeconomic Environment 1980 to 2017*

| | India | | | | China | | | |
|---|---|---|---|---|---|---|---|---|
| *Macroeconomic Indicators* | *1980* | *1990* | *2005* | *2017* | *1980* | *1990* | *2005* | *2017* |
| Gross Domestic Savings | 15.5 | 22.6 | 29.7 | 29.8 | 35.0 | 39.9 | 49.0 | 47.4 |
| Gross Capital Formation | 18.7 | 24.1 | 33.4 | 31 | 35.4 | 36.4 | 43.5 | 44 |
| Merchandise Trade as % of GDP | 12.4 | 13.1 | 28.5 | 28.7 | 20.1 | 32.5 | 63.6 | 33.5 |
| Average Tariff Rate (%) | 99.4 | 61.9 | 38.3 | 6.3 | 38.8 | 39.9 | 20.9 | 3.5 |
| Exports of Goods and Services as % of GDP | 6.0 | 6.9 | 19.3 | 18.9 | 6.0 | 15.9 | 33.7 | 19.8 |
| Imports of Goods and Services as % of GDP | 9.1 | 8.3 | 22 | 21.8 | 6.6 | 13.7 | 29.2 | 18.0 |
| Trade Deficits (Surplus) as% of GDP | -3.1 | -1.4 | -2.7 | -5.3 | -0.6 | 2.2 | 4.5 | 4.4 |
| FDI Net Inflows as % of GDP | 0.04 | 0.07 | 0.82 | 1.5 | 0.03 | 1.0 | 3.54 | 1.4 |
| Government Deficits | -5.1 | -7.8 | -3.7 | -3.5 | -13.7 | -2.8 | -0.7 | -3.5 |
| Tax Revenue as % of GDP | NA | 9.8 | 9.9 | 7.5 | 12.7 | 11.7 | 16.7 | 16.3 |
| External Debt (Billions of US$) | 21 | 85 | 121 | 514 | 5.8 | 55 | 281 | 1710.6 |
| External Debt as % of GDP | 11.07 | 26.07 | 14.50 | 19.78 | 3.05 | 15.36 | 12.38 | 13.97 |
| Inflation Rate (Consumer Prices) | 11.4 | 9.0 | 4.2 | 4.9 | NA | 3.1 | 1.8 | 2.0 |
| Lending Interest Rate | 16.5 | 16.5 | 10.8 | 9.55 | 5.0 | 9.4 | 5.6 | 4.35 |
| Unemployment Rate | NA | 4.3 | 4.4 | 3.5 | NA | 4.9 | 4.1 | 4.7 |
| Total Reserves (Billions of US$) | 12.09 | 5.6 | 138 | 400 | 10.09 | 34.4 | 831 | 3088 |

*Source:* World Development Indicators (2017), available at http://www.chinatax.gov.cn/eng/n2367736/index.html

India's fiscal deficits have been much higher than China's during post liberalization period. In 1980, India's fiscal deficit stood at 5.1 per cent against China's 13.7 per cent. However, thereafter, China's fiscal discipline has been far more impressive than India, even though tax revenues of both the countries are similar, hovering around 10 per cent of GDP.

In India, the interest rate, which is crucial for investments, has been as high as 16.5 per cent through 1980s and has consistently remained high. China had kept the lending rate much lower to boost investments and borrowing, which was crucial to achieving high growth. Similarly, the inflation rate has been too high in India throughout time, whereas China effectively managed inflation at a very low level to boost growth. Despite such huge differences in inflation, unemployment rate remained similar for both the countries.

Due to trade liberalization and fiscal discipline, as envisaged in Washington Consensus, China had much less external debt, whereas India had borrowed extensively to finance its recurring trade deficits. In 1990s, when India had a BOP crisis, the external debt went up to 26.07 per cent of GDP, which has fallen since to 20.66 per cent in 2014. However, China's external debt has been far too less due to its trade surplus and huge FDI inflows.

The total reserves for India have gone up to USD 325 billion in 2014 from a low of USD 5.6 billion in 1990, whereas China has amassed an impressive USD 3.9 trillion in reserves in 2014, up from USD 34.4 billion in 1990. It may be noted that the reserves accumulated by India have been due to capital account surplus, whereas Chinese reserves were built with a major contribution from current account surplus. This provides more robustness to the Chinese economy as compared to India.

The attainments of Chinese macroeconomic parameters have come in the backdrop of its decision to strengthen its infrastructure that was crucial for growth. Though India emphasized the importance of infrastructure, until recently, it did not embrace the Chinese single-minded goal of infrastructure development that is built ahead of time in anticipation of future demand. China had built infrastructure to facilitate production in manufacturing much ahead of time. That enabled them to become the manufacturing hub of the world. India started with a balance between growth and equitable distributive policies based on socialist principles in the mid-fifties, but changed course with greater emphasis on redistribution during critical periods of growth. For example, in the power sector, village electrification was a priority for farms and not necessarily for households. Emphasis on connectivity without economic efficiency meant financial burden on the government budget. Having a centralized political system with complete State control helped China to take risks to modernize its infrastructure, which would have been difficult under alternate political paradigms. In the telecom sector, India was committed to allow growth of access of service and connectivity through entry of private sector. The reforms in telecom sector have provided wider connectivity with a large population being connected. Table 2.3 summarizes the infrastructure development since 1980.

As evident from Table 2.3, India has built more roads as compared to China during post liberalization period and remains ahead of China in this segment. But the percentage of paved roads in China is better than India implying much better road infrastructure. In railways, China has increased the lines route length by 32.7 per cent since 1980 as compared to India's 5.2 per cent, though India had early advantages to strengthen its rail infrastructure. India had a vast railway network with railways owning real estate in prime locations in most of the Indian cities. But Indian railways could not capitalize on these advantages to strengthen the network and rail infrastructure. Similarly, in the energy sector, China has moved far ahead of India in production and consumption.

The impressive growth of these two countries is not devoid of challenges. They face serious challenges in sustaining the growth in 21st century in the wake of environmental concerns. The following section examines environmental degradation and costs and their implications to sustainability of economic development.

## Environmental Degradation and Costs

China and India are endowed with large amounts of cheap labour and natural resources, but in the past, they lacked the necessary capital to exploit them. In China, comparative advantages mostly existed in

Table 2.3 *Basic Infrastructure Sector Performance Indicators (1980 to 2017)*

| | *India* | | | | *China* | | | |
|---|---|---|---|---|---|---|---|---|
| *Infrastructure Indicators* | *1980* | *1990* | *2005* | *2017** | *1980* | *1990* | *2005* | *2017** |
| Telephone Connections per 1000 persons | 2.3 | 5.07 | 40 | 20 | 4.3 | 11.1 | 270 | 140 |
| Mobile Phones per 1000 persons | NA | 0 | 148 | 870 | NA | 0.02 | 348 | 1050 |
| Power Capacity (1000 mwh) | 33.3 | 71.8 | 137.6 | 326.8 | 65.9 | 126.6 | 442.4 | 1,770.00 |
| Power Generation (Billion kwh) | 119.3 | 275.5 | 661.6 | 1,160.14 | 285.5 | 590.3 | 2371.8 | 6,412.0 |
| Energy Use (Kg of Oil equivalent Per capita) | 294 | 363 | 472 | 624 | 610 | 767 | 1717 | 2,143 |
| Energy Intensity of Primary Energy | NA | 8 | 6 | 5 | NA | 21 | 10 | 7 |
| Roads (in 1000 Kms) | 644 | 2,000 | 2,526 | 4,865 | 883 | 1,181 | 1,931 | 4,460 |
| Paved Roads (% of total Roads) | NA | 47 | 57 | 53.8 | NA | NA | 40.8 | 63.7 |
| Rail Lines Route Length (Kms) | 61,240 | 62,367 | 63,465 | 64,460 | 49,940 | 53,378 | 62,200 | 67,092 |
| Safe Drinking Water (% of Population with Access) | 42 | 71 | 86 | 94 | NA | 67 | 86 | 95 |
| Sanitation (% of Population with Access) | 7 | 17 | 31 | 44 | NA | 48 | 65 | 75 |

* 2017 or the latest data

*Source:* World Development Indicators (2017)

the form of labour-intensive goods and in India, the advantage lay in natural resources. After economic reforms, many MNCs had set up their factories to take advantage of cheaper labour and increased access to natural resources. FDI flew in at a large scale and the economy began to export raw materials and low value merchandise. With open markets, people in these countries have more choices in finished goods, which are imported from developed countries. With rising income levels fuelled by growth, domestic consumption and production have increased manifold, resulting in further depletion of natural resources. The arguments of weak sustainability further resulted in depletion of natural and environmental resources.

It is interesting to note that despite increased awareness levels and advocacy by world bodies, depletion of natural resources is not accounted for in the existing framework of National Income Accounts. In the absence of institutional interference and accounting framework, over-exploitation and excessive pollution levels have assumed alarming proportions. Among all countries, USA's contribution to pollution and degradation has been the highest, both in absolute and per capita terms. For example, the carbon dioxide emissions per capita in the US was 17 kg per USD GDP, while it was only 6.7 kg for China and 1.7 kg for India. However, China's contribution to methane and nitrous oxide emissions is far worse than USA's, whereas India's emissions are the least among these three countries. As for greenhouse emissions, USA's emissions are far higher than China's, whereas India pollutes the least. So, India fares far better than China in these environmental sustainability parameters. Table 2.4 summarizes sustainability indicators for the three major economies discussed above.

The energy consumption levels adversely affect the environment and threaten sustainability of development. As evident, energy use (Kg of Oil equivalent per capita) of USA has been 6,909 kg against China's 2,143 kg and India's 624 kg. However, energy consumption in China and India has gone up by around two or three times since 1990. Similarly, electric consumption in USA stands at 12,954 kWh per capita against China's 3,475 and India's 744. It may be noted that power consumption in China has gone up close to seven times since 1990, whereas India's consumption has gone up by less than three

Table 2.4 *Sustainability Indicators and Environment: India and China*

| *Indicators of Sustainability* | *India* | | | | |
|---|---|---|---|---|---|
| | *1980* | *1990* | *2000* | *2010* | *2017** |
| Carbon dioxide emissions | 314,016.211 | 619,154.615 | 1,031,853.46 | 1,719,690.99 | 2,238,377.14 |
| Carbon dioxide emissions per capita | 0.450 | 0.711 | 0.979 | 1.397 | 1.730 |
| Methane emission (kilo tonne of carbon dioxide equivalent) | 444,528 | 513704 | 561,733 | 621,480 | 636,395.827 |
| Nitrous oxide emission (thousand metric tons of carbon dioxide equivalent) | 114,802.92 | 169,598.52 | 207,700 | 234,135.87 | 239,755.131 |
| Greenhouse gas emission | 929,414.77 | 1,387,371.82 | 1,885,189 | 2,771,456.76 | 3,002,894.93 |
| Pump price for diesel per liter (USD) | | | 0.39 | 0.82 | 0.81 |
| Pump price for gasoline (USD) per liter | | | 0.6 | 1.15 | 0.97 |
| Electric power consumption (kWh per capita) | 142.148 | 273.046 | 394.963 | 642.111 | 805.599 |
| Fossil fuel energy consumption (% of total) | 39.383 | 53.763 | 63.727 | 71.404 | 73.463 |
| Energy use (Kg of oil) | 287.054 | 351.340 | 418.684 | 563.159 | 637.428 |
| Energy intensity | | 8.291 | 6.949 | 5.353 | 4.730 |
| Forest area | | 21.505 | 21.993 | 23.473 | 23.773 |

*(Continued)*

*(Continued)*

| Indicators of Sustainability | China | | | | |
|---|---|---|---|---|---|
| | *1980* | *1990* | *2000* | *2010* | *2017** |
| Carbon dioxide emissions | 1,467,193.37 | 2,442,431.02 | 3,405,179.87 | 87,760,400.42 | 10,291,926.9 |
| Carbon dioxide emissions per capita | 1.49525075 | 2.15157091 | 2.69686243 | 6.56052001 | 7.543 |
| Methane emission (Kt of carbon dioxide equivalent) | 869,136 | 1,016,910 | 1,043,400 | 1,642,260 | 1,752,290.14 |
| Nitrous oxide emission (thousand metric tons of carbon dioxide equivalent) | 237,185.34 | 340,451.3 | 414,138.3 | 550,296.5 | 587,166.366 |
| Greenhouse gas emission | 2,757,430.09 | 3,892,675.16 | 5,082,325.6 | 11,183,810.6 | 12,454,710.6 |
| Pump price for diesel per liter (USD) | | | 0.45 | 1.04 | 0.81 |
| Pump price for gasoline (USD) per liter | | | 0.4 | 1.11 | 0.96 |
| Electric power consumption (kWh per capita) | 281.624 | 510.619 | 992.943 | 2,943.589 | 3,927.044 |
| Fossil fuel energy consumption (% of total) | 69.074 | 75.709 | 79.841 | 88.198 | 87.480 |
| Energy use (Kg of oil) | 609.455 | 766.995 | 898.987 | 1954.722 | 2236.729 |
| Energy intensity | | 21.179 | 10.233 | 8.679 | 6.690 |
| Forest area | | 16.738 | 18.853 | 21.368 | 22.189 |

* 2017 or the latest data
*Source*: World Development Indicators (2017)

times during the same period. The energy intensity (MJ/$2011 PPP GDP) in China is too high compared to USA and India, which makes Chinese GDP much less green.

The vehicular pollution contributes to environmental degradation to a large extent. The number of motor vehicles and fuel prices are major determinants of pollution levels. In USA, motor vehicles per 1000 people stands at 809, China is at 113 and India is at 18. Higher fuel prices[5] in India result in lesser fuel consumption and subsequently lesser vehicular pollution. China, on the other hand, faces steep challenges to save their environment as compared to India since their per capita income is five times that of India.

Environmental degradation has been taking a heavy toll on aquatic and plant life. The loss of species has been significant and all the countries need to devote a lot of resources to safeguard aquatic and plant life from possible extinction that ultimately threatens the global ecosystem. However, the forest area of all three major economies of the world is increasing since 1990 due to proactive interventions.

The economic growth over last two decades has contributed to natural resources degradation and global warming. As the environmental resources become scarcer due to their overuse, accountability norms in a more stringent nature are in line to be enforced in respective countries to contain environmental depletion. Such institutional measures will pose challenges to the existing development models of China and India, as environmental costs will raise the costs of production and thereby reduce the competitiveness of products. In such a scenario, the export led growth experienced by China over last two decades will suffer huge setbacks, given the very high energy intensity of Chinese production. India will also find it difficult to maintain a lower energy intensity in the face of rising environmental costs in the 21st century.

## Challenges of Sustaining Economic Development

The prime source of development has primarily been economic growth, as higher levels of income enables economies to allocate more for social infrastructure. The key drivers have been adoption of an investment centric neoclassical growth model and pursuing the policy reforms as envisaged in Washington Consensus. China's homogeneous and skilled workforce and India's talent in the IT sector has been a major determinant of attracting foreign investments. However, in the coming years, both these countries will find it hard to sustain their high growth rates as resources deplete at a faster rate. Due to enhanced mobility, factors of production will become more expensive, thereby raising the overall cost of production. Chinese economy had excelled due to low cost production by exploiting its resources, mainly labour. With extensive and intensive globalization and factor markets becoming more international, competitiveness of Chinese manufacturing will be challenged by other developing countries. The decline in export competitiveness of China will adversely affect its growth. In an increasingly concerned world, conscious of global warming, environmental costs will soon be accounted for with responsibility fixed at source. China, with high energy intensity levels, will no longer be competitive. The demographic dividends, primarily responsible for Chinese growth over the last three decades, will not be same with China's one child policy and an ageing population with increasing LEB. To sustain its growth rate, China has to innovate to produce high value products to replace its low-cost low-value products.

India's achievements in economic development parameters have been much less as compared to China despite its high growth rates over the last two decades. India's economic reforms process, which was pursued a decade after China, is not yet complete. India will do well in completing the reforms process and by putting more emphasis on execution. The low achievements of India in development parameters provide an opportunity to maintain a higher growth rate than China. India, with low energy intensity, has better prospects to cope with future environmental regulations. India is likely to reap the demographic dividends as it will have the largest young workforce in the world in the coming years. India's 'Make in India' campaign, envisaged by Prime Minister Narendra Modi, will focus on high end manufacturing. This campaign, if executed well, will provide much needed impetus to the India's quest for higher economic achievements that has remained elusive in the last few decades. However, both the countries will have to shift their focus from low-cost, low-value economic activities to knowledge-based, high value-addition economic activities to sustain their development in 21st century.

## Conclusions

The high growth rates attained by China and India in the last few decades have transformed them into economic powerhouses. Their economic development since the 1980s has been significant. With more than one third of the world's productive workforce, these two economies will occupy the center-stage in the 21st century. The Sino-Indian economic development model, based on a neoclassical framework, pursued the reforms process as envisaged in the Washington Consensus. However, with the rising threat to environment and increasingly globalized factor markets, both China and India face challenges to sustain higher levels of economic development. This study finds that India has an advantage over China to sustain high growth rates in the 21st century due to its young workforce and a determined new political paradigm that puts so much emphasis on the execution of economic reforms.

## Notes

1. Though the Human Development Index (HDI), estimated by UNDP does not include many of these social dysfunction and environmental depletion parameters, it goes beyond income by including education and health parameters.
2. Despite a paradigm that focused on income redistribution and an equal society, inequality in Chinese economy is much higher with a Gini coefficient of 42.1 against India's 33.6.
3. As India follows a system of 'Common Law', where the Judiciary is independent, property rights are clearly defined and are respected by the State.
4. All the figures are in US Dollars, if not otherwise specified.
5. Relative to income levels; India's PCI is one fifth of China's PCI.

## References

Acemoglu, D., S. Johnson, and J. A. Robinson. 2002. 'Reversal of Fortune: Geography and Institutions in the Making of the Modern World Income Distribution.' *The Quarterly Journal of Economics* 117, No. 4, 1231–1294.

Bass Hans, H. 2008. 'Ragnar Nurkse's Development Theory: Influences and Perceptions.' http://www.hs-bremen.de/internet/hsb/struktur/mitarbeiter/bass/publikationen/downloadangebote/nurkse_book_2008_bass.pdf

Baran, Paul A. 1957. *The Political Economy of Growth*. New York: Monthly Review Press.

Cao, Y., Y. Qian, and B. Weingast. 1999. 'From Federalism, Chinese Style to Privatization, Chinese Style.' *Economics of Transition* 7, 103–131.

De Soto, H. 2000. *The Mystery of Capital: Why Capitalism Triumphs in the West and Fails Everywhere Else.* New York: Basic Books.

Furtado, C. 1964. *Development and Underdevelopment – A Structuralist View of the Problems of Developed & Underdeveloped Countries.* Berkeley: University of California Press.

Hirschman, Albert O. 1998. *The Strategy of Economic Development.* New Haven: Yale University Press.

Jie, Gan. 2008. 'Privatization in China: Experiences and Lessons.' Hong Kong University of Science and Technology. http://english.ckgsb.edu.cn/sites/default/files/privatization_in_china.pdf;

Marx, Karl. 1867. *Capital: A Critique of Political Economy* https://www.marxists.org/archive/marx/works/download/pdf/Capital-Volume-I.pdf

Moyo, D. 2009. *Dead Aid: Why Aid Is Not Working and How There Is Another Way for Africa.* London: Allen Lane.

Nurkse, Ragnar. 1953. *Problems of Capital Formation in Underdeveloped Countries.* Oxford: Oxford University Press.

Prescott, C. Edward. 1988. 'Robert Solow's NeoClassical Growth model: An Influential Contribution to Economics.' *Scandinavian Journal of Economics* 90, No.1, 7–12.

Ramo, Joshua Cooper. 2004. 'The Beijing Consensus. The Foreign Policy Centre.' http://fpc.org.uk/fsblob/244.pdf

Ricardo, David. 1817. *The Principles of Political Economy and Taxation.* https://books.google.bg/books?id=cUBKAAAAYAAJ&dq=editions:y8vXR4oK9R8C&pg=PR1&hl=bg#v=onepage&q&f=true

Romer, P. M. 1986. 'Increasing Returns and Long Run Growth.' *Journal of Political Economy* 94, 1002–1038.

Rostow, W. W. 1960. *The Stages of Economic Growth: A Non-Communist Manifesto.* Cambridge: Cambridge University Press.

Santos–Paulino, Amelia U. 2010. 'China and India: Country Role Models of Development Success?' UNU-WIDER Working Paper No2010/121.

Schumpeter, J. A. 2011. *The Theory of Economic Development: An Inquiry into Profits, Capital, Interest and the Business Cycle.* New Jersey: Transaction Books.

Sen, Amartya A. 2005. 'Human Rights and Capabilities.' *Journal of Human Development* 6, No. 2, 151–166.

Singh, Nivikar. 2008. 'India's Development Strategy: Accidents, Design and Replicability.' MPRA Paper No.12453. https://mpra.ub.uni-muenchen.de/12453/1/MPRA_paper_12453.pdf

Solow, R. M. 1956. 'A Contribution to the Theory of Economic Growth.' *The Quarterly Journal of Economics* 70, No.1, 65–94.

Wei, Pan. 2007. *The Chinese Model of Development.* http://fpc.org.uk/fsblob/888.pdf.

Williamson, John. 2004. *The Washington Consensus as Policy Prescription for Development.* http://www.iie.com/publications/papers/williamson0204.pdf

World Bank. 2017. World Development Indicators. http://data.worldbank.org/indicator

Yao, Yang. 2008. 'The Disinterested Government: An Interpretation of China's Economics Success in the Reform Era.' http://policydialogue.org/files/events/Yao_Disinterested_Government_China.pdf

Zhang, Ming. 2014. 'The Transition of China's Development Model.' In *China's Economic Development: Institutions, Growth and Imbalance*, edited by Ming Lu, Zhao Chen, Yongqin Wang, Yang Zhang, Yuan Zhang, Changyuan Luo, Edward Elgar and Cheltenham, pp. 52–56. Edward Elgar: UK.

CHAPTER 3

# BCIM Economic Corridor from the Perspective of Sino-Indian Cooperation

Xiaojuan Zhou

## Characteristics of BCIM Economic Corridor and its Construction

The BCIM economic corridor covers a wide range of regions, including Bangladesh, northeast India, Myanmar and southwest China, covering an area of 1.65 million square meters and a population of about 440 million people, covering 40 per cent of the world's population.[1] All the proposed regions under BCIM are border regions of the countries with most regions being underdeveloped areas. The special regional position of BCIM economic corridor determines the different initial conditions for its construction. Unlike other regional cooperation mechanisms, BCIM economic corridor is a regional cooperation mechanism based on the poorest assembly zone in the world. In this section we make an attempt to provide an overview of these countries based on parameters like economic progress, industrial development, human capital, infrastructural development and international trade openness to justify the usefulness of the BCIM Economic Corridor to these countries.

1. **Economic attainments.** GDP per capita in 2017 of various countries in the path of the BCIM Economic Corridor was as follows: Bangladesh USD 1,517; China USD 8,827; India USD 1,940; Myanmar USD 1,299; these countries rank 147th, 73th, 139th and 154th, respectively, in the world.[2] The average level of economic development in eastern India and Yunnan Province of China (the core regions) substantially lag behind the average level in the respective countries. These regions house the most poverty-stricken population of India and China.
2. **Industrial development.** From the perspective of industrial development, Bangladesh and Myanmar are two countries with very weak industrial sectors and they rely on the agricultural sector to boost their economic growth. Eastern Indian States and Yunnan Province of China are predominantly traditional agricultural regions of India and China, respectively. Northeast India mainly depends on industries like processing units of primary products, which are labour intensive, for its growth. The area's share of average industrial production is less than 30 per cent of the total output and most of the labour forces are employed in the traditional agricultural sector. Similarly, Yunnan Province of China is heavily dependent on the agricultural sector with 66 per cent of employment being generated in the agricultural sector while the level of industrialization is lower than the national average.
3. **Human capital.** Human Development Index (HDI) in BCIM Economic Corridor regions lags behind the average and the quality of life and development attainments are very low. HDI in various countries of BCIM Economic Corridor in 2017 was as follows: Bangladesh 0.608; China 0.752; India 0.640; Myanmar 0.578; these countries rank 136th, 86th, 130th and 148th in the world.[3] Additionally, the adult literacy rate as a percentage of people aged 15 years and above in India was only 69.3 per cent in 2017, ranking last among the four countries—China, India, Bangladesh and Myanmar. The literacy rate is especially low in the eastern part of India, except in Mizoram and Tripura. In comparison, the literacy rate of adults aged 15 years and above as recorded in 2017 was 95.1 per cent in China, 75.6 per cent in Myanmar and 72.8 per cent in Bangladesh.[4]

4. **Infrastructural development.** Spatial distribution of BCIM Economic Corridor presents highly ecologically fragile regions with complex and precipitous terrains characterized by remote and rocky mountains, dominated by an occlusive environment with poor infrastructure. Compared to global standards, information communications infrastructure in developing regions of China and India lags far behind. The total competitiveness score of infrastructure in China and India is separately 77.9 and 68.1, respectively, ranking the 36th and 70th in the world (as illustrated in Table 3.1). The efficiency of air transport services and exposure to unsafe drinking water are the main indicators affecting China's global ranking in infrastructure, separately ranking 66th and 74th in the world. Road connectivity and electricity supply quality are

Table 3.1 *The Global Competitiveness of Infrastructure*

| | *China* | | *India* | |
|---|---|---|---|---|
| | *Score* | *Rank* | *Score* | *Rank* |
| **Infrastructure** | **77.9** | **36** | **68.1** | **70** |
| **1. Transport infrastructure** | **68.9** | **24** | **66.4** | **28** |
| 1.1 Road connectivity | 95.7 | 10 | 75.8 | 72 |
| 1.2 Quality of road infrastructure | 59.7 | 45 | 58.6 | 48 |
| 1.3 Railroad density | 17.9 | 61 | 56.6 | 39 |
| 1.4 Efficiency of train services | 59 | 24 | 57 | 30 |
| 1.5 Airport connectivity | 100 | 2 | 100 | 4 |
| 1.6 Efficiency of air transport services | 60.7 | 66 | 64.3 | 59 |
| 1.7 Liner shipping connectivity | 100 | 1 | 59.9 | 25 |
| 1.8 Efficiency of seaport services | 58.6 | 52 | 59.1 | 49 |
| **2. Utility infrastructure** | **86.9** | **65** | **69.8** | **103** |
| 2.1 Electricity access | 100 | 2 | 87.5 | 105 |
| 2.2 Electricity supply quality | 99 | 18 | 85.8 | 108 |
| 2.3 Exposure to unsafe drinking water | 83.6 | 74 | 49.9 | 106 |
| 2.4 Reliability of water supply | 64.9 | 68 | 55.9 | 96 |

*Source:* Compiled from the Global Competitiveness Report 2019

the main indicators affecting India's global ranking in infrastructure, with a much lower ranking at 72nd and 108th, respectively.[5]

5. **International trade openness.** Core regions of BCIM Economic Corridor are mainly inland frontier regions, which are surrounded by land and are unable to contact the adjacent markets resulting in lesser level of economic globalization compared to the countries' average. The frequency of international trade, investment, information and culture exchange between various countries is generally lower than the world average. The globalization index in various countries of BCIM Economic Corridor in 2017 was as follows: Bangladesh: 51.26, China: 65.11, India: 62.25 and Myanmar: 43.93; the countries rank 155th, 84th, 100th and 192nd in the world, respectively.[6] Additionally, most regions in the Yunnan Province and Northeast India belong to the typical domestic oriented economy with very low degree of economic openness. The foreign trade volume in Yunnan Province in 2018 was USD 29.8 billion, accounting for 0.5 per cent of the trade volume of China. Similarly, the foreign trade volume in Northeast India is nearly negligible compared to overall trade volume of India.

## Significance of BCIM Economic Corridor for China and India

It is advantageous for both China and India, the largest rising economies in the world to maintain a peaceful coexistence, boost economic development with economic cooperation by opening up their border through BCIM Economic Corridor construction project, which can boost transportation and infrastructure. From the perspective of economic development, BCIM Economic Corridor can potentially impact 40 per cent of the population of the world and can create nearly USD 11 trillion GDP with its vast natural resources such as animals, plants, crude oil and minerals. China and India are emerging powers with their own advantages. China has advanced technologies in the fields of manufacturing, power and telecommunication, equipment and engineering as well as a powerful and rich management experience in the field of infrastructure. India has the core advantage in the information industry, software outsourcing and pharmaceutical industry (Li Shuyao, 2014). BCIM Economic Corridor will provide institutional arrangement of trade convenience for products with comparative advantages relative to market demand potential in China and India, which will increase investment potentially resulting in a reduction in India's trade deficit with China. This project shall connect markets of both China and India and can potentially create more job opportunities for sustainable development in both countries. Additionally, BCIM Economic Corridor is coherent with China's 'Westward Opening' and India's 'Look East Policy'. The ensuing international trade has the potential to extend itself to east Asia, South Asia, Southeast Asia and other Asiatic regions. This will also promote the 'networking' of interregional cooperation mechanisms, further expand the common economic space between China and India, cultivate new economic growth points and form an open economic belt. Therefore, the BCIM Economic Corridor is of great significance from the prospective of Sino-Indian economic cooperation.

## Sino-Indian Position on BCIM Economic Corridor

### Economic and Political Cooperation between China and India and the BCIM Economic Corridor

Sino-Indian sub-regional economic cooperation based on the BCIM Economic Corridor may not only realize the 'absolute benefit' of win-win cooperation economically, but it will also help to win the 'comparative benefit' by mutual political trust. After assuming office in 2014, the Indian Prime Minister, Narendra Modi, strengthened the 'Look East Policy', which had been implemented for more than 20 years in the form of 'Act East Policy'. It further emphasized the aspiration and decision to participate in the economic affairs concerning the Asian-Pacific regions, greatly enhancing the compatibility and blending relationship with China. With this development, Sino-Indian relations entered the best period in the countries' political history, when mutual favour and cognition between the two countries significantly improved through repeated exchange visits of leaders of China and India. In April 2018, Prime Minister Modi visited China for the first informal meeting between the leaders of China and India in Wuhan, demonstrating the determination of the two countries to expand economic and trade cooperation. In 2019, President Xi Jinping went to Chennai, India, to hold the second informal meetings with Prime Minister Modi, laying the foundation for a new step in bilateral relations (Vikram Misri, 2019).

## Sino-Indian Economic Cooperation and BCIM

According to the Asian infrastructure construction forecast report, released by the Asian Development Bank in 2012, if about USD 320 billion is invested into transportation and communication field each year between 2010 and 2020, the improvement of communication and transportation will reduce one-fifth of trade costs for India, and one-seventh for China; improvement on means of communication will reduce 11.2 per cent of trade cost for India.[7] Therefore, at present, China and India have basically the same understanding on the issues of BCIM economic corridor cooperation, that is, the construction of BCIM economic corridor mainly emphasizes on strengthening economic cooperation, mutual benefit and the win-win situation. Interconnection construction, as the current priority area of cooperation, includes traffic connection, system connection and human to human connection. Among these, transportation connection in BCIM is currently the most important basis to push the regional economic cooperation between China and India. However, the development focus of interconnection between China and India in the short term is mainly on traditional traffic connection—construction of highways, railways, aviation and water transport. In terms of Sino-Indian road connection, the construction of Nathu La highway made the road connection between China's Tibet and India's Kolkata a reality in July 2006. The distance from Tibet's Nathu La to India's Kolkata was shortened by about 1200 km. In terms of Sino-Indian aviation connection, Kunming–New Delhi business-chartered airplane realized its first flight in December 2000, ending the long-term blank history of aviation connection between China and India. Beijing–Shanghai–Delhi airline was opened in 2002, Beijing–Delhi non-stop flight was opened in 2006, Kunming–Calcutta airline was opened in 2007, Chengdu–Bangalore non-stop flight was opened in 2010 and Chengdu–Bombay flight was opened in 2012. These developments are very promising for future economic cooperation between India and China.

## Strengthening of Bilateral Trade and Economic Cooperation

With India dominating the services industry and China dominating the manufacturing industry, development of Sino-Indian relations lie in driving mutual beneficial cooperation in other fields with economics and trade cooperation. It has been argued that China and India should enhance economic and trade cooperation through complementary advantages and facilitate positive and stable development of bilateral relations with a core focus on economic and trade cooperation. Since the proposal of BCIM Economic Corridor strategy in 2013, the level of cooperation among the four stakeholder countries has been increasingly strengthened. India, Bangladesh and Myanmar become three of 25 countries whose economic and trade scale with China exceed USD 10 billion along 'One Belt and One Road', of which India is the largest trade partner of China among countries along the BCIM Economic Corridor. In 2018, bilateral trade volume between China and India increased to USD 95.54 billion, an increase of 13.2 per cent over the same period in the previous year.[8] India is the seventh largest export market for China. In 2017, the export volume from China to India exceeded USD 34 billion.[9] Meanwhile, China is the largest trading partner and the largest import source and the third largest export market for India. India's overseas direct investment stock at the end of 2017 in China had reached USD 4.75 billion. Sino-Indian trade volume accounted for 11.4 per cent of foreign trade volume in India.[10] China was the only country with imports accounting for more than 10 per cent of India's total imports, with imports accounting for 14.4 per cent amounting to USD 16.35 billion. India's exports to China accounted for about 5.1 per cent. These figures are encouraging for a strong bilateral trade relationship between the two fastest growing economies in the world. BCIM Economic Corridor will help achieve greater cooperation.

## Challenges to BCIM Economic Corridor

BCIM Economic Corridor is the sub-regional economic cooperation strategy of China and India. Theoretically, China and India should have lots of related potential cooperation avenues, however, they are still not realized to their full potential. Besides, relevant cooperation contents launched by BCIM Economic Corridor haven't been implemented, and only generated a limited progress on bilateral economic and trade cooperation between China and India. Objectively, BCIM Economic Corridor is still within a difficult cooperation range (Zhu Cuiping, 2015) and China and India are mainly confronted with the following problems and challenges during BCIM Economic Corridor construction.

### Cooperative Mechanism: Highly Uncertain.

1. **Weighting of cooperation benefit.** Allocation of cooperation benefit produced by cooperative mechanism is the key to continuous cooperation. However, in terms of BCIM Economic Corridor construction, though China and India have a mutual interest in promotion of sub-regional economic integration, they also have reached a consensus on gaining profits through development potential and economic cooperation. China and India may be easily sensitive to comparative benefit, especially in any arrangement involving northeast regions. India is more inclined to focus on the comparative benefit rather than absolute benefit as the position of BCIM regions become more important. In this case, India will inevitably choose the negative attitude of 'Slow Down Pace' for BCIM Economic Corridor construction. This may result in making BCIM economic cooperation highly uncertain.
2. **Low institutional level of cooperative mechanism.** From the perspective of BCIM Economic Corridor cooperation practice, the two parallel 'mechanisms' in this region are highly uncertain. Dialogue between think-tanks is legitimate to a certain extent, but faces the problem of poor effectiveness and that the government authorization can be recalled at any time. Yunnan has been the centre of BCIM Regional Cooperation Forum in China and

Sichuan, Guangxi, Guizhou, Tibet and other western areas barely participate in it. Such phenomenon also occurs in India. Northeast India didn't take part in the regional forum dominated by Chinese Research Institute in New Delhi in 2015. In the meanwhile, though a series of issues have been mapped out since its establishment, no consensus has been reached on the priority of issues. In addition, the government working-level talk of BCIM Economic Corridor was initiated in 2013 and is still at the preliminary stage. It is easily influenced by the fluctuating political relations between countries since the support of the government of each country may be recalled at any time.

## Pathway Construction: Hard in the Long Run

1. **China and India haven't completely reached a consensus on traffic corridor line.** Pathway construction has always been the key problem of BCIM Economic Corridor and is also regarded as the most difficult problem currently. At present, during a discussion at the Bangladesh China India Myanmar regional economic forum, the traffic corridor routes of BCIM economic corridor basically reached a consensus on the 'three lines', namely, 'The North Line' (Stilwell Highway), 'The Middle Line' (Kunming-Dali-Baoshan-Ruili-Mandalay-Tamu-Sippar-Shillong- Dacca-Calcutta) and 'The South Line' (connecting the deep sea port). However, at the government level in China and India, only a basic consensus has been reached on the middle line, which is considered to be a relatively easy route to realize connectivity at present. Due to security threats, geopolitics and other reasons, the north line and the south line, with the lowest construction cost and the most convenience, are still under discussion.
2. **Lack of funds for infrastructure investment.** Although China has basically completed the construction of roads in the country, Northeast India and other regions along the line are featured by lots of alpine and gorge regions and backward infrastructure, so capital investment is very large. Though China and India are seeing rapid economic growth, they are still developing countries with limited economic resources, which are further

compromised with rising state deficits. Currently, New Delhi declared that India is facing USD 1 trillion of capital construction deficit. Though China has proposed to invest USD 20 billion for infrastructure and special economic zones construction in India, it only remits the infrastructure investment scale of BCIM Economic Corridor. It is impossible for Chinese and Indian government or public sectors to bear all investments. While the intervention of private enterprises is never fully encouraged, the development of capital market lags behind. Besides, huge funding gap also delay the formation of 'Hard Connection' of BCIM Economic Corridor to a large extent.

## Lack of Convergence in Economic Interests

1. **Imbalance in trade between China and India.** In term of trade balance, only the intra-regional trade of China has maintained a surplus in BCIM, while India has been in deficit for a long time. Although the Sino-Indian trade deficit eased down by 3.6 per cent, China remained the largest source of India's trade deficit—USD 57.22 billion in 2018.The continuous sharp increase of Sino-Indian trade deficit triggers the panic button for India for the potential competition from China, which also restrains India's positivity to further enhance the Sino-Indian bilateral trade through BCIM Economic Corridor.
2. **Intra-regional FDI influence on Sino-Indian development.** China's direct investment into India increases rapidly, however, China's direct investment in India only accounts for a little more than 2 per cent of China's total foreign investment. India's investment into China also only accounts for 1.3 per cent in India's total foreign investment outflow. Most states in Northeast India belong to internal-oriented economy areas and are rarely associated with the external economic entities except for a small amount of cross-border trade. The import volume of Northeast India is very low except for West Bengal and Meghalaya, who are involved in exports to foreign countries..

In addition, the exports from China and India are mainly labour-intensive products such as plastics, rubber, ore, raw materials and textiles. The export products have low value-addition and strong substitutability. Meanwhile, the advantages of raw materials and labour force of China and India overlap partially. Homogeneous competition will hinder bilateral trade between China and India.

### Trade Liberalization Needs Improvement

1. **Regulations in tariff levels.** China and India have reached a consensus on 42.5 per cent duty-free commodities in term of bilateral trade, but the tariff restriction can be further broadened. India still requires to pay 9.5 per cent tariff to enter the Chinese market, and China requires to pay 14 per cent tariff to enter the Indian market. Moreover, from the perspective of overall tariff structure, the proportion of products with over 10 per cent tariff is still quite high—37.2 per cent in China and 18.5 per cent in India.[11]
2. **Non-tariff barrier influence on Sino-Indian economic and trade cooperation.** As far as non-tariff barriers are concerned, Sino-Indian trade structure is still highly restrictive. India hopes China could eliminate the non-tariff barriers in such fields as agricultural products and medicine. However, India has a more serious restriction in fields such as technology, sanitary and phytosanitary measures[12] and cargo clearance barriers. Additionally, India has imposed lots of trade barriers in intellectual property, government procurement, import quotas and other aspects. It is estimated that bilateral port efficiency, customs environment and regulations environment of China and India have trade facilitation level of 0.59 and 0.51 respectively, which are not high when compared to the 24 countries along Maritime Silk Road, ranking 8th and 14th, respectively (Zhou Yan and Chen Shumei, 2016).[13]

## Conclusion

In order to make the BCIM Economic Corridor a successful venture, institutional breakthrough and improvement will be required, which can be achieved through cooperative mechanisms, cooperative fields, cooperative benefits and cooperative targets, so as to resolve the cooperation dilemma between China and India to expedite BCIM Economic Corridor.

Both the countries can adopt multiple ways to enhance Sino-Indian exchange and communication at the government level, scholar level and at the level of general public. At government level, definite formulations of the bilateral exchange mechanism of BCIM Economic Corridor should realize the connection between policy and plan, and carry out pragmatic cooperation, particularly that India has agreed to develop the north line and south line of its northeast regions by cooperating with China in principle. However, India is still worried because of high sensitivity in the northeast regions. Therefore, China and India should further strengthen the bilateral exchange and increase political mutual trust based on cooperation and mutual security. At academic level, the researchers should provide an intellectual platform for BCIM Cooperation Forum to enhance the cooperation and exchange of Sino-Indian academic institutions, especially think-tanks. This can be achieved by building a team of researchers specializing in the Indian economy, society and culture to further investigate the details regarding the surrounding countries. At the level of general public, a mechanism should be put in place for cultural exchanges between these two countries, which would provide a platform to push folk cultural exchange to increase mutual understanding between China and India.

Domestic and foreign funds can be mobilized to strengthen BCIM; it would be ideal to continue the construction of roads, communication and other infrastructures and reduce the dilemma of shortage of resources for this project. To attract foreign funds, active participation in international construction and actively seeking funds from institutions like the World Bank, Asian Development Bank and Asian Infrastructure Investment Bank should be done. On the domestic side, the government should encourage large enterprises and consortia to make direct investment or joint development of interconnection projects, promote capital connectivity through infrastructure export construction and deepen regional value linkage. At the same time, the government should actively set up diversified development funds for

BCIM economic corridor, strengthen policy support for interconnection projects and provide special fund support or preferential loans for the development of BCIM.

Both the countries should exploit their comparative advantages to deepen the intra-regional professional division system and enhance the convergence of interests between China and India via the production network of complementary advantages (Wang Bo, Cheng Nuo and Lin Guijun, 2019). On the basis of existing BCIM bilateral and multilateral trade contacts and the priority demand of Sino-Indian economic and trade development, core industries such as agriculture, metallurgical mineral, gardening and handcrafts in India and its northeast regions should be strengthened. Other sectors like agricultural produce, tourism, new energy and other aspects should be the focus areas to continue to expand the Sino-Indian trade contacts and promote complementary resources by using BCIM Economic Corridor (Yu Zheng, Sheng Minhui and Wang Qiong, 2014). Under the platform and framework of economic corridor, both the countries should actively drive the projects in medical, Infrastructure, IT and other fields through mutual cooperation between China and India. Both the economies should take the lead in creating a batch of iconic early harvest programs with effective cooperation. To enhance the cooperation and mutual trust between China and India, India should reduce its attention on comparative benefit in the specific field of BCIM Economic Corridor to advance pragmatic cooperation.

Both the countries should improve the institutionalized subregional economic cooperation of BCIM Economic Corridor by creating free trade zones. This will absorb the construction experience of China-ASEAN free trade zone and India-ASEAN free trade zone to push the negotiation and research on China–India Free Trade Agreement. This will further improve the percentages of the bilateral trade tariff elimination and elimination of the non-tariff barrier as well. Both the economies should drive mutual opening of various sectors like medical treatment, finance, culture and manufacturing. Both countries should strengthen the port and service system construction of BCIM Economic Corridor by building modern parks to cater to the needs of the manufacturing industry, IT, agriculture and animal husbandry, logistics and medicine to promote trade facilitation and economic cooperation between the two countries.

## Notes

1. Data source: World Bank WDI Database 2018.
2. Data source: China Statistics Press, International Statistical Yearbook-2018, 2018
3. Data source: The United Nations, Human Development Report 2018, 2018
4. Data source: World Bank Database, last updated date 2018
5. Data source: World Economic Forum, The Global Competitiveness Report 2019
6. Data source: KOF Swiss Economic Institute, KOF Globalization Index 2018
7. Data source: Asian Infrastructure Construction [M]. Academy of Asian Development Bank, Beijing: Social Sciences Academic Press, 2012
8. Data source: Chinese Ministry of Commerce 2019
9. Data source: 2018 China Trade and External Economics Statistical Yearbook Editorial Staff
10. Data source: WTO, Global Trade Data and Prospects 2019
11. Data source: calculated based on the HS2012 version 6-digit tariff data in WTO Tariff Database.
12. The Agreement on the Application of Sanitary and Phytosanitary Measures (SPS) is a multilateral trade Agreement under the jurisdiction of the world trade organization. It is both a separate agreement and part viii of the agriculture agreement.
13. Data source: Economic Effect Analysis of Trade Liberalization and Facilitation of the 21st Century Maritime Silk Road, Asia-pacific Economic Review, January 2016.

## References

Li Shuyao. 2014. 'Study on Trade Relations and Development Potential of BCIM Economic Corridor.' Yunnan University of Finance and Economics master's thesis.

Misri, Vikram. 2019. 'From WuHan to Chennai, India Promotes Win-Win Cooperation.' *Global Times* 10, No. 11, 14.

Qing, Yonghong. 2013. 'The overall framework of institutionalization in China–India relations.' *South Asian Studies Quarterly* 4, No. 155, 61–67.

Wang Bo, Cheng Nuo, and Lin Guijun. 2019. 'Value-added trade network of manufacturing industry in countries along 'One Belt And One Road' and its influencing factors.' *Journal of International Trade* 3, 85–100.

Yu Zheng, Sheng Minhui, and Wang Qiong. 2014. 'China–India FTA Trade Fundamentals and Economic Effects.' *South Asian Studies* 2, 12–27.

Zhou Yan, and Chen Shumei. 2016. 'Economic Effect Analysis of Trade Liberalization and Facilitation of the 21st Century Maritime Silk Road.' *Asia-pacific Economic Review* 1, 50–56.

Zhu Cuiping. 2015. *BCIM Economic Corridor Construction: China-India perspective*. Social Sciences Academic Press.

CHAPTER 4

# A Comparative Analysis of Poverty Reduction Patterns of China and India

Zujun Liao and Delang Song

## Introduction

China and India are countries with the largest number of poor people in the world. There are many similarities and significant differences in the problem of poverty reduction. Similarities are mainly reflected in various aspects—both are big developing countries with a vast national land area and with a huge population base endowed with abundant natural resources. Also, both China and India are the major emerging economies among the 'BRIC countries', which have had a remarkable contribution to the growth of global economy in recent years. At the same time, differences between China and India are mainly embodied in the political system, economic system, economic structure and history and culture. Through the comparative analysis of the Sino-Indian poverty reduction pattern, it is beneficial for the two countries to exchange experiences to effectively implement their strategies in their endeavour to reduce poverty.

# Poverty Reduction Strategies between China and India

## China: Government-oriented Poverty Alleviation Pattern

The key task of targeted poverty alleviation is to ensure that the poor masses have adequate food and clothing, with the aim of speeding up poverty alleviation and prosperity, improving ecological environment, improving development ability, narrowing the development gap and realizing the goal of building a moderately prosperous society in an all-round way. This would improve the ecological environment and enhance the development capacity by narrowing the development gap so as to achieve a moderately prosperous society (Liu, 2016). Precise poverty alleviation is a new pattern of poverty alleviation with Chinese characteristics of 'government-led, market dynamic, social participation' by incorporating the concept of fine management, integrated synergy and sustainable regeneration as a guide. This is done by adopting scientific methods of co-ordination and classification by insisting on the whole process of responsibility management. Implementation of a new comprehensive management form of accurate identification, precise policy, precise support, precise management for poverty alleviation targets is the premise of this policy. The essence of its theory is as follows: first, identify the 'roots of poverty', find out a suitable remedy for it and implement targeted therapy; second, change the traditional 'inclusive and social movement-based poverty alleviation' as precise poverty alleviation of combining 'inclusive and appropriate competition'; third, to achieve accuracy in six aspects including supporting objects, project arrangement, fund use, implementation of measures, sending people to villages, and assessing effects of poverty alleviation.

## India: NGO-oriented 'Relief +Technology' Poverty Alleviation Pattern

P.O.O.R.[1] is also led by many non-governmental organizations (NGO), which use science and technology to address poverty alleviation, mainly focusing on ecological protection (Devi 2013), cultural quality, economic development, health and gender equality. Its goal is to improve the ecological environment of the poor in rural areas so as to enhance the vitality of rural economy, create opportunities of employment, improve health conditions of rural population and ensure women are actively involved in rural governance to promote gender equality, all of this through scientific research, effective use of local resources, promotion of applicable technology products and provision of technical guidance and training to achieve technology and capacity upgrading (Oki-Okogbuo 2015). There are many representative Indian NGOs including the Bharatiya Agro Industries Foundation (BAIF), the Indian Development Research Foundation, the Children's Development Khazana (CDK), Bharatiya Samruddhi Investments and Consulting Services (BASIX), the SYEDHASH IM, etc. The Indian Government is mainly responsible for the implementation of relief-oriented poverty alleviation. Before 2013, they were involved in disbursement of 25 kg of rice or wheat per household as a basic living allowance. However, from that year till now, they subsidize benefits ₹30,000 to ₹40,000 per household, which can be directly accessed by the beneficiaries in their bank account.

In comparison, the Poverty Alleviation Strategies (patterns) between China and India have a fundamental difference in the power of poverty reduction. China's poverty alleviation pattern shows that the core force is the government with government-led social participation. While in India, NGOs are the main force with non-governmental organization-led and government-guided poverty alleviation. While the government mainly provides the basic relief funds for the extremely poor people, NGOs guide and coordinate to carry out poverty relief in India.

## Poverty Identification in China and India

### Comparison of Poverty Standards

1. **Poverty standards in China and poor people identification.** National Bureau of Statistics of China defines poverty for individuals or families, which rely on labour income and other lawful income that is not sufficient to maintain the basic survival needs. The poor areas refer to region of poor population.
   **The poverty line:** China has set the annual income per person of rural residents under USD 324.54 (2010 constant price)[2] as the

national poverty alleviation standard. In 2015, actual poverty standard of living expenses has reached around USD 2.12 per person per day in China, which has been higher than the international absolute poverty standard of USD 1.9 (Yang and Ma, 2016).

2. **Poverty standards in India.** India has different poverty lines for urban and rural areas. The rural poverty line refers to rural residents' income reaching 2435 calories per person per day, which amounts to USD 0.4045 according to the US dollar exchange rate of 2019; the urban poverty line refers to urban residents' income reaching 2095 kcal, which amounts to USD 0.4944 according to the US dollar exchange rate of 2019 (Kumari, 2013).[3]

## Comparison of Poverty Identification Methods

1. **Poverty identification methods in China.** China uses a combination of village participation and multidimensional comprehensive evaluation for poverty identification. China, for identification of its poor, follows the process of 'group assessment → village discussion → village township check → county confirm → group publicity' (Wang, 2016). This establishes a recognition mechanism that is divided into three levels, namely, poor population, poor households and poor cities. In order to avoid the defect assessment of the single standard, China adopts a combination of quantitative analysis by means of the comprehensive indexes and qualitative assessment by means of considering six aspects in the assessment of the poor population and poor households. Constructing detailed indexes from the housing situation, production conditions, asset accumulation, labour force status, education, present situation and other aspects, the system achieves comprehensive evaluation on poverty and ensures that the evaluation is fair and open. Generate a card for poor families and input them into the database of poverty population (Chen and Zhang, 2016). The poverty population database is adjusted dynamically according to the cycle.
2. **Poverty identification in India.** Poverty identification in India is carried out mainly in terms of national sampling survey, which is based on people's consumption expenditure and the proportion of population. An NSS sample survey is the main method for identification of poor households. Through a comprehensive survey which

includes the residents' housing conditions, income, safe drinking water, communication conditions, etc., the Indian government determines the poor households and accordingly provides ration cards.

Both China and India adopt absolute indicators of poverty. However, the poverty line in China is far higher than in India and the methods of poverty identification in China are more specific and effective than in India.

## Poverty Reduction Measures in China and India

### China's Poverty Alleviation Measures

Based on precise assessment, China optimizes the allocation of resources to achieve precision in poverty alleviation of the residents in rural households.

#### *Precise Information and Management of Poverty*

Precision in management is the guarantee of removal of poverty. China has established a complete information management platform for poverty alleviation, including food, clothes, houses, etc. Focus on the utilization and comprehensive information resources, targeting data sharing and interaction platform, it builds an information service platform. The Poverty Alleviation Cloud, supported by Internet applications and services helps this cause. According to information docking platforms, the information management platform for poverty alleviation achieves precision, dynamic and scientific management of poverty alleviation, helps in dynamic recognition of poor and intelligent determination of the poverty level and undertakes constant announcement of poverty alleviation information to finally achieve poverty elimination (Xiaohai Deng et al., 2015).

### Cadres Move into the Village to Ensure Precision

Village cadres constitute the main force in effecting poverty alleviation. Cadres are sent to the villages to assist impoverished villages' mayors and secretaries to carry out poverty alleviation work and play an active role in giving suggestions for poverty elimination.

Through the integration of resources, the introduction of quality projects and the execution of these projects, it accelerates the process of poverty alleviation. In strict accordance with 'if poverty is not eliminated, the village cadres will not leave', the work requirements effectively promotes the implementation of the policies and improves the efficiency of using the resources earmarked for this purpose.

### *Poverty Alleviation and Implementation of Policies*

According to the level of poverty-stricken objects and the causes of poverty, targeted assistance plans are formulated; assistance projects are formulated according to local agricultural production and farmers' production capacity. Overall planning for the poverty alleviation, urbanization, traffic and the development of characteristic industry, it achieves the organic combination of farmers and industry. According to local conditions, it improves local infrastructure and promotes the income growth of the farmers by imparting knowledge on agricultural science and use of technology.

## Poverty Alleviation Measures in India

1. **Non-governmental organizations provide technical support.** Through technical training and promotion, non-governmental organizations improve the poor people's income, provide welfare benefits and social status in agricultural development, assist in women empowerment and children's relief. For example, the agricultural industry foundation of India (BAIF) uses the rural cluster development method to establish self-help groups for the poor to guide them and launch various income generating activities and community development activities to reduce the incidence of poverty.
2. **Non-governmental organizations provide life relief.** Deepak Foundation (DF) provides relief services to the poor by undertaking maternal and child safety projects (to provide free child delivery service and prenatal and postnatal maternal examination service), women self-help engineering (which establishes women self-help production teams, mainly making handicrafts and producing milk,

to help women create an income), disaster relief and reconstruction projects (to provide relief to the victims) (Wang, 2009).

3. **Non-governmental organizations provide financial help.** SYEDHASH IM family foundation is a charity that aims at relieving the poor and helping the poor get rid of poverty. It gives out relief funds to orphans (₹200 per month), disabled persons and old persons (₹100 to 150 per month). They also provide interest free loans of about ₹1 to 100,000 to the poor who have technologies and the ability to produce (Lian Zhong, 2006).
4. **The government provides the necessary relief.** The government directly transfers funds to the beneficiaries' bank accounts. The usual transfers are between ₹30,000/year and ₹40,000/year for every family, which is about USD 407.38 to USD 544.52 (Xiaohai Deng et al., 2015). Such bank transfers can reduce corruption embedded in the process of distribution of materials/supplies, thereby increasing the poverty reduction rate. It promotes overall development of children in nutritional health, mental health, education and other aspects by Integrated Child Development Services (ICDS) (Zhong, 2006).

## Effectiveness of Poverty Reduction in China and India

### Effectiveness of Poverty Reduction in China

1. **A significant decline in the number of poor people.** According to the National Bureau of Statistics, the population living under poverty in China reduced over the years from 2013 to 2017 (Figure 4.1). The pattern of poverty alleviation is declining year by year. By the end of 2018, the number of rural poor in the country had decreased from 98.99 million in 2012 to 16.6 million, a cumulative decrease of 82.39 million; the incidence of poverty fell from 10.2 per cent in 2012 to 1.7 per cent in 2018, a cumulative decrease of 8.5 percentage points.[4]
2. **The living conditions of poor have improved.** Poverty-stricken rural infrastructure such as road, water, electricity, housing, etc., have been comprehensively improved. Administrative villages have achieved full coverage of broadband and many public centre

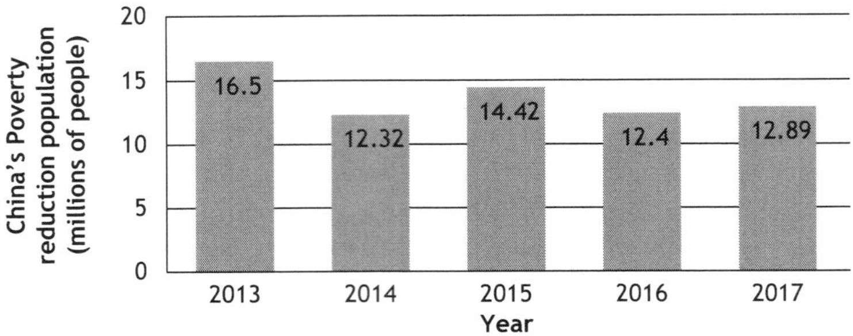


Figure 4.1 *Change in Population (in Millions) Living Under Poverty in China (2013–2017)*

kindergartens are set up in the township. Additionally, as of 2018, the proportion of poor households participating in the new rural cooperative system has reached 98.22 per cent, the patency rate of poor country roads has reached 89.3 per cent, access to tap water for the households reached 92 per cent and the coverage rate of standardized clinics in poor villages and the comprehensive cultural activity centres has reached 84 per cent and 72 per cent, respectively.

## Effectiveness of Poverty Reduction in India

1. **Children's health.** The proportion of underweight children of less than five years of age in 2013–2014 was 30.7 per cent, which has significantly improved because of several government programs to reduce malnutrition. This includes the Integrated Children's Development Service (CDS) and the National Rural Health Service. The proportion of India's underweight children has dropped 13 percentage points in 2017–2018 from 2007–2008.
2. **Education.** The Indian government has made some progress in improving the enrolment rate of disadvantaged groups and promoting gender equality. The enrolment rate for children in 2018 increased to 99.73 per cent as compared to 77.45 per cent in 1990, an increase of 20 per cent. The percentage of women in secondary education increased from 39.74 per cent in 2000 to 47.98 per cent in 2013, an increase of 8.214 per cent. The proportion of literate

adult women has increased year on year. In 2018, the literacy rate of female adults in India reached 69.277 per cent, nearly 3.3 times higher than that in 1980.

3. **Health.** The Government of India and non-governmental organizations continue to increase spending on public health, which accounts for 40.03 per cent of total medical expenditure in 2018, an increase of 6 per cent in about 10 years. The three-level network of medical care services, including health care stations, primary health care centres and community health centres, meet the basic medical needs of most Indians. At the same time, since 2005, India has begun to implement the 'National Rural Health Service Project', which is provided for free as part of universal immunization programs and other medical services for the general poor. In the 1990s, the success rate of tuberculosis was only 25 per cent, while by 2014, the success rate of tuberculosis treatment rose to 95 per cent, nearly 3.7 times higher than before.

## Learnings from Poverty Reduction in China and India

### Provide Better Autonomy to NGOs to Reduce Poverty

At present, non-governmental organizations (NGOs) are also involved in the process of poverty alleviation in China and India. To a certain extent, NGO intervention is required because of its function in terms of promoting public welfare and characteristic with respect to its flexibility which can make up for the lack of functions of the government and market entities to a certain extent, and have incomparable advantages in coverage and management efficiency. Furthermore, NGOs try to enhance the poor's entrepreneurial capacity and benefits through financial support, technical training, establishment of mutual aid organizations, etc., which are helpful to enhance the capacity of managing the poor population to achieve sustainable development. However, it is necessary to further strengthen NGOs resources, deepen NGOs participation in poverty alleviation and guide NGOs to fight poverty. Diversification would help in poverty alleviation and enhance the efficiency and effectiveness of poverty alleviation eventually.

## Strengthen the Accountability of Poverty Alleviation Funds

The accountability of poverty alleviation funds is a key factor in determining the effectiveness of poverty alleviation. For example, the Indian government has had poor ability of financial supervision in the past years, resulting in the loss of funds for poverty alleviation and therefore, the programs have been less effective. Not only in India, but in China also, their efforts to reduce poverty have met with problems such as the interference of cadres, filing of false claims, corruption and so on. It is necessary for the countries to further strengthen the publicity of the alleviation project and improve the transparency related to the use of financial funds. We should also strengthen the audit team and give full autonomy to the auditors as gatekeepers in the management of public financial funds. Besides, it is necessary to expose problems relating to the use of funds, to crack down on illegalities and irregularities by strengthening the supervision by auditors for quality improvement, to prevent corruption, which can be termed as the 'darkness under the lights'. The government should keep the balance between fund supervision and fund use, and set supervision standards according to the actual use of funds.

## Effectiveness of Poverty Identification

Poverty identification is the basis for accurately implementing poverty policy and improving the effectiveness of poverty alleviation. India adopts the pattern of poverty identification of 'general identification + fuzzy recognition, which lacks pertinence and effectiveness. For accurate identification, China also faced many problems, such as information transmission error, missing poor problem and high cost of identification. Poverty identification should be performed effectively to further innovate the identification mechanism and combine comprehensive evaluation and core standards through qualitative observation and quantitative indicators of evaluation. They should distinguish the differences in terms of region and community, plan a rational identification path, summarize the recognition rules, implement home visits and third-party verification in identification of poverty groups, the causes of poverty and poverty levels.

## Conclusion

As emerging figures for world economic development, China and India are an important part of the world economic map. At the same time, China and India still have huge numbers of impoverished people. They are committed to the reduction of poverty and undertaking innovation in poverty alleviation models. Through the comparison of China–India poverty reduction models, we find that China's absolute poverty line is much higher than India's. The method of poverty identification is more specific than that of India. The government has played an important role in China's poverty alleviation. At the same time, India is an important force for social relief and poverty alleviation. In the future, it is necessary to further exert the poverty reduction role of non-governmental organizations, strengthen their supervision and performance management of poverty alleviation funds, effectively and economically.

## Notes

1. P.O.O.R. is a small NGO working in India to address some of the problems faced by the rural poor. (http://www.poor.org.in/about.html)
2. On September 1, 2019, the middle rate of RMB exchange rate in the interbank foreign exchange market is: 1 US dollar = 7.1543 RMB, 1 RMB = 0.1398 US dollars.
3. On September 1, 2019, the middle rate of RMB exchange rate in the interbank foreign exchange market is: 1 US dollar = 7.1543 RMB, 1 RMB = 0.1398 US dollars.
4. See The State Council Leading Group Office of Poverty Alleviation and Development http://www.cpad.gov.cn/

## References

Devi, R. U. 2013. 'An Analytical Study on the Role of NGOS in the Poverty Reduction of India.' *Researchers World* 4 (4), 127–137.

Hui, Chen, and Zhang Quanhong. 2016. 'Poverty Precision Identification and Precision Poverty Alleviation Measures Based on Multidimensional Poverty Measurement—In the Mountains of Northern Guangdong as an Example.' *Journal of Guangdong University of Finance and Economics* 31 (3), 36–43.

Kumari, L. 2013. 'Poverty Eradication in India: A Study of National Policies, Plans and Programs.' *Researchers World* 4 (2), 68–80.

Lian, Zhong. 2006. 'India to Benefit Millions of Disadvantaged Children's CDS Project.' *Press of Early Childhood Education and Education Science* 11, 46–52.

Obi-Okogbuo, J. 2015. 'Science, Technology, and Globalization: A Re-appraisal in the Philosophy of Science and Technology.' *European Scientific Journal* 11 (14), 32–41.

Xiaohai, Deng, Zeng Liang, and Luo Mingyi. 2015. 'Precise Identification of Tourism Poverty Alleviation under the Background of Precision Poverty alleviation.' *Ecological Economy* 4, 94–98.

Xiaolin, Wang. 2016. 'Precise Poverty Alleviation Identification for Object and Precise Helping Research—Case Study of the Southwest of Guizhou.' *Finance and Economics of Contemporary Rural* 3, 70–89.

Zhanyong, Liu. 2016. 'Connotation Characteristics of Precision Poverty Alleviation Thought and Its Enlightenment to the Practice of Poverty Alleviation.' *Jianghan Academic* 4, 49–60.

Zhengwei, Yang, and Ma Hailong. 2016. 'Accurate Understanding of Poverty Standards.' *Economic Daily*, 2016-09-14.

Zhong, Wang. 2009. 'The Study of NGOs on the Social Assistance to Replace the Role of Complementary.' Beijing Jiaotong University.

CHAPTER 5

# Migrant Workers' Well-Being

## *A Comparative Study Based on China and India*

**Xiwei Huang**

## Introduction

Migration is a crucial dimension of human civilization. It provides an example of how human beings strive for a better life (Abbas and Varma, 2014). Migration has been an important feature of the Chinese society. Especially after decades of migration controls, there has been a sudden upsurge in the number of migrants (Pieke, 2014). Many migrants come to cities from rural areas in search of a more friendly life-environment. According to National Bureau of Statistics of China (2018), the population of migrant workers has reached 286 million, which account for approximately 20 per cent of China's total population. Scholars have identified various factors motivating people to migrate from rural areas to urban cities, such as a lack of equality in urban–rural income (Zhang & Song, 2003), labour surplus in agriculture (Wong, Li, & Song, 2007), urbanization of the countryside (Iredale, Bilik, Su, Guo, & Hoy, 2001) and the dissolution of state-owned enterprises and a modernized market economy (Iredale et al., 2001). These migrants might very well take up less favourable jobs, work with poorer social protection and live in worse housing conditions than urban workers (Wong, Li, & Song, 2007). Having limited access to public services, they are also generally believed to be highly vulnerable in terms of mental health status (Zhong et al., 2017).

Internal migration in India is primarily spurred by employment and marriage. It has great influence on India's society in many aspects. According to United Nations in India (2018), nearly one-third of India's population is migrant and nearly half of the migrants in India have been driven by poverty. Though some well-educated Indian citizens migrate internally and earn a higher wage than local residents in urban cities (Khan, 2016), this chapter focuses specifically on the disadvantaged population driven by poverty from rural areas to urban areas. The migration flows can be permanent, semi-permanent or seasonal (Abbas & Varma, 2014). In spite of the differences in the duration of their stay, all migrants are often vulnerable and exploited. They face multiple challenges at their workplace destinations.

## Comparison of Structural Oppression

Despite the difference between countries of origin, migrant workers face similar structural oppression, which makes it hard to promote their well-being. This study analyzes and compares the difficulties that migrant workers face in China and India, and hopefully shed some light on how to overcome the obstacles of promoting their well-being.

### Comparison of Identity Dilemma

China's *hukou* system serves as a household registration system that regulates population distribution and rural to urban migration by managing domestic passports. This has divided the rural and urban populations in China and has adversely affected millions of rural residents and deprived them of their rights to settle legally in cities (Chan, 2010).

In China's context, the term 'migrant worker' refers to industrial and service worker with rural *hukou*. Migrant workers are not eligible for the same welfare benefits and other rights as urban *hukou* holders, such as access to urban health insurance, urban pension plans and public housing. Regardless of their length of urban life, they remain legally rural *hukou* holders.

Most migrant workers are trapped in heavy labour and service jobs. Their legal rural *hukou* status and their ineligibility for urban *hukou* make them easily vulnerable to exploitation. What is worse, some decrees have been issued by local authorities to forbid migrant workers from taking up jobs other than heavy labour and service jobs. Thus, the system has inevitably created an easily exploitable and highly flexible industrial workforce for China's export economy (Chan, 2010).

There is no *hukou* system in India, but structural oppression about identity exists in a different form. In rural or remote areas, many Indian citizens are born at home. So, they do not have birth certificates that are issued in hospitals or clinics. The overall birth registration rate in India is 34.7 per cent while regional differences remain significant. For example, Uttar Pradesh and Bihar, the major states of labour exportation have birth registration rates of 6.5 per cent and 1.6 per cent respectively. This has led to the result of numerous undocumented migrant workers in the receiving urban community (Abbas and Varma, 2014).

Birth certificate is the fundamental document that can be used to acquire ration cards, voter cards and so on. It ensures that a person can benefit from state-provided rights and welfare. Without a birth certificate, it becomes a serious issue for migrant workers to prove their identity when they arrive in a new place. This issue could keep on troubling them for years or even decades after their migration (Abbas and Varma, 2014). For example, the hardship of acquiring ration card could be one of the consequences caused by this issue. It can be used to buy grocery at ration shops and it is often needed to access many public resources (Abbas and Varma, 2014). With no birth certificate to acquire a ration card, migrant workers have no access to public services and are forced to buy groceries at higher market prices. They also have problems accessing traditional educational channels for their children.

Migrants are legally entitled to a new ration card by national policy, but in reality, it has become a tricky dilemma. First, it has become an unsolvable loop that many migrant workers have never received a birth certificate and ration card in their home state when the policy requires them to delete their names from original ration cards. Second, many migrant workers do not have the knowledge or access to knowledge of the correct procedure to obtain a new ration card. Third, officials are often not willing to cooperate with the migrant workers as regards the procedural requirements. For different reasons such as discrimination or seeking bribes, some officials refuse to accept the provided documents from migrant workers. As a consequence of this uncertainty, a lot of migrant workers choose to not take the risk of deleting their names from the original ration cards issued to them in their home state (Abbas and Varma, 2014).

### Comparison of Migrant-resident Income Gap

China's *hukou* system is also suggested to be one of the fundamental reasons why there is such a rural–urban income gap in the country (Lu and Song, 2006). Migrant workers usually work for extremely long hours and earn very low wages. Since 1990s migrant workers' average work hours have been about 63 hours a week, while urban workers work only for 43 hours a week (Meng, 2014). Another research (Lu and Song, 2006) suggests that about 95 per cent of migrant workers earn less than 1500 yuan for a month while only 68 per cent of urban workers earn within the same bracket.

In India, scholars (Duraisamy and Narasimhan, 1997; Sharma, 2014; Srivastava & Sasikumar, 2005) have revealed that migrant workers often take up low-skilled jobs and face discrimination at the destination. According to research carried out over the years (Duraisamy and Narasimhan, 1997; Sharma, 2014; Srivastava and Sasikumar, 2005), they are paid lower than local residents who do the same kind of work and are also less likely to be covered by the social welfare system.

## Comparison of Housing Conditions

According to a research (Luo and Deng, 2014), in 2012, the average living space per capita of China's urban residents reached 32.9 square meters. Migrant workers' average living space per capita is less than

10 square meters. The average living space per capita of some migrant workers who live in relatively good housing condition is about eight square meters but most migrant workers live in shared accommodation or low-priced dormitories in which the average living space per capita is less than four square meters. Luo and Deng (2014) concluded three features of migrant workers' housing condition—extremely limited living space, poor facilities and equipment and the lack of security. It is a cruel fact that most migrant workers cannot afford appropriated housing, not to mention that they still have to save up to support their families back home.

Another scholar (Hu, 2008) indicated that over half of the migrant workers live in accommodations provided by employers, such as dormitories, construction sites or the workplace. Approximately 43.9 per cent of migrant workers rent low-priced dormitories by themselves and only 1.5 per cent can afford self-owned apartments. More than 10 per cent live in unstable housing and face the risk of eviction anytime.

The central government has emphasized the importance of solving migrant workers' issues from economic policy perspective but has not released any specific policies solving migrant workers' housing problems. On the other hand, many local governments in urban cities have delivered a series of policies seeking to solve the problem. Unfortunately, these policies have been criticized by scholars (Lu and Zhou, 2008) for two reasons. First, specific policies for migrant worker's housing problem are still too few to make a real difference. Second, all the policies have not yet taken concrete shape in a systematic manner.

In India, migrant workers mostly live in slums due to low wages. Larger demand for labour does not necessarily come with an increased capacity to accommodate every migrant. Approximately 68 million Indians lived in slums in 2011 (Abbas and Varma, 2014). Low-income population in urban areas lacks access to adequate rehabilitation or public housing, so they end up in slums. Things are even worse for some other migrant workers who cannot afford the rents in slums either. They have no choice but to live in shopping pavements, open areas or at their workplaces. Without safe housing, these migrant workers have become even more vulnerable than before (Abbas and Varma, 2014).

## Comparison of Education Resources

Social public services have many dimensions such as health care, senior services and most importantly, children's education. This study intentionally focuses on the education of migrant workers' children.

A majority of migrant workers in China have to leave their families behind in the rural villages and work in other places (Meng, 2014). A survey from the RUMiCI project (as cited in Meng, 2014, p. 383) indicates that in China only 63 per cent of married migrants bring their spouse with them and around 56 per cent of children under 16 years of age are left behind in the migrant workers' rural hometowns. The total number of the children left behind has been estimated at about 58 million (China Youth Research Center, 2006). However, despite the challenges, in Sa's study (as cited in Lai et al., 2014, p. 68) it appears that an increasing number of migrants have chosen to bring their children with them. The total number of children who are brought with their parents reached 19 million in 2000 and 43.8 per cent of them are between the age of 6 and 14 years (China Youth Research Center, 2006). Some of the children come along with their migrant parents while some are left behind with elderly relatives and brought over at a later date.

As one of the consequences of the *hukou* system, migrant workers have to pay a much higher price for their children to attend urban schools close to where they work. The price is often too high to afford considering migrant workers' low wages (Kong and Bao, 2009). A case study in Shanghai (Zhang and Wang, 2010) indicates that migrant workers who have no urban *hukou* have to pay school fees several times higher than Shanghai *hukou* holders for their children's education.

Rural residents' children are more likely to grow up in poverty and attend far less equipped schools located in less developed areas than their urban peers (Yang, 2010). Due to the rural–urban gap in educational resources, urban students usually have better academic performances and achieve higher educational attainment (Wang et al., 2011). Rural students also face various barriers even when successfully transferred to urban schools because urban schools usually adopt different editions of textbooks that are more academically advanced than rural schools (Kong and Bao, 2009).

In India, although migration has drawn wide attention internationally, migrants' children have been still understudied. The instability caused by the migration process makes it hard for these children to keep attending school (Pang-Ben Bella, 2014).

There have been major attempts to solve the problem, such as the enactment of the Right of Children to Free and Compulsory Education Act, 2009. Unfortunately, some ambiguities and loopholes in the 2009 Act have led to the consequence of failing to offer universal education for all including migrant workers' children (Pal, 2014). Even for those who successfully enrolled in rural schools in their hometown, some of them could still drop out because they have been absent from school when they migrate with their parents (Pal, 2014).

## Discussion

As a response to social problems related to internal migration, governmental policies and initiatives have profound influence on promoting migrant workers' well-being in China. Provincial local governments have been emboldened by China's central government to experiment with different approaches to serve citizens, especially migrant workers.

On a macro level, there have been various reforms in the *hukou* system both by the central government and provincial local government in order to deal with migrant workers' essential issues caused by structural oppression. In 1983, the rules were relaxed and for the first time, rural residents were allowed to sell their agricultural produce outside of their hometowns and live outside of their hometowns. In a document released by the central government, it was stated that a certain degree of mobility of labour was acceptable (Cai and Wang, 2008). From the mid-1980s, rural *hukou* holders were allowed to migrate to cities and take up a job or even run their own business. They were issued a special kind of *hukou*, Zilikouliang, which meant self-sufficient in foods (Wu, Zhang and Chen, 2010). During the same time, some local governments in major cities implemented a 'blue-stamp' *hukou* strategy, which allowed certain rural residents preferred by government to migrate legally. One type of the preferred populations was those who bought an apartment in the city or invested in local businesses (Xu, 2015).

A remarkable change took place in 1997 when policies were approved by the State Council allowing rural residents to obtain an urban *hukou* if they had a stable income and a permanent residency address in the city. However, these policies had only begun to be widely implemented in small towns and cities. Reports in the predominant state television channel suggest that the real and more radical change had not taken place until 2014. The reform was approved by the state government and has aimed at stopping *hukou* restrictions in small cities, lower restrictions in mid-sized cities and set appropriate terms in big cities (Xu, 2015). The reform would eliminate the segregation between urban and rural *hukou*. It has been expected to ease the structural oppression and help migrant workers gain access to their rightful social welfare and protection (Branigan, 2014). Unfortunately, the reform was criticized for its ambiguity because practical plans to carry out the reform were not available. It seems that the central government has remained extra careful and cautious when it comes to the *hukou* system reform and decided to take step-by-step policies according to different urban volumes of various cities (Xu, 2015).

The provincial local policy has been another impact factor on *hukou* system reform. Considering the fact that the ultimate cost for the reform is paid by local governments, the central government has encouraged local governments to create different policy reforms accordingly (Xu, 2015). Researchers have made suggestions to local governments. For example, Cai and Wang (2008) proposed that the government should only provide limited employment, public services and social welfare for citizens in small towns and small cities in order to not attract too many new residents. In this way, the influx caused by the reforms could be kept under control. As for major cities, abundant job opportunities, comprehensive social welfare system and better public services are all attracting numerous migrants from all over the country. Intense pressure has been put on these cities' economic and social infrastructure. Zhengzhou, the capital city of Henan Province, revised some *hukou* policies in 2003. The incoming migrants flooded into the city and exceeded the city volume very quickly (Xu, 2015). Next year, the government had to announce a withdrawal of the reform because of the burden caused by the influx of migrants. As a result, Xu (2015) suggested that the local governments in major cities should set strict terms for migrants accessing urban *hukou*.

With a long history of system reforms, China has been engaging in promoting migrant workers' well-being constantly from policy perspective. On a micro level, there have been various approaches helping migrant worker individuals as well. Social work positions have been created and set within the existing social service system (Gao and Yan, 2015). In 2009, Chengdu Civil Affairs Center (CCAC) was founded by Chengdu Civil Affairs Bureau and since then CCAC has taken on supervisory responsibilities for the professional development of social work in Chengdu city. CCAC identifies difficulties and problems of local community social service organizations and helps them deal with the issues by multiple methods, such as training and workshop. CCAC also initiates leading programs as a demonstration to other organizations. School social workers have only begun to be recognized in China. Cooperating with Chengdu Association of Social Workers, CCAC has selected three elementary schools in which at least over 50 per cent of students are migrant workers' children. CCAC has launched a leading school-social-work program in the three schools since 2014, especially monitoring the needs of migrant workers' children (Chengdu Civil Affairs Center and Chengdu Association of Social Works, 2015).

China has reacted actively on governmental level. Social change has taken place from top to bottom. On the other hand, social change in India has taken a rather different path.

In spite of collecting evidence of positive outcomes of migration for the low-income population, national policymakers have drawn a conclusion that internal migration should be prevented by implementing strategies such as rural employment programs (Abbas and Varma, 2014). With no further research to prove positive outcomes of migration, urban development projects have been designed to keep migrant workers out. Migrant workers are considered to be almost illegal residents and thus often harassed by the police (Abbas and Varma, 2014).

There has been some policy reform in India regarding the issue of migrant workers. The Government of India made an enactment under the name of 'Inter-State Migrant Workmen (Regulation of Employment and Conditions of Service) Act of 1979'. It aimed to address migrant workers' unjust working conditions. Migrant workers have to seek employment through middleman contractors or agents who often fail to pay wages timely as promised and many of them work in unsafe and unprotected environment without being informed of the job's risks. The Act made a list of employers' and contractors' responsibilities and made it very clear that wages must be timely-paid and be equal or higher than the minimum wage. Employers and contractors must provide appropriate housing, medical assistance, protective clothing and they must inform accidents or even causalities to certain authorities and migrant workers' kin. Migrant workers could return home periodically without losing jobs or wages. They could also raise industrial disputes. In order to enforce the Act, penalties were set as rules. However, employers and contractors were provided with an escape route if they could prove that they were not aware of such transgressions (Sarde, 2018). Meanwhile the Act has been overwhelmingly ignored by state governments (Abbas & Varma, 2014). Not surprisingly, the Act has remained empty talk and never reached the goal to better policy environment for migrant workers on a governmental level. Almost no record of dispute settlement or prosecution could be found (Sarde, 2018).

In 2005, National Rural Employment Guarantee Act, 2005 (Ministry of Law and Justice, 2005) was issued. It allows 100 days of employment for all enrolled workers, including migrant workers, in a financial year. The daily wage must be no less than the minimum wage within a certain territory. However unfortunately, despite the good will of the Act, an Indian scholar (Sarde, 2018) stated that the Act has not taken off the ground in reality. There has not been strong political will or social commitment to make it happen. It has only been implemented successfully in very few places. Criticism has been made by other scholars in history as well (Bhalla, 2014; Narayanan, 2017). From a trade union perspective, Sarde (2018) believes that this was due to the lack of organizational structures, awareness and desire.

While macro responses from the governmental level have failed to contribute much to migrant workers' well-being, non-governmental organizations (NGO) have played an active role to cope with these social issues. Their practice and innovations in migration practice have helped migrant workers transform challenges into more stable livelihood options in recent years.

In order to provide services, support and security to seasonal migrant workers, Aajeevika Bureau, a non-governmental and non-profit initiative was founded in 2005 in Udaipur, Rajasthan. Based on a hypothesis that rural–urban migration is inevitable in India's socio-economic transition, Aajeevika Bureau aims at helping migrant workers live a better life in the receiving community. Aajeevika Bureau has built up a number of walk-in service centers in migrant workers' original community and arriving community. It has been one of the most important operational strategies that makes resources more easily accessible for migrant workers. Services provided at Aajeevika Bureau include issuing registration documentation, offering skills training, legal aid and literacy programs and assistance accessing banking and social security.

Some other NGOs have been working to enable education for children of migrant workers. Initiatives and programs have been designed and implemented in both original and arriving communities to have children of migrant workers included.

By unionizing migrant workers, NGOs like PRAYAS Center for Labour Research and Action have worked with migrant workers in vulnerable occupations with the rights-based strategy. PRAYAS has helped migrant workers' families achieve considerable success in negotiating wage increases and successfully reducing the number of child workers. PRAYAS' work in preventing child trafficking has inspired the foundation of a joint governmental task force to prevent child trafficking in the cotton pollination season (PRAYAS Center for Labour Research and Action, 2012).

Some NGOs have facilitated labour programs seeking to build institutional linkages between migrant workers and the urban labour market. For example, LabourNet in Bangalore has been providing services such as membership registration, certified training and job placement. It has built a system that acts as a coordinator between employers and certified workers. In addition, LabourNet also helps migrant workers to gain access to social security and financial resources.

Rationing Kruti Samiti (RKS), a group organization of mainly slum-based NGOs in Mumbai, has successfully influenced government policy to entitle migrant workers' rights to access subsidized rations in urban communities. RKS has sought to make a better policy environment for the poor by helping them gain access to food entitlement in urban arriving communities. The network built by RKS has actively involved both providers and policymakers (Jenkins and Goetz, 2002). It contributed to the passing of a government resolution, which not only proclaims obstacles faced by migrant workers while acquiring identity and residency proofs, but also proposes certain relaxations for migrant workers. Following this government resolution, a leading voluntary organization named Disha (Abbas and Varma, 2014) helped seasonal migrant workers apply for temporary ration cards for four to twelve months with more flexible document requirements.[1]

## Conclusion

China and India have taken different paths to cope with migrant workers' issues. NGOs in India have played an elementary role in migration history promoting migrant workers' well-being. In many ways, NGOs have influenced national decision-makers from bottom to top. Considerable progress has been achieved because of NGOs. However, NGOs in China have not been contributing much in migration history due to multiple reasons. The late occurrence of social work profession development and its accelerated growth has led to the consequence that social work theories, methods and techniques being used by Chinese NGO's are not firmly rooted in the local community (Shi, 2013). There has been a tendency of Chinese NGOs to rely on Western social work theory (Yan & Tsang, 2005). This is in opposition to the experiences of Indian NGOs whose works and theories have been grounded in the needs and requirements of the local community. Compared to western world, Indian environment and issues are much more similar to China's as both are developing countries. Numerous Indian NGOs' success stories can serve as examples to inspire China and also make China privy to the Indian NGOs' thinking perspective, strategies and frameworks.

Despite loopholes, ambiguity and sometimes a lack of operability, China's government has always diligently engaged in dealing with problems and endeavoured to make a change for migrant workers' lives. While achieving extraordinary economic development, China's government has come to realize the fact that labour migration is vital and inevitable for economic growth and stopped seeing migration as a problem. Internal migration could be both an opportunity and a challenge to the country and its citizens. Hopefully, the Chinese government's path could offer some inspiration to India.

## Note

1. Data source: 'About Us' on dishaindiasociety.org/

## References

Aajeevika, Bureau. 2018. *Vision, Mission and Approach.* http://www.aajeevika.org/about_us.php

Abbas, R., and D. Varma. 2014. *Internal Labor Migration in India Raises Integration Challenges for Migrants.* https://www.migrationpolicy.org/article/internal-labor-migration-india-raises-integration-challenges-migrants

Bhalla, S. S. 2014. 'No Proof Required: Move from NREGA to cash transfers.' *Indian Express* indianexpress.com/article/opinion/columns/no-proof-required-move-from-nrega-to-cash-transfers/

Branigan, T. 2014. 'China Reforms Hukou System to Improve Migrant Workers' Rights.' *The Guardian*, 1–4. Beijing. http://www.theguardian.com/world/2014/jul/31/china-reform-hukou-migrant-workers

Cai, F., and D. Wang. 2008. 'Impacts of Internal Migration on Economic Growth and Urban Development in China.' In *Migration and Development Within and Across Borders: Research and Policy Perspectives on Internal and International Migration*, 245–272.

Chan, K. W. 2010. 'The Household Registration System and Migrant Labor in China: Notes on a Debate.' http://faculty.washington.edu/kwchan/Chanhukou.pdf

Chengdu Civil Affair Center and Chengdu Association of Social Works. 2015. '*Shehui gongzuo fazhan baogao – 2014 nian shehui gongzuo zhuanyerencai dui-wujianshe jihua*' [Report on Social Work Profession Development—Growth of Social Work Professionals in 2014]. Chengdu, China: Chengdu Civil Affair Center.

China Youth Research Centre (CYRC). 2006. *China's Children and Juveniles Statistical Handbook*. Beijing, China: Science Press.

Duraisamy, P., and S. Narasimhan. 1997. 'Wage Differentials between Migrants and Non-migrants and Discrimination in Urban Informal Sector in India.' *Indian Journal of Labour Economics* 40 (2), 223–235.

Gao, J. G., and M. C. Yan. 2015. 'Social Work in the Making: The State and Social Work Development in China.' *International Journal of Social Welfare* 24 (1), 93–101. https://doi.org/10.1111/ijsw.12089.

Hu, Z. 2008. '*Chengdu nongmingong zhufang yanjiu*' [A Study of Urban Migrant Workers' Housing Condition] Doctoral dissertation.

Iredale, R. R., N. Bilik, W. Su, F. Guo, and C. Hoy. 2001. *Contemporary Minority Migration, Education, and Ethnicity in China*. Cheltenham, UK: Edward Elgar Publishing Limited.

Jenkins, R., and A. Goetz. 2002. 'Civil Society Engagement and India's Public Distribution System: Lessons from the Rationing Kruti Samiti in Mumbai.' In *Making Services Work for Poor People. World Development Report (WDR) 2003/04 Workshop Held at Eynsham Hall, Oxford*, (October 2002), 1–23. http://eprints.cscsarchive.org/260/1/Civil_Society_Engagement_and_India's_Public_Distribution_System_22489_jenkinsgoetzWDR.pdf

Khan, M. I. 2016. 'Migrant and Non-migrant Wage Differentials: A Quintile Decomposition Analysis for India.' *Indian Journal of Labour Economics* 59 (2), 245–273. https://doi.org/10.1007/s41027-017-0054-7.

LabourNet. 2018. *About LabourNet*. https://www.labournet.in/about/

Lai, Fang, Chengfang Liu, Renfu Luo, Linxiu Zhang, Xiaochen Ma, Yujie Bai, Brian Sharbono, and Scott Rozelle. 2014. 'The Education of China's Migrant Children: The Missing Link in China's Education System.' *International Journal of Educational Development* 37, 68–77. 10.1016/j.ijedudev.2013.11.006.

Lu, P., and T. Zhou. 2008. '*Nongmingong zhufang baozhang wentirenshi yu duicey-anjiu – jiyu chengben-xiaoyi fenxi*' [Identify and Countermeasure on Housing Security of Rural Migrant Worker Based on Cost-Benefit Analyses]. *Urban Studies* 15(3):110–113.

Lu, Z., and S. Song. 2006. 'Rural-Urban Migration and Wage Determination: The Case of Tianjin, China.' *China Economic Review* 17 (3), 337–345. https://doi.org/10.1016/j.chieco.2006.04.007.

Luo, R., and D. Deng. 2014. 'Chengshihua beijingxia nongmingong zhufangwenti tanxi' [A Study of the Migrant Worker Housing Problem in the Background of Urbanization].' *Journal of Guangdong University of Foreign Studies* 5:99–102.

Meng, X. 2014. 'Rural-Urban Migration in China.' In *The Oxford Companion to the Economics of China*, edited by S. Fan, R. Kanbur, S. Wei and X. Zhang, 382–387. Oxford, United Kingdom: Oxford University Press.

Ministry of Law and Justice of India. 2005. *National Rural Employment Guarantee Act, 2005*. http://nrega.nic.in/rajaswa.pdf

Narayanan, R. 2017. 'Communalism Has Been Injected Even in Bread and Butter Issues of Jharkhand.' https://thewire.in/caste/communalism-has-been-injected-even-in-the-bread-and-butter-issues-ofjharkhand

National Bureau of Statistics of China. 2018. '*2017nian nongmingong jiance diaochabaogao*' [The 2017 Report on the Surveillance of China's Rural-to-Urban Migrant Workers]. www.stats.gov.cn/tjsj/zxfb/201804/t20180427_1596389.html

Pal, S. D. 2014. 'Anakuran: A Proposed Path to Education for Children of Migrant Construction Workers in India.' *International Journal of Education & Development Using Information & Communication Technology* 10, 96–106.

Pang-Ben Bella. A. 2014. 'Migrating across Generations: Education Choices amongst Migrant Families in India' Paper Presented at the Annual Meeting of the 55th Annual Conference of the Comparative and International Education Society, Fairmont Le Reine Elizabeth, Montreal, Quebec, Canada. http://citation.allacademic.com/meta/p492815_index.html

Pieke, F. N. 2014. 'Introduction: Chinese Migrations Compared.' In *Internal and International Migration: CHINESE Perspectives*, edited *by* H. Mallee and F. N. Pieke, 1–26. London, United Kingdom: Routledge.

PRAYAS Center for Labor Research and Action. 2012. 'Child Labor in Cottonseed Production: Investigation and Advocacy.' https://www.laborrights.org/sites/default/files/publications-and-resources/Child%20Traffiking%20in%20Cotton%20Seed%20Report.pdf

Sarde, S. R. 2018. 'Migration in India: Trade Union Perspective in the Context of Neo-Liberal Globalization.' http://www.scribd.com/doc/102667602/migrant-workers-in-india

Sharma, V. 2014. 'Wage Differentials between Local and Migrant Permanent Farm Servants in Punjab.' *Indian Journal of Labour Economics* 57 (1), 157–167.

Shi, B. 2013. 'New Century: The Dilemma Confronting Social Work Education in China.' *Chinese Education & Society* 46 (6), 56–68.

Srivastava, R., and S. K. Sasikumar. 2005. 'An Overview of Migration in India: Its Impacts and Key Issues.' In *Migration and Development: Pro-poor Policy Choices*, edited by Tasneem Siddiqui. Dhaka, 157–216, India: The University Press.

Wang, X., C. Liu, L. Zhang, R. Luo, T. Glauben, Y. Shi, S. Rozelle, and B. Sharbono. 2011. 'College Education and the Poor in China: Documenting the Hurdles to Educational Attainment and College Matriculation.' *Asia Pacific Education Review* 12 (4), 533.

Wong, D. F. K., C. Y. Li, and H. X. Song. 2007. 'Rural Migrant Workers in Urban China: Living a Marginalised Life.' *International Journal of Social Welfare* 16 (1), 32–40. https://doi.org/10.1111/j.1468-2397.2007.00475.x.

Wu, K., L. Zhang, and X. Chen. 2010. 'The Obstacles of the Hukou Reform: A Analysis Based on Settled Requirements.' *Chinese Population Science* 1, 66–74.

Xu, J. 2015. 'Rural Migrant Workers' Integration into City Under the Reform of Household Registration (Hukou) System in China—A Case Study of Zhenjiang city.' Master's thesis. https://core.ac.uk/download/pdf/38685923.pdf

Yan, M. C., and A. K. T. Tsang. 2005. 'A Snapshot on the Development of Social Work Education in China: A Delphi Study.' *Social Work Education* 24 (8), 883–901.

Yang, X. 2010. 'Access to Higher Education for Rural-Poor Students in China.' *Educational Research for Policy and Practice* 9 (3), 193–209.

Zhang, K. H., and S. Song. 2003. 'Rural–urban Migration and Urbanization in China: Evidence from Time-Series and Cross-section Analyses.' *China Economic Review* 14 (4), 386–400. https://doi.org/10.1016/j.chieco.2003.09.018.

Zhang, Li, and Guixin Wang. 2010. 'Urban Citizenship of Rural Migrants in Reform-Era China.' *Citizen-ship Studies* 14 (2), 145–166.

Zhong, B., S. S. Chan, T. Liu, D. Jin, C. Hu, and H. F. Chiu. 2017. 'Mental Health of the Old- and new-generation Migrant Workers in China: Who Are at Greater Risk for Psychological Distress?' *Oncotarget* 8 (35), 59791–59799.

United Nations in India. 2018. *Decent Work for Migrant Workers in India*. http://in.one.un.org/page/decent-work-for-migrant-workers-in-india/

CHAPTER 6

# A Comparative Study of the Pension Systems in China and India

Yufei Wei

## An Overview of Pension Systems in China and India

Social welfare is a concept with very wide extension. It has been given different meanings in different contexts. Understanding social welfare from the perspective of social systems, such as 'welfare state' (Lin Yi, 2013), means that the state maintains and improves the level of people's material and cultural life. At the macro level, in the social welfare model, pension system arrangement is the most important facet with implications on the welfare of the elderly population. The pension system is also the cornerstone of protection for the elderly in their final years of life. This chapter makes a comparative study of China and India's pension systems, and helps to understand the differences between China and India's pension systems and puts forward the learnings from the study of both systems.

The pension systems in China and India have many similarities. There are some similar backgrounds in pension system arrangement in

China and India. For example, unbalanced development exists between urban and rural areas in China and India, both of which are 'urban and rural development gap' (Qi, 2003), implying there are super-large cities (such as: Shanghai, Mumbai) and poor rural areas. China and India are developing countries where prevalence of the pension system has a relatively short history. As a result, the system has many imperfections that need to be improved. In any of the countries and regions, the arrangement of the pension system is based on the history and tradition of the area, economic and social development, population and the demographic profile of the ageing population; these are all important parameters to determine the structure of a specific pension system. Depending upon the results of these parameters, along with the similarities, there are also many differences in the constitution of the pension systems prevailing in India and China.

## The Difference of the Process of Establishing a Market Economic System

There are differences in the functioning of the market economy system of the two countries. In 1991, before India carried out economic reforms, it was a mixed economy. In fact, India is the first country to implement a mixed economic system among developing countries. The Rao Government in 1991, conducted comprehensive economic reforms and since then India's economy entered into a transitional phase. The Indian government changed its economic development model and management system to promote a market economy and overall, the basic economic system has been regulated by the market. For China, the establishment of the market economy system had to break the original planned economic system to integrate into a market economy system so that the original planned economic system coexisted with the market economy.

## Differences in Levels of Economic Development

Since the reform and opening up, Chinese gross domestic product (GDP) has maintained a rapid growth, economic development level has been far higher than India. In 2015, Chinese GDP touched USD 11.06 trillion with a per capita income of USD 8,069 as compared to Indian GDP of USD 2.102 trillion and per capita income of USD

1,606. However, since May 2014, India's economic growth rate gradually slowed down even though the GDP growth rate has been more than the Chinese growth rate in consecutive years (7.4% in 2014 and 8.2% in 2015 [World Bank]). There is a great potential for economic development for both the economies. Since a long period of time, however, China's GDP and per capita income figures are far higher than that of India.

## Differences in Demographic Development

The population in China is aging at a faster pace as compared to India and if the population policy does not change, the proportion of the elderly population will nearly double in 2050 and the elderly population of over 60 years old and 65 years old will reach 35 per cent and 26 per cent of the total population, respectively. In 2015, China introduced the option of having two children. According to the current estimates, China has entered into the phase of 'low birth rate'. The implementation of a comprehensive two child policy does not appear to increase growth of birth rate so far. According to the forecast, as a result of the 'two child' policy implementation in China, the proportion of the elderly population by 2050 may be lowered only by two to four per cent. China's economy will eventually be burdened with a large proportion of elderly people as compared to the current demographic dividends it has yielded to develop its economy, for instance, some funds of the government will have to be invested into the pension industry instead of being invested in the production field.

India is one of the youngest countries in the world with a median age of the population of only 26.8 years (in 2015) (Statista 2019). In 2025, the proportion of the working age population is likely to be as high as 55 per cent (Shen Qiuhong, 2014). According to the PADIS-INT forecast, in 2030, India's working-age (between 15–64) population will exceed China's working age population by one billion (Shen Qiuhong, 2014) with a much younger population compared to China. However, India soon will also be affected by the problem of an aging population; the PADIS-INT predicts that India will enter the aging period in 2025, when the elderly dependency ratio will start to rise slowly. So, there is a huge difference in the demographic profiles and patterns of China and India. Whereas China has already entered the aging phase with a larger percentage of aging population, India is likely to enter this phase by 2025.

## Comparative Analysis of Pension Systems of India and China

The pension system is mainly divided into two systems—payment pension system, where an individual contributes to the pension fund and the non-payment pension system, where the State pays the entire pension to the individuals. In the latter, individual beneficiaries need not contribute to the pension fund and national treasury pays for the entire pension amount. The contributory pension system is more dominant in the national pension system covering largest number of beneficiaries of the population. The State contribution to beneficiaries has immense effect on the social redistribution and helps address the issues of inequality and poverty; it is a kind of institutional arrangement by the State to provide for the elderly poor.

Chinese pension system is typical of a social democracy mode in the planned economy era (Scandinavian model, with nuances of the system present in Denmark and Sweden). The main feature is based on common social security for all citizens, but in reality, it only protects a special group, such as civil servants and workers of state-owned enterprises. After the introduction of market economy system, the pension system became a conservative welfare system (a typical representative of Germany and France), where the family is at the core. This is based on advance payment (such as pension, unemployment insurance, etc.) which highlights the responsibility of the individual, with compulsory pay and savings. Because of the continuity of this system, China's pension system is characterized by hybrid characteristics, while India's pension system follows the United States' Remedial pension system, with general protection to the civil servants with mixed characteristics.

### Privileges of the Civil Servants

In the employee contributory pension system arrangement, there are some similarities between China and India, namely, the establishment of a certain class of privileged civil servants. Whether it is the legacy of the planned economy in China or the dominance of India's bureaucratic elite class, the contribution of the State in pension payments in their post retirement pensions is higher than others. Because of retirement system of government departments and institutions, civil servants' pension system has a unified financial payment, so-called 'chihuangliang'. The payment financed by the state treasury, where individuals do not have to contribute anything, the benefits are much higher than the contributory pension. In 2014, the Chinese government carried out the reform of endowment insurance system for institutional staff, where the basic endowment insurance system divides into social accounts and individual accounts, and the social accounts are paid by the employers and individual accounts are paid by individuals, which gradually reduces the privilege of civil servants class in the pension system.

India's payment pension system mainly includes the government social security plan, the public sector security plan and occupation pension plan, retirement demission plan and voluntary savings plan. One of the most notable features is tendency of welfare on the government social security plan. Although the states governments in India can make plans in accordance with the conditions of civil servants' pension independently, but in reality, most of the states follow the central government's approach, implementing the same social security pension plan. It benefits the employees of the federal governments and state governments. In 2003–2004, the civil service pension scheme was promulgated, which established a new access to the central government sector employees (excluding military) involved in the contributory fixed pension plan, respectively by employers and employees to pay 50 per cent of the last drawn salary (Qin Yonghong and Zhang Wei 2011).

## Coverage and Differences in Pension Systems of India and China

China's contributory pension system has a tendency to focus on 'basic security' and the main goal is to expand the coverage of basic pension for all urban enterprises' employees, people and urban individuals working in the industrial sector and commercial establishments as well as the households. The pension system requires that employers pay 20 per cent into social accounts and individuals pay 8 per cent into individual accounts, and pay the full 15 years or reach the retirement age upon which one can receive a pension. This is basic provision in the design of the system on urban labour population encompassing all of the pension system. At the same time, in China, the pension system is incorporated into the urban residents who never paid the pension fund. As long as urban residents reach retirement age, they can receive pensions. The system reached the target of the basic security with a wide coverage. But it is undeniable that the pension system mainly concentrates on including more individuals in an aging society where disbursements of pensions face major challenges.

In the pension system in India, there are differences across industries, mainly embodied in the formal organization and informal organization. The contributory pension system mainly includes the public sector, the public sector enterprise social security plan, including insurance companies, the Reserve Bank of India, the public power sector, oil and gas companies and industries. Most of these enterprises have their own relatively independent social security pension plan and the occupation pension plan or retirement severance plan, mainly, is set by the employer's pension plan, which provide regular retirement income to employees in the formal sector. Although, four/fifths of the working class in India work in the informal sector and need to be protected by welfare organizations, communities and non-governmental organizations through some form of pension plan post their retirement. The country has not designed the system of basic pension coverage for the people of the informal sector (Qin Yonghong and Zhang Wei, 2011)

## Comparative Analysis of Non-contributory Pension System with Universal Security

The non-payment pension system with universal security belongs to third level model (redistribution, saving, insurance) of the World Bank (1994) and the fifth level mode non-contributory social assistance system, in order to guarantee minimum living where the first level of old-age security includes social protection with an effective integration of family security along with land security. The formation of an effective old-age security function and social-security-function based protection under universal security layer, the non-contributory type in the settlement of low-income and redistribution of old-age security system is far more effective for the elderly people.

## China's Inclusive Pension System

Inclusive pension system refers to the pensions provided to senior citizens residing in urban and rural areas who reach the required eligible age. They receive pension benefits without contributing to the pension fund themselves. The decision to participate in the pension system requires family income levels as a precondition to avail the benefits. Regardless of people's income, wealth and working life, under unified pension payment system, inclusive pension system avoids cost of the household survey to prepare the list of beneficiaries. China provides subsidies with full coverage for the elderly upon reaching a threshold age. According to the Ministry of Civil Affairs, in 2016, the country had 26 provinces (autonomous regions and municipalities) which have introduced the policy. They will soon achieve national coverage. The new rural social pension insurance scheme is a guarantee to ensure a basic life for elderly rural residents. With a combination of government subsidies, pension treatment in the form of a combination of the 'basic pension + personal account' provides better benefits to the senior citizens. As per the norm, the national treasury pays a minimum sum when people attain 60 years of age, specifically to those who did not enjoy the urban basic insurance. This reflects the new agricultural insurance as part of the inclusive pension system. Objectively speaking, China's new rural insurance benefits are low, which can only be used as a supplement to the family, but is never really enough to realize the basic life guarantee for the rural elderly.

## The Pension System for the Elderly in India

In 1995, India had included non-contributory pension and social assistance programs for the elderly, which were included in the central budget NSAP (National Social Assistance Program), NOAPS (National Old Age Pension Scheme), NFBS (National Family

Benefit Scheme) and NMBS (National Maternity Benefit Scheme) (Qin Yonghong and Zhang Wei, 2011). The national pension plan is a welfare system that is aimed at reduction of poverty. Based on the household survey to give out cash allowances, central government and state government funds were used. Eligibility criteria for this pension system requires the beneficiary to be more than 65 years of age without any fixed income from family members. In April 2000, with the introduction of the s Ananapurna Scheme, grains were distributed among poor households. Its implementation was aimed at reducing incidences of malnutrition and poverty. In 2007, the IGNOAPS (Indra Gandhi National Old Age Pension Scheme) was implemented to provide cash for the elder from families living under the poverty line. People aged between 60 and 79 years were given a pension of ₹200 a month and people above the age of 80 were given ₹500 a month (Qin Yonghong and Zhang Wei, 2011. So far, through two levels of government financing and multi-level management, including cash and in kind, two types of welfare delivery and non-contributory pension system were put to practice. It can be said that India's welfare delivery has certain advantages, which helps the disadvantaged with some cash in hand.

The non-contributory pension system reflects a national social welfare for the elderly. While the United States is a representative of the remedial model to provide for pensions, Northern Europe follows an inclusive model. India follows the American model of non- contributory pension schemes based on national survey of households, whereas in China, is the pension system is based on inclusive welfare as practiced in Northern Europe.

## Common Goals Pension Systems in China and India

### Expansion of Coverage to Achieve Greater Inclusiveness

One of the problems of China and India's pension system is to expand the coverage. In China, the design of policy is aimed at full coverage of the people. The statistics from the Ministry of Civil Affairs, from 2009 to 2012 showed that China had completed full coverage of the social endowment insurance system, but in practice, the pension disbursements did not achieve full coverage. First, the pension system in China has not covered the entire population, so there are more than 200 million people who are out of the pension system. Second, the enthusiasm for paying insurance among the migrant workers, who constitute a huge labor group in society, is low. Last, flexible employees are departing from the insurance system since flexible employment has become an obstacle to take the benefits in insurance. In the future, China's pension system must expand the actual coverage to achieve greater inclusiveness.

It is difficult for the pension system to expand its coverage in India. The pension system still focused on covering employees of formal sector rather than employees of informal sector. India should gradually include the informal sector workers into the pension system to achieve greater inclusiveness, which can ensure elimination of poverty and help the elderly to enjoy the basic living standards with certain dignity.

## Fairness of the Contributory Pension System

The establishment of contributory pension system should be uniform, which is a common problem faced by China and India. There existed imbalances within the pension system in China. The target group of the next pension reform should be civil servants, the cost of reform (all contributions from the Treasury) is still arduous. There are the differences between urban and rural pension benefits. There is some equality in the design of the system of new rural insurance system and city residents pension insurance, but there still remains a large gap. The focus of the reform of the pension system should aim at equality of pension provisions irrespective of occupation and urban–rural divide in China.

There are differences between urban and rural areas and between formal organizations and informal organizations, in pension system. The central and state government employees contribute nothing but can enjoy generous pensions. From 2003 to 2004, the Indian government launched a new civil servants' pension system. However, in India differences between the formal sector and the informal sector are still large. In the future, pension system should focus on the design of the system of 'equality', with the establishment of a multi-level social security system, so that all citizens can benefit from the pension system and play a role in social development.

## Pension System Reforms in China and India

### Possible Influence of China's Pension System Reform on India

China's pension reforms are directed towards the system of 'equality' and the design is to include all people. Chinese government is integrating the pension insurance of city residents and rural residents (these two pension insurance are totally different in payment standard and fund management). The author surmises that India can learn from the reforms that are introduced in China. With the Modi administration, India's pension system reform has begun in February 2015, with India's finance minister Mr Arun Jaitley announcing that India will set up a national security system to provide social security to all the people of India, especially the poor people.

### Potential Learnings and Possible Influence of India's Pension System on China

Reference to India's pension system mainly manifests in two aspects—first, to improve India's old-age insurance management efficiency, the introduction of competition mechanism, the gradual introduction of private pension funds in the pension industry and expansion of the pension insurance investment channels pension fund management. China can learn from India's experiences in pension system reforms. It is very important to note that investment in pensions is a long-term phenomenon. China's endowment insurance fund lacks security, stability and high returns on investment. Without the introduction of specialized management institutions to manage pension fund in China, returns cannot be increased (Xiao Yanhua, 2011). In the future, China can consider introduction of a private pension insurance fund and introduce competition in the sector, so as to expand the investment of pension fund channels to improve efficiency of investment fund. Second, India follows provision of cash as well as goods. The way to avoid cash provision is to ensure the money used for the welfare of really poor elderly population. China can learn from India by implementing cash and goods, which can further guarantee the dignity of life to the elderly.

## Conclusion

China and India are developing countries with large populations. Although the economic system and demographic profiles are different, they will be housing large number of elderly people in their countries with average age increasing steadily. Both the countries can learn from each other's experiences in the establishment of the pension system to improve their social security programs so that elderly people in both the countries can lead a dignified life post their retirement form work-life.

## Reference

Lin, Yi. 2013. *Social Insurance (3rd ed)*. Beijing: China Finance Press.

Qi, Minzhu. 2003. 'Population Change and Economic Growth: A Comparison between China and India.' *Demography Studies* 37 (3): 93–101.

Qin, Yonghong, and Wei. 2011. 'The Reform of Social Security System in India and Its Enlightenment to China.' *South Asian Studies Quarterly* (5), 99.

Statista. 2020. 'India: Average Age of the Population from 1950 to 2050 (Median Age in Years)'. https://www.statista.com/statistics/254469/median-age-of-the-population-in-india/

Shen, Qiuhong. 2014. 'Population Development and Population Policy in India.' *Demography journal* (2), 97.

Xiao, Yanhua. 2011. 'China's Population Aging and Pension Insurance Personal Account Reform in 21 Century.' *Shanghai Economic Research* (12), 104.

CHAPTER 7

# Sino-Indian Manufacturing Based on Malmquist Index Decomposition

Ying Cao

## Introduction

For a country or region's manufacturing sector, the input and structure of different factors (including technology, capital and labour) will inevitably lead to differences in overall output efficiency, which will subsequently impact the overall economic performance of the country or region and finally reshape its development model. It is generally believed that the high growth of China's manufacturing industry is driven by high investment and the export of labour-intensive products, in which the technical elements occupy only a small share and the growth rate is not so good. In recent years, China's supply-side reforms have been partly reflected in the focus and advancement of the latter. On the side of India, the manufacturing sector has long been known for its potential, along with its private enterprises' level of involvement in domestic and foreign markets (Chen and Huang, 2008). Moreover, India's information technology and service industry, especially the software industry, provides strong support for the development of India's manufacturing (Li, 2016). On the other hand, issues have also been troubling India's economy frequently, such as path dependence and instability of growth rate (Ren and Qiu, 2014).

Hence, it becomes imperative to find out the root cause of the rapid growth in the Indian subcontinent. This is especially so in the light of the fact that Indian manufacturing was often considered as a relatively under-developed sector in the past. This raises several questions—Is it from labour growth or capital drive or is it caused by total factor productivity? If it's the latter, then the imperative is to find out what the overall efficiency is and what the rate of technological progress is.

In present times, both China and India are facing the possibility of deepening reforms. It may be a significant attempt to learn from each other's strength. This study makes use of the Data Envelopment Analysis method to explore the productivity of the manufacturing industry in both countries from the perspective of input and output, and to decompose the total productivity of the two countries' manufacturing industries through the Malmquist Index Method. Simultaneously it goes on to explore factors responsible for the relative differences affecting the technological progress rate and technological efficiency growth of the manufacturing industry in both countries. Finally, based on this, it proposes a response and development strategy from the macro direction.

## General Indicators of Manufacturing Development in China and India

The manufacturing sector has always played a key role for both the developed and developing countries. Its scale, growth rate and GDP (Gross Domestic Products) ratio are generally used to indicate and reflect the development of certain kind of manufacturing. In terms of manufacturing's share in GDP, the data in Table 7.1 shows that in 12 years (2004–2016), India was about 16 per cent and China was about 30 per cent. In terms of growth rate, China's manufacturing had increased 1.7 times in 2016 as compared to 2005, with an average growth rate of 9.31 per cent annually, while India's manufacturing had increased 1.3 times, with an average annual growth rate of 7.80 per cent. However, the growth rate in the past five years has decreased (India and China had reached an average annual growth rate of 5.29 per cent and 5.70 per cent respectively), and India was only 0.41 percentage points behind China. In terms of the scale of manufacturing, the gap between the two countries is still growing. As shown in Table 7.1, in 2005, the value added from the manufacturing sector of China was 6.3 times that of India while in 2016 the figure was 10.6 times. Above results on growth rate are calculated based on the items from Table 7.1.

## Study Methodology

Generally, there are three major methods used for the study of total factor productivity (TFP) changes—Solow residuals approach, data envelopment analysis (DEA) and stochastic frontier analysis (SFA) (Hulten, 2000; Coelli et al., 2005). Among them, the DEA method has the advantages of requiring no prior assumption of the production function structure, no need to estimate parameters, allowing inefficient behaviour and the ability to decompose TFP changes. Thus, more attention and use has been on the DEA method.

DEA is a non-parametric method that can measure and evaluate production performance or efficiency changes, which was developed by Charnes, Cooper and Rhodes (1978), and is known as the CCR or C2R method (named by using the initial letter of the three authors' name). Subsequently a number of methods have been proposed, such as BCC (Banker et al., 1984) and C2GS2 (Charnes et al., 1985) method. Amongst these methods, C2R is the basic one and most widely used.

The C2R model assumes that there are 'n' kinds of Decision-Making Units (DMUs) prepared to be compared. Each DMU has 'm' kinds of inputs and 's' kinds of possible outputs. For the selected

Table 7.1. *General Indicators of Manufacturing in China and India*

(USD 100 million)

| *India* | | | | *China* | | | |
|---|---|---|---|---|---|---|---|
| *Statistical Year* | *Value Added* | *Index* | *GDP Ratio* | *Statistical Year* | *Value Added* | *Index* | *GDP Ratio* |
| 2004-05 | 1008.7 | 100.0 | 15.25% | 2005 | 6317.2 | 100.0 | 27.63% |
| 2005-06 | 1178.4 | 109.5 | 15.39% | 2006 | 7541.3 | 112.7 | 27.40% |
| 2006-07 | 1401.7 | 120.0 | 16.06% | 2007 | 11502.5 | 128.7 | 32.37% |
| 2007-08 | 1820.0 | 131.2 | 15.99% | 2008 | 14764.3 | 141.2 | 32.09% |
| 2008-09 | 1779.4 | 140.0 | 15.43% | 2009 | 16120.4 | 154.5 | 31.55% |
| 2009-10 | 1944.7 | 152.0 | 15.10% | 2010 | 19251.8 | 170.8 | 31.55% |
| 2010-11 | 2353.0 | 165.5 | 14.80% | 2011 | 24223.8 | 187.1 | 31.98% |
| 2011-12 | 2942.4 | 176.6 | 17.39% | 2012 | 26900.1 | 201.8 | 31.42% |
| 2012-13 | 2890.7 | 186.2 | 17.09% | 2013 | 29365.7 | 217.6 | 30.55% |
| 2013-14 | 2832.2 | 197.5 | 16.53% | 2014 | 31845.5 | 233.5 | 30.38% |
| 2014-15 | 3081.4 | 211.7 | 16.41% | 2015 | 32499.5 | 249.6 | 29.38% |
| 2015-16 | 3039.2 | 228.5 | 16.57% | 2016 | 32261.3 | 266.3 | 28.82% |

*Source:* Statistical yearbooks of China and India. The data of China's manufacturing sector is derived from the website of the National Bureau of Statistics of China (website: http://data.stats.gov.cn/easyquery.htm?cn=C01), and India's data is taken from the Indian Ministry of Statistics and Project Implementation's (MOSPI) (website: http://mospi.nic.in/publication/statistical-year-book-india). Data showed in Table 7.1 have been compiled and calculated.

DMU, the radial DEA model to judge its effectiveness can be expressed as:

$$\min\left[\theta-\varepsilon\left(\sum_{i=1}^{m}s_i^{-}+\sum_{r=1}^{s}s_r^{+}\right)\right]$$

$$s.t.\sum_{j=1}^{n}\lambda_j x_{ij}+s_i^{-}=\theta x_{ij0},\ i=1,2,..,m \tag{1}$$

$$\sum_{j=1}^{n}\lambda_j y_{rj}-s_r^{+}=y_{rj0},\ r=1,2,..,s$$

$$\lambda_j\geq 0, j=1,2,...,n; s_i^{-}\geq 0, s_r^{+}\geq 0$$

In the above formula (1), $s_i^{-}$ and $s_r^{+}$ are surplus variables and slack variables respectively, $\varepsilon$ is non-Archimedes infinitesimal variable, which is usually valued $\varepsilon = 10^{-6}$, $\theta$ is the effective value of a certain DMU, When $\theta = 1$ the DMU is DEA effective, and if $\theta < 1$ the DMU is DEA invalid.

## Introduction to Malmquist Index Based on DEA

Malmquist index was first proposed by Sten Malmquist (1953). Further, Caves et al. (1982) first applied this index to the measurement of productivity performance change. Since then, combined with the DEA methodology established by Charnes et al. (1978), it has been widely accepted as a sound method to assess productivity performance measurement. However, in empirical analysis, the Malmquist index based on DEA established by Färe et al., has been widely adopted by researchers.

The Malmquist productivity index has three main advantages. Firstly, there is no need for relevant price information, and thus this makes it easy to subject it to empirical analysis. This becomes an advantage as factor prices are often difficult to attain. Secondly, the method permits sample analysis of multiple countries or regions in different periods with ease. Thirdly, it can be further decomposed into technical efficiency change index and technical progress index. The equations and brief explanations are as follows:

From period 't' to period 't+1', the Malmquist index can be expressed as follows formula (2):

$$M_0(x_{t+1}, y_{t+1}, x_t, y_t) = \left[ \frac{d_0^t(x_{t+1}, y_{t+1})}{d_0^t(x_t, y_t)} \times \frac{d_0^{t+1}(x_{t+1}, y_{t+1})}{d_0^{t+1}(x_t, y_t)} \right]^{1/2} \quad (2)$$

In the above equation, $d_0^t(x_{t+1}, y_{t+1})$ represents technical efficiency level in the period of (t+1), which is referred to the period of (t); $d_0^t(x_t, y_t)$ represents technical efficiency level in the period of (t) referred to the period of (t); $d_0^{t+1}(x_{t+1}, y_{t+1})$ represents technical efficiency level in the period of (t+1) referred to the period of (t+1).

The equation can be explained as follows. When the index is greater than 1, it indicates that the TFP is increasing from time (t) to time (t+1); when it is equal to 1, it indicates that the TFP is stagnant in this period; and when it is less than 1, it indicates that the TFP is decreasing in the study period.

According to the above treatment, the Malmquist index obtained has good properties, which can be decomposed into the Technical Efficiency Change index (EC) and Technical Progress index (TP) under the assumption of constant scale return (Färe et al., 1992, 1994). The decomposition process may be represented through equation (3) as follows:

$$M_0(y_{t+1}, x_{t+1}, y_t, x_t) = \frac{d_0^{t+1}(x_{t+1}, y_{t+1})}{d_0^t(x_t, y_t)} \times \left[ \frac{d_0^t(x_{t+1}, y_{t+1})}{d_0^{t+1}(x_{t+1}, y_{t+1}C)} \times \frac{d_0^t(x_t, y_t)}{d_0^{t+1}(x_t, y_t)} \right]^{1/2} = EC \times TP \quad (3)$$

The EC can be further decomposed into Pure Technical Efficiency Change index (PC) and Scale Efficiency Change index (SC).

Further, in order to measure the Malmquist productivity index, a linear programming method is needed to calculate various distance functions of input and output. For the TFP change of a certain DMU from time 't' to time 't+1', the following four DEA-based distance functions needs to be calculated as following formula (4):

$$
\begin{array}{ll}
\left[d_0^t(x_t, y_t)\right]^{-1} = \max_{\phi,\lambda} \phi & \left[d_0^{t+1}(x_{t+1}, y_{t+1})\right]^{-1} = \max_{\phi,\lambda} \phi \\
\text{s.t.} \quad -\phi y_{it} + Y_{t+1}\lambda \geq 0 & \text{s.t.} \quad -\phi y_{i,t+1} + Y_{t+1}\lambda \geq 0 \\
\quad x_{it} - X_{t+1}\lambda \geq 0 & \quad x_{i,t+1} - X_{t+1}\lambda \geq 0 \\
\quad \lambda \geq 0 & \quad \lambda \geq 0 \\
\left[d_0^t(x_{t+1}, y_{t+1})\right]^{-1} = \max_{\phi,\lambda} \phi & \left[d_0^{t+1}(x_t, y_t)\right]^{-1} = \max_{\phi,\lambda} \phi \\
\text{s.t.} \quad -\phi y_{i,t+1} + Y_t\lambda \geq 0 & \text{s.t.} \quad -\phi y_{it} + Y_{t+1}\lambda \geq 0 \\
\quad x_{i,t+1} - X_t\lambda \geq 0 & \quad x_{it} - X_{t+1}\lambda \geq 0 \\
\quad \lambda \geq 0 & \quad \lambda \geq 0
\end{array} \tag{4}
$$

## Data Sourcing and Processing

Thus, to assess the productivity indices across the two countries the following data sources and processing was carried out.

### Data Source

The data used in this study, including data on manufacturing in China and India, has been taken from the MOSPI and China National Bureau of Statistical (NBS) website. Among them, the Indian manufacturing data used in the article was ascertained from the Annual Survey of Industries. The price index used in the calculation was taken from the Indian Statistical Yearbook[1]. The Chinese manufacturing data and related price indices used in the study are sourced and obtained through query requests from the website of National Bureau of Statistics of China[2].

### Data Processing

The manufacturing data of the two countries are related to input indicators such as fixed assets and current assets, labour and employment and output indicators such as output value and profit. The above indicators were subjected to adjustment basis their respective price indices before the calculation. The Indian data was adjusted based on the price of the statistical year of 2003–2004. The Chinese data was adjusted based on the 2004 price[3]. In addition, the fixed assets were reduced using the Fixed Asset Price index; in terms of liquid assets, the Chinese data was reduced by the producer price index (PPI), and the Indian data was reduced using the Primary Articles Indices; China's output value data was reduced by the PPI, India's data was reduced by Manufactured Products Indices, and profit data was all reduced by the consumer price index (CPI). Considering the identity, comparability and measurability of the indicators of the two countries, the data of India's manufacturing is selected from statistical year of 2008–2009 to 2012–2013, comparing with China's manufacturing data from the year of 2009 to 2013. In this process, all the sectorial data of the two countries are categorized and sorted. For India, the sectorial data of post-production processing activities of agricultural products, salt extraction products, commodity and equipment repair, precious metal manufacturing and cultural and sports products are removed, while China's some sectorial data such as the equipment and goods repairs, sports and other industrial supplies are also removed. At the same time, the data of automobile, railway equipment and shipbuilding data are combined into one sector for the sake of comparison with that of India's. Finally, series of comparable manufacturing panel data of 27 sub-sectors of the two countries are formed. Additionally, China's data from 2003 to 2008 and 2014 to 2016 are only used to judge its manufacturing trends, not for comparison with India (see Table 7.3).

Table 7.2 *India's Manufacturing Malmquist Index and its Decomposition*

| *Year/ Item* | *Technical Efficiency Change (EC)* | *Technology Progress Change (TP)* | *Pure Technology Progress Change (PC)* | *Scale Efficiency Change (SC)* | *Total Factor Productivity Change (TFP)* |
|---|---|---|---|---|---|
| 2009-10 | 1.2730 | 0.7410 | 1.2180 | 1.0460 | 0.9430 |
| 2010-11 | 1.0500 | 0.9350 | 1.0390 | 1.0100 | 0.9810 |
| 2011-12 | 0.8290 | 1.2540 | 0.8770 | 0.9460 | 1.0400 |
| 2012-13 | 0.8790 | 1.0760 | 0.9450 | 0.9300 | 0.9460 |
| **Average** | **0.9940** | **0.9830** | **1.0120** | **0.9820** | **0.9770** |

*Source:* Calculated based on DEA2.1 by the author

Table 7.3 *China's Manufacturing Malmquist Index and its Decomposition*

| *Year/ Item* | *Technical Efficiency Change (EC)* | *Technology Progress Change (TP)* | *Pure Technology Progress Change (PC)* | *Scale Efficiency Change (SC)* | *Total Factor Productivity Change (TFP)* |
|---|---|---|---|---|---|
| 2004 | 1.0440 | 1.0380 | 0.9920 | 1.0520 | 1.0840 |
| 2005 | 0.9400 | 1.1360 | 1.0340 | 0.9090 | 1.0680 |
| 2006 | 1.0990 | 0.9650 | 1.0000 | 1.0990 | 1.0600 |
| 2007 | 0.9400 | 1.1530 | 1.0720 | 0.8770 | 1.0830 |
| 2008 | 1.1400 | 0.9050 | 0.9790 | 1.1650 | 1.0320 |
| 2009 | 1.0440 | 0.9830 | 1.0520 | 0.9920 | 1.0260 |
| 2010 | 0.8670 | 1.2100 | 1.0020 | 0.8650 | 1.0490 |
| 2011 | 1.1470 | 0.9310 | 1.0100 | 1.1360 | 1.0670 |
| 2012 | 0.9760 | 1.0350 | 0.9660 | 1.0100 | 1.0090 |
| 2013 | 1.0210 | 1.0110 | 1.0170 | 1.0040 | 1.0320 |
| 2014 | 1.0240 | 0.9950 | 1.0320 | 0.9930 | 1.0190 |
| 2015 | 0.9930 | 1.0340 | 1.0130 | 0.9800 | 1.0270 |
| 2016 | 0.9980 | 1.0230 | 1.0000 | 0.9980 | 1.0210 |
| **Average** | **1.0150** | **1.0290** | **1.0130** | **1.0020** | **1.0440** |

## Analysis and Results

Once the above data was processed, DEAP2.1 software was used to automatically compare the growth rate of manufacturing TFP and all the sub-indicators including TP, EC and PC and SC of the two countries by using the Malmquist index decomposition method. At the same time, the sub-sectors of the two countries' manufacturing were also compared.

### Average Malmquist Index and its Decomposition

The obtained results have been shown in Tables 7.2 and 7.3. As can be observed, in terms of the indicator of TFP change, the geometric mean value of China's TFP is higher than India's by about 6.2 percentage points during the measurement period. Annual data shows that only in 2011–2012 India was about three per cent higher than China. Results also show that between 2009 and 2013, the TP change in China's manufacturing was higher than that in India. The decomposition of the Malmquist index shows that India's manufacturing industry, except the PC was 1.4 per cent higher than China, while other sub-items were all lower than China. The annual EC growth rate, except for 2010, is higher in India than in other years; and meanwhile, the rate of TP demonstrated a reverse trend, that is, China's manufacturing TP was lower than India except for 2010. In terms of the indicator of PC, India was higher than China in the first two measurement years, and lower than China in the latter two years; in terms of SC, India was lower than China in 2009–2010, and the rest of the measurement year was lower than China.

Table 7.3 shows China's manufacturing Malmquist index and its decomposition from 2004 to 2016. It can be deduced from the results that the geometric mean of the Malmquist index and its decomposition were relatively higher for China than that of India.

Hence, it can be seen that overall, in a comparable period (2010–2013), China's manufacturing industry was more efficient and progressive than India. However, it is also apparent that India's technological progress rate is catching up with China. Moreover, in terms of the growth rate of total factor productivity and the growth rate of each decomposition item, in recent years, China's numerical value has stabilized, although this does not mean that the growth rate of China's manufacturing industry, which includes technology scale, etc., is reducing. For the Indian manufacturing sector scale efficiency should be given more emphasis.

## Malmquist Index of Segmented Industries in China and India and their Decomposition

As shown in Tables 7.4a and 7.4b, the results of the calculations reveal that in the manufacturing industry, India's total factor productivity growth rate in chemical fiber, fur products, petroleum processing, instrumentation and other four industries are higher than that of China. On the other hand, the other twenty-three industries are lower than the ones in China. Among them, ferrous metal manufacturing,

Table 7.4a *Malmquist Index and Its Decompositions of India's Manufacturing Sectors*

| *Malmquist Index Decompositions* / *Industry Sectors* | *Technical Efficiency Change (EC)* | *Technology Progress Change (TP)* | *Pure Technology Progress Change (PC)* | *Scale Efficiency Change (SC)* | *Total Factor Productivity Change (TFP)* |
|---|---|---|---|---|---|
| Electrical Equipment et al. | 0.954 | 0.989 | 0.958 | 0.995 | 0.944 |
| Apparels & Garments | 1.027 | 0.953 | 1.040 | 0.987 | 0.978 |
| Textile Goods | 1.080 | 0.969 | 1.084 | 0.996 | 1.047 |
| Non-metallic Products | 0.974 | 0.988 | 0.980 | 0.994 | 0.963 |
| Material Recovery & Waste Disposal | 0.954 | 0.998 | 1.000 | 0.954 | 0.952 |
| Basic Iron & steel | 0.902 | 1.007 | 0.904 | 0.998 | 0.909 |
| Man-made Fibers | 1.046 | 1.002 | 1.087 | 0.962 | 1.048 |
| Chemical Products | 1.016 | 0.995 | 1.018 | 0.998 | 1.011 |
| Computer, Communication & Consumer Electronics Products | 0.947 | 0.980 | 0.974 | 0.972 | 0.929 |
| Furniture | 0.935 | 0.955 | 0.974 | 0.960 | 0.893 |
| Transport Equipment | 1.025 | 0.981 | 1.027 | 0.999 | 1.006 |
| Metal Products | 0.909 | 0.984 | 0.914 | 0.995 | 0.894 |
| Beverage | 0.944 | 0.993 | 0.967 | 0.976 | 0.938 |
| Products of Wood et al. | 1.068 | 0.956 | 1.111 | 0.961 | 1.021 |

| | | | | | |
|---|---|---|---|---|---|
| Post-harvest Crop Activities & Processing of Meat et al. | 0.962 | 0.973 | 0.964 | 0.998 | 0.935 |
| Leather & Fur Products | 1.093 | 0.953 | 1.123 | 0.973 | 1.042 |
| Coke & Petroleum Products | 1.000 | 1.088 | 1.000 | 1.000 | 1.088 |
| Food & Diary Products | 1.048 | 0.962 | 1.052 | 0.996 | 1.008 |
| General Purpose Machinery | 0.953 | 0.986 | 0.963 | 0.990 | 0.940 |
| Rubber & Plastic Products | 0.991 | 0.986 | 0.997 | 0.994 | 0.978 |
| Tobacco & Cigar Products | 0.939 | 0.953 | 0.971 | 0.967 | 0.895 |
| Pharmaceuticals, Medicinal et al. Products | 1.026 | 0.987 | 1.032 | 0.994 | 1.013 |
| Measuring & Testing et al. Products | 1.078 | 0.965 | 1.169 | 0.922 | 1.040 |
| Publishing & Media Products | 1.076 | 0.971 | 1.108 | 0.972 | 1.045 |
| Basic Precious & Non-ferrous Metals Products | 0.941 | 1.006 | 0.948 | 0.992 | 0.946 |
| Paper & Paper Products | 1.018 | 0.988 | 1.037 | 0.982 | 1.006 |
| Special-purpose Machinery | 0.964 | 0.984 | 0.974 | 0.990 | 0.949 |
| AVERAGE | 0.994 | 0.983 | 1.012 | 0.982 | 0.977 |

*Source:* Author's calculations based on DEA2.1.

Table 7.4b *Malmquist Index and its Decompositions of China's Manufacturing Sectors*

| *Malmquist Index* / *Decompositions Industry Sectors* | *Technical Efficiency Change (EC)* | *Technology Progress Change (TP)* | *Pure Technology Progress Change (PC)* | *Scale Efficiency Change (SC)* | *Total Factor Productivity Change (TFP)* |
|---|---|---|---|---|---|
| Electrical Equipment et al. | 0.978 | 1.037 | 0.961 | 1.018 | 1.014 |
| Apparels & Garments | 0.975 | 1.039 | 0.981 | 0.994 | 1.013 |
| Textile Goods | 1.013 | 1.041 | 1.020 | 0.993 | 1.055 |
| Non-metallic Products | 1.011 | 1.034 | 1.011 | 1.000 | 1.045 |
| Material Recovery & Waste Disposal | 1.000 | 1.041 | 1.000 | 1.000 | 1.041 |
| Basic Iron & steel | 1.000 | 1.037 | 1.000 | 1.000 | 1.037 |
| Man-made Fibers | 0.985 | 1.042 | 0.985 | 1.000 | 1.026 |
| Chemical Products | 1.009 | 1.042 | 1.036 | 0.974 | 1.052 |
| Computer, Communication & Consumer Electronics Products | 0.982 | 1.037 | 1.000 | 0.982 | 1.019 |
| Furniture | 0.972 | 1.041 | 0.977 | 0.995 | 1.012 |
| Transport equipment | 0.992 | 1.042 | 0.996 | 0.996 | 1.034 |
| Metal Products | 0.997 | 1.030 | 0.996 | 1.001 | 1.027 |
| Beverage | 0.993 | 1.039 | 0.993 | 1.000 | 1.032 |
| Products of Wood et al. | 1.022 | 1.042 | 1.017 | 1.004 | 1.064 |

| | | | | | |
|---|---|---|---|---|---|
| Post-harvest Crop Activities & Processing of Meat et al. | 1.000 | 1.032 | 1.000 | 1.000 | 1.032 |
| Leather & Fur Products | 0.962 | 1.039 | 0.960 | 1.003 | 0.999 |
| Coke & Petroleum Products | 1.000 | 1.076 | 1.000 | 1.000 | 1.076 |
| Food & Diary Products | 1.000 | 1.030 | 0.999 | 1.001 | 1.029 |
| General Purpose Machinery | 0.988 | 1.038 | 0.984 | 1.004 | 1.026 |
| Rubber & Plastic Products | 1.002 | 1.034 | 1.001 | 1.001 | 1.035 |
| Tobacco & Cigar Products | 1.004 | 1.127 | 1.000 | 1.004 | 1.132 |
| Pharmaceuticals, Medicinal et al. Products | 1.012 | 1.041 | 1.012 | 1.000 | 1.053 |
| Measuring & Testing et al. Products | 0.999 | 1.031 | 1.001 | 0.999 | 1.030 |
| Publishing & Media Products | 1.046 | 1.033 | 1.043 | 1.003 | 1.081 |
| Basic Precious & Non-ferrous Metals Products | 1.006 | 1.039 | 1.007 | 1.000 | 1.046 |
| Paper & Paper Products | 0.990 | 1.038 | 0.991 | 1.000 | 1.027 |
| Special-purpose Machinery | 0.989 | 1.035 | 0.989 | 0.999 | 1.024 |
| AVERAGE | 0.997 | 1.042 | 0.998 | 0.999 | 1.039 |

*Source*: Author's calculations based on DEA2.1.

non-ferrous metal manufacturing, metal products, furniture manufacturing and other industries are all below 10 per cent and the tobacco manufacturing industry is 23 per cent lower than China. Other industries such as electronic equipment manufacturing, wine and beverage manufacturing, agricultural and sideline products processing and general equipment manufacturing are also lower than in China.

When one looks at decomposition, in terms of technical efficiency of the industry, India has 12 industries in 27 sub-sectors with higher growth rates than China, including fur products, instrumentation equipment manufacturing, textile industry, chemical fiber manufacturing, textile and garment, food manufacturing, wood processing, shipping equipment, printing media, paper and paper products, pharmaceutical manufacturing and chemical products. India's technical efficiency in the above-mentioned industries is higher than that of China. This is mainly attributable to the growth rate of its pure technological progress rate and yet, as stated earlier its contribution to scale efficiency is relatively small, which includes both 'pure technological advances' and 'scale efficiency'. The corresponding effect can be seen on the decomposition results (see Table 7.3). In addition, in terms of the rate of technological progress, India's oil and other sectors are higher than the corresponding indicators for China.

Thus, in terms of the various manufacturing sectors India's better performance is reflective of its efficiency in technology application, which is a major contributor to the growth of total factor productivity. The rate of technological advancement in the sectors is the main contributor to total factor productivity; at the same time there is still room for improvement in the efficiency of its technical application. Conversely, the technological advancement of some industries is insufficient and this needs to be addressed as it may otherwise have a negative impact on the country's manufacturing growth.

## Conclusion

The manufacturing industries of China and India have been expanding year by year in terms of the scale difference, but the annual growth rate of Indian manufacturing has begun to approach and surpass China since 2015. In terms of TFP, China has performed better than India in recent years. However, when looking into the sub-indicators of TFP, the indicator of China's TP did not perform as well as that of India. In terms of EC and its sub-indicators, India's manufacturing PC had been growing faster than China in recent years yet reflecting its low SC (scale efficiency change), which might be the major reason why India's TFP had been lagging behind China during these years. The performance of the two countries' manufacturing in their 27 sub-sectors was like that of the TFP change. Therefore, from a macro perspective, China should pay more attention to the improvement of technological progress in the future, including its technology level and especially its technical literacy of employees, that is, the improvement of human capital. For India's manufacturing industries, more attention should be paid to the improvement of the technical efficiency, especially its scale efficiency in the future days.

## Notes

1. Statistical Year Book India 2017. Retrieved form: http://mospi.nic.in/publication/statistical-year-book-india.
2. National Bureau of Statistics of China. Retrieved form: http://data.stats.gov.cn/easyquery.htm?cn=C01.
3. As real growth rates of manufacturing products have been calculated based on the data from Table 7.1 in the previous text, where the price base period was chosen, 2003–2004 for India and 2004 for China, for the comparability, uniformity and consistency of the data, base period for comparison and measurement here is decided.

## References

Banker, R. D., A. Charnes, and W. W. Cooper. 1984. 'Some Models for Estimating Technical and Scale Inefficiencies in Data Envelopment Analysis.' *Management Science* 30 (9),1078–1092. https://doi.org/10.1287/mnsc.30.9.1078.

Caves, D. W., and L. R. C. E. Diewert. 1982. 'The Economic Theory of Index Numbers and the Measurement of Input, Output, and Productivity.' *Econometrica* 50 (6),1393–1414. https://doi.org/10.2307/1913388.

Charnes, A., W. Cooper, and E. Rhodes. 1978. 'Measuring the Efficiency of Decision-making Units.' *European Journal of Operational Research* 2,429–444. https://doi.org/10.1016/0377-2217(78)90138-8.

Charnes, A., W. W. Cooper, and B. Golany. 1985. 'Foundations of Data Envelopment Analysis for Pareto-Koopmans Efficient Empirical Production Functions.' *Journal of Econometrics* 30 (1–2),91–107. https://doi.org/10.1016/0304-4076(85)90133-2.

Chen, F., and M. Huang. 2008. 'A Comparative Study on the Manufacturing Competitiveness of China and India.' *Asia-Pacific Economic Review* 3,88–97, 152.

Coelli, T. J., D. S. P. Rao, C. J. O'Donnell, and G. E. Battese. 2005. *An Introduction to Efficiency and Productivity Analysis.* New York: Springer.

Färe, R., S. Grosskopf, B. Lindgren, and P. Roos. 1994. 'Productivity Developments in Swedish Hospitals: a Malmquist Output Index Approach'. In *Data Envelopment Analysis: Theory, Methodology, and Applications* (253–272) edited by A. Charnes, W. W. Cooper, A. Y. Lewin, and L. M. Seiford. New York: Springer.

Färe, R., S. Grosskopf, M. Norris, and Z. Zhang. 1992. 'Productivity Growth, Technical Progress, and Efficiency Change in Industrialized Countries.' *American Economic Review* 84 (1), 66–83.

Hulten, C. R. 2000. 'Total Factor Productivity: A Short Biography.' *NBER Working Papers* 51 (3), 3–16.

Li, L. 2016. 'An Analysis of the 'Make in India' Campaign and India's Economic Prospects.' *Contemporary International Relations* 9:46–53.

Malmquist, S. 1953. 'Index numbers and indifference surfaces.' *Trabajos de Estadistica* 4(2):209–242. https://doi.org/10.1007/BF03006863.

Ren, J., and X. Qiu. 2014. 'The Evolution of Indian Industrial Policy Since 1948 and the Impact on the Development of Manufacturing Sector.' *South Asian Studies* 2:106–121.

CHAPTER 8

# Impact of Manufacturing Intelligence on Employment of Labourers Shifted from Agriculture in China and India

Jixiang Chen

## Connotation, Characteristics and Focus of Manufacturing Intelligence

### Connotation of Manufacturing Intelligence

In the 1980s, the concept of manufacturing intelligence was put forth and studied in the United States, but its definition was not generally recognized and its connotation and characteristics were approached in different ways (Shuzi Yang, 2012). Since the 21st century, especially after the initiatives, viz., Germany's 'Industry 4.0' and China's 'Made in China 2025' were proposed, manufacturing intelligence has made its sensational appearance and received extensive attention in various circles. The definition of manufacturing intelligence was introduced by two American scholars, Wright and Bourne. According to them, 'manufacturing intelligence intends to integrate knowledge engineering (including manufacturing technology and skills, and experts' knowledge), manufacturing software system, robot visual and machine control, to realize the small-scale production without artificial interference' (P. K. Wright and D. A. Bourne, 1988). Along with the rapid development of artificial intelligence and information technology, manufacturing intelligence has covered a much wider range than the above definition. In many studies, manufacturing intelligence has been regarded as the focus for development of manufacturing automation and an integrated human-machine intelligent manufacturing system consisting of intelligent machines and human experts. It is also considered as the application of artificial intelligence in each link of product life cycle, including manufacturing intelligence technology and manufacturing intelligence system (Liu Jianping and Ye Bangyan, 2004). Based on its path of development, manufacturing intelligence can be actually defined as an advanced manufacturing system that is formed by intelligent machines and human experts, based on the extensive interconnection of humans, machines and materials, and carried by manufacturing systems to achieve the capabilities of autonomous sensing, learning, analysis, decision making, communication and coordination control to some extent and the ability to dynamically adjust to the changing environment for manufacturing and realize independent optimization of objectives. By embracing manufacturing intelligence, the traditional manufacturing industry will develop with a focus on high performance, high accuracy, high sensitivity, high stability, high reliability, high environment-friendliness and long service life, while new and advanced manufacturing technologies will be miniaturized, integrated, packaged, electronic, digital, multifunctional, intelligent, networked, computerized, comprehensively automated and combined with optical, mechanical and electronic devices. Moreover, production service will become specialized, convenient, maintenance-free, automated in assembly, dust-free (or super clean) and customized (Sun Bolin, 2013).

## Characteristics of Manufacturing Intelligence

Manufacturing intelligence provides support for a profound reform in the traditional manufacturing industry. It has the following characteristics:

### *Manufacturing Intelligence Is based on the Development of Artificial Intelligence Technology*

Unlike a common system operating only in a designer-programmed way, artificial intelligence is a system that can think, study and make decisions like a human being. A common system is relatively static, but artificial intelligence, which relies on deep learning based on big data, can drive reasonable sensing, planning, reasoning and self-optimization of machines and lead to reasonable decisions. Manufacturing equipment based on artificial intelligence will have the capability of intelligent production. Obviously, the development of artificial intelligence technology lays a foundation for manufacturing intelligence.

### *Manufacturing Intelligence Can Independently and Dynamically Adjust to the Changing Environment for Manufacturing and Independently Realize Independent Optimization for Objectives*

Manufacturing intelligence is based on the immense development of artificial intelligence. With manufacturing intelligence, factories can maintain the operation of production equipment by networking equipment, visualizing production data, making production documents paperless, realizing transparent production process, assigning no worker at production site, relying on self-learning for production decisions and making diverse and customized products. Hence, manufacturing intelligence can independently and dynamically adjust to the changing environment for manufacturing and autonomously realize independent optimization of objectives.

## Manufacturing Intelligence is Green

In the 21st century, being green and intelligent has become a trend in the industrial sector around the world. It is also a main characteristic of manufacturing intelligence and a great reflection of and response to actual industrial demand at present. Green manufacturing is a modern manufacturing model that addresses the environment and resource efficiency comprehensively. The model intends to minimize the environmental impacts of products and maximize the utilization of resources in its whole life cycle covering design, manufacturing, packaging, transportation, use, decommissioning and disposal, so as to constantly enhance the level of sustainable development.

## Manufacturing Intelligence is Easily Customized

For intelligent production, manufacturing intelligence must be easily customized. 'Intelligence' refers to a person's ability to think, identify and make use of regularities and resolve problems. Intelligent system features 'personified intelligence', implying its self-adaption, self-learning, self-calibration, self-coordination, self-organization, self-diagnosis and self-recovery. Hence, manufacturing intelligence satisfies the production of diverse customized products.

### Development Focus of Manufacturing Intelligence

Manufacturing intelligence will cause a profound adjustment to the cost structure of traditional manufacturing industry and will further lower the proportion of labour cost for the manufacturing industry and greatly improve the efficiency of production. Under this circumstance, it will be more convenient and expedient to customize. Hence, advanced development of manufacturing intelligence will certainly change the path of industrial transfer in traditional manufacturing industry in a profound way, affect the reshaping of the world economy and exert a deep influence on employment around the world. Manufacturing intelligence is developed together with the artificial intelligence technology and information technology, so that it can evolve from intelligent equipment manufacturing to manufacturing intelligence ecosystem. Obviously, it is very much possible for the countries having advantages in intelligent equipment manufacturing in each sector of manufacturing industry to take the lead in the establishment of manufacturing intelligence ecosystem and keep their advantageous positions in the field of manufacturing intelligence, so that these countries are able to control the high-end of value chain in manufacturing industry. For this reason, major industrial countries around the world have given priority to the development of manufacturing intelligence, which will result in more fierce global competition in intelligent equipment manufacturing and intelligent information transfer in the future. Based on the prediction of intelligent technology and equipment manufacturing development in various countries, it will take 20–25 years even for Germany, with its profound industrial background, to realize manufacturing intelligence. China has developed the strategic initiative of Made in China 2025, showing very high attention to intelligent manufacturing industry, but it is still behind Germany, the United States and quite a few other countries in such fields like artificial intelligence technology and intelligent equipment manufacturing to some extent. Therefore, China will find it very difficult to obtain advantages in the key sectors of manufacturing intelligence within a short period.

## Development Status of Manufacturing Intelligence in China and India

On 19th May 2018, China Economic Information Service officially released the *Global Manufacturing Intelligence Development Index Report 2017* in Changzhou, classifying 22 typical countries into four tiers, with China in the second tier and India in the fourth tier. The first tier consists of three 'leading' countries in manufacturing intelligence, that is, the United States, Japan and Germany. The second tier has nine countries with 'advanced' manufacturing intelligence, namely, Britain, South Korea, China, Switzerland, Sweden, France, Finland, Canada and Israel. The third tier covers five countries with 'potential' for manufacturing intelligence, including Austria, Belgium, Italy, Russia and Spain. The fourth tier includes five countries with 'fundamental' manufacturing intelligence, namely, Turkey, India,

South Africa, Brazil and Nigeria. Obviously, China and India should both speed up to catch up with other countries in the field of manufacturing intelligence.

## Development Status of Manufacturing Intelligence in China

China has attached great importance to manufacturing intelligence, especially to high-end intelligent equipment manufacturing. Therefore, the Chinese government has developed a number of action plans, for example, *Made in China 2025*, *Green Industrial Development Plan (2016–2020)* and *Guideline for Implementation of Green Manufacturing (2016–2020)*. China is facilitating the rapid development of manufacturing intelligence in three aspects, that is, innovation and industrial application of key technology for high-end intelligent remanufacturing, research and development and industrial application of intelligent remanufactured equipment and establishment of industrial collaboration system for high-end intelligent remanufacturing. It is due to the Chinese government's promotional activities and the active participation of enterprises that manufacturing intelligence could develop to quite some extent in China. According to the *Global Manufacturing Intelligence Development Index Report 2017*, China occupied the sixth rank in the global manufacturing intelligence development index (Xinhuanet.com. 2018).

## Development Status of Manufacturing Intelligence in India

After assuming office, Modi launched the 'Make in India' initiative in 2014, which was the most important plan in India. To fulfill this initiative, the Modi administration energetically attracted foreign direct investments (FDI). Manufacturing intelligence being an inevitable development trend of manufacturing industry, India spares no effort to advocate and support its development. India has not only actively attracted FDI towards manufacturing intelligence, but also strengthened its cooperation with other countries and paid more attention to the scientific research capability of local enterprises. In 2017, India was ranked number 18 comprehensively in global manufacturing intelligence development index. India has great potential for the development of manufacturing intelligence, while its global reputation for IT and advanced IT will greatly drive its manufacturing intelligence.

## Application of Manufacturing Intelligence and its Impacts on Employment of Labourers Transferred from Agriculture in China and India

At present, manufacturing intelligence is still in the primary stage in the two countries, but its impact on manufacturing industry and labourer demand structure has been gradually noticed along with its rapid development. As two countries with a large population, both China and India have very low rate of urbanization,[1] and face a heavy pressure from employment of numerous labourers trying to move out of agriculture, which affects their development significantly. Nowadays, manufacturing intelligence is mainly reflected in the application of intelligent equipment in manufacturing industry, and its impact on labourer demand from the point of view of creation and replacement of jobs.

## Applications of Manufacturing Intelligence

In any sector, the application of intelligent equipment depends on two factors. One is whether the cost of intelligent equipment is lower than the labour cost, and the other is the difficulty of realizing intelligent production in the sector. For instance, manufacturing intelligence is promoted very fast in industrial sectors featuring high labour cost and easy application of intelligent equipment. In manufacturing sectors, it is very difficult to achieve manufacturing intelligence due to the difficulty in application of intelligent equipment. Globally, in terms of salary level and difficulty of automated production under current technical conditions, the Boston Consulting Group predicted that 85 per cent of production related positions in four sectors namely traffic and transportation, electronic products, electrical equipment and mechanical equipment might be taken over by intelligent equipment very soon since the level of salary is higher there and it is also easy to realize automation. Cai Xiuling and Gao Wenqun (2017) mentioned that in the next decade, industrial robots would be installed in these sectors, which might exceed 75 per cent of total industrial robots installed in the manufacturing industry. Moreover, the sector for plastic and plastic products might also face the overwhelming impact of manufacturing intelligence due to its easy realization of automated production regardless of lower labour cost. However, it has been difficult to push forward manufacturing intelligence in sectors like furniture, apparel, food, textile and construction where it was difficult to realize automation.

## Applications of Manufacturing Intelligence in China and India at Present

The number of industrial robots installed in China is increasing fast. China has the fastest and largest market for industrial robots around the world. In 2014, up to 50,000 industrial robots were installed in China's manufacturing industry.[2] The domestic sale of industrial robots in China reached 87,000 in 2016 and soared to 156,000 in 2018. Meanwhile, the production of robots in China witnesses a high growth rate as well. In 2018, China produced up to 165,000 industrial robots. Regardless of the high sales growth in industrial robots in recent years, China still shows a much lower application of industrial robots than the world's average level. In 2018, China had an application rate of only 88 industrial robots, slightly higher than the average level of the world, but much lower than that of South Korea (631), Singapore (488) and Germany (309). Obviously, China still has much room for growth in industrial robots compared to developed countries in the future.

The application of industrial robots is expanding fast in India. Since the beginning of the 21st century, the number of robots used by Indian companies has rocketed. However, such a dramatic growth is achieved at a lower level in India. In 2016, India had only 16,026 industrial robots, accounting for just 0.1 per cent of industrial labourers (Bhattacharya 2018). The application rate of robots in India soared from less than one robot per 10,000 manufacturing workers in 2000 to nearly 10 robots in 2016. As one of the countries with lower application rate of robots around the world, India's robot industry will have a bright future compared to other countries.

## Impacts of Manufacturing Intelligence on Employment

The main impact of manufacturing intelligence on employment is reflected in the structure of employment. Manufacturing intelligence leads to a more advanced manufacturing system based on a new generation of information technology; it is essentially the progress of manufacturing technology. However, there is no specific conclusion on whether technological progress could increase or decrease employment rate. Technological progress is accompanied with 'replacement' and 'creation' of jobs. Marx argued that machines replacing workers would lower the percentage of labourers in the process of production, while reproduction on an extended scale would increase the demand for labourers. In other words, technological progress would result in the relative decrease and absolute increase of workers concurrently (Zhao Li, 2009). As a matter of fact, technological innovation will change the economic structure, resulting in the change in employment structure. Hence, technological progress affects employment structurally in a noticeable way in most countries. On one hand, it leads to decrease in demand for labourers with insufficient skills. On the other hand, the demand for highly skilled labourers tends to soar. Actually, the impact of technological progress on employment in modern times has evolved from the 'binary' relation, that is, mutual replacement of capital and labour, in the early stage of industrialization, to the 'ternary' relation involving capital, unskilled labourers and skilled labourers (Luo Rundong, 2006). Manufacturing intelligence is essentially technological progress, and 'replacement' and 'creation' of jobs tends to affect the demand for unskilled and highly skilled labourers. Therefore, manufacturing intelligence imposes a structural impact on employment. In other words, extensive development and wide application of manufacturing intelligence will significantly affect the employment structure of labourers.

## Impacts of Manufacturing Intelligence on Employment of Labourers Transferred from Agriculture in China and India

With regard to process, manufacturing intelligence replace jobs mainly in intelligent production, packaging and transportation, while intelligent design, intelligent equipment manufacturing and intelligent service will generate a large number of professional, technical and service positions. With regard to industrial chain, manufacturing intelligence exerts an influence from the point of view of employment replacement mainly on the sector of manufacturing assembly in the lower part of industrial value chain, while creating jobs mainly in sectors like research and development, design, brand and after-sale service in the upper part of the industrial value chain. China and India rely on cost advantage for development and growth, so that most of their manufacturing sectors belong to the lower end of the global value chain for manufacturing industry, and employ a very large proportion of unskilled labourers represented by labourers shifted from agriculture. It is therefore predicted that manufacturing intelligence will dramatically impact the employment of labourers who have moved out of agriculture to the manufacturing industry in China and India.

### Impact of Manufacturing Intelligence on Employment of Labourers Moving Out of Agriculture in China

China has a very large number of labourers from agriculture (peasant workers), which is still increasing, but the percentage of labourers shifting from agriculture to manufacturing industry is decreasing due to the progress of manufacturing intelligence. Labourers transferred from agriculture form an important but special group of workers in the manufacturing industry of China. Since 2013, value of China's manufacturing industry output has maintained a growth rate of around seven per cent. In 2016, the gross output value of manufacturing industry reached RMB 22.35 trillion, accounting for 30 per cent of gross domestic product (GDP) and up 6.80 per cent on a year-on-year basis. In 2017, the growth rate was 6.9 per cent. Regardless of the large output value and fast growth of manufacturing industry in China, the growth rate of labourers shifting from agriculture to manufacturing industry was negative. In 2015, China had 277.47 million peasant workers, which increased to 281.71 million in 2016, up by 4.24 million, a 1.5 per cent increase. In 2017, the number of peasant workers in China reached 286.52 million, up by 4.81 million and 1.7 per cent, compared to 2016. The total number of peasant workers was increasing, but the proportion of these peasant workers accepted in manufacturing industry was decreasing due to the progress of manufacturing intelligence. In 2015, China had 86 million peasant workers in manufacturing industry, accounting for 31.1 per cent of total peasant workers. In 2016, the proportion dropped to 30.5 per cent, down by 0.6 per cent. In 2017, it further decreased by 0.6 per cent to 29.9 per cent.[3]

## Impact of Manufacturing Intelligence on Employment of Labourers Who Are Shifting from Agriculture in India

For many reasons, manufacturing industry creates fewer jobs in India regardless of high growth rate. The continuous promotion of manufacturing intelligence is undoubtedly one of the key factors. From 1994 to 2017, the industry achieved an average growth rate of 6.61 per cent in India. From 2014 to 2016, the growth rate of manufacturing industry reached 7.1 per cent in India. However, enterprises with more than 10 employees had 460 million employees in total in 2016, which dropped from 480 million in 2014. Among all sectors, only wholesale and retail created more jobs. In the meantime, the number of employees in manufacturing industry (whether enterprises had joined trade union or not) dropped from 51.4 million to 48.1 million.[4] With the desire to utilize India's population dividend, Modi administration borrowed the successful experience from China's reform and opening up policy to create more jobs by revitalizing 'Make in India' and narrow the social gap between rich and poor, so as to achieve the rise of India. As a matter of fact, India has a relatively lower level of manufacturing on the whole, and its industry is highly replaceable in terms of manufacturing intelligence. For this reason, the number of industrial robots is soaring in India. Hence, the manufacturing value added increases fast, but it needs fewer and fewer employees. According to the prediction based on the scale and level of manufacturing in India, the extensive application of industrial robots will cause very slow growth of employment in manufacturing industry, and the number of employees in manufacturing may drop significantly in a decade.

## Comparison of the Impact between China and India

### Similarities in Employment of Labourers from Agriculture between China and India in Terms of Manufacturing Intelligence

#### *China and India Face Tremendous Pressure from Employment of Labourers Transferred from Agriculture*

More and more labourers are transferred from agriculture, causing tremendous pressure of employment. In 2017, China had 286.52 million peasant workers, up 4.81 million and 1.7 per cent compared to 2016. Among them, there were 171.85 million migrant peasant workers, up 2.51 million and 1.5 per cent, compared to 2016. Among migrant peasant workers, 137.1 million peasant workers entered cities, up 1.25 million and 0.9 per cent, compared to 2016. In India, agriculture employs a large number of labourers, and unemployment is a serious issue in cities, creating tremendous pressure of employment for labourers from agriculture as well. In 2017, India had up to 650 million people in the labour force (ages 18–60), 49 per cent of which were employed in agriculture contributing to approximately 13 per cent of its GDP. Due to seasonal employment of agriculture, there were not enough job opportunities for rural people. In 2016, India's unemployment rate was 7.15 per cent in rural areas, and 9.62 per cent in urban areas. According to the 2017 report of International Labour Organization, India's employment level was much lower than its economic growth rate, and it was expected that employment would not be improved in 2017 and unemployment rate would increase together with the decrease of employment rate in manufacturing industry in 2018.

### *China and India Will Witness Decrease in Number of Employees in Manufacturing Industry Due to the Promotion of Manufacturing Intelligence*

With the promotion of manufacturing intelligence, the number of employees and growth rate of employment in manufacturing industry will decrease constantly in both China and India. Around the world, the application of industrial robots will cause a lower number of employees needed to create the same output value in manufacturing industry. For instance, in 2010, the United States had a gross output value of manufacturing industry only 0.4 per cent lower than that of China due to its high level of intelligence, while China's manufacturing industry employed 114.445 million workers compared to only 11.5 million workers in the United States, which was only 10 per cent of China's workers. Considering the domestic condition in China and India, the growth rate of employment in manufacturing industry decreases significantly compared to other sectors, and it even becomes negative in India. In 2017, the number of employees in agriculture, manufacturing, construction and service industries increased by 6.56 per cent, 4.57 per cent, 10.25 per cent and 6.29 per cent, respectively, in China. Obviously, the growth rate of employment in manufacturing industry is lower than other industries in China. According to the forecast on the development trend of manufacturing in India, the number of employees in manufacturing industry might decrease by 30 per cent to 40 per cent in the next decade. As a matter of fact, the number of employees in manufacturing industry had already dramatically decreased from 51.4 million to 48.1 million in India from 2014 to 2016.

### *The Number of Employees Decreases in Manufacturing Industry in India and China on the Whole But Increases Gradually in the Tertiary Industry Due to the Rapid Spread of Industrial Robots*

In 2016, China's tertiary industry had up to 337.57 million employees, which portrayed an increase by 60.57 million compared to the figure in 2012. Meanwhile, the number of employees in the primary and secondary industries decreased by 42.77 million and 8.91 million, respectively. During 2012–2016, the proportion of employees in the tertiary industry to total employees increased from 36.1 per cent to

43.5 per cent, up 7.4 per cent, so that the tertiary industry created the largest number of job opportunities in China. In the meanwhile, the proportion of employees in the primary and secondary industries dropped from 33.6 per cent and 30.3 per cent to 27.7 per cent and 28.8 per cent, respectively.[5] In 2017, the proportion of three industries in India was agriculture 13 per cent, industry 18 per cent and services sector 69 per cent, respectively. On the whole, the number of employees in industry decreased in India, but the number of employees in service sector increased fast. In 2011, India had 49 per cent employees in agriculture, 24 per cent in the secondary industry and 27 per cent in the tertiary industry. In 2017, it was 49 per cent in agriculture, 21 per cent in the secondary industry and 30 per cent in the tertiary industry.

## Differences in Employment of Labourers from Agriculture between China and India in Terms of Manufacturing Intelligence

### *Employment as a Whole Increases Rapidly in China, But Very Slowly in India*

In 2016, China created 13.14 million new jobs in urban areas. By the end of 2017, 10.34 million new jobs were added in urban areas of China. Throughout the country, 27.7 per cent of total employees were in the primary industry, 28.8 per cent in the secondary industry and 43.5 per cent in the tertiary industry, in 2016. In 2017, it was 27 per cent in the primary industry, 28.1 per cent in the secondary industry and 44.9 per cent in the tertiary industry.[6] Thanks to the rapid growth in employment, China had an unemployment rate of approximately 4.5 per cent in urban and rural areas during 2014–2017. Meanwhile, employment increased slowly in India with unemployment rate of 7.2 per cent in rural areas and up to 9.6 per cent in urban areas during 2014–2017.

### *It is Easier for Labourers Shifting From Agriculture to Get Employed in Industry in China than India, Revealing Much Higher Urbanization Rate in China*

In urban areas, as more than 10 million job opportunities are created in China, a large number of peasant workers are attracted to cities for employment. China achieves a much faster process of urbanization than India. In 1990, China had an urbanization rate of 26.44 per cent, while it was 25.55 per cent in India. By 2017, while it reached 58.52 per cent in China, it has been 32.41 per cent in India. Clearly, China's urbanization rate was 26.11 per cent higher than India's.

### *Different Bases for Creation of Job Opportunities in Manufacturing Industry between China and India.*

Firstly, the scale of manufacturing industry is different in China and India, leading to difference in the number of job opportunities. In 2017, the output value of China's manufacturing industry was approximately USD 4 trillion, accounting for 30 per cent of that around the world and equivalent to the sum of the output values in manufacturing industry in the United States, Germany and Japan. The scale of manufacturing industry in China was large and increasing fast. In 2017, the growth rate of manufacturing industry was 6.8 per cent. In the financial year 2017–2018, the output value of manufacturing industry in India was approximately USD 400 billion, up 4.6 per cent on a year-on-year basis. Regardless of large scale, China's manufacturing value added per-capita has been only 35.5 per cent of the United States', 27.8 per cent of Germany's and 33.4 per cent of Japan's. Due to the large scale and low per-capita added value of China's manufacturing industry, there is still much room for its development and great potential to accept new labourers. India's manufacturing industry has a small scale, leading to the limited capacity of employment. Meanwhile, India's manufacturing value added per-capita is only 12 per cent of China's and four per cent of the United States', showing much room for further expansion. In recent years, the number of employees in India's manufacturing industry is decreasing, but it may still increase significantly if India could delve into the development potential of manufacturing industry.

### *Difference between China and India in Terms of Levels of Infrastructure for Creation of Employment*

As a leading industry, infrastructure exerts a huge influence on industrial development and employment structure. Large-scale construction of infrastructure facilitates the transfer of labourers from agriculture to manufacturing and service industries. Due to the construction and rapid development of infrastructure, service industry is developing fast in China and creates much more job opportunities than manufacturing and agriculture. Hence, it has become a main industry receiving labourers from agriculture. By the end of 2017, China's service industry had approximately 358 million employees, accounting for 46.21 per cent of China's employed population. In 2017, the tertiary industry had 4.794 million new registered enterprises, up 7.5 per cent on a year-on-year basis, accounting for 78.9 per cent of China's new registered enterprises and realized a growth rate of employment at four per cent. Among them, tourism created 79.9 million jobs whether directly or indirectly for 10.28 per cent of China's employed population.[7] In India, comparatively backward infrastructure has obstructed its economic development and improvement in employment. Therefore, its unemployment rate has been always high. In 2017, tourism provided around 51.9 million jobs whether directly or indirectly, but its abundant tourist resources have not been effectively utilized due to backward infrastructure.

### *Difference in Qualities of New Labourers Accepted in Manufacturing Industry in China and India*

Since 2010, the number of new jobs created has dropped from 25 million and it is predicted to reach 13 million by 2020. China's literacy rate is around 90.9 per cent, and approximately six million students graduate each year. Additionally, China has trained about 200 million industrial workers since its 'reform and opening up' policy was announced. India has an illiteracy rate of 30 per cent and less than 50 million industrial workers. China has a population of relatively higher quality than India, thus it could offer enough jobs to lower the unemployment rate with the increase in the industrial scale.

## Conclusion and Recommendations

Manufacturing intelligence is an inevitable trend for the development of manufacturing industry. China and India should both follow the historic trend and assiduously promote the development of manufacturing intelligence. Due to its effect with respect to employment replacement and creation, both countries should make full use of their advantages in resource, industry and talent and guide the coordinated development of manufacturing intelligence and other industries so as to create more jobs as much as possible, provide job opportunities for their huge population qualified for employment and lower the unemployment rate. For this reason, recommendations are given as follows:

1. **Manufacturing, a key engine to a country's industry, lays a foundation for its development and provides a way for its revitalization.** Both China and India should assiduously develop their manufacturing industry to solidify the foundation for industrial development and drive the healthy development of the tertiary industry to improve employment rate.

   Firstly, China and India should draft policy to guide and promote the application of manufacturing intelligence and internet of things and lower labour cost and cost of sales for enterprises. In this way, China could facilitate the green development and customization of traditional manufacturing industry, upgrade traditional industries and prevent the massive outbound transfer of traditional industries such as clothing and shoemaking. Again, this will help India accept the transferred industries from other countries and further develop its manufacturing industry.

   Secondly, assiduously promoting manufacturing intelligence can help China and India nurture high-end equipment manufacturing industry and move towards the upper end of the value chain of manufacturing industry. China's manufacturing industry is transforming from labour-intensive, heavy chemical industry to capital-intensive and technology-intensive. Speeding up the promotion of manufacturing intelligence can facilitate the development of new and high-tech industries such as semiconductor, information, new material, new energy and bio-pharmaceutical in China, as well as lead to the optimization and upgradation of industries. India could accelerate the development of manufacturing intelligence to give full play to its advantages in terms of the IT industry and talents, get into the world's industrial chain of intelligent equipment manufacturing and enhance its capability of intelligent equipment manufacturing.

Thirdly, both China and India should assiduously push forward the development of manufacturing intelligence to create more positions in research and development and design, which would help improve employment level and salary, achieve leading innovation capability and significant competitive advantage in main sectors of manufacturing industry and construct the world's leading technical and industrial system.

2. **China and India should speed up the development of productive service industry to facilitate adjustment and upgrade of industrial structure.** Both countries should consider the demand for industrial transformation and upgradation to further speed up the development of productive service industry, guide the expansion of enterprises to the upper end of value chain and facilitate the gradual transformation from productive manufacturing to productive service. China and India have a strong foundation of information technology, which should be taken as the basis for accelerating the combination of productive manufacturing with information and network technology to promote modernization of agricultural production and industrial manufacturing. Moreover, both countries should improve the delivery system for means of production in agriculture and the information-based and networked sale of agricultural products and drive the development of specialty agriculture, factory-style agriculture and the like. With regard to manufacturing industry, China and India should push forward research and development and application of basic process, basic material, basic elements, system integration, internet of things and intelligence software for industrial cluster and small and medium enterprises. Additionally, both countries should develop specialized services including technical support, equipment monitoring, maintenance, repair, renovation to enhance the quality of equipment operation and improve the level of green manufacturing.
3. **China and India should further strengthen the construction of infrastructure and assiduously drive the development of the tertiary industry.** Manufacturing intelligence can create jobs, and its promotion will lead to a large number of research and development

and design positions and drive the development of related productive service industry, so as to further bring new job opportunities. Nevertheless, manufacturing intelligence can improve labour productivity significantly as revealed from the development of countries with advanced manufacturing intelligence (e.g. the United States, Germany, Japan), but its development will reduce the positions in manufacturing industry while generating the same output value. Hence, China and India should consciously drive the development of the tertiary industry to alleviate the tremendous pressure from employment while promoting the development of manufacturing intelligence.

4. **China and India should strengthen industrial cooperation to jointly delve into their industrial potentials and improve their industrial level, so as to create more job opportunities.** China and India are highly complementary to each other, allowing cooperation among themselves in many aspects. India has relatively backward infrastructure, while China possesses advantages from the point of view of technology, equipment and fund for infrastructure construction. Therefore, the two countries can assiduously cooperate in this field. India has well-developed IT and bio-pharmaceutical industries, so China can attract relevant investments from India to drive the development of related domestic industries. Additionally, both countries have ancient civilization, abundant natural and cultural heritages and tourism resources, making it possible to cooperate in the tourism sector. For this reason, China and India should promote the development of tourism to create more jobs related to tourism, so as to alleviate unemployment pressure due to the progress of manufacturing intelligence.

## Notes

1. The rate of urbanization in developed countries normally exceeds 80 per cent, but in 2017 it was 58.5 per cent in China and 32.4 per cent in India, which is much lower than the former. what is the source of this information?
2. China robot industry development report (2018) issued by the Ministry of industry and information technology of China.
3. Data are calculated based on the documents released by the National Bureau of Statistics including the *Monitoring and Survey Report on Peasant Workers*

*in 2015*, the *China Statistic Yearbook 2015*, the *Statistical Communiqué of the People's Republic of China on the 2017 National Economic and Social Development*, and the *Monitoring and Survey Report on Peasant Workers in 2017*.
4. Surveys in 2017 and February 2018 by the National Sample Collection Center of India Statistics Office.
5. Data released by the National Bureau of Statistics of China.
6. *Statistical Communiqué on Human Resources and Social Security Development in 2017* released on May 21, 2018.
7. The *Report on Tourism Market and Comprehensive Contribution in 2017* by the National Tourism Data Center.

## References

Bhattacharya, Pramit. 2018, May. 'How Many Factory Workers in India Have Lost Their Jobs to Robots?' *Livemint*. https://www.livemint.com/Home-Page/tAZPQyqg8dhaagFWhpziNM/How-many-factory-workers-in-India-have-lost-their-jobs-to-ro.html

Cai, Xiuling, and Wenqun Gao. 2017. 'Impacts of Manufacturing Intelligence on Employment of Labors Transferred from Agriculture in China.' *Journal of Fujian Normal University (Philosophy and Social Sciences Edition)* 2 (1), 35.

Liu, Jianping, and Bangyan Ye. 2004. 'The Summarization of the Development Trends of Intelligence Manufacturing and its Application.' *Journal of Shanghai University (English Edition)* 3 (s1), 64.

Luo, Rundong. 2006. 'The Impact of Modern Technological Change On employment.' *Comparative Economic & Social Systems* 2 (4), 47.

Shuzi, Yang. 2012. *A Collection of Yang Shuzi's Papers on Science and Technology, Vol. I, Wuhan*: Huazhong University of Science and Technology, 213–25.

Sun, Bolin. 2013. 'Commentary of the Development Trend for Intelligent Equipment Manufacturing Industry in the Future.' *Process Automation Instrumentation* 34 (1), 2.

Wright, P. K., and D. A. Bourne. 1988. 'Manufacturing Intelligence.' *Robotics and Computer-Integrated Manufacturing* 4 (1/2), 293.

Xinhuanet.com. 2018, May 19. (Wu Qiong, Chen Hanzhe), China Economic Information Service releases the *Global Manufacturing Intelligence Development Index Report 2017* in Changhzou. Xinhuanet.com. http://www.js.xinhuanet.com/2018-05/19/c_1122857490.htm.

Zhao, Li. 2009. 'Impacts of Technological Progress on Employment Based on the Analysis of Shandong Province.' Tianjin: Doctoral Dissertation of Tianjin University, p. 25.

CHAPTER 9

# Comparison of Management Control Frameworks for Modern Day Organizations

Devesh Baid

## Introduction

This study explores the developments in discourse relating to management control systems (MCS) over the last sixty years. It compares various definitions by authors and how these definitions have broadened the scope of subject over the years. Also, MCS frameworks suggested by many researchers are compared on numerous parameters. The objective is to identify the appropriate framework that is relevant in today's organizational formats and may be applied for empirical investigation of control practices in these organization.

Researchers have defined MCS in different ways and there exists no one definition and framework acceptable to all (Merchant, 1998; Strauß and Zecher, 2013). The distinction comes as MCS has drawn support from numerous theoretical perspectives such as systems theory, sociology, transaction cost economics, etc., (Strauß and Zecher, 2013).

Two major functions of control systems are information function and control function (Davila, 1997). Anthony's (1965) framework is the most applied MCS framework. However, researchers have currently criticized this framework due to its solitary focus on formal controls in manufacturing industry making it irrelevant for new, present day organizational structures with focus on the service industry (Otley, Broadbent and Berry, 1995; Strauß and Zecher, 2013). Ahrens and Chapman (2004) and Alvesson and Kärreman (2004) have reported that both types of controls, that is, formal and informal MCS are found across various types of organizations.

The structure of the chapter is divided into four parts. This first part gives introduction to the study.Part two describes in detail about MCS definitions and frameworks. Part three compares various frameworks and identifies most appropriate framework for studying organizational controls in organizations. The last part concludes the study and provides direction for future research.

## MCS Definitions and Frameworks

Anthony (1965) defined MCS as 'the process by which managers assure that resources are obtained and used effectively and efficiently in the accomplishment of organizations objectives.' This definition focuses on the formal aspects of management controls in a business entity and demarcates MCS from strategy formulation and operational control. The control process includes activities of strategic planning, preparing budgets, execution and evaluation of performance. It is a cybernetic model where each activity leads to the next and collectively, they make a closed loop system. It is focused only on formal accounting-based controls and does not include contextual variables that restrict its applicability. Anthony's controls are more appropriate for middle managers.

Ouchi (1979) defines organizational control as 'the mechanism through which an organization can be managed so that it moves towards its objectives.' Based on transaction cost economics it identifies three types of control mechanisms—market, bureaucratic and clan control. In market control each employee can be rewarded in the ratio of his contribution and, therefore, market acts as a very efficient mode of control. In bureaucratic control, employees are constantly monitored and directed by people higher up in the hierarchy. Specific rules are laid down with detailed information for completing any process or achieving any levels of output or quality. Clan control is based on the concept of socialization at the organization level.

Flamholtz, Das and Tsui (1985) take a broader view of management controls based on theories drawn from discipline of sociology, psychology, administrative science, etc. They prefer using the term organizational control over management control and define it as 'attempts by the organization to increase the probability that individuals and groups will behave in ways that lead to the attainment of organizational goals' and defines control systems as 'techniques and processes to achieve goal congruence and may be designed for all levels of behavioural influence: individuals, small groups, formal subunits and the organizational as a whole'. Their model has two parts. The inner part constitutes of essential control systems which makes closed loop and the outer part identifies contextual factors that resembles an open system. The core system consists of the planning element, the operational subsystem, the outcome element, the measurement element, the feedback element and the evaluation reward element. It is enveloped in the contextual variables of an entity internal framework, its culture, and the relevant outer world settings. This conceptualization of Management Controls is better than Anthony's (1965) as it includes only formal controls and does not suggest any types of control.

Simons (1995) had brought a new dimension to the study of MCS. He has identified different objectives MCS achieves in an organization and how top management uses controls to achieve these objectives. His definition of MCS is 'formal, information-based routines and procedures managers use to maintain and alter patterns in organizational activities'. At the center of the framework lies business strategy. Next layer consists of '*core values, risks to be avoided, critical performance variable and strategic uncertainties*'. This layer is implemented in organization by using what Simmons call a lever. Core values are managed by lever of belief systems of an organization while *risk to be avoided* by an organization is managed by boundary systems. Similarly levers of interactive MCSs and diagnostic MCSs are applied for managing strategic uncertainties and critical performance variable. First and third levers are considered as positive controls while second and fourth levers are considered as negative controls. This framework is flexible to support innovation, which helps in evolving strategies bottom up. It is based on formal controls although it includes soft controls like values but only to the extent they are written and formalized. It does not classify types of control explicitly.

Tessier and Otley (2012) have developed a framework to overcome limitations of Simons' framework. At the center of this framework are the social and technical controls. The inner ring comprises of four different systems categorized into two types. One is related to performance classified as operational MCS and strategic performance MCS while the second is related to compliance classified as operational boundaries and strategic boundaries. The middle ring refers to managerial intentions about using controls interactively or diagnostically, in enabling manner or constraining manner and the reward and punishment for performance and compliance requirement. The outer ring of the framework refers to presentation of control and relates it to employee's perception of controls.

Merchant (1998) deviates from the old, narrower view of MCS based on simple cybernetic system and defines control as 'all the devices managers use to ensure that the behaviours and decisions of people in the organization are consistent with the organization's objectives and strategies'. Personal limitations of employees, low or no motivation and feeling directionless are stated by him as three main reasons for having controls. He identified employees' actions, employees' outcomes, organization personnel control policies and cultural controls policies as 'objects of control'. Each type of control can be used tightly or loosely. Overall objective of this framework is to control human behaviour. Results control 'influence actions because they cause employees to be concerned about the consequences of their actions they take'. Action controls are 'the most direct form of management control because they involve taking steps to ensure that employees act in the organizations' best interests by making their actions themselves the focus of control'. They are applied in many ways such as imposing behavioural restrictions, doing reviews of decisions before actions, making people accountable for actions and creating redundancy in organizations. Personnel controls 'are based on the employee's natural tendencies to control and/or motivate themselves' and involve setting and implementing of policies for ensuring proper selection, placement and training of employees, suitable job design to facilitate proper work and providing required resources. Cultural controls 'are designed to encourage mutual monitoring, a powerful form of group pressure on individuals who deviate from the group norms and values' and are enforced by creating codes of conduct, making provisions for group based rewards, doing transfers within organizations, providing for fair physical and social measures to all employees and commitment of the upper management of the entity to its organization's values.

Malmi and Brown (2008) differentiate management controls from MCSs. According to them, policies and practices written or unwritten, which management puts in place in an entity to direct employees behaviour forms management controls in that organization. 'If these are complete systems, as opposed to a simple rule (for example not to travel in business class) then they should be called MCSs.' Mostly organizations have many MCSs and if they are 'designed and coordinated intentionally' then it can be described as MCS system. They further state that distinct members in entity at various times introduce distinctive systems so MCSs in an organization are not a single system but multiple systems working as a package of systems to achieve desired results. Their study identifies five categories of control and places them at three levels. Cultural controls are at the top consisting of three sub-controls identified as clan, values and symbols. Middle layer includes three different forms of controls in an order. The order starting from left consists of planning followed by cybernetic controls and reward and compensation to the right. Controls related to planning consist of both long period and short time action-oriented planning. They are tightly linked to practice. Cybernetic controls comprise of financial (including budgets), non-financial and hybrid measurement systems. Base of the framework consists of administrative controls and provides arrangements in which middle layer controls are exercised. It includes structures of governance in the organization, its own organization structure and policies and procedures. At the top are cultural controls. They represent broad yet important controls, which takes long time to change. They provide a boundary in which other controls are implemented.

Grabner and Moers (2013) differentiate the terms MCS systems and MCS packages stating that 'MC practices form a system if the management control practices are interdependent and the design choices take these interdependencies into account'. In contrast, MCS package comprises of a holistic pack of control practices put in an organization irrespective of whether they are dependent on each other or not and the design of control practices takes their relationship into consideration or not. It implies that the MC package is either consisting of a number of MC systems and/or of a number of independent MC practices, which are addressing difficulties related to controls not related to each other. If the objective is to study linkages among MC practices, in that case, study of MC package is entirely not suitable to study at all.

Whitley (1999), based on sociological approach, has identified bureaucratic, output, delegated and patriarchal as different forms of control systems in an organization. These systems are based on four characteristics of the control system, which differ considerably among organizations. They are organizations dependence on clearly stated rules, regulations and practices; control over business transactions to be executed, subordinates' participation and influence in designing and managing control system and comprehensiveness of the control system. These are linked to various ways of how work is organized, types of firm and institutional features.

Otley (1999) owing to his disagreement with the economic and agency theory presented a new 'performance management framework'. It is designed to address five issues that cover all relevant features of management control in organizations. These issues are addressed in the form of five following questions:

1. Identify the important objectives that are very essential in determining success of an organization in future years and what are the measures used for assessing the performance of its objectives.
2. Identify business strategies and plans put in place by organizations and also identify processes and activities required for successfully

implementing them. In what ways does it access and measure the performance of action taken.
3. Determine the extent of performance needed to achieve objectives and strategies identified by the organization and what is the process used for fixing adequate performance targets for the organization.
4. What are the awards or penalties, that employees will get for completing or not being able to meet the performance standards set above.
5. Identify the necessary movement of information within organization for achieving learning from its past experience and accordingly change its existing behaviour.

This framework was drawn from inductive approach. It was based on contingency theory. It used traditional approach of command and control based on formal controls and did not consider role of strategy formulation as important.

Ferreira and Otley (2009) have preferred using broader terminology of Performance Management Systems (PMS) in place of MCS as they felt these words cover holistically all facets of organizational controls and performance. They define PMS as combination of formal and informal policies and practices applied by an entity to convey goals and objectives to be achieved by its employees. These processes are not static and evolve and change over time in an organization. These mechanisms, systems or by whatever name called assist in strategy implementation and day to day management of the entity. It includes elements of planning, measurement, control and reward for achieving set targets. This supports and promotes learning and change in an organization.

This framework integrates Simons' (1995) and Otley' (1999) frameworks and puts forward 12 questions relating to 'vision and mission, key success factors, structure, strategies and plans, key performance indicators, target setting, performance evaluation criteria, reward, information flows, systems and networks, PMSs use, PMSs change and strength and coherence'. It explicitly excludes factors of culture and context because organizations have limited control over them. Broadbent and Laughlin (2009) elaborate the PMS by including context and different forms of rationality, which were not considered by Ferreira and Otley. They also elaborates on questions relating to flow of information in organization, its systems and networks and the use of PMSs.

Different types of MCS frameworks are summarized in Table 9.1. MCS definitions and frameworks have moved from bounded rational system to open natural system models.

The closed system models ignored external environment as contingent variables, which can affect MCS while open system models considered external environment. Organizations are considered as rational systems if they are carefully designed for achieving pre-defined objectives, whereas they are considered as natural systems when unplanned and unexpected processes influences rational models.

Merchant and Simon give a broad view to management controls. Merchant recognizes the behavioural side as well as aspects of contingency framework and thus his work is placed on the line differentiating models based on closed natural and open rational approaches (Otley et al., 1995). Simon's use of interactive systems, which take care of strategic uncertainties in business leading to emergent strategies, places his framework in open rational approach.

The word Management Accounting (MA), Management Accounting Systems (MAS) and MCS are often applied interchangeably in literature as conveying the same meaning. Chenhall (2003) has explained that the three are different on the basis of scope of activities. MA refers to group of techniques such as variance analysis, inventory control or job costing; MAS uses these techniques of MA to achieve organizational objectives. Same MAS can be used for different objectives. MCS is a much broader concept than MAS as it covers other types of controls including informal controls such as clan controls. It may be most effective when formal and organic controls operate in combination'. As organic (informal) controls are very flexible they help in maintaining employee's commitment and builds in them a sense of innovation. At the same time formal controls help to inculcate financial discipline in employees and achieve economic viability by developing an effective and efficient workforce.

Table 9.1 *Types of MCS Framework*

| *Criteria of Comparison* | *Anthony (1965)* | *Ouchi (1979)* | *Flamholtz, Das and Tsui (1985)* | *Simons (1995)* | *Merchant (1998)* |
|---|---|---|---|---|---|
| Discipline | Sociology | | Organizational Psychology, Sociology and Administrative Theory | Psychology Based | Psychology Based |
| Theory | Agency Theory | Transaction Cost Economics | Contingency Theory | Agency Theory | Agency Theory |
| Contextual Variables | Nil | External Environment (Price Requirement for Market and Social Condition for Clan) | Organizational structure, organisational culture and the relevant external environment | External Environment | Recognized some aspects of contingency framework |
| Open/Closed Systems | Closed Systems (Cybernetic Systems) | Open Systems | Open Loop | Open Loop (Interactive control systems) | At boundary of natural and rational systems (Otley et al., 1995) |
| Rational/ Natural Systems | Rational Models | Rational Models | Natural Systems (Talks of Ex-post Controls) | Rational approach (Talks of Strategic Uncertainties) | At boundary of closed and open systems approach (Otley et al., 1995) |
| Formal/ Informal | Formal Accounting based | Both Formal and Informal Controls | Formal Controls | Formal controls including soft controls like values but only to the extent they are written and formalized | Both Formal and Informal Controls |

*(Continued)*

*(Continued)*

| *Criteria of Comparison* | *Anthony (1965)* | *Ouchi (1979)* | *Flamholtz, Das and Tsui (1985)* | *Simons (1995)* | *Merchant (1998)* |
|---|---|---|---|---|---|
| Types of Controls | Nil | Market, Bureaucratic and Clan Control | Nil | Belief Systems, Boundary Systems, Interactive Controls and Diagnostic Controls | Action Controls, Results Controls, Personnel Controls and Cultural Controls |
| Process Dimensions | Strategic Planning, Budget Preparation and Execution and Evaluation of Performance | Knowledge of the Transformation Process and Ability to Measure Output | Planning element, the operational subsystem, the outcome element, the measurement element, the feedback element and the evaluation reward element. | Core values, risk to be avoided, critical performance variable and strategic uncertainties | Looseness and Tightness of Control |
| Inclusion/ Exclusion | Excluded Strategy Formation & Operational Control from design of controls | | | Strategy at the Core | Separate Management control from Strategic Control |
| Applicability | Middle Managers | | Individuals, small groups, formal subunits and the organization as a whole | Senior Management | |

| *Criteria of Comparison* | *Otley (1999)* | *Whitley (1999)* | *Malmi and Brown (2008)* | *Ferreira and Otley (2009)* | *Broadbent and Laughlin (2009)* | *Tessier and Otley (2012)* |
|---|---|---|---|---|---|---|
| Discipline | Inductively generated framework drawing from extant body of knowledge in the field and on his research experience | Sociological Approach | A Typology based on synthesis of 40 years of literature. | Integrates Simons (1995) and Otley (1999) framework | Elaborates on PMS framework given by Ferreira and Otley (2009) | Revised version of Simons LOC Framework. At the periphery they have managerial intentions for controls and employees performance of controls |
| Theory | Contingency Theory | Rely on Role of Societal Institutions and Agencies | | Contingency Theory | | Agency Theory |
| Contextual Variables | External Environment, Organizational Culture, Social Controls and History | Six institutional factors including business dependence on the state, extent of formal regulation of markets and economic conditions | Nil | Contextual Factors and Culture | Both Internal and External Environment | External Environment |

(Continued)

*(Continued)*

| *Criteria of Comparison* | *Otley (1999)* | *Whitley (1999)* | *Malmi and Brown (2008)* | *Ferreira and Otley (2009)* | *Broadbent and Laughlin (2009)* | *Tessier and Otley (2012)* |
|---|---|---|---|---|---|---|
| Open/Closed Systems | Open Systems (Organizations operate in context that are continuously changing) | Open Systems | Closed Loop | Open Systems | Open Systems | Open Systems |
| Rational/ Natural Systems | Rational Systems (Static perspective - giving a snapshot at a point in time) | Natural Systems (Control systems characteristics change when nature and power among various interest groups in workplace change) | Rational Systems | Natural systems (How has the PMS altered in the light of change dynamics of the organization and its environment) | | Rational approach (Strategic performance and control systems focuses on strategic uncertainties) |
| Formal/ Informal | Formal Controls | Both Formal and Informal Controls | Both Formal and Informal Controls | Both Formal and Informal Controls | | Both Formal and Informal Controls |
| Types of Controls | Focussed on what Simons (1995) calls Diagnostic Control Systems | Bureaucratic, Output, Delegated and Patriarchal | Cultural, Planning, Cybernatic Controls, Reward & Compensation, and Administrative Controls | Nil | Transactional PMS and Relational PMS | Social and Technical controls |

| | | | | | | |
|---|---|---|---|---|---|---|
| Process Dimensions | Five issues relating to objectives, strategies & plans, performance targets, reward systems and type of information flows | Extent of reliance on formal rules and procedures, extent of control over how economic activities are to be carried out, involvement and influence of subordinates in control systems and scope of control systems | Cultural control is at the top while administrative control is at bottom | Has 10 'what' and 2 'how' questions relating to vision & mission, key success factors, organizational structure, strategies & plans, key performance measures, target setting, performance evaluation, reward systems, information flow systems & networks, PMS use, PMS change and strength & coherence. | Considers communicative rationality and instrumental rationality | Four control systems - operational performance control systems, strategic performance contrl systems, operational (or business conduct boundaries) and strategic boundaries. |
| Inclusion/ Exclusion | Excludes role of strategy formulation. Applicable to both for profit and not for profit organization. | | Excludes pure decision support systems | | | |
| Applicability | Transmission of control across organizational hierarchy | Individuals/work groups level and the organizational subunit level | | Transmission of control across organizational hierarchy | | Senior Management |

*Source:* Prepared by author based on Review of Literature.

According to Alvesson and Kärreman (2004), 'Management control typically includes an apparatus for specifying, monitoring and evaluating individual and collective action. It focuses on worker behaviour and output and/or the minds of the employees. Sometimes it attempts to focus on all three.' They classify controls broadly as socio-ideological and technocratic. Technocratic controls directly control people's behaviour by working with 'plans, arrangements and systems focusing behaviour and/or measurable outputs'. Socio-ideological control focuses on employees' relations, their identity and philosophy to control people's mindsets through establishing norms, beliefs and values, which influence behaviour indirectly. These controls have been covered in literature earlier as normative, cultural, ideological and concertive (team-based self-control mechanism) controls.

Tucker and Parker (2013) have given a comprehensive definition of informal controls. In the case of these controls, communication among employees happens based on common values, beliefs and traditions. These are not applied by consciously designing clear and valid measures. Rather these are unwritten practices of the organization that direct and guide the actions of various stakeholders in an organization. These informal controls essentially have their origin in or are proof of the unique culture of an organization also known as cultural control.

Based on the above literature it can be very well said that MCS definitions and frameworks differ broadly on account of using only formal or both formal and informal controls to control only subordinates' behaviour (managerial control) or both subordinates behaviour and work processes (organizational control) in the organization. Either they are narrow in scope covering only types of control or broad, covering not only about types of control but also covering ways controls are administered to assist strategy formulation, strategy implementation and operational control. Frameworks have also moved from closed rational systems to open natural systems. It will be a good idea to evaluate each of these definitions and frameworks to understand the scope and limitations of various frameworks.

## Comparison of MCS Frameworks

This section tries to evaluate various MCS frameworks discussed in the previous section. Frameworks are evaluated in terms of their scope, clarity of construct definition, application in various academic studies, limitations of the frameworks and relevance in current organizational context. It is evident that Anthony's (1965) is the most applied MCS framework. However, researchers have currently criticized this framework due to its focus only on formal controls in the manufacturing industry making it irrelevant for new organizational structures of present days which focus on the service industry.

Anthony's framework was suitable for large, stable and hierarchical organizations, which are not relevant organizational formats today. It also tended to emphasize accounting based controls such as budgeting and variance analysis as the prime way to implement control processes in an organization (Otley, Broadbent and Berry, 1995; Strauß and Zecher, 2013). Contemporary organizations are subject to considerable uncertainties, have relatively fewer middle management roles, require flexibility, adaption and continuous learning to occur. This brings into question whether Anthony's relative narrow definition of management control is still appropriate (Otley, 1994).

Otley et al. (1995) identify three major limitations of Anthony's framework. First, Anthony does not pay attention to important problems of ambiguity and uncertainty in defining strategies, goals and objectives. Second, he also does not address operational control problems relating to the process of production or service delivery. Finally, he focuses on planning and control using accounting methods and provides miniscule discussion on socio-psychological or behavioural issues despite recognizing their importance in organizational controls.

Control framework by Simons (1995), instead of identifying various control types present in an organization, asserts how organizations devote their time managing numerous control systems applied to ensure proper behaviour of employees. Management can decide to use a control system either diagnostically or interactively. Prior studies have used this framework to formulate and implement strategy and change management. Tessier and Otley (2012) state that Simons' (1995) framework is discussed very prominently in the MCS discipline but at the same time acknowledges that researchers have criticized this framework. Its concepts are not precisely defined and appear too vague and ambitious. Chenhall, Hall and Smith (2010) see the classification of Simons Levers of Control (LOC) Framework similar to enabling and coercive controls.

Malmi and Brown (2008) compare their framework with Merchant's (1998) controls framework. They conclude that their MCS as a Package (MCSPF) framework covers all elements of 'Objects of Control (OCF)' framework (except providing utmost required resources which as per them is necessary for accomplishing work and so cannot be considered as part of controls) with certain changes. Planning in their framework is classified as separate control while in OCF, it is a subtype of financial results control. MCSPF 'provides a more complete conception of the administrative tools managers use to control behavior as compared to their objects of control framework'. However, according to Grabner and Moers (2013), MCSPF furnishes a list of 'non–exhaustive' practices, which are grouped in various categories to assist future research but does not have a theory that can explain possible interdependencies between them. Although the package follows a particular order of presenting controls, it is not clear whether they have any interdependence that leads to internal consistency among them.

Sandelin (2008) compares various frameworks for identifying the most suitable framework for his study on control packages. According to this study, Ferreira and Otley (2009) and Otley (1999) take systems view of an entity and focus on applying more formal MCS in an organization. They do not emphasize informal means to motivate and control employees' behaviours. They also reported Simons' (1995) work on MCS relating to formal MCS practices. This framework helps to study the ways managers in the organization are using MCS to apply strategy in place of types of MCS practices. Flamholtz et al. (1985) framework is not very specific though it focuses on the requirement to coordinate control policies and practices in an entity. Sandelin (2008) further goes on to clarify that although Merchant's (1998) framework is rich in terms of identifying control practices, it does not elaborate upon the linkages between control elements. 'It focuses on the spectrum of control practices, but still provides sufficient rigidity with the specific control objects of culture, personnel, action and results.'

Abernethy and Brownell (1997) in their study classify controls as accounting-based controls, behaviour controls and personnel controls and draws reference to Merchant's conceptualizations of control while explaining these control terms. Strauß and Zecher (2013) in their review of MCS, prepared a map of MCS landscape on which they have ranked Merchant's objects of control framework highest on comprehensive coverage of MCS emphasizing on both formal and informal controls to achieve desired outcomes from employees of an entity. Abernethy and Stolewinder's (1995) work relating to specialized service organizations such as consulting, medical profession and universities states that 'professional control is similar to Ouchi notion of clan control in that it is based on social and self-control processes'. Malmi and Brown (2008) suggest that cultural control can be implemented by applying processes relating to clan controls in an organization. Berry et al. (2009) in their review, acknowledge that Merchant's and Simons' works draw from agency theory and psychology. They deviate from the narrow definition of MCS by recognizing that management controls are indeed much broader than conceptualized in past.

According to Tucker and Parker (2013), organizations today apply all types of controls (including informal controls) simultaneously to achieve organizational objectives. This is in line with the current view according to which a variety of such controls add up together to make a package of controls. Controls in such packages may either act as complement or as substitute to each other. Some of them may also be in opposition.

## Conclusion

From the above comparison of these frameworks it is clear that Merchant's framework is very broad as it encompasses major types of control; it also considers that these controls are being applied tightly or loosely in an organization. It is also empirically used in numerous research studies. All other frameworks of MCS discussed given by various authors and researchers are very broad based and have not received much needed theoretical and empirical support in research studies. Hence this study proposes Merchant's framework for further research and investigation in area of management controls in modern day organizations.

## References

Abernethy, M. A., and P. Brownell. 1997. 'Management Control Systems in Research and Development Organizations: The Role of Accounting, Behavior and Personnel Controls.' *Accounting, Organizations and Society* 22 (3–4), 233–248.

Abernethy, M. A., and J. U. Stoelwinder. 1995. The Role of Professional Control in the Management of Complex Organizations. *Accounting, Organizations and Society* 20 (1), 1–17.

Ahrens, T., and C. Chapman, 2004. Accounting for Flexibility and Efficiency: A Field Study of Management Control Systems in a Restaurant Chain. *Contemporary Accounting Research* 21 (2), 271–301.

Alvesson, M., and D. Kärreman. 2004. 'Interfaces of Control. Technocratic and Socio-ideological Control in a Global Management Consultancy Firm.' *Accounting, Organizations and Society* 29 (3–4), 423–444.

Anthony, R. N. 1965. 'Planning and Control System: A Framework for Analysis. Division of Research', Graduate School of Business Administration, Harvard University.

Berry, A. J., A. F. Coad, E. P. Harris, D. T. Otley, and C. Stringer. 2009. 'Emerging Themes in Management Control: A Review of Recent Literature.' *The British Accounting Review* 41 (1), 2–20. http://doi.org/10.1016/j.bar.2008.09.001

Broadbent, J., and R. Laughlin. 2009. 'Performance Management System: A Conceptual Model.' *Management Accounting Research* 20 (4), 283–295.

Chenhall, R. H. 2003. 'Management control systems design within its organizational context: Findings from contingency-based research and directions for the future.' *Accounting, Organizations & Society* 28 (2/3), 127–168.

Chenhall, R. H., M. Hall, and D. Smith. 2010. 'Social Capital and Management Control Systems: A Study of a Non-government Organization.' *Accounting, Organizations & Society* 35 (8), 737–756. http://doi.org/10.1016/j.aos.2010.09.006

Davila, A. 1997. *The Information and Control Functions of management Control Systems in Product Development: Empirical and Analytical Perspectives (D.B.A.).* Harvard University, United States, Massachusetts. Accessed June 20, 2015, from http://search.proquest.com/pqdthss/docview/304340657/abstract/A3C44D6C2BE845FEPQ/1?accountid=27540

Ferreira, A., and D. Otley. 2009. 'The Design and Use of Performance Management Systems: An Extended Framework for Analysis.' *Management Accounting Research* 20 (4), 263–282.

Flamholtz, E. G., T. K. Das, and A. S. Tsui. 1985. 'Toward an Integrative Framework of Organizational Control.' *Accounting, Organizations and Society* 10 (1), 35–50.

Grabner, I., and F. Moers. 2013. 'Management Control as a System or a Package? Conceptual and Empirical Issues.' *Accounting, Organizations and Society* 38 (6–7), 407–419.

Malmi, T., and D. A. Brown. 2008. 'Management Control Systems as a Package—Opportunities, Challenges and Research Directions.' *Management Accounting Research* 19 (4), 287–300.

Merchant, K. A. 1998. *Modern Management Control Systems: Text and Cases.* New Jersey: Prentice-Hall.

Otley, D. 1994. 'Management Control in Contemporary Organizations: Towards a Wider Framework.' *Management Accounting Research* 5 (3/4), 289.

Otley, D. 1999. 'Performance Management: A Framework for Management Control Systems Research.' *Management Accounting Research* 10 (4), 363–382.

Otley, D., J. Broadbent, and A. Berry. 1995. 'Research in Management Control: An Overview of its Development.' *British Journal of Management* 6 (special issue), S31–S44.

Ouchi, W. G. 1979. 'A Conceptual Framework for the Design of Organizational Control Mechanisms.' *Management science: Journal of the Institute for Operations Research and the Management Sciences* 25 (9), 833–848.

Sandelin, M. 2008. 'Operation of Management Control Practices as a Package—A Case Study on Control System Variety in a Growth Firm Context.' *Management Accounting Research* 19 (4), 324–343.

Simons, R. 1995. *Levers of Control: How Managers Use Innovative Control Systems to Drive Strategic Renewal.* Boston: Harvard Business School Press.

Strauß, D. E., and C. Zecher. 2013. 'Management Control Systems: A Review.' *Journal of Management Control* 23 (4), 233–268. http://doi.org/10.1007/s00187-012-0158-

Tessier, S., and D. Otley. 2012. 'A Conceptual Development of Simons' Levers of Control Framework.' *Management Accounting Research* 23 (3), 171–185.

Tucker, B. P., and L. D. Parker. 2013. 'Out of Control? Strategy in the NFP Sector: The Implications for Management Control.' *Accounting, Auditing & Accountability Journal* 26 (2), 234–266. http://doi.org/10.1108/09513571311303729

Whitley, R. 1999. 'Firms, Institutions and Management Control: The Comparative Analysis of Coordination and Control Systems.' *Accounting, Organizations and Society* 24 (5), 507–524.

CHAPTER 10

# Ethics and Privacy Concerns in Today's 'Digital India'

Mudit Gera

## Introduction

Human beings demand trust from their family members, friends, co-workers and from anyone they transact with in their day to day life which makes their relationship stronger leading to longevity of the relationship. Same is the case in a digital environment, considering a user and a service provider, in which a user becomes more loyal to that business entity which preserves his trust and keeps him delighted by providing reliable services, with no compromise on business ethics.

In a digital environment, a user is more concerned for his privacy, security of his personal data being compromised, ethical behaviour of the businesses and various other trust issues. Malhotra et al. (2004) found that internet users' privacy concerns are solely determined by three factors, namely, how their data is collected, how important they consider being aware of the data collected and the control users perceive to have over this collection of data. The more a user is worried about these factors, the higher their privacy concerns will be.

In the last couple of years, the issue of privacy concerns has gained much importance due to massive data breaches worldwide. According to Statista (2018), millions of data records were leaked in the United States between 2005 and 2017. In 2017, the personal information of millions of consumers of Equifax was leaked to outsiders (Equifax, 2017), which conveys a need for an effective data protection global framework.

Although, different governments worldwide have put in place various data protection laws such as the European Union's Data Protection Directive and General Data Protection Regulation–European Directive EC 95/461995, the United States Federal Trade Commission's Fair Information Practice Principles, the Organization for Economic Cooperation and Development's guidelines on the Protection of Privacy and Transborder Flows of Personal Data and Malaysia's Personal Data Protection Act 2010, but the compliance to these regulations to protect user privacy still remains a challenge faced by various organizations across the globe (Gan et al., 2019).

Ethics and privacy in a digital environment have been widely brought into practice across the United States and United Kingdom (Martin, 2016), but across developing nations it still remains a wide grey area due to many issues such as user's acquaintance with the subject, exponential digital penetration with high online risks, insufficient and immature government regulations, etc.

It has been found out that if a firm meets its consumers' privacy expectations then it also increases their purchase intentions and likelihood to transact with that firm (Cases et al., 2010; Eastlick et al., 2006), which ultimately increases trust in that firm (McCole et al., 2010).

This research paper primarily talks about ethics and privacy concerns in a digital world particularly in the Indian domain. It begins with literature review of the subject in concern, followed by research gaps and objectives of this research, design and methodology followed by results, findings and implications of this research work. It would be primarily useful for advertising managers, digital marketers, government agencies as well as marketing students who have interest in the challenging issue of privacy and ethics in this digital era.

## Literature Review

While browsing internet, users are under the impression that their activity over internet is secure, which in reality is far from the truth. The moment a user is connected via the internet, he/she gets tracked by various third-party cookies and the user's digital footprints are logged behind without consent, making it dangerous. According to Smith et al. (1996), privacy concern refers to 'the concern that individuals have with the information privacy practices of organizations, which could compromise the individuals' ability to control his personal information' and about sixty nine per cent of consumers feel that they have lost control of their data online (Laczniak and Murphy, 2006).

Information privacy concerns are also found to vary according to the user's demographic profile. In general, men have higher privacy concerns than women, however, if age is also taken in consideration, women in the age group of forties and younger, tend to exhibit higher privacy concerns whereas men in the age group of fifties and older exhibit higher privacy concerns. Income and education also have been found to impact privacy concerns such that higher the income and education of a customer, higher will be his/her information privacy concerns (Lee et al., 2019). In fact, how much a user has knowledge of and experience with technology, also affects his privacy concerns. Martin (2018) studied that users who are well informed about or proficient in the use of computers and internet tend to place higher importance on privacy factors than the users who are not knowledgeable about the computers and internet. Teens are one of the most active users in this digital landscape. Gogus and Saygın (2019) found out that eighty-seven per cent of teens believe that it is essential to protect their personal information whereas fifty four per cent of high school students get uncomfortable when they get to know that their activities are tracked online by third party websites the moment they start using internet.

Users in digital environment frequently face the dilemma of 'Privacy Paradox', according to which users become anxious about their privacy online but at the same time continue to share their personal information to enjoy the benefits of a more personalized experience and monetary compensation (Barnes, 2006; Norberg et al., 2007).

However, users can only pay for a certain amount of privacy, but as privacy continues to wear down, the quality of value provided in exchange declines. While discussing the effects and determinants of online privacy concerns in context of e-commerce, Anic et al., (2019) found out that the users in this case would like to have more control over their personal information and where government regulations are found out to be ineffective, online privacy concerns increase. Although it was proven that there is no direct relationship between online privacy concerns and online purchases, online privacy concerns affect attitudes toward online shopping which ultimately drives online purchases.

Smartphones have now become an indispensable part of a user's life and these are incomplete without apps installed in it. Mobile apps, which are generally free to install and use, serve the user with advertisements, gather their private data such as their location, contact list, usage behaviour with the help of search terms, history, etc., which demonstrates that no apps are so called 'free apps' and users pay a hefty price in return for their privacy online. It has been found out that online advertisers gather as much as ninety per cent of the users' information in just three weeks (Wang et al., 2019).

The literature presents few models discussed with regard to online privacy and ethical concerns. Thus, Chang et al., (2018) studied the role of privacy policy on users' perceived privacy and proposed a Privacy Boundary Management Model (PBMM), which explains how users formulate and manage their privacy boundaries and concluded that the elements of Fair Information Practice Principles, namely, Enforcement, Security, Notice and Access have significant impact on perceived effectiveness of privacy policy. Similarly, Román and Cuestas (2008) proposed the Consumer Perception Regarding Ethics of Online Retailers Model (CPEOR Model), which states Security, Privacy, Fulfilment and Non-deception as the important factors for users while shopping online. Users are generally more conscious in an online setting and when a user is knowledgeable and has a general internet expertise, CPEOR significantly improves, since user's expertise partially alleviates information deficit. It is found that for a user, security of transactions is the most important factor. The CPEOR Model was termed as an effective means of getting new online shoppers.

One of the key innovations in the last few years has been the Internet of Things (IoT), which enables multiple devices to seamlessly communicate with each other, with an objective to improve the quality of human life. IoT devices are built on a common architecture of repetitive sensing and forwarding of information thus forming a time–series data, which keeps the client aware and updated about the changing parameters thus enabling him to react accordingly (Asif et al., 2018). However, benefits of IoT devices come at a huge cost of major privacy and ethical concerns and data breaches. It is found that if a user is able to control the amount of information being shared by each individual IoT device, he/she will be able to trade-off between the level of users' data privacy and the utility of the resultant IoT device (Asif et al., 2018).

A new emerging marketing technique called Programmatic Advertising, is applied to the internet these days (Leal-Rodríguez et al., 2015). The Programmatic Advertising algorithm analyses real time data, which allows advertisements to accurately reflect the interests of a user at the moment at which they are most likely to make a purchase or click on an advertisement (Huang, 2018; Belanche et al., 2017; Oikarinen and Söderlund, 2016). The effects of Programmatic Advertising on users' privacy concerns have been studied by Palos-Sanchez et al. (2019). The research concluded that users admit that advertising on the web is much more interesting than traditional advertising. The perceived usefulness of Programmatic Advertising has a direct influence on the users' concern for privacy, which increases when users realize how this type of advertising works because it makes them an active part of the advertising method.

Users in today's digital landscape are much more vulnerable to covert marketing, in which firms use various tactics to secretly market their products and services to their prospective customers, which raise ethics and privacy concerns in the mind of users. According to Milne et al. (2009), it has been found out that when users become aware that they have been the targets of covert marketing by firms, it lowers the purchase likelihood of users by almost 29 per cent. Users are worried in such a case since they are targeted without their knowledge of commercial intent behind the covert tactics.

## Research Gaps

Earlier studies have put forth various challenges in the domain and there exists a wide grey area in the subject of online privacy and ethics in Indian digital environment, which when studied in depth can provide useful information to various stakeholders such as concerned businesses, users and government agencies to keep a check on the business environment prevailing in India.

Previous works have also discussed about unethical behaviour of companies to discourage unprofitable customers based on behavioural targeting and cutting-edge technologies such as geo-fencing, and various important factors, which help in elevation of consumer trust in a digital environment along with the effect of demographic factors on judgement of consumers regarding online retailers (Laczniak and Murphy, 2006; Martin, 2016). However, many of these challenges are not yet addressed in the Indian context and hence this study will attempt to throw light on such issues.

The main challenge in this digital world lies in making consumers aware of the processes that are in place to protect consumer interest and enforcing quality standards. There is a need of better collaboration between the marketers and government agencies globally. Marketers need to think about the new ways of advertising, recognizing what is best for the consumers, safeguarding their interests and at the same time maintaining marketing effectiveness.

## Objectives of the Study

The exploratory study has the following broad objectives in the Indian context:

1. To assess consumer attitude towards company related factors, namely, promises kept by the company, quick resolution offered by the company, a company understanding its customers and transparency offered by the company.
2. To assess whether the company related factors, namely, promises kept by the company, quick resolution offered by the company, a

company understanding its customers and transparency offered by the company varies as a function of consumer demographics—age, gender, education and city of residence.

3. To assess whether the company related factors, namely, promises kept by the company, quick resolution offered by the company, a company understanding its customers and transparency offered by the company varies as a function of the purpose for which the consumer uses the digital environment.

## Constructs under Study: Definition of the Proposed Relationships

In today's digital world, consumers use digital platforms for various purposes such as Online Shopping, Online Banking or Social Networking, thereby making their life easy and fulfilling at the same time. To improve user experience on the web, this research explores the relationship of various constructs as described below with regard to consumers' trust in the Indian context.

**Promises kept:** Firms should do their best to live up to their customer's expectations and never commit something they cannot accomplish. Customers always crave service consistency from the businesses they transact with, which in turn helps the firms to retain their customers' loyalty. But when firms fail to deliver what they promise, their customers will not trust them anymore and will look forward to services from their competitors.

**Quick Resolution:** Trust originates from the customer's first contact with the company and ends with business's quality delivery, care and support. At each step of the customer's journey within the system, businesses can either improve or damage the customer experience, hence it is very important to deal with customer issues and concerns promptly and effectively at the same time so as to boost up their transaction confidence and help businesses create a sense of differentiation with regard to their competitors in the mind of their customers.

**Customer Understanding:** Understanding the customers is an integral part of any business. Hence, firms should always listen to what their customers want and make use of the feedback mechanism to serve them better. Once a firm has an idea about his customer behaviour, it will be easier to convince them and make them their loyal customers.

**Transparency:** Firms should always remain transparent to their customers about their products and services in the real sense. It helps to build firm's brand mantra and at the same time acts as a differentiation strategy with regard to its competitors.

## Methodology of the Study

A simple questionnaire with nineteen questions was framed keeping in mind demographic profiles of various audience and rolled out online. With regard to scale of measurement, nominal scale was used with regard to the variables such as City of Residence (Metro, Non-Metro), Gender (Male, Female), Age (Less than 30 years, Greater than 30 years), Qualification (Tenth, Twelfth, Diploma, Graduate, Post Graduate, Doctoral), Usage (Online Shopping, Banking Services, Social Networking, Others) and a five-point interval scale was used with regard to questions pertaining to consumers in a digital environment. A total of valid 60 respondents' data was collected and analyzed in this research, out of which 70 per cent were from urban areas. With regard to gender and age, there was an equal proportion of male-female respondents and almost 70 per cent of respondents were less than 30 years of age. As far as qualification level is concerned, 65 per cent of total respondents were post-graduates, 25 per cent were graduates and rest had other qualification levels. It was interesting to know that almost half of the respondents use digital platforms primarily for the purpose of social networking and just 20 per cent use it for online shopping and rest for various other online applications.

In this study, convenience sampling is used to collect user data. The target group comprised of Indians who actively transact in a digital environment for various purposes such as online shopping, online banking, social networking and various other online applications. As far as data analysis is concerned in this paper, variety of techniques are

Table 10.1 *Reliability Statistics*

| *Cronbach's Alpha* | *No. of Items* |
|---|---|
| 0.8 | 12 |

Table 10.2 *Test of Normality*

| *Constructs* | *Significance* |
|---|---|
| Promises | 0.168 |
| Quick Resolution | 0.141 |
| Transparency | 0.073 |
| Customer Understanding | 0.054 |

applied for testing the objectives framed for the study. Next, based on the data collected using a questionnaire, one sample t-test, independent sample t-test and one-way ANOVA are used as Parametric tests if data is found to be Normal.

Before proceeding with the statistical testing, reliability of data which was collected is tested and the value for Cronbach's alpha was found to be 0.800 as shown in Table 10.1, which concludes that items have relatively high internal consistency. Afterwards, normality of data collected was tested to gauge whether to proceed with Parametric or Non-parametric statistical tests.

From Table 10.2, it can be clearly understood that since the significance value of all the Shapiro-Wilk tests of the four constructs were found to be greater than 0.05, it was concluded that the data was Normal.

## Results

The statistical testing was carried out using IBM SPSS Statistics (Version 23), the results of which are described in detail as follows.

Table 10.3 *Objective 1: Assessing the Consumer Attitude*

| *Constructs* | *p-value* |
|---|---|
| Promises | 0.366 |
| Transparency | 0.897 |
| Quick Resolution | 0.000* |
| Customer Understanding | 0.000* |

*Significant difference $p < 0.05$.

Initially the first objective of the study, which was to assess the consumer attitude towards company related factors, namely, promises kept by the company, quick resolution offered by the company, a company understanding its customers and transparency offered by the company in a digital environment, was tested and the p-values were calculated using the Parametric tests.

From Table 10.3, looking at the p-values, it can be said that for both the constructs namely, Promises and Transparency, population means were statistically significantly indifferent and hence it can be concluded that consumers in a digital environment have a neutral attitude towards Promises and Transparency. Whereas, in the case of constructs namely, Quick Resolution and Customer Understanding, population means were statistically significantly different and hence it can be concluded that consumers in a digital environment do not have a neutral attitude towards Quick Resolution and Customer Understanding.

The second objective of the study was to assess whether the company related factors, namely promises kept by the company, quick resolution offered by the company, customer understanding and transparency offered by the company vary as a function of consumer demographics—age, gender, education and city of residence; the company related factors were tested and the p-values were calculated using the Parametric tests.

Looking at the p-values in Table 10.4, in the case of Gender, it can be said that for all the constructs namely, Promises, Transparency,

Table 10.4 *Group Means Analysis (Gender)*

| *Constructs* | *p-value* |
|---|---|
| Promises | 0.413 |
| Transparency | 0.114 |
| Quick Resolution | 0.434 |
| Customer Understanding | 0.332 |

Table 10.5 *Group Means Analysis (Age)*

| *Constructs* | *p-value* |
|---|---|
| Promises | 0.054 |
| Transparency | 0.167 |
| Quick Resolution | 0.764 |
| Customer Understanding | 0.943 |

Quick Resolution and Customer Understanding, Group means are statistically insignificantly different and hence it can be concluded that, Promises, Transparency, Quick Resolution and Customer Understanding variables do not vary across Gender.

Looking at the p-values in Table 10.5, in the case of Age also, it can be seen that for all the constructs namely, Promises, Transparency, Quick Resolution and Customer Understanding, Group means are statistically insignificantly different and hence it can be concluded that, Promises, Transparency, Quick Resolution and Customer Understanding variables do not vary across Age.

In the case of City of Residence, as seen from Table 10.6, for all the constructs namely, Promises, Transparency, Quick Resolution and Customer Understanding, Group means are statistically insignificantly different and hence it can be concluded that, Promises, Transparency, Quick Resolution and Customer Understanding variables do not vary across City of Residence.

Table 10.6 *Group Means Analysis (City of Residence)*

| *Constructs* | *p-value* |
|---|---|
| Promises | 0.396 |
| Transparency | 0.326 |
| Quick Resolution | 0.618 |
| Customer Understanding | 0.709 |

Table 10.7 *Group Means Analysis (Qualification)*

| *Constructs* | *p-value* |
|---|---|
| Promises | 0.100 |
| Transparency | 0.029* |
| Quick Resolution | 0.023* |
| Customer Understanding | 0.174 |

From Table 10.7, it can be seen with regards to qualification that for the constructs, namely, Transparency and Quick Resolution, Group means are statistically significantly different and hence, it can be concluded that both Transparency and Quick Resolution vary across Qualification. However, for the constructs namely, Promises and Customer Understanding, group means are statistically significantly indifferent and hence, it can be concluded that both Promises and Customer Understanding do not vary across Qualification.

The third objective of the study to assess whether the company related factors, namely, promises kept by the company, quick resolution offered by the company, customer understanding and transparency offered by the company vary as a function of the purpose for which the consumer uses the digital environment, was tested and the p-values were calculated using the Parametric tests.

It can be seen from Table 10.8 that for all the constructs namely, Promises, Transparency, Quick Resolution and Customer

Table 10.8 *Group Means Analysis (Purpose of using digital environment)*

| *Construct* | *p-value* |
|---|---|
| Promises | 0.781 |
| Transparency | 0.303 |
| Quick Resolution | 0.512 |
| Customer Understanding | 0.765 |

Understanding, Group means are statistically insignificantly different and hence, Promises, Transparency, Quick Resolution and Customer Understanding variables do not vary across purpose of using digital environment.

## Discussion of Findings and Research Implications

As discussed in the previous sections of this research, consumers in a digital environment are much more concerned about how their data is collected, how much they are aware of the data collected and about how much control they perceive to have over this collection of data and it is said that more a consumer is worried about these factors, the higher their privacy concerns will be. This study tries to assess the general attitude of Indian consumers in a digital ecosystem to some extent.

The results of this study confirm the findings of the previous researches that in developing nations like India, the subject of Ethics and Privacy Concerns still remains a wide grey area due to less knowledge of the customers on the subject. A company understanding its customers does not vary across customers' demographics nor with purpose of using digital environment. Also, less user acquaintance with the subject demonstrates an urgent need for an effective data protection framework globally along with effective compliance of these regulations to protect customers' interest.

Previous researches, as described in earlier sections of this study, show that information privacy concerns vary according to customer's demographic profiles. However, in the Indian context, this study refutes the claim of previous researches done in the global context. The results of this research conclude that except the qualification levels of Indians, none of the users' demographic factors namely Gender, Age and City of Residence affect the privacy concerns of Indians, their attitude in general remains neutral.

This research confirms that Indian customers in a digital environment continue to face the dilemma of 'Privacy Paradox', according to which users become anxious about their privacy online but at the same time continue to share their personal information to enjoy the benefits of more personalized experience and monetary compensation. Indian consumers in a digital environment do not value Promises made by firms and Transparency offered by them as important factors while transacting online. Also, all the four constructs such as Promises, Transparency, Customer Understanding and Quick Resolution do not vary across purpose of using digital environment.

As far as the Academic Implications are concerned with regard to this research work, there is still lack of quality research in the domain of 'Ethics' and 'Privacy', which highlights the need for more theoretically grounded rigorous work. Users' less acquaintance with this subject coupled with exponential technological advances in this area pose challenges to the academic researchers globally. One of the viable solutions to bridge this gap is a need for collaborations between academic researchers within a global framework to undertake research in this area more effectively by reducing the time taken for research and generating more quality output making a generous contribution to the community.

This study also conveys some Managerial Implications, such as the results of this research will aid active industry practitioners in identifying gaps related to 'Ethics' and 'Privacy' and fill them appropriately with respect to their line of businesses, which will help them in designing better products and services and to further target those to their customers. Keeping in view the rising technological advances in this area, they need to act swiftly to win their customers' confidence in them, which ultimately will increase trust in their businesses, leading to rise in their service volumes and revenue figures. However, the most challenging task for industry practitioners is to make their customers aware of this subject as much as they can. They should try to understand their customers more closely, deliver what they promise to their customers and most importantly they should be absolutely transparent about their policies and service offerings to their customers.

## Limitations and Future Research

In line with other research studies, this study too suffers from various limitations as described below in this section.

This research work was conducted using limited number of sixty respondents, hence, can be considered to be a small-scale study, which may or may not capture the overall picture of the online consumers in India. As India is progressing towards major digital revamp, the results of this study may change over time due to technological innovations in this area and thus need to be updated in terms of testing the objectives again after a gap of few years with a different and larger data set.

In future studies, how these four constructs namely Promises, Transparency, Quick Resolution and Customer Understanding affect consumers' trust in a digital environment, can also be studied.

This study incorporated the route of convenient sampling into consideration due to various resource constraints, however, future studies can take into consideration various other sampling methods to collect data inputs of various other stakeholders.

To gain a holistic view of Ethics and Privacy Concerns in developing/emerging economies, data from various nations can be collected in future studies, since in this research data from only Indian respondents were taken into consideration.

In terms of digital ecosystem, this research primarily focused on Online Shopping, Online Banking Services, Social Networking as major service offerings, however, today a digital consumer uses internet for various other services like online food delivery such as 'Zomato' 'Swiggy', etc., online travel booking such as 'Uber', 'Ola', which can be studied in future.

## Appendix A. Questionnaire

**Q1. Do you work for any of these organizations?**

A) Market Research
B) Advertising Agency
C) Media Agency
D) Digital Media Company
E) E-commerce Firm
F) Pure Digital Firm
G) Others

**Q2. Did you participate in a market research survey in the past one month?**

A) Yes
B) No

**Q3. Please indicate your city of residence.**

A) Metro
B) Non- Metro

**Q4. Please indicate your gender.**

A) Male
B) Female

**Q5. Please indicate your age.**

A) Less Than 30 Years
B) More Than 30 Years

**Q6. Please indicate your qualification.**

A) 10th
B) 12th
C) Diploma
D) Graduate
E) Post-Graduate
F) Doctoral

**Q7. For what purpose do you use the internet primarily for?**

A) Online Shopping
B) Banking Services
C) Social Networking
D) Others

**Q8. The websites you visit deliver what they intend to up to your satisfaction level?**

A) Strongly Disagree
B) Disagree
C) Neutral
D) Agree
E) Strongly Agree

**Q9. The website tells you that your data is safe with them, and you feel a sense of security?**

A) Strongly Disagree
B) Disagree
C) Neutral
D) Agree
E) Strongly Agree

**Q10. The website tells you that they will never sell your data to third party websites for marketing purposes?**

A) Strongly Disagree
B) Disagree
C) Neutral
D) Agree
E) Strongly Agree

**Q11. The website has a dedicated communication support channel via telephone (toll-free), e-mail, social media handles, etc.?**

A) Strongly Disagree
B) Disagree
C) Neutral
D) Agree
E) Strongly Agree

**Q12. In case of a failure to provide the services, the company has a very quick first response time (Acknowledgement of Issue)?**

A) Strongly Disagree
B) Disagree
C) Neutral
D) Agree
E) Strongly Agree

**Q13. In case of a failure to provide the services, the company has a very quick resolution time (Solving of Issue)?**

A) Strongly Disagree
B) Disagree
C) Neutral
D) Agree
E) Strongly Agree

**Q14. Websites display a notice telling how they collect user data using cookies, for what purpose and whether data is being shared with a third party for marketing purposes?**

A) Strongly Disagree
B) Disagree
C) Neutral
D) Agree
E) Strongly Agree

**Q15. Terms and conditions regarding return policies, exchange, cashback, etc., mentioned on the websites are clear to understand?**

A) Strongly Disagree
B) Disagree
C) Neutral
D) Agree
E) Strongly Agree

**Q16. The website shows actual prices (prices shown are inclusive of taxes, shipping charges are labelled correctly, if any)?**

A) Strongly Disagree
B) Disagree
C) Neutral
D) Agree
E) Strongly Agree

**Q17. Websites offer customized promotions and solutions?**

A) Strongly Disagree
B) Disagree
C) Neutral
D) Agree
E) Strongly Agree

**Q18. Website is user friendly in terms of appearance, speed and functionality both when visited through mobile/tablet or desktop/ laptop?**

A) Strongly Disagree
B) Disagree
C) Neutral
D) Agree
E) Strongly Agree

**Q19. In case of any issue, the customer care representative can understand your problem and provide a solution adequately?**

A) Strongly Disagree
B) Disagree
C) Neutral
D) Agree
E) Strongly Agree

# Appendix B. Responses Data

The websites you visit deliver what they intend to up to your satisfaction level

60 responses

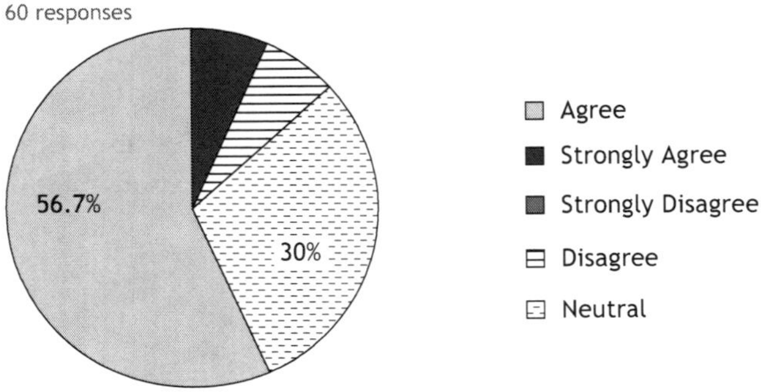


The website tells you that your data is safe with them and you feel a sense of security

60 responses

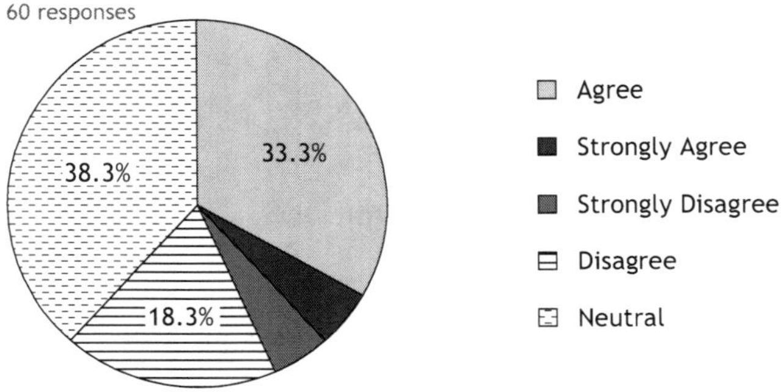


The website tells you that they will never sell your data to 3rd party websites for marketing purpose

60 responses

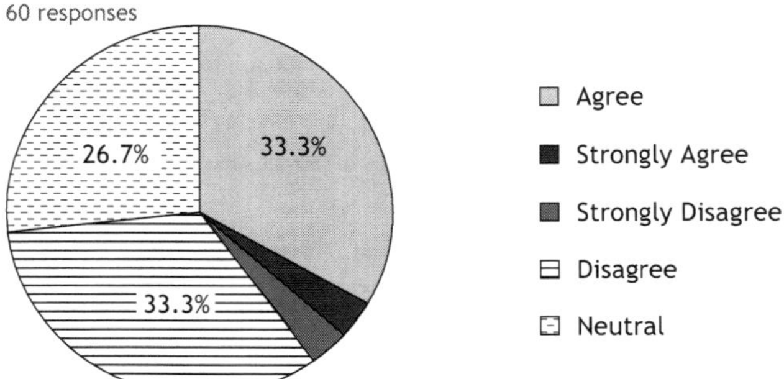

The website has dedicated communication support channel via Telephone (Toll-Free), E-mail, Social Media handles etc.

60 responses

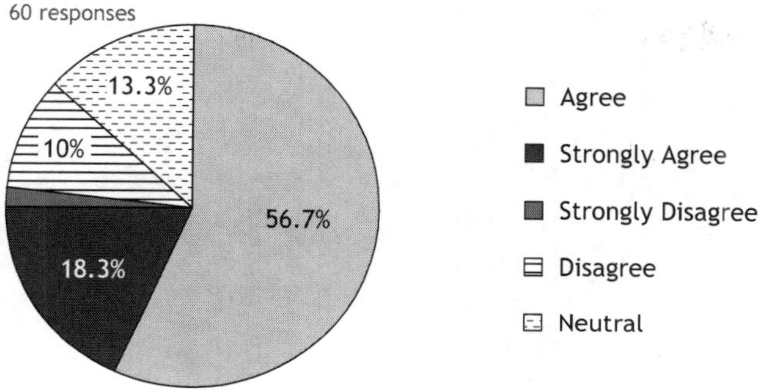


In case of a failure of providing the services, the company has a very quick first response time (Acknowledgement of Issue)

60 responses

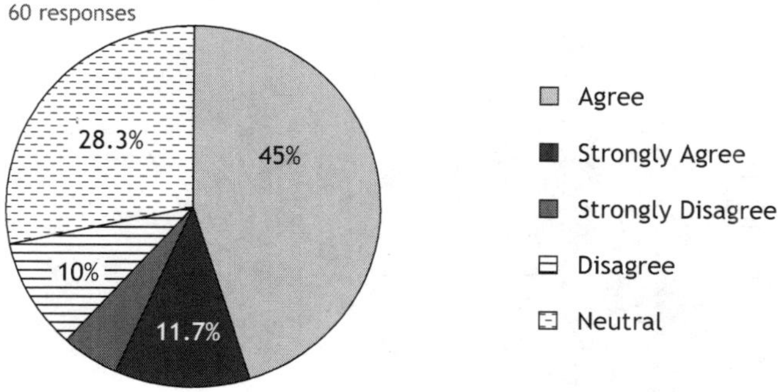


In case of a failure of providing the services, the company has a very quick resolution time (Solving of Issue)

60 responses

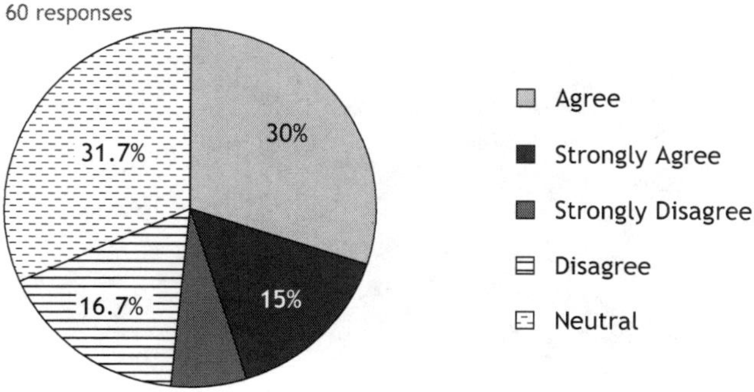

Websites display a notice telling how they collect user data using cookies, for what purpose and whether data is being shared with 3rd party for marketing purpose

60 responses

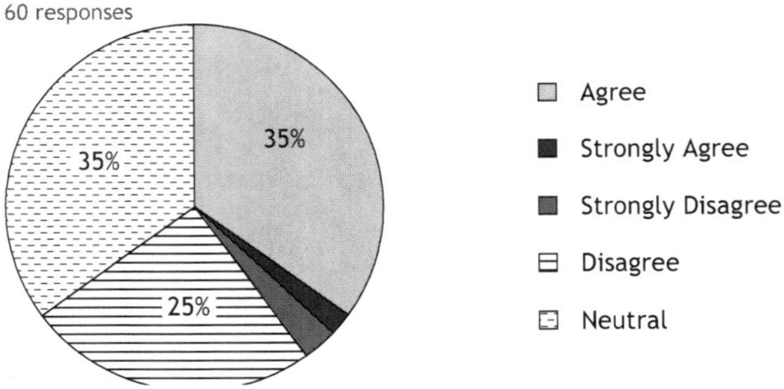


Terms & Conditions regarding return policies, exchange, cashback et mentioned on the websites are clear to understand

60 responses

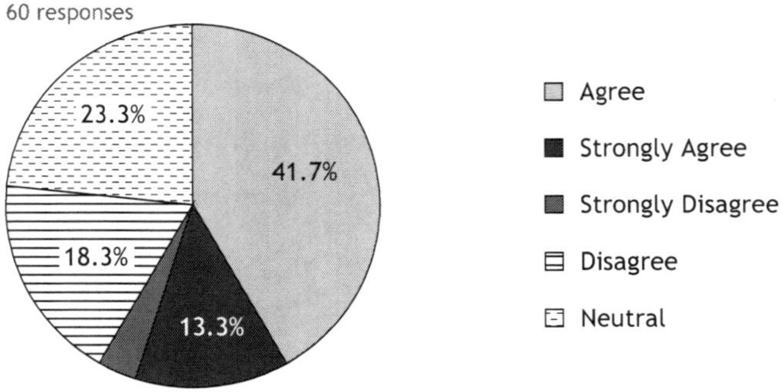


The website shows actual Prices (Prices shown are inclusive of taxes, Shipping charges are labelled correctly, if any)

60 responses

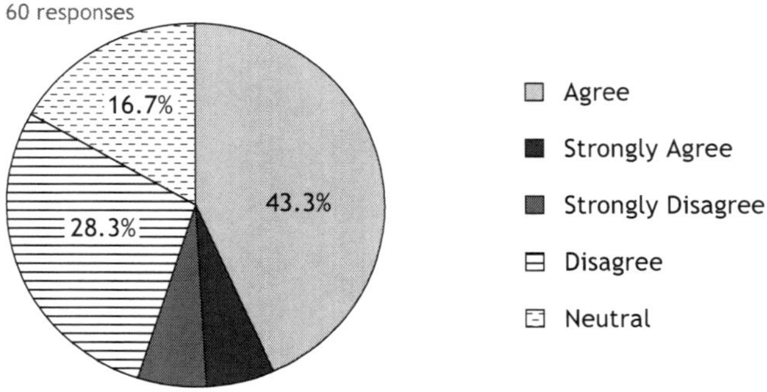

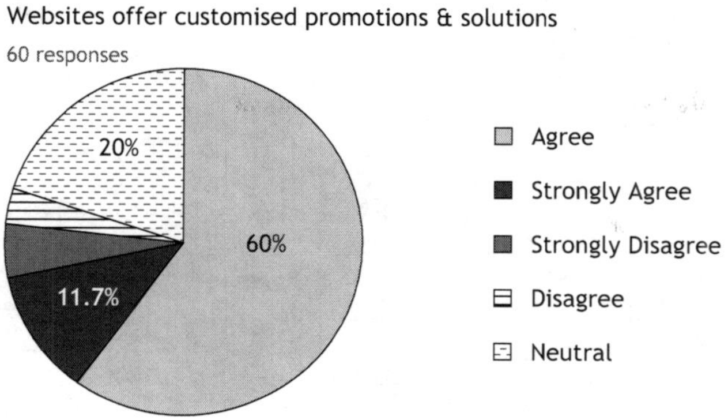


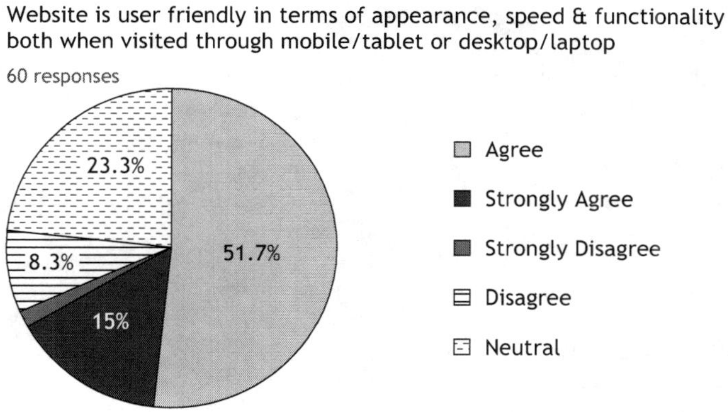


## References

Anic, Ivan-Damir, Vatroslav Škare, and Ivana Kursan Milaković. 2019. 'The Determinants and Effects of Online Privacy Concerns in the Context of E-commerce.' *Electronic Commerce Research and Applications* 36 (100868).

Asif, Waqar, Muttukrishnan Rajarajan, and Marios Lestas. 2018. 'Increasing User Controllability on Device Specific Privacy in the Internet of Things.' *Computer Communications* 116, 200–211. https://doi.org/10.1016/j.comcom.2017.11.009.

Barnes, Susan B. 2006. 'A Privacy Paradox: Social Networking in the United States.' *First Monday* 11 (9). https://doi.org/10.5210/fm.v11i9.1394.

Belanche, Daniel, Carlos Flavián, and Alfredo Pérez-Rueda. 2017. 'Understanding Interactive Online Advertising: Congruence and Product Involvement in Highly and Lowly Arousing, Skippable Video Ads.' *Journal of Interactive Marketing* 37, 75–88. https://doi.org/10.1016/j.intmar.2016.06.004.

Cases, Anne-Sophie, Christophe Fournier, Pierre-Louis Dubois, and John F. Tanner Jr. 2010. 'Web Site Spill Over to Email Campaigns: The Role of Privacy, Trust and Shoppers' Attitudes.' *Journal of Business Research* 63 (9–10), 993–999. https://doi.org/10.1016/j.jbusres.2009.02.028.

Chang, Younghoon, Siew Fan Wong, Christian Fernando Libaque-Saenz, and Hwansoo Lee. 2018. 'The Role of Privacy Policy on Consumers' Perceived Privacy.' *Government Information Quarterly* 35 (3):445–459. https://doi.org/10.1016/j.giq.2018.04.002.

Eastlick, Mary Ann, Sherry L. Lotz, and Patricia Warrington. 2006. 'Understanding Online B-to-C Relationships: An Integrated Model of Privacy Concerns, Trust, and Commitment.' *Journal of Business Research* 59 (8), 877-886. https://doi.org/10.1016/j.jbusres.2006.02.006.

Equifax. 2017. 'Cybersecurity Incident & Important Consumer Information.' equifaxsecurity2017.com. https://www.equifaxsecurity2017.com/consumer-notice/#notice (accessed September 12, 2019).

Gan, May Fen, Hui Na Chua, and Siew Fan Wong. 2019. 'Privacy Enhancing Technologies Implementation: An Investigation of Its Impact on Work Processes and Employee Perception.' *Telematics and Informatics* 38, 13–29. https://doi.org/10.1016/j.tele.2019.01.002.

Gogus, Aytac, and Yücel Saygın. 2019. 'Privacy Perception and Information Technology Utilization of High School Students.' *Heliyon* 5 (5), e01614. https://doi.org/10.1016/j.heliyon.2019.e01614.

Huang, Yi-Ting. 2018. 'The Female Gaze: Content Composition and Slot Position in Personalized Banner Ads, and How They Influence Visual Attention in Online Shoppers.' *Computers in Human Behavior* 82, 1–15. https://doi.org/10.1016/j.chb.2017.12.038.

Laczniak, Gene R., and Patrick E. Murphy. 2006. 'Marketing, Consumers and Technology: Perspectives for Enhancing Ethical Transactions.' *Business Ethics Quarterly* 16 (3), 313–321. https://doi.org/10.5840/beq200616330.

Leal-Rodríguez, Antonio Luis, Stephen Eldridge, José Luis Roldán, Antonio Genaro Leal-Millán, and Jaime Ortega-Gutiérrez. 2015. 'Organizational Unlearning, Innovation Outcomes, and Performance: The Moderating Effect of Firm Size.' *Journal of Business Research* 68 (4), 803–809. https://doi.org/10.1016/j.jbusres.2014.11.032.

Lee, Hwansoo, Siew Fan Wong, Jungjoo Oh, and Younghoon Chang. 2019. 'Information Privacy Concerns and Demographic Characteristics: Data from a Korean Media Panel Survey.' *Government Information Quarterly* 36 (2):294–303. https://doi.org/10.1016/j.giq.2019.01.002.

Malhotra, Naresh K., Sung S. Kim, & James Agarwal. 2004. 'Internet Users' Information Privacy Concerns (IUIPC): The Construct, the Scale, and a Causal Model.' *Information Systems Research* 15 (4), 336–355. https://doi.org/10.1287/isre.1040.0032.

Martin, Kirsten. 2016. 'Understanding Privacy Online: Development of a Social Contract Approach to Privacy.' *Journal of Business Ethics* 137 (3), 551–569. https://doi.org/10.1007/s10551-015-2565-9.

Martin, Kirsten. 2018. 'The Penalty for Privacy Violations: How Privacy Violations Impact Trust Online.' *Journal of Business Research* 82, 103–116. https://doi.org/10.1016/j.jbusres.2017.08.034.

McCole, Patrick, Elaine Ramsey, and John Williams. 2010. 'Trust Considerations on Attitudes towards Online Purchasing: The Moderating Effect of Privacy and Security Concerns.' *Journal of Business Research* 63 (9–10), 1018–1024. https://doi.org/10.1016/j.jbusres.2009.02.025.

Milne, George R., Andrew Rohm, and Bahl Shalini. 2009. 'If It's Legal, Is It Acceptable?' *Journal of Advertising* 38 (4), 107–122. https://doi.org/10.2753/JOA0091-3367380408.

Norberg, Patricia A., Daniel R. Horne, and David A. Horne. 2007. 'The Privacy Paradox: Personal Information Disclosure Intentions Versus Behaviors.' *Journal of consumer affairs* 41 (1), 100–126. https://doi.org/10.1111/j.1745-6606.2006.00070.x.

Oikarinen, Eeva-Liisa, and Magnus Söderlund. 2016. 'The Effects of Humour in Online Recruitment Advertising.' *Australasian Marketing Journal (AMJ)* 24 (3), 180–186. https://doi.org/10.1016/j.ausmj.2016.02.005.

Palos-Sanchez, Pedro, Jose Ramon Saura, and Felix Martin-Velicia. 2019. 'A Study of the Effects of Programmatic Advertising on Users' Concerns about Privacy Overtime.' *Journal of Business Research* 96, 61–72. https://doi.org/10.1016/j.jbusres.2018.10.059.

Román, Sergio, and Pedro J. Cuestas. 2008. 'The Perceptions of Consumers Regarding Online Retailers' Ethics and their Relationship with Consumers' General Internet Expertise and Word of Mouth: A Preliminary Analysis.' *Journal of Business Ethics* 83 (4), 641–656. https://doi.org/10.1007/s10551-007-9645-4.

Smith, H. Jeff, Sandra J. Milberg, and Sandra J. Burke. 1996. 'Information Privacy: Measuring Individuals' Concerns about Organizational Practices.' *MIS Quarterly* 20 (2), 167–196.

Statista, 2018. Annual Number of Data Breaches and Exposed Records in the United States from 2005 to 2018 (in millions). Accessed September 12, 2019, from https://www.statista.com/statistics/273550/databreaches-recorded-in-the-united-states-by-number-of-breaches-and-records-exposed/.

Wang, Yan, Yingying Chen, Fan Ye, Hongbo Liu, and Jie Yang. 2019. 'Implications of Smartphone User Privacy Leakage from the Advertiser's Perspective.' *Pervasive and Mobile Computing* 53, 13–32. https://doi.org/10.1016/j.pmcj.2018.12.006.

CHAPTER 11

# Impact of Indian Festivals on Imports from China

*An Exploratory Study*

Rohit Vishal Kumar

## Introduction

It is a well-known fact that the two major emerging economies in the world are India and China. Both the countries have faced similar economic trajectories till the 1980s having around a 4 per cent economic growth rate. But since then, both have followed a different set of paradigms, which has put China far ahead of India in almost all socio-economic parameters. In 1978, China began to focus on economic reforms and started opening its economy to integrate with the world economy. India, on the other hand, kept its focus on maintaining a tight regime of central control and started opening up in 1991 when it faced severe macro-economic crises (Economic Research and Training Foundation, 2015). However, both the countries have faced different growth trajectories since then. China has maintained a consistent 10 per cent economic growth rate since 2000s whereas Indian economic growth rate has hovered around 7 per cent. China presently accounts for approximately 10 per cent of all global exports while India accounts for less than 1 per cent of the global exports (Tian and Yu, 2012). The reasons for such performance of these two major economies are well researched in literature.

As China has gained confidence in international trade, Chinese made products have started entering the international markets and India has not remained untouched by the influx of Chinese products and services. However, with Chinese goods entering Indian markets, Indian media and buyers have shown xenophobic tendencies—specially propagating that the Chinese products and services are inferior in quality. The bogey of '*ban Chinese products*' seems to get renewed from time to time in various media platforms. For example, the leading newspaper in India, *The Hindu*, carried an article in which various industry captains had claimed that low cost products from China would hamper Indian production process specially in the small and medium enterprise sector (Subbu, 2000). A casual search on the web using the term 'ban Chinese products' throws up a plethora of articles on the subject. For example, there is a change.org petition addressed to the Ministry of External Affairs requesting for a ban on Chinese products in the Indian markets (Change.org, 2017). In 2017, the debate for ban on Chinese products reflected in almost all the major news magazines in India. Business Today (Sharma, 2017), Economic Times (Sachitanand and Goyal, 2016) and Bloomberg and NDTV (Nag, 2017) carried articles for and against the ban. It should also be noted that playing to populist sentiments, the Government of India had already banned the import of electronic items, specific mobile phones, milk and milk products and some steel products on 25 April 2016 (Indiatoday.in, 2016). Another specific thing to note is that the voices demanding ban of Chinese products peaks at around the time of major Indian festivals and then dies down. In this paper, we look at the monthly import data of Chinese products to see whether there is some truth in the said observations.

## Review of Literature

A lot of work has been done on studying the relationship between India and China in economic aspects. A large number of studies in a similar vein can be found on the existing sources (Kalirajan, Wang,

Yu and Singh, 2013; Kumari and Malhotra, 2014; Mitra, 2016; Panagariya, 2006).

Marelli and Signorelli (2011) analyzed the economic growth of China and India in terms of integration in the global economy and found that the effect on economic growth (in terms of GDP per capita) remains positive for both openness and foreign direct investments. They conclude that by opening up their economies both China and India have seen a positive net effect on growth. Singh and Santpal (2014) analyzed the major trends in India–China exports and concluded that the bilateral trade between these two countries is unfavorable to India. Ores, slag and ash (HS26) dominated India's export whereas electrical machinery and equipment and parts thereof (HS85) dominated the India's import from China. Balance of trade was unfavourable to India. In another study it was found that the backwardness in the eastern parts of India can be attributed to the closure of trade between the two countries post Indian independence. The study suggests that proximity and complementarity of the people in the eastern region lead to high cross border trade between the two countries prior to Indian independence (Banik and Chatterjee, 2016).

In a working paper of the European Central Bank, the author dealt with the question of whether the rise of key emerging economies such as China and India and their increasing role in world export markets represents positive or negative news for advanced countries and concluded that the competition from the Indian and Chinese manufacturers has been beneficial for the world economy. The study also found that the countries with a lower share of employment in manufacturing and lower employment protection legislation have benefited comparatively more from the rise of China and India as have the countries, which have pre-existing links to India and China (Stracca, 2013). Another study focusing on African counties, but in the same vein, found that imports from India and China provide cheaper goods, which benefits the African customers. The impact on poverty depends on whether the poor consume the goods that are imported from Asia, and whether there is a negative effect on employment opportunities for unskilled workers. Countries that import a relatively high proportion of basic consumer goods from China and India such as Ghana, Uganda and Tanzania found that the real income of the poor tended to increase; but in the case of Ethiopia and Nigeria, however, there have been negative effects on poverty (Banerjee, 2005)

However, studies pertinent to the work at hand are hardly there. There is a huge amount of literature in terms of how to measure the impact of an economic event on the local event (Crompton and McKay, 1994; Strydom, Saayman and Saayman, 2006). The only relevant literature we could find for our purpose was that of Srikanth and Maloth (2013) who studied the Diwali effect on the trading of the Indian National Stock Exchange. The authors studied all the 100 stocks that make up the BSE-100 index, 10 working days preceding Diwali and 10 working days succeeding Diwali. The study has employed Wilcoxon test, a non-parametric test, to analyze the impact of Diwali on the Indian stock market. The study concluded that the Diwali effect is not statistically significant on the stock market in India and results of Run test reveals that average abnormal returns are random during the study period.

Given the nature of the study, no major literature was forthcoming. As such, it was decided to forge ahead with the traditional mode of analysis using seasonal dummies. For dummy regression analysis the months in which the two major festivals of India, Diwali and Dusshera, occurred were identified and coded as dummy variables. As per the Hindu traditions, Dusshera is celebrated to commemorate the victory of Lord Rama over the evil Ravana and Diwali is celebrated to commemorate the arrival of Lord Rama to his kingdom Ayodhya after 14 years of banishment. As such, Dusshera precedes Diwali, normally by a difference of 21 days, subject to variations in the lunar calendar. Most years Dusshera occurs in the month of October whereas Diwali occurs in the month of November.

## Data Analysis

The Chinese import data was collected from Department of Commerce, Ministry of Commerce and Industries, Government of India via their website (http://commerce-app.gov.in/eidb/). All data was collected in constant US dollar million terms starting from April 2006 to March 2018 covering a total of 144 monthly data points. The summary statistics of the dataset is presented in Table 11.1 along

Table 11.1 *Descriptive Statistics of Indian Imports from China (USD)*

| *Summary Statistics* | *Amount (USD Million)* |
|---|---|
| Arithmetic Mean | 3,957.00 |
| Median | 4,143.70 |
| Minimum | 1,047.00 |
| Maximum | 6,961.10 |
| Standard Deviation | 1,442.90 |
| Coefficient of Variation | 36.46% |
| Skewness | -0.13250 |
| Excess Kurtosis | -0.88520 |

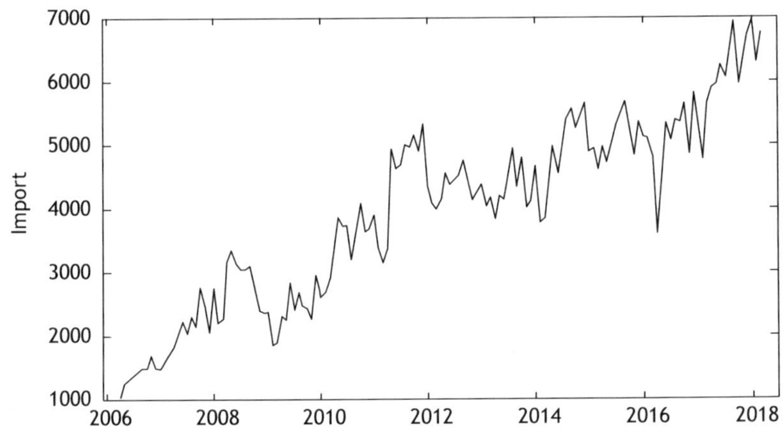


*Source:* Calculated from data collected from Department of Commerce, Ministry of Commerce, Government of India. Data available at: http://commerce-app.gov.in/eidb/

with the time series plot of the data. Analysis was done using Gretl software (Cottrell and Lucchetti, 2020). Two approaches to analysis were utilized.

## Seasonal Dummies Approach

In the first approach, the 11 seasonal dummies for the months of January to November were created and regressed with the relevant time series. The following three time series were used:

*Level of the Series:* The level of the import series was used under the assumption that the data points represented the money value of imports. As such it was hypothesized that if there is an influx of Chinese goods in the Indian marketplace then the landed values would be higher for the months of July, August and September, the months preceding the festival.

*First Difference of the Series:* The first difference of the series would indicate the value change in imports of Chinese products to the Indian markets. As such, again we would expect the changes to be significant for the months preceding the festivals.

*Seasonal Irregular Component of the Series:* The series was de-seasonalized using the X-12-ARIMA protocol and the seasonal irregular component was saved. It is assumed that once the trend cycle has been eliminated then the seasonal irregular component would show the effects only due to the presence of additional imports in the months prior to the festivals.

The X-12-ARIMA output suggested the ARIMA (0,1,1) (0,1,1) model for forecasting purpose. The parametric test for seasonality assuming stability and the non-parametric test for seasonality were found to be significant at 0.1 per cent level suggesting that the series had stable seasonality. No evidence was found of moving seasonality in the series. Similarly, residual seasonality was also not seen in the test. This suggested that the imports from China are fairly stable with respect to seasonality; giving hope that the use of irregular component would be a good approach. The seasonal indexes calculated by X-12-ARIMA are presented in Figure 11.1.

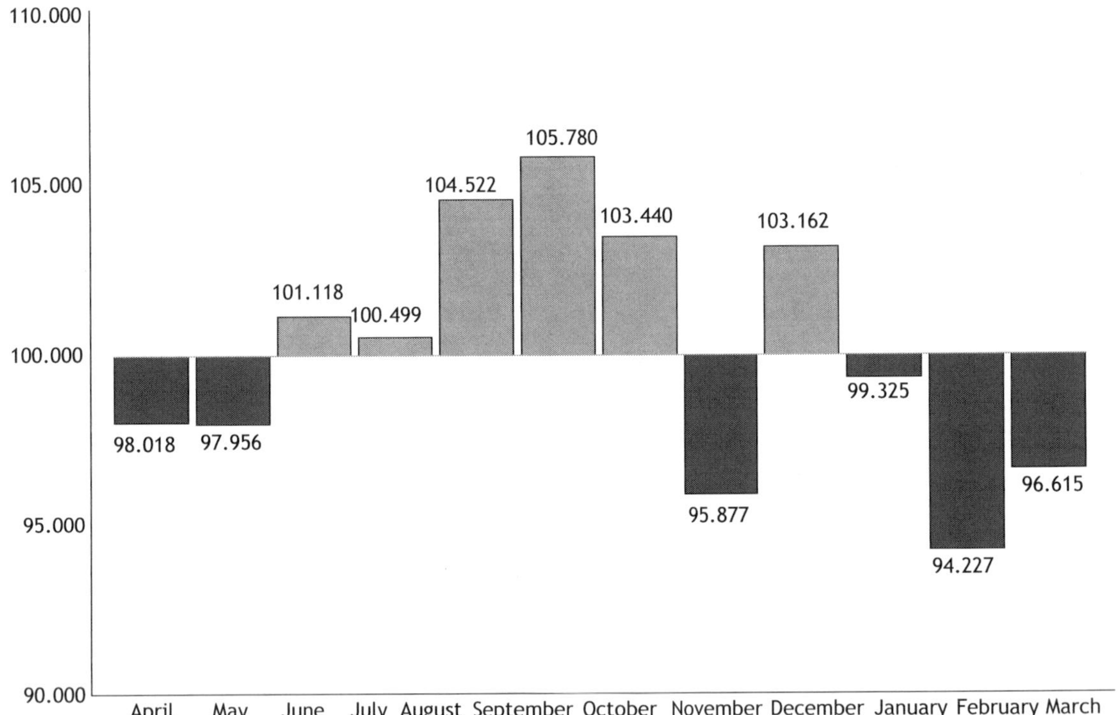


Figure 11.1 *Seasonal Index of Chinese Imports*

The plots of seasonal index show that the seasonal indexes are greater than 100 for the months of June to October and December and below 100 for the remaining the months. This tended to provide credence to the belief that the Indian markets imported more during the months preceding the major festive months. What was needed was the statistical support to identify whether the effects were significant or not. The results of the analysis are presented in Tables 11.2–11.4).

Looking at the outputs and specially the F values, it was seen that the r-squared and the adjusted r-squared were very low for all the three

Table 11.2 *Seasonal Dummy Regression on Level of Imports*

| | *Coefficient* | *Std. Error* | *t-ratio* | *p-value* |
|---|---|---|---|---|
| Const | 4153.4900 | 429.1471 | 9.6785 | 0.0000 *** |
| dm1 | -91.6067 | 606.9056 | -0.1509 | 0.8803 |
| dm2 | -436.6033 | 606.9056 | -0.7194 | 0.4732 |
| dm3 | -338.4358 | 606.9056 | -0.5576 | 0.5780 |
| dm4 | -665.1042 | 606.9056 | -1.0959 | 0.2751 |
| dm5 | -247.6875 | 606.9056 | -0.4081 | 0.6839 |
| dm6 | -193.5050 | 606.9056 | -0.3188 | 0.7504 |
| dm7 | -196.3975 | 606.9056 | -0.3236 | 0.7467 |
| dm8 | 2.5083 | 606.9056 | 0.0041 | 0.9967 |
| dm9 | 48.8017 | 606.9056 | 0.0804 | 0.9360 |
| dm10 | 16.8175 | 606.9056 | 0.0277 | 0.9779 |
| dm11 | -257.0342 | 606.9056 | -0.4235 | 0.6726 |

| | | | |
|---|---|---|---|
| Mean dependent var | 3956.9694 | S.D. dependent var | 1442.8598 |
| Sum squared resid | 291720841.8179 | S.E. of regression | 1486.6090 |
| R-squared | 0.0201 | Adjusted R-squared | -0.0616 |
| F(11, 132) | 0.2461 | P-value(F) | 0.9934 |
| Log-likelihood | -1249.8748 | Akaike criterion | 2523.7495 |
| Schwarz criterion | 2559.3873 | Hannan-Quinn | 2538.2307 |
| Rho | 0.9614 | Durbin-Watson | 0.0845 |

*Source:* Author's calculations from the collected data.

Table 11.3 *Seasonal Dummy Regression on First Difference of Imports*

| | *Coefficient* | *Std. Error* | *t-ratio* | *p-value* |
|---|---|---|---|---|
| Const | 257.0342 | 118.3019 | 2.1727 | 0.0316 ** |
| dm1 | -348.6408 | 167.3041 | -2.0839 | 0.0391 ** |
| dm2 | -602.0308 | 167.3041 | -3.5984 | 0.0005 *** |
| dm3 | -158.8667 | 167.3041 | -0.9496 | 0.3441 |
| dm4 | -92.9360 | 171.0643 | -0.5433 | 0.5879 |
| dm5 | 160.3825 | 167.3041 | 0.9586 | 0.3395 |
| dm6 | -202.8517 | 167.3041 | -1.2125 | 0.2275 |
| dm7 | -259.9267 | 167.3041 | -1.5536 | 0.1227 |
| dm8 | -58.1283 | 167.3041 | -0.3474 | 0.7288 |
| dm9 | -210.7408 | 167.3041 | -1.2596 | 0.2100 |
| dm10 | -289.0183 | 167.3041 | -1.7275 | 0.0864 * |
| dm11 | -530.8858 | 167.3041 | -3.1732 | 0.0019 *** |

| | | | |
|---|---|---|---|
| Mean dependent var | 40.0357 | S.D. dependent var | 444.4014 |
| Sum squared resid | 22000672.2321 | S.E. of regression | 409.8098 |
| R-squared | 0.2155 | Adjusted R-squared | 0.1496 |
| F(11, 131) | 3.2713 | P-value(F) | 0.0006 |
| Log-likelihood | -1056.8855 | Akaike criterion | 2137.7711 |
| Schwarz criterion | 2173.3252 | Hannan-Quinn | 2152.2186 |
| Rho | -0.3800 | Durbin-Watson | 2.7442 |

*Source:* Author's calculations from the collected data.

series, but the F values presented a different picture. In the level of the series and in the irregular components the F value was not rejected. The F value was only significant in the difference of the import series indicating that the overall regression was significant. Another interesting thing to note in the difference of the series was that the imports in the month of October and November were significant at 10 per cent and 1 per cent levels respectively. This certainly indicated that there is an influx of imports in the Indian markets during the time of Dusshera and Diwali. The inflow in the month of January and

Table 11.4 *Seasonal Dummy Regression on Seasonal Irregular Components of Imports*

| | *Coefficient* | *Std. Error* | *t-ratio* | *p-value* |
|---|---|---|---|---|
| Const | 3.4688 | 72.2097 | 0.0480 | 0.9618 |
| dm1 | 33.2508 | 102.1199 | 0.3256 | 0.7452 |
| dm2 | -17.7133 | 102.1199 | -0.1735 | 0.8626 |
| dm3 | -2.8039 | 102.1199 | -0.0275 | 0.9781 |
| dm4 | -148.2611 | 102.1199 | -1.4518 | 0.1489 |
| dm5 | 57.4716 | 102.1199 | 0.5628 | 0.5745 |
| dm6 | 16.2993 | 102.1199 | 0.1596 | 0.8734 |
| dm7 | -6.9275 | 102.1199 | -0.0678 | 0.9460 |
| dm8 | -50.1923 | 102.1199 | -0.4915 | 0.6239 |
| dm9 | 3.4727 | 102.1199 | 0.0340 | 0.9729 |
| dm10 | -43.8451 | 102.1199 | -0.4293 | 0.6684 |
| dm11 | 28.4677 | 102.1199 | 0.2788 | 0.7809 |

| | | | |
|---|---|---|---|
| Mean dependent var | -7.4296 | S.D. dependent var | 245.6577 |
| Sum squared resid | 8259350.6521 | S.E. of regression | 250.1416 |
| R-squared | 0.0429 | Adjusted R-squared | -0.0368 |
| F(11, 132) | 0.5381 | P-value(F) | 0.8743 |
| Log-likelihood | -993.2343 | Akaike criterion | 2010.4685 |
| Schwarz criterion | 2046.1063 | Hannan-Quinn | 2024.9497 |
| Rho | -0.1341 | Durbin-Watson | 2.2656 |

*Source:* Author's calculations from the collected data.

February were also found to be significant, but it is difficult to ascribe them to festivals as no major Indian festivals take place during that time. Most likely the reason for such a high import is that the Indian budget is presented in the month of February and as such importers want to take advantage of the existing import rules, duties and taxes in a bid to avoid any uncertainty in the upcoming budget. The above analysis shows that the quantum of imports goes up during the months before the festivities. Once imported, the products would be routed to the markets for sale leading to higher than normal availability of the products in the marketplace in the festival months. This may lead to the augmentation of the belief that Chinese products flood the Indian markets and may well lead to media cries for banning Chinese imports during Dusshera and Diwali.

## Dummy Regression Approach

In the second approach, dates of Diwali and Dusshera were identified from various calendars and the corresponding months were coded using dummy variables. The ordinary least squares (OLS) regressions were run using imports as the dependent variable and Diwali and Dusshera as the independent variables. It was hoped that these would show up as significant in the regression, giving credence to the belief. The outputs are presented in Tables 11.5–11.7.

Again, we get comparable results with the difference in imports showing a significant F value. Also, we can see that Diwali imports are significant at 1 per cent level in the difference of the series and the

Table 11.5 *Dummy Regression with Diwali and Dusshera on Imports*

| | *Coefficient* | *Std. Error* | *t-ratio* | *p-value* |
|---|---|---|---|---|
| Const | 3945.4625 | 128.6901 | 30.6586 | 0.0000 *** |
| Diwali | -179.2536 | 469.5147 | -0.3818 | 0.7032 |
| Dusshera | 317.3364 | 469.5147 | 0.6759 | 0.5002 |

| | | | |
|---|---|---|---|
| Mean dependent var | 3956.9694 | S.D. dependent var | 1442.8598 |
| Sum squared resid | 296697637.1163 | S.E. of regression | 1450.5994 |
| R-squared | 0.0034 | Adjusted R-squared | -0.0108 |
| F(2, 141) | 0.2391 | P-value(F) | 0.7877 |
| Log-likelihood | -1251.0927 | Akaike criterion | 2508.1855 |
| Schwarz criterion | 2517.0949 | Hannan-Quinn | 2511.8057 |
| Rho | 0.9519 | Durbin-Watson | 0.0922 |

*Source:* Author's calculations from the collected data.

## Table 11.6 *Dummy Regression with Diwali and Dusshera on Difference of Imports*

| | *Coefficient* | *Std. Error* | *t-ratio* | *p-value* |
|---|---|---|---|---|
| Const | 73.9872 | 37.8579 | 1.9543 | 0.0527 * |
| Diwali | -532.1855 | 137.5971 | -3.8677 | 0.0002 *** |
| Dusshera | 127.5959 | 137.5971 | 0.9273 | 0.3554 |

| | | | |
|---|---|---|---|
| Mean dependent var | 40.0357 | S.D. dependent var | 444.4014 |
| Sum squared resid | 25293809.0670 | S.E. of regression | 425.0530 |
| R-squared | 0.0981 | Adjusted R-squared | 0.0852 |
| F(2, 140) | 7.6109 | P-value(F) | 0.0007 |
| Log-likelihood | -1066.8588 | Akaike criterion | 2139.7177 |
| Schwarz criterion | 2148.6062 | Hannan-Quinn | 2143.3296 |
| Rho | -0.2989 | Durbin-Watson | 2.5844 |

*Source:* Author's calculations from the collected data.

## Table 11.7 *Dummy Regression with Diwali and Dusshera on Irregular Components of Imports*

| | *Coefficient* | *Std. Error* | *t-ratio* | *p-value* |
|---|---|---|---|---|
| Const | -1.5032 | 21.6290 | -0.0695 | 0.9447 |
| Diwali | -158.2502 | 78.9117 | -2.0054 | 0.0468 ** |
| Dusshera | 87.1327 | 78.9117 | 1.1042 | 0.2714 |

| | | | |
|---|---|---|---|
| Mean dependent var | -7.4296 | S.D. dependent var | 245.6577 |
| Sum squared resid | 8381041.9072 | S.E. of regression | 243.8032 |
| R-squared | 0.0288 | Adjusted R-squared | 0.0150 |
| F(2, 141) | 2.0918 | P-value(F) | 0.1273 |
| Log-likelihood | -994.2874 | Akaike criterion | 1994.5747 |
| Schwarz criterion | 2003.4841 | Hannan-Quinn | 1998.1950 |
| Rho | -0.1389 | Durbin-Watson | 2.2767 |

*Source:* Author's calculations from the collected data.

irregular series, pointing to some justification in the belief that Chinese products flood the Indian markets prior to the major festivities.

In order to check the models for consistency, the following tests were performed: (a) Ramsey's RESET Test for model specification (Ramsey, 1969) with the null hypothesis that the model specification is adequate in linear form; (b) White's Test for Heteroscedasticity (White, 1980) with the null hypothesis that heteroscedasticity is not present; (c) Normality of Residuals using Jarque-Bera test and (d) test for autocorrelation using the standard DW test. The p-values are summarized in the Table 11.8.

Looking at the p-values for the different tests we can conclude that the difference in imports series shows the most promise and that has been seen in the regressions. One interesting thing to note is that the coefficient of Dusshera is positive (but not significant) indicating that there may be more imports in the months preceding Diwali. The Diwali month coefficients are negative and significant, indicating that imports show a deep dip once the festival season is over.

## Conclusion

Based on the data analysis, it is observed that the difference in imports series and the seasonal indexes does point toward increases in imports during the pre-Dusshera and pre-Diwali months. The seasonal indexes do not show a significant jump and remain well within +/- 5 per cent change levels. Also, the differenced series points to some increase in imports during the festival months. But whether the quantum of import is significant enough to create such an outcry needs to be understood using psychology rather than economics. Forbes.com estimates that the Dusshera and Diwali market in India is alone worth a staggering USD 3.9 billion in 2017 (Kaur, 2017) or approximately ₹30,000 crores. Given the size of the market and the growing demand for products and services in the Indian economy, Indian importers turn to countries from where products can be cheaply and readily imported to satisfy the demand in the domestic market. One major beneficiary of such an import pull is China. This is primarily because the Chinese products and services are much cheaper to import than

Table 11.8 *P-values of Various Test*

| | *Analysis Type* | *Series Type* | *RESET* | *White* | *JB Test* | *DW Test* |
|---|---|---|---|---|---|---|
| | Null Test of >> | | Specification | Heteroscedasticity | Normality | Auto Correlation |
| Table 11.2 | Seasonal Dummies | Level | 0.000 | 0.996 | 0.076 | 0.000 |
| Table 11.3 | Seasonal Dummies | Difference | 0.841 | 0.433 | 0.175 | 0.999 |
| Table 11.4 | Seasonal Dummies | Irregular | - | 0.368 | 0.000 | 0.947 |
| | | | | | | |
| Table 11.5 | Dummy Regression | Level | 0.006 | 0.819 | 0.071 | 0.000 |
| Table 11.6 | Dummy Regression | Difference | 0.890 | 0.895 | 0.093 | 0.999 |
| Table 11.7 | Dummy Regression | Irregular | 0.911 | 0.856 | 0.000 | 0.956 |

*Source:* Author's calculations from collected data.

their counterparts from USA or EU. This is primarily because the exchange rates are more favourable with Chinese Yuan as compared to US dollar or Euro. This in turn leads to Chinese products and services being imported and distributed in the Indian markets for sale prior to and during the festival months. However, Indian psychology is mistrustful of the Chinese government. Capture of Tibet (1959), Indo–China war (1962), Nathu-La clashes (1967), Chinese Indian skirmish (1987) and the Doklam Plateau incident (2017) has made Indians distrustful of the Chinese government and policy. Given the huge presence of Chinese products and services in the marketplace, it is believed that this distrustfulness and animosity translates to poplar public demand for banning of imports of Chinese products and services, even though there is no economic rationale for doing so.

## References


Banerjee, S. 2005. *The Effect of China and India's Growth and Trade Liberalisation on Poverty in Africa*. London: Department for International Development.

Banik, A., and R. Chatterjee. 2016. 'Trade Openness, Conflicts and Sino-Indian Relations: Identifying Impacts on Poverty in Eastern India.' In *12th Asia Pacific Economic Conference*. Symposium conducted at the meeting of International Management Institute Kolkata, Kolkata.

Change.org 2017. 'Ban Chinese Product in India, No Trade with China.' Change.org. https://www.change.org/p/narendra-modi-ban-chinese-product-in-india-no-trade-with-china

Cottrell, A., and R. J. Lucchetti. 2020. 'Gretl - Gnu Regression, Econometrics And Time-Series Library.' http://gretl.sourceforge.net/

Crompton, J. L., and S. L. McKay. 1994. 'Measuring the Economic Impact of Festivals and Events: Some Myths, Misapplications and Ethical Dilemmas.' *Festival Management and Event Tourism* 2 (1), 33–43. https://doi.org/10.3727/106527094792335782

Economic Research and Training Foundation. 2015. *India-China Trade Relation*. Mumbai India. http://www.imcnet.org/cms/public/content/ertf_thoughtpaper/2.%20India-China%20Trade%20Relation.pdf

Indiatoday.in 2016. 'India Bans Import of Goods from China: List of Top 5 Imports of India.' *India Today*. https://www.indiatoday.in/education-today/gk-current-affairs/story/india-bans-import-of-goods-from-china-320275-2016-04-27

Kalirajan, K., Y. Wang, M. Yu, and K. Singh. 2012. China and India: A Comparative Analysis of Trade and Investment Performance. Available at http://mjyu.ccer.edu.cn/EABER_Routledge%20chapter_2.pdf

Kaur, T. 2017. 'Festival of Lights: All You Need to Know About Diwali.' *Forbes*. https://www.forbes.com/sites/tarandipkaur/2017/10/18/festival-of-lights-all-you-need-to-know-about-diwali/ForbescomRetriev

Kumari, D., and N. Malhotra. 2014. 'Trade-led Growth in India and China: A Comparative Analysis.' *Journal of International and Global Economic Studies* 7 (2), 68–88.

Marelli, E., and M. Signorelli. 2011. 'China and India: Openness, Trade and Effects on Economic Growth.' *The European Journal of Comparative Economics* 8 (1), 129–154.

Mitra, D. 2016. 'Trade Liberalization and Poverty Reduction.' *IZA World of Labor*. Advance online publication. https://doi.org/10.15185/izawol.272

Nag, A. 2017. 'Flood of Cheap Chinese Imports May Hurt India's Factories.' *NDTV*. https://www.ndtv.com/india-news/flood-of-cheap-chinese-imports-may-hurt-indias-factories-1738045Retriev

Panagariya, A. 2006. *India and China: Trade and Forign Investments*. PDF Manuscript.

Ramsey, J. B. 1969. 'Tests for Specification Errors in Classical Linear Least Squares Regression Analysis.' *Journal of the Royal Statistical Society: Series B*, 31 (2)

Sachitanand, R., and M. Goyal. 2016. 'Why the Threat of a Boycott of Chinese Products Is More Bark than Bite.' *Economic Times*. https://economictimes.indiatimes.com/news/economy/foreign-trade/why-the-threat-of-a-boycott-of-chinese-products-is-more-bark-than-bite/articleshow/55133257.cmsRetriev

Sharma, S. 2017. 'Ban Chinese goods: Can India do to China what China Does to Other Countries?' *Business Today*. https://www.businesstoday.in/current/economy-politics/ban-chinese-goods-can-india-do-to-china-what-china-does-to-other-countries/story/256282.html

Singh, J., and Santpal. 2014. 'A Comparative Study of India-China Bilateral Trade.' *International Journal of Commerce, Business and Management* 3 (2).

Srikanth, P., and R. R. Maloth. 2013. 'Economic Impact of Festivals: Evidence from Diwali Effect On Indian Stock Market.' *Researchers World: Journal of Arts, Science and Commerce* IV (2), 27–37.

Stracca, L. 2013. 'The Rise of China and India Blessing or Curse for the Advanced Countries?' Working Paper No. 1620. Frankfurt, Germany: European Central Bank.

Strydom, A. J., M. Saayman, and A. Saayman. 2006. 'The Economic Impact of the Volksblad Arts Festival.' *Acta Commercii* 6 (1). https://doi.org/10.4102/ac.v6i1.97

Subbu, R. 2000. 'Threat Perception over Imports from China.' *The Hindu*. https://www.thehindu.com/thehindu/2000/11/30/stories/0630000a.htm

Tian, W., and M. Yu. 2012. 'China and India: Trends in Trade Over the Last Decade.' *The Journal of China and Global Economics* 1 (1), 27–38.

White, H. 1980. 'A Heteroskedasticity-Consistent Covariance Matrix Estimator and a Direct Test for Heteroskedasticity.' *Econometrica* 48 (4). https://doi.org/10.2307/1912934.

# Part II

# Sectoral Insights

China enjoys cost competitiveness in the manufacturing sector and has become a manufacturing hub in the world producing one fifth of the global output. While China has strengthened its manufacturing sector over years, India has been dominating the service sector with its unique cost competitiveness led by IT and ITES sectors. India has been able to retain its unique position of exports of software services, which is in excess of USD 80 billion and accounts for more than 25 per cent of total exports from the country. The software exports have also helped reduce current account deficits of India. Similarly, China's exports have crossed USD 2 trillion in recent years. Manufactured goods constitute a substantial portion of China's total merchandise exports, which has helped strengthen the Chinese economy with a significant current account surplus in recent years.

The chapters in this section on 'Sectoral Insights' cover a wide range of topics from manufacturing to services. The chapters cover the sectors such as banking, manufacturing, insurance, retail, film culture and medical tourism of both the countries. Chapter 12 of this section deals with marketing strategies of firms in manufacturing and service industries. The study probes into the differences in marketing strategy for various sectors like FMCG, consumer durables, industrial products, software, banks, services and telecom. The study finds interesting insights regarding fulfilment of consumer expectations of different sectors of an economy. Chapter 13 of the book examines manufacturing–services nexus and deliberates on a global value chain analysis for India and China. The study analyses sectoral composition of Indian economy, which has witnessed a substantial structural shift over the last decades explaining its journey from a socialist to market driven economy through a bold set of reforms. Chapter 14 analyses performance and profitability of Sino-Indian banks and emphasizes the need to curb ballooning non-performing assets with stringent monitoring and rehabilitation of accounts for better risk management. Chapter 15 provides an overview of deposit insurance systems in India and China. The study finds that while deposit insurance systems in India have been well established, China requires effective legislation to attain the same level of deposit insurance systems prevailing in other countries. Chapter 16 analyses the price dispersion in unorganized retail markets in India and provides insights into reducing price dispersion with growing presence of online marketplace. The study finds that price dispersion is much higher in unorganized retail as compared to organized retail because of higher search cost and lack of information. Chapter 17 draws a comparative analysis of performance of retail sector in India and China and elaborates on the growth and development of retailing in both the countries. Chapter 18 deals with the entertainment sector in India and China with a special emphasis on film industry by outlining their development over the decades. The study calls for effective government intervention for optimal utilization of resources available with the industry through scientific and technological cooperation between these two countries to fulfil the twin objectives of strengthening cultural ties and the economy. It claims that such cooperation would result in sustainable development of the film sector, which contributes significantly to the national income of both the countries. Finally, Chapter 19 looks at the practice of traditional Chinese and Indian medical systems. A comparative analysis of the initiatives taken by the two countries in promoting their ancient and traditional medical tourism for holistic wellness is detailed and is followed by recommendations for further development.

Majority of the chapters in this section emphasize on better Sino-Indian ties to strengthen their specific economic sectors, which can boost economic cooperation and progress. The analytical rigour of these chapters provides greater insights for policy makers of both the countries and calls for greater cooperation to boost economic and cultural ties.

CHAPTER 12

# Marketing Strategy and Performance of Firms in India

Rahul Gupta Choudhury

## Introduction

Industries may be divided into various sectors depending on the products or services they produce. These firms have the primary objective of fulfilling the needs of their customers/consumers. In order to do this, they adopt strategies which encompass the various functions of the firm. These strategies differ across sectors as well as at the individual level. This is primarily because of the difference in the needs of customers as well as the macro-economic environment. The present study attempts to identify the strategic differences among diverse industries and understand their consequent influence on the performance of these industries. It is pertinent here to mention that there has been a lot of deliberation on whether firm-specific strategy is more relevant than industry strategy. The concepts of SCP (structure-conduct-performance) and the RBV (resource-based view) has for a long time dominated the discourse on the functioning and performance of firms and industries. In the present study, the functioning and performance of the industry is being considered keeping in mind that it is the structure of the industry and its characteristics that influence the strategies undertaken by the firms in a given industry. At an aggregate level, there are many similar strategies that firms belonging to a particular industry follow, irrespective of the firm's position in the industry. Normally it is observed that in any given industry, there are outstanding performers who elevate the overall performance of the industry. Then there are average performers and still further down are the laggards who pull down the performance of the industry. The methodology of this study precludes the consideration of firm-level differences and, instead, highlights the overall differences among industries in terms of strategy (primarily marketing). The study also attempts to study the strategic factors in individual industries that may influence their performance.

## Review of Literature

It has been reported by Hawawini et al. (2000) that most prior studies had concluded that firm-specific factors compared to industry effects were more dominant in explaining firms' profitability. However, they also found that, for most firms (i.e., those who are not notable leaders or losers in their industry), the industry effect turns out to be more important for performance than firm-specific factors. Andrus et al. (1988) compared the marketing strategy between industrial and consumer goods industry. They found that industrial goods manufacturers paid less attention to monitoring of efficiency of trade channels and also felt that their advertisements were less effective than those of consumer goods. Also control procedures for achieving annual plan objectives of industrial goods manufacturers were less adequate than those of consumer goods manufacturers. Industrial product firms were also more interested in international expansion and increasing the geographical spread of their products. O'Connor (1994) studied the differences in marketing strategies and operating efficiencies in surviving and failed industries. Firms that survived diversified in to related product-markets and commanded a higher market presence in their chosen industries than failing firms. The authors also found that failing firms likewise diversified, even though market penetration in each of their chosen industries was significantly lower than their surviving counterparts'. Their cost of operations were much higher, and their reinvestment in fixed asset bases was considerably lower than their surviving counterparts. In a comparative analysis (Shih, 2010) of marketing strategies for manufacturers' and retailers' brands, the author found that manufacturers' brands follow high quality and high price strategies. They also pursue the right kind of promotion strategies and develop brand equity in accordance with the buying behaviour of consumers. It was also found that brand endorsement strategies without a careful evaluation process is disadvantageous to manufacturers. For the retail store brands, the positive influencers are low prices, promotion activities, brand endorsement strategies and improving store images. This helps in building brand equity and consumer purchase intentions of retailer store brands.

In a paper on economic development and marketing strategies, Sarathy et al. (2014) study the marketing strategies of firms from emerging markets under different models of economic development. The two broad models of development can be classified as socialism and capitalism. Socialism can be further classified as Soviet Communism and Fabian Socialism. Thus, the general thrust has been in the direction of pro-market reform, in different degrees. The authors point out that there is a need to study the reverse innovation strategies of firms from emerging markets trying to make inroads in to developed countries; and that too, not on the basis of low prices alone. The markets are being targeted with better price-performance ratios so as to serve the mass market better. It is possible for firms from emerging markets to obtain sustainable competitive advantage only when marketing strategy is complemented with related strategies such as cost efficiency.

Stoicic et al. (2013) found that market share of firms in transition economies was positively related to restructuring behaviour, which included improvements in cost efficiency, labour productivity, investment and increasing experience. Vorhies et al. (2009) investigates the relationships between strategic business unit (SBU) product-market strategy and scope, marketing capabilities and the business unit performance. The objective of the authors was to augment understanding of how critical firm-level marketing capabilities enable the realization of strategy. The authors found strong evidence that both architectural and specialized marketing capabilities and their integration, positively mediate the product-market strategy and derived business unit performance relationship.

Gupta et al. (2014) studied the linkage between organization's strategy and structural dimensions. They found that there are significant differences among the organizations in terms of structural dimensions and the strategy used. Prospector strategy is used more in the IT industry, analyzer strategy in the banking industry and reactor strategy in power industry. Vertical linkages and formalization are more used in the power sector, horizontal linkages in automobile sector and centralization in banking sector. When the firm uses reactor as the dominant strategy, vertical linkages and formalization are perceived more. Horizontal linkages are more prevalent in the organization using prospector strategy and organizations using the analyzer strategy were found to be high on centralization. Some of the explanations offered by the authors are: IT uses prospector strategy as there is a lot of untapped market in this sector and there is lot of scope for innovation and growth. Banking industry pursues a combination of defender and prospector strategies as it helps them to perform its traditional role of monetary transactions and enables them to come up with new products and services to fulfill the needs of the customers.

## Study Objective

Thus, it is evident that firms pursue different strategies that may be formulated on the basis of the internal as well as external factors. As has been discussed earlier, there has been considerable debate and discussion on whether firm-specific attributes or industry characteristics have a more significant role to play in the business strategies of the firm. This study, however, does not enter in to that debate. The attempt here is more concentrated on finding out whether different industry affiliations produce distinct strategies, which are more similar to the given characteristics of the industry rather than firm-specific factors? The study considers the overall strategies of firms belonging to certain sectors and compares that with the strategies pursued by firms operating in diverse sectors. As a corollary, it is also the aim of the study to link the strategies with their corresponding performance parameters. The objective here is to observe and find out the specific strategic factors which are influencing the performance of the firms across sectors.

## Study Methodology

In order to understand the strategies pursued by different firms, the study made use of a detailed structured questionnaire. The questionnaire was designed on the basis of an extant literature review.

The questionnaire is divided into the following ten sections: background, market, target audience, competition, offering, sales and buying process, pricing, strategy issues, impact of marketing strategy and marketing strategy decisions. In the questionnaire, questions were formulated on a wide range—from markets to quality as well as research and development (R&D). The objective was to ascertain the direct as well as indirect impact of business strategy on various aspects of the functioning of the firm—from defects and waste to inventory, from customer management to personnel and from labour to risk management. A particular area is devoted to questions pertaining to product, from design to development, and from technology to performance. Strategic competitive goals were also discussed wherein questions were asked regarding particular marketing strategies like lower selling prices, distribution, product, delivery, advertisement and sales promotion. The questionnaire had a combination of open as well as close-ended questions, such that executives were not required to divulge confidential information on one hand, and on the other hand, no constraints were put on them in terms of answering questions they felt they needed to answer in detail.

The details of the relevant sections of the questionnaire are:

1. *Areas influenced by strategy:* Intended to elicit opinion about the influence marketing strategy-making has on various business benchmarks. The benchmarks are: focusing on strong markets,

entering foreign markets, marketing planning activities, entering new business areas, decision on marketing expenditures, product strategies/introduction of new products, number of products, provision of R&D budget, quality, promotion strategies and promotion budget, size of sales force, sales training.

2. *Indirect impact of strategy implementation:* Degree of indirect impact that marketing strategy has on the various business benchmarks. The benchmarks are: improvement of quality, reduction in repair, reduction in defects, average mending manpower wage bill, reduction in waste, reduction in defect times, reduction in inventory, reduction in inventory carrying costs and increased efficiency in production.
3. *Impact of marketing strategy on business success:* Elicits opinion on impact on some pertinent parameters of business success. The parameters are: aligned with market drivers, focus on consumer satisfaction factor (CSF), competitive advantage, customer management complaints, customer satisfaction, customer spread/region spread, product spread, product age, product/brand awareness, repeat purchase trial, barriers to entry, stakeholder objectives, marketing communication, corporate governance, production service supply, supplier spread ration, joint planning, supplier satisfaction, capacity utilization, total quality management (TQM), SBU manpower planning, knowledge center approach, formal planning by top down/bottom up, labour turnover, span of control, skills, labour productivity, disciplinary levels, working conditions, health and safety, risk management, compensation, contingency planning, portfolio analysis, investment appraisal, debt management, impact analysis and cost management and control.
4. *Success factors:* Elicits opinion on: (a) whether the factors are relevant for the success of marketing strategy and (b) whether they are practised in their organization. The factors are: product/service has sufficient market demand, product/service does the job that it is intended to do, product/service meets the customer needs or wants, product/service is able to stay up with current technology, company staff is competent and technologically current, company has the resources to stay competitive in the

market, product/service is ready for the market, product/service has sufficient customer development support, product/service has a well-established technological base and newer versions of product/service perform as expected.

5. *Strategic competitive goals:* Elicits opinion from respondents on which goals are important (and not important) for their organization. The goals are: have lower selling prices, offer superior product/ service design and quality, deliver excellent product/service conformance to specifications, have superior customer service (after-sales and/or technical support), provide a greater variety of products/services, offer a greater number of new products/services, have shorter time-to-market for new products/services, offer greater customization, offer faster deliveries, offer more dependable deliveries, have better distribution strength, have better sales force and have a higher promotion/advertisement budget.

**Population Studied and Sampling Process:** In order to establish the business strategy across various firms, responses were required from executives of organizations who were aware of the strategic direction of their firms and the consequent results they have obtained. The responses were obtained by administering the above questionnaire to top executives (mostly general managers and above) of companies operating in India.

The scope of the study encompassed firms across the entire spectrum of the Indian industry. The questionnaire was pre-tested on corporate and academic experts. Post the pilot testing, it was administered to top executives through e-mail. The study sources the firms listed with Confederation of Indian Industry (CII) and the Associated Chambers of Commerce of India (ASSOCHAM). Thus, email invitations were sent to these firms to participate in the survey. Reminders were sent to the target firms after a gap of 15 days. The data obtained were a fair representation of the Indian industry sectors and hence could be used for further analysis. A total of 105 complete responses were received from the target sample of 7,000 firms. Out of the 105 responses received, 33 per cent were firms of international origin and 67 per cent were domestic. Industry wise break-up of responses are the following: 34 per cent from Services, 33 per cent from Industrial Products, 9 per cent from Consumer Durable, 8 per cent from Software, 5 per cent from Fast Moving Consumer Goods (FMCG), 4 per cent from Banks, 3 per cent from Pharmaceuticals, 3 per cent from Automobiles and 2 per cent from Telecom. The method obtained for identifying the industry in cases where it was a well-diversified conglomerate was that the respondent who filled the questionnaire belonged to the largest division (by revenues) of the conglomerate. In some cases, the respondent answered on the basis of the division he/she belonged to.

## Data Analysis and Study Findings

The obtained responses were initially analyzed by using One-Way Analysis of Variance. The industry sectors are coded in the following fashion: (a) FMCG; (b) Consumer Durable; (c) Industrial Products; (d) Software; (e) Pharmaceuticals; (f) Telecom; (g) Banks; (h) Automobiles; (i) Others/Services. The discussion on the findings are based on the factors where significant differences were observed. The findings of the analysis for the factor, 'focusing on strong markets', are presented in Table 12.1A and Table 12.1B.

Table 12.1A *Descriptive for 'Focusing on Strong Markets'*

| *Industry* | *N* | *Mean* | *Std. Dev.* | *Std. Error* |
|---|---|---|---|---|
| FMCG | 6 | 4.1667 | .40825 | .16667 |
| Consumer Durable | 9 | 4.5556 | .52705 | .17568 |
| Industrial Products | 37 | 4.2703 | .87078 | .14316 |
| Software | 8 | 3.5000 | .53452 | .18898 |
| Telecom | 2 | 4.0000 | .00000 | .00000 |
| Banks | 4 | 3.7500 | .95743 | .47871 |
| Others/Services | 37 | 3.7568 | .86299 | .14187 |
| Total | 103 | 4.0194 | .83994 | .08276 (F=2.597) |

Table 12.1B Post Hoc Least Significant Differences (LSD) for 'Focusing on Strong Markets'

| *Industry 1* | *Industry 2* | *Std. Error* | *Significance* |
|---|---|---|---|
| FMCG | 2 | .42326 | .361 |
| | 3 | .35344 | .770 |
| | 4 | .43371 | .128 |
| | 6 | .65571 | .800 |
| | 7 | .51838 | .424 |
| | 9 | .35344 | .249 |
| Consumer Durable | 1 | .42326 | .361 |
| | 3 | .29848 | .342 |
| | 4 | .39023 | .008 |
| | 6 | .62779 | .378 |
| | 7 | .48259 | .098 |
| | 9 | .29848 | .009 |
| Industrial Products | 1 | .35344 | .770 |
| | 2 | .29848 | .342 |
| | 4 | .31313 | .016 |
| | 6 | .58301 | .644 |
| | 7 | .42269 | .221 |
| | 9 | .18671 | .007 |
| Software | 1 | .43371 | .128 |
| | 2 | .39023 | .008 |
| | 3 | .31313 | .016 |
| | 6 | .63489 | .433 |
| | 7 | .49178 | .612 |
| | 9 | .31313 | .414 |
| Telecom | 1 | .65571 | .800 |
| | 2 | .62779 | .378 |
| | 3 | .58301 | .644 |
| | 4 | .63489 | .433 |
| | 7 | .69549 | .720 |
| | 9 | .58301 | .677 |

*(Continued)*

*(Continued)*

| *Industry 1* | *Industry 2* | *Std. Error* | *Significance* |
|---|---|---|---|
| Banks | 1 | .51838 | .424 |
| | 2 | .48259 | .098 |
| | 3 | .42269 | .221 |
| | 4 | .49178 | .612 |
| | 6 | .69549 | .720 |
| | 9 | .42269 | .987 |
| Others/Services | 1 | .35344 | .249 |
| | 2 | .29848 | .009 |
| | 3 | .18671 | .007 |
| | 4 | .31313 | .414 |
| | 6 | .58301 | .677 |
| | 7 | .42269 | .987 |

Among the various business benchmarks, significant differences were observed in four parameters. They are as follows: focusing on strong markets (.022), decision on marketing expenditures (.053), provision of R&D budget (.088), and sales training (.069). Table 12.1C and 12.1D show the values for each of the factors.

Table 12.1C

| *Factors* | *F - Values* | *Significance* |
|---|---|---|
| Focusing on strong markets | 2.597 | .022 |
| Entering foreign markets | .929 | .478 |
| Marketing planning activities | .980 | .443 |
| Entering new business areas | .435 | .854 |
| Decision on marketing expenditures | 2.165 | .053 |
| Product strategies/Introduction of new products | .984 | .441 |
| Number of products | .705 | .646 |
| Provision of R&D budget | 1.906 | .088 |
| Quality | 1.244 | .291 |
| Promotion strategies & Promotion budget | 1.754 | .117 |
| Size of sales force | .461 | .836 |
| Sales training | 2.032 | .069 |

Table 12.1D *Descriptive Statistics*

| | N | Range | Mean | | Std. Deviation |
|---|---|---|---|---|---|
| | Statistic | Statistic | Statistic | Std. Error | Statistic |
| Focusing on strong markets | 103 | 4.00 | 4.0194 | .08276 | .83994 |
| Entering foreign markets | 103 | 4.00 | 3.1650 | .13096 | 1.32914 |
| Marketing planning activities | 103 | 4.00 | 3.8350 | .08627 | .87556 |
| Entering new business areas | 103 | 4.00 | 3.5437 | .09233 | .93700 |
| Decision on marketing expenditures | 103 | 4.00 | 3.2427 | .08557 | .86847 |
| Product strategies/ Introduction of new products | 103 | 4.00 | 3.7379 | .08612 | .87404 |
| Number of products | 103 | 4.00 | 3.2330 | .08528 | .86550 |
| Provision of R&D budget | 103 | 4.00 | 3.0194 | .10043 | 1.01923 |
| Quality | 103 | 3.00 | 4.2718 | .07582 | .76944 |
| Promotion strategies and Promotion budget | 103 | 4.00 | 3.3883 | .08419 | .85443 |
| Size of sales force | 103 | 4.00 | 3.4757 | .08375 | .84997 |
| Sales training | 103 | 4.00 | 3.6019 | .08871 | .90032 |
| Valid N (listwise) | 103 | | | | |

Consumer durable firms and Industrial Product firms place a lot of importance on focusing on strong markets and in that they are significantly (at 5% level) different from firms in other industries. Difference between consumer durable firms and banks are at 10 per cent significance level in this parameter. Consumer durable firms place a lot of importance on decisions on marketing expenditures. In this factor, they are significantly different from all other industries. FMCG and industrial product firms give much more importance to provision of R&D budget when compared to service industry firms. FMCG and industrial product firms also place significantly more importance on sales training, compared to all other industries. Service industry give more importance to sales training compared to industries like telecom (at 10% significance level). Differences were observed in factors relevant for success of marketing strategy as well.

Banks give significantly more importance compared to all other industries, in the following two parameters: product/service meets the customer needs or wants, and product/service is ready for the market. However, software industry, in comparison with all other industries, places significantly more importance to the parameter of 'product/service has sufficient customer development support'. Among factors practised in the organization, banks, again, place significantly more importance compared to all other industries in the parameter of 'company has the resources to stay competitive in the market'. However, FMCG firms give more significance in this parameter, compared to industrial products. On the parameter of 'product/service does the job that it is intended to do', banks give significantly more importance compared to all other industries. In this, telecom industry also places significantly more importance compared to services, industrial products, and FMCG. Even software industry gives significantly more importance to this parameter than does industrial products industry. When important strategic competitive goals were considered, significant difference in five factors were observed. FMCG industry places significantly more importance on the parameter of 'have more promotion/advertisement budget', compared to all other industries. Similarly, banks placed the least significant importance to 'have better sales force', especially in comparison with FMCG, consumer durable and industrial products. It is significantly more important for industrial products to offer greater customization, compared to FMCG, consumer durables and services. Even software industry places significantly more importance compared to FMCG in this parameter. Banks, however, place significantly less importance on the parameter of 'have shorter time to market for new products/services', compared to all other industries. Consumer durable industry places significantly more importance to 'lower selling prices', when compared to FMCG and services industry. Software also gives more significant importance to this parameter compared to the services industry.

Analysis was also done on factors which are based more on functions rather than marketing, like manufacturing and operations. It was observed that consumer durable industry gives a lot of importance to reduction in inventory, reduction in defects and reduction in repair. In this parameter, they were significantly different from the service industry as well as telecom. Industrial products also placed significantly more importance on this parameter, compared to the service industry. Software industry placed significantly more importance on reduction in defects, compared to the service industry.

Industrial products considered alignment with market drivers as significantly more important for business success in comparison with all other industries. They, along with consumer durables industry, gave significantly more importance to customer satisfaction, compared to software and telecom industries. They also gave significantly more importance to barriers to entry as well as stakeholder objectives, when compared to all other industries. When suppliers are considered, FMCG, consumer durables and industrial products place significantly more importance to supplier spread ratio and supplier satisfaction in comparison to all other industries. In terms of debt management, FMCG, consumer durables as well as industrial products place significantly more importance on them compared to the software industry. Again, consumer durables, industrial products and banks place significantly more importance on investment appraisal, as compared to services. The phenomenon remains the same in case of portfolio analysis as well. Span of control is significantly more important to FMCG, consumer durables and industrial products compared to software and telecom industries. It is significantly more important for banks and service industries as well, especially when compared to telecom and software.

There is no significant difference among industries in case of all other parameters studied in the questionnaire.

Based on the above analysis, Table 12.2 summarizes the main strategic thrusts of the different industries. From this, a clear view of the strategic differences among the industries emerge.

In the next step, all the parameters were tested for their influence on performance with all industries responses put together—through regression analysis. As an illustration of the results of the analysis, the correlation coefficients along with their corresponding significance values for the 'Areas Influenced by Strategy' has been depicted in Tables 12.3A–12.3C.

Table 12.2

| *Industry* | *Strategy* |
|---|---|
| **FMCG** | **Marketing:** Provision of R&D budget, Sales Training, Company has the Resources to stay Competitive in the Market, have more Promotion/Advertisement Budget, Have Better Sales Force<br>**Operations:** Supplier Spread Ratio, Supplier Satisfaction, Debt Management, Investment Appraisal, Portfolio Analysis, Span of Control |
| **Consumer Durable** | **Marketing:** Focusing on Strong Markets, Decision on Marketing Expenditures, Have Better Sales Force<br>**Operations:** Supplier Spread Ratio, Supplier Satisfaction, Debt Management, Customer Satisfaction, Reduction in Inventory and Defects and Repair, Investment Appraisal, Portfolio Analysis, Span of Control |
| **Industrial Products** | **Marketing:** Focusing on Strong Markets, Provision of R&D Budget, Sales Training, Have Better Sales Force, Offer Greater Customization, Lower Selling Prices<br>**Operations:** Supplier Spread Ratio, Supplier Satisfaction, Debt Management, Reduction in Inventory and Defects and Repair, Customer Satisfaction, Alignment with Market Drivers, Barriers to Entry, Stakeholder Objectives, Span of Control |
| **Software** | **Marketing:** Offer Greater Customization, Lower Selling Prices, Product/Service has Sufficient Customer Development Support, Product/Service does the job that it is intended to do<br>**Operations:** Reduction in Defects |
| **Banks** | **Marketing:** Company has the Resources to stay Competitive in the Market, Product/Service does the job that it is intended to do, Product/Service meets the Customers' needs or wants, and Product/Service is ready for the Market<br>**Operations:** Investment Appraisal, Portfolio Analysis, Span of Control |
| **Service** | **Marketing:** Sales Training<br>**Operations:** Span of control |
| **Telecom** | **Marketing:** Product/Service does the job that it is intended to do |

Table 12.3A *Correlation Coefficients for 'Areas Influenced by Strategy'*

| | *Profits* | *1* | *2* | *3* | *4* | *5* | *6* | *7* | *8* | *9* | *10* | *11* | *12* |
|---|---|---|---|---|---|---|---|---|---|---|---|---|---|
| Profits | 1.000 | | | | | | | | | | | | |
| 1 | -.086 | 1.00 | | | | | | | | | | | |
| 2 | -.114 | .199 | 1.00 | | | | | | | | | | |
| 3 | -.056 | .391 | .243 | 1.00 | | | | | | | | | |
| 4 | -.091 | .223 | .124 | .302 | 1.00 | | | | | | | | |
| 5 | -.131 | .289 | -.010 | .479 | .210 | 1.00 | | | | | | | |
| 6 | -.075 | .287 | -.072 | .276 | .295 | .253 | 1.00 | | | | | | |
| 7 | -.049 | .156 | .017 | .271 | .217 | .250 | .509 | 1.00 | | | | | |
| 8 | -.003 | .263 | .417 | .256 | .369 | .150 | .281 | .271 | 1.00 | | | | |
| 9 | -.023 | .007 | -.035 | .213 | .106 | .076 | .078 | .022 | .118 | 1.00 | | | |
| 10 | -.086 | .058 | .098 | .349 | .015 | .506 | .085 | .049 | .171 | .017 | 1.00 | | |
| 11 | -.066 | .262 | -.009 | .265 | .115 | .187 | .209 | .181 | .091 | .085 | .256 | 1.00 | |
| 12 | -.063 | .296 | -.092 | .277 | .096 | .238 | .265 | .133 | .083 | .228 | .126 | .557 | 1.00 |

1: Focusing on strong markets; 2: Entering foreign markets; 3: Marketing planning activities; 4: Entering new business areas; 5: Decision on marketing expenditures; 6: Product strategies/Introduction of new products; 7: Number of products; 8: Provision of R&D budget; 9: Quality; 10: Promotion strategies and Promotion budget; 11: Size of sales force; 12: Sales training.

Table 12.3B *Significance (1 – tailed) of the correlation coefficients for 'Areas influenced by Strategy'*

| | *Profits* | *1* | *2* | *3* | *4* | *5* | *6* | *7* | *8* | *9* | *10* | *11* | *12* |
|---|---|---|---|---|---|---|---|---|---|---|---|---|---|
| Profits | – | | | | | | | | | | | | |
| 1 | .194 | – | | | | | | | | | | | |
| 2 | .126 | .022 | – | | | | | | | | | | |
| 3 | .286 | .000 | .007 | – | | | | | | | | | |
| 4 | .180 | .012 | .106 | .001 | – | | | | | | | | |
| 5 | .094 | .002 | .462 | .000 | .017 | – | | | | | | | |
| 6 | .226 | .002 | .235 | .002 | .001 | .005 | – | | | | | | |
| 7 | .310 | .058 | .431 | .003 | .014 | .005 | .000 | – | | | | | |
| 8 | .488 | .004 | .000 | .004 | .000 | .066 | .002 | .014 | – | | | | |
| 9 | .410 | .472 | .364 | .015 | .144 | .222 | .217 | .414 | .117 | – | | | |
| 10 | .194 | .281 | .161 | .000 | .439 | .000 | .196 | .312 | .042 | .433 | – | | |
| 11 | .255 | .004 | .462 | .003 | .123 | .029 | .017 | .034 | .180 | .196 | .005 | – | |
| 12 | .263 | .001 | .178 | .002 | .166 | .008 | .003 | .091 | .201 | .010 | .102 | .000 | – |

1: Focusing on strong markets; 2: Entering foreign markets; 3: Marketing planning activities; 4: Entering new business areas; 5: Decision on marketing expenditures; 6: Product strategies/Introduction of new products; 7: Number of products; 8: Provision of R&D budget; 9: Quality; 10: Promotion strategies and Promotion budget; 11: Size of sales force; 12: Sales training.

Table 12.3C *Model Summary*

| *R* | *R Square* | *Adjusted R Square* | *Std. Error* | *Durbin - Watson* | *F - Value* | *Significance* |
|---|---|---|---|---|---|---|
| .236 | .056 | -.070 | 1.61610 | 2.364 | .443 | .942 |

From these tables, it can be seen that none of the factors of 'Areas Influenced by Strategy' have a significant correlation with profits. The rest of the factors are also then regressed with profits and the results are enumerated in the following paragraphs.

The following ten factors were found to be significant: reduction in defects (.002), average mending manpower wage bill (.000), focus on CSF (.053), competitive advantage (.012), product/brand awareness (.008), marketing communication (.049), corporate governance (.019), capacity utilization (.031), labour turnover (.007), and product/service has sufficient customer development support (.030). This is obtained by regression in the 'backward' method. The final results are depicted in Table 12.3D and Table 12.3E.

The next step was to identify the differences in parameters that influence performance of the various industries. This was done by regression analysis. First, parameters belonging to the non-marketing functions were considered. Four industries showed perfect correlation between certain parameters and their performance (R-square = 1).

The parameters influencing performance are different for different industries. The four industries that showed perfect correlation are FMCG, consumer durable, industrial products and software. For industrial products, very few parameters were excluded, that is, very few parameters did not influence the performance. Those parameters are not being enumerated as it is irrelevant at this stage of the discussion. The parameters that influenced the performance of FMCG industry are reduction in inventory, TQM, contingency planning, portfolio analysis and cost management and control. The parameters that influenced performance of consumer durables are reduction in inventory carrying costs, aligned with market drivers, competitive advantage, customer spread/region spread, barriers to entry, joint planning, SBU manpower planning and cost management and control. The parameters that influenced

Table 12.3D

| Model | Unstandardized B | Coefficients Std. Error | Std. Coeff. Beta | t | Sig. |
|---|---|---|---|---|---|
| (Constant) | 6.047 | 1.396 | | 4.333 | .000 |
| Reduction in defects | -.407 | .131 | -.295 | -3.108 | .002 |
| Average mending manpower wage bill | .665 | .147 | .475 | 4.532 | .000 |
| Focus on CSF | -.387 | .197 | -.168 | -1.960 | .053 |
| Competitive advantage | -.572 | .224 | -.227 | -2.551 | .012 |
| Product/Brand Awareness | -.525 | .195 | -.252 | -2.691 | .008 |
| Marketing Communication | .457 | .229 | .179 | 1.993 | .049 |
| Corporate governance | .357 | .150 | .235 | 2.385 | .019 |
| Capacity utilization | .332 | .152 | .220 | 2.187 | .031 |
| Labour turnover | -.513 | .187 | -.296 | -2.746 | .007 |

Table 12.3E *Model Summary*

| R | R Square | Adjusted R Square | Std. Error | Durbin - Watson | F - Value | Significance |
|---|---|---|---|---|---|---|
| .607 | .368 | .307 | 1.30041 | 2.297 | 6.023 | .000 |

performance of software industry are reduction in repair, average mending manpower wage bill, reduction in waste, customer satisfaction, product spread, product age and cost management and control.

So, for FMCG industry, keeping costs under control is a major issue. While that holds good for consumer durable industry as well, being market and customer oriented is equally important. It is quite understandable that for industrial products, a wide variety of operational parameters will influence performance. Software industry is more focused on products and customer while keeping costs under control.

Then the marketing parameters were considered for their influence on performance of different industries. In case of FMCG and consumer durables industry, no correlation was observed between success factors (relevant and/or practised) and performance. In case of industrial products, the following parameters influenced their performance: product/service is ready for the market (.029), product/service meets the customers' needs or wants (.048) and company has the resources to stay competitive in the market (.038). The final result of the regression analysis for the industrial products category is depicted in Table 12.3F. For the software industry, the significant influencers are product/service does the job that it is intended to do (.070), and company

Table 12.3F

| | *Unstandardized* | *Coeff.* | *Std. Coeff.* | | |
|---|---|---|---|---|---|
| *Model* | *B* | *Std. Err* | *Beta* | *T - Value* | *Sig.* |
| (Constant) | -1.083 | 1.477 | | -.733 | .469 |
| Product/service meets the customer needs or wants - Practised | 1.942 | 1.068 | .290 | 1.818 | .078 |
| Product/service is able to stay up with current technology - Practised | .505 | .639 | .130 | .790 | .435 |
| Company has the resources to stay competitive in the market - Practised | 1.442 | .794 | .295 | 1.815 | .079 |
| (Constant) | -.887 | 1.448 | | -.613 | .544 |
| Product/service meets the customer needs or wants - Practised | 2.129 | 1.035 | .318 | 2.056 | .048 |
| Company has the resources to stay competitive in the market - Practised | 1.629 | .754 | .334 | 2.160 | .038 |

staff is competent and technologically current (.070). In the telecom industry, the only parameter that influences performance is 'newer versions of product/service perform as expected' (perfect fit). Banks also returned perfect fit with R-square equaling one. The parameters are as follows: product/service meets the customer needs or wants, company has the resources to stay competitive in the market, newer versions of the product/service perform as expected, company staff is competent and technologically current and product/service has a well-established technological base. In the services sector, the influencers are as follows: product/service has sufficient customer development support and the company has the resources to stay competitive in the market.

So, while FMCG and consumer durables industry are not influenced by the success factors, industrial products industry is influenced by product, customer and resources. Software is influenced by product as well as right quality of people. Telecom is influenced by product alone, while banks are influenced by a combination of all these parameters.

The next factor to be tested was the various strategic business benchmarks. Overall, there were 12 parameters and the objective again was to observe their influence on performance of the various industries. It was observed in the FMCG industry that five parameters had a perfect fit with performance with R-square value of one. These five factors are marketing planning activities, entering new business areas, decision on marketing expenditures, number of products and sales training. Consumer durable industry also had a R-square value of one, but with larger number of parameters. The eight parameters are focusing on strong markets, entering foreign markets, decision on marketing expenditures, product strategies/introduction of new products, number of products, provision of R&D budget, promotion strategies and promotion budget and sales training. In case of industrial products, all parameters were included with a R-square value of 0.541. Software industry showed similar results with consumer durable industry. With a R-square value of one, the parameters which were significant are focusing on strong markets, marketing planning activities, number of products, provision of R&D budget, quality, promotion strategies and promotion budget and sales training. Telecom industry had a perfect fit but with only one parameter, which is sales training. Banks also had a perfect fit with three parameters. They are number of products, promotion strategies and promotion budget and sales training. There are a lot of similarities between service industry and banks. Service industry had a R-square value of 0.309 and included all parameters.

So, performance of all the industries was influenced by sales training. Other than sales training, FMCG industry placed a lot of importance on planning activities (strategizing) as well as products and expenses on marketing. In addition to all these parameters, consumer durables were influenced by R&D expenditures as well. Software industry focused on all the parameters of consumer durable industry as well as quality.

Then important strategic competitive goals were considered. This factor again had thirteen parameters. The objective was the same—to find out different parameters which influence performance of different industries. In this again, FMCG, consumer durables and software industries had a lot of similarities in spite of their differences. The strategic competitive goals of the different industries followed the same pattern as in the case of the earlier factor, which was business benchmarks.

Industrial products were completely different, and so were the other industries like banks and service sectors. For FMCG industry, R-square value was one and five parameters were significant. The five parameters are as follows: offer superior product/service design and quality, deliver excellent product/service conformance to specifications, offer a greater number of product/service, offer greater customization and have a higher promotion/advertisement budget. Consumer durable industry also showed a R-square value of one, with eight parameters. The focus of the consumer durable industry was however more on logistics and distribution. The eight parameters are as follows: offer superior product/service design and quality, offer a greater number of product/service, have shorter time-to-market for new product/service, offer greater customization, offer faster deliveries, offer more dependable deliveries, have better distribution strength and have a higher promotion/advertisement budget. For industrial products, there was only one significant parameter—have lower selling prices. In case of software industry, R-square value was one. It has seven significant parameters, which are as follows: offer superior product/service design and quality, offer a greater number of new product/service, have shorter time-to-market for new product/service, offer faster deliveries, have better distribution strength, have better sales force and have a higher promotion/advertisement budget. Telecom industry also has a R-square value of one, with only one parameter—have better sales force. Banks again had a R-square value of one, with the following three parameters: offer faster deliveries, offer more dependable deliveries and have a higher promotion/advertisement budget. The service industry is quite close to the banking industry with the following three factors: offer greater customization, offer more dependable deliveries and have a higher promotion/advertisement budget.

So, in this part of the analysis also, it is observed that there is a consistency of responses across all industries and the parameters also reflect the differences in strategy between the industries. The results in this part of the study is in consonance with the results that were obtained in the first part of the study.

## Discussion and Contribution

It was observed in the literature survey that a few studies were inclined to believe that firm specific strategies are creating the real differences in performance of firms. However, off late, the views seem to be veering towards the belief that firms operating in a given industry share a lot of commonalities in their strategies and that this industry-wide difference in strategies is responsible, in some ways, for the differences in their performances. The findings of this study support the later view, wherein it is clearly established that industry specific strategies are distinct and more often than not play a very important role in the performance of the firms. For example, the assumption that advertisements are crucial for the consumer product companies does not hold good any more, though the traditional belief was that advertisements are one of the most crucial aspects for the performance of the consumer product companies. It is seen from the outcomes of this research that advertisements remain important for FMCG companies, but not for consumer durable companies. Consumer durable companies rely much more on their sales force than on their advertisement strategy. However, sales training has considerable influences on the performance of firms—in FMCG as well as consumer durable industries. This research has considered the factors that are important as well as high in influence of performance, in great detail. The author has not come across any other study which has considered the strategic differences among the various industries in such detail. This is definitely a value add to the literature on this area. In the marketing strategy literature, there is an absence of comparison among all these industries simultaneously and hence, this study takes the literature forward in this area. Further detailed studies may be undertaken to identify the key crucial factors responsible for performance of the firms in different industries. Also, the study is confined to the emerging market of India and may be replicated and specifically tested in other emerging markets as well as the developed world. The practicing managers will also get a good idea about the important factors impacting the performances in their industries and may then decide to work accordingly. The factors identified in this study will act as a guide for the practicing managers whereby they may decide to concentrate on the factors which are crucial in their industries.

## Conclusion

It is quite clear that different industries pursue different strategies in order to fulfill their goals in the market place. However, there is no getting away from the fact that each and every industry is trying hard to satisfy the customers. In order to achieve that goal, different industries are adopting different strategies, which are in tune with their internal as well as external environments and circumstances. A point which comes across significantly is that only the FMCG industry places a lot of importance to market planning. This industry also places a lot of importance on advertisement, adequate resources and sales force. Consumer durables and industrial products industry focus on many operational parameters, in addition to their marketing parameters. They concentrate on reduction of defects and keep repairs low. Software industry also keeps defects low, but is also concerned with keeping prices low. So, they are more particular about the technological capabilities of their work force. As is expected, service industry and banks are quite different from the rest of the industries. While banks are more concerned about meeting the needs and wants of customers, service industry is more focused on training their sales force and having proper control. Telecom, on the other hand, is more focused on the product as there is lot of demand in the market as well as high customer expectations regarding the performance of their product.

## References

Andrus, David, Joseph Bellizzi, Wayne Norvell, and Shalini Gogumalla. 1988. 'Marketing Strategy Differences Between Industrial and Consumer Goods Companies Among Fortune 500 Companies.' *American Business Review.*

Fu, Long. 2001. 'A Differentiation Focus Strategy Provoked by Changing Environments: The American Life Insurance Industry Approaching Asian Americans.' *Management Research News* 24 (½); ABI/INFORM Complete; 1.

Gupta, Bindu, and Ajay Singh. 2014. 'Strategy and Structural Dimensions – A Comparative Study of Four Industries.' *Indian Journal of Industrial Relations* 50 (1), 180–192.

Hawawini, G., V. Subramanian, and P. Verdin. 2000. Is Profitability Driven by Industry—or Firm-Specific Factors? A New Look at the Evidence. INSEAD Working Paper Series. INSEAD, Fontainebleau, France.

O'Connor, and Gina Colarelli. 1994. 'Differences in Marketing Strategies and Operating Efficiencies in Surviving and Failed Organizations.' *Journal of Strategic Marketing* 2, 1–28. https://doi.org/10.1080/09652549400000001.

Sarathy, Ravi, and Elitsa R. Banalieva. 2014. 'Economic Development and Marketing Strategies: A Comparative Lens, Organizations and Markets in Emerging Economies.' 5 (1, 9).

Vorhies, Douglas W., Robert E. Morgan, and Chad W. Autry. 2009. 'Product-Market Strategy and the Marketing Capabilities of the Firm: Impact on Market Effectiveness and Cash Flow Performance.' *Strategic Management Journal* 30 (12), 1310–1334. https://doi.org/10.1002/smj.798

CHAPTER 13

# Manufacturing–Services Nexus

## *A Global Value Chain Analysis for India and China*

**Arnab K. Deb and Kalpana Tokas**

## Introduction

In the last few decades, the world has witnessed an enormous economic shift, with India and China emerging as superpowers to reckon with. Both countries have a common past, with a comparable cultural history and economic institutions to give shape to their interesting economic journey. However, when one considers their transition from a closed to an open economy, the two countries have adopted very dissimilar growth models for the purpose. As the two countries underwent structural reforms, with the common objective to move towards a market economy and grow sustainably, China's transition was characterized by growth in the manufacturing sector while India took the path of service led growth and emerged as the leading service exporter of the world.

If one examines these growth patterns, the three-sector model of growth posits that typically an economy, while moving on a growth path, transits from primary to secondary to the tertiary sector.

Allan (1939), Clark (1940) and Chenery and Syrquin (1975) focused on the tripartite division of the economy into primary, secondary and tertiary sector. According to them, the distribution of economic activity (output, employment, productivity) of a nation shifts from the primary sector to the secondary sector and finally to the tertiary. Kaldor (1961) emphasized on the role of the relation between manufacturing growth and Gross Domestic Products (GDP) growth and the growth of manufacturing output and the productivity of the sector. According to him, growth in services sector depended upon rising incomes as well as input demand of the manufacturing sector. Romer (1987), Ciccone and Matsuyama (1996), Fafchamps and Helms (1996), Rodriguez-Clare (1996) highlighted

> [I]n developing economies, the lack of local support industries forces the use of relatively simple production methods in downstream industries, which in turn implies a small market size for specialized inputs, which prevents a network of support industries from springing up in the economy. In contrast, rich countries are characterized by a network of highly specialized firms producing a wide range of products.

However, contrary to theory, in the Indian scenario the economy shifted directly from the agriculture to the service sector and hence bypassed the important stage of expansion and stabilization of the manufacturing sector. Natural outcome of this type of structural change is the emergence of a large service sector in India. The service sector, currently contributing 55.2 per cent to the nation's GVA (gross value added) and 72.5 per cent of the GVA growth in 2017–2018, largely stands as the key driver of Indian economic growth story over the post-reform years. Along with the rising contribution of service sector to the domestic sector of Indian economy; a considerable change in the ratio of services exports to goods exports from 35.8 in 2000–2001 to 58.2 per cent in 2016–2017 (Economic Survey of India, 2017) clearly portrays the vital role this sector is playing in changing India's trading relationship with trade partners and hence the trade balance of this country. Nevertheless, emergence of this sector and the subsequent boost to the growth of the economy is clearly an aberration from traditional growth theory.

Interestingly, even if the primary objective of India's shift (through major economic reforms of 1991) towards a market-oriented economy was to restructure Indian manufacturing, the contribution of this sector to the nation's Gross Value Added (GVA) stands at 29.6 per cent in the year 2018–2019 and has shown relatively slow real growth (6.9%) as compared to the service sector of the country (share of service sector in GVA is 54.3 per cent in 2018–2019 and real growth rate is around 7.5%).[1] Literature refers to this phenomenon as 'pre-mature deindustrialization', wherein a developing country has a very small share of their peak GDP attributable to manufacturing, and they reach this state at a much lower level of income than the traditional industrialized nations (Rodrik, 2015). Further, the growth of the services sector in India has not been very employment intensive, as it accounts for only 34 per cent of the employment share, which is much in contrast with other developing economies such as China, Mexico and Brazil.[2] Further, since the employment generation is largely confined to the high-skilled workforce, this sector fails to absorb the workforce migrating from the primary sector of the economy. Nevertheless, in the contemporary world economy, characterized by global value chains and international production networks spread across geographies, especially in sectors such as automotive and electronics, there exists evidence that the services sector and manufacturing sector cannot grow in isolation. This is because of the existence of upstream and downstream linkages between these sectors. In the context of Indian economy this is of significant importance for industries like Information Technology (IT) and IT enabled services (ITES) since these industries form the backbone of Indian services exports contributing to 41 per cent of the services exports in 2017–2018.[3]

In contrast, China emerged as a global manufacturing hub accompanied with a growing and vibrant services sector that contributed to 52.2 per cent of the GDP in 2018–2019[4] and employing 46.3 per cent of the total population.[5] China's phenomenal growth story has been ushered by a scorching pace of export driven approach and a strong manufacturing base to work on. Across sectors and industries, the competency and the competitiveness developed by China has indeed been noteworthy. Innovation centers, design labs and a strategic thrust to developing a culture of strong research and development focus are key steps the nation has taken in the last decade. These steps are bound to create a strong and superior atmosphere of output, which will scale China to the league of the developed nations. The start-up culture is already agog in the country and there is more than a fair share of the same in the country. The prosperous and active economic zones spreading across the ports of China are a boost to the already burgeoning economy.

Miroudot and Cadestin (2017), using input-output data from the Trade in Value Added (TiVA) database (1995–2011), show that in global value chains, services do not only link activities across countries but also create value in the context of the 'servicification' of manufacturing. The results of that study suggest that services account for a large share of exports, whether as products directly exported, as inputs embodied in exports of goods or as activities within manufacturing firms. A new stylized fact that emerged from that study is that service activities contribute about 40 per cent of value creation within manufacturing firms. It means that the contribution of services is even higher than previously measured. For the manufacturing sector alone, value-added service goes up from 37 per cent to 53 per cent in gross exports when considering the in-house provision of services. Further adding exports of services firms, the overall contribution of services value-added to gross exports is close to two-thirds. Given the rising importance of cross linkages (both way) between manufacturing and service sectors in sustaining growth it is essential to understand how India and China stand with respect to the strength of such linkages. Therefore, in this chapter, we aim to portray a comparative analysis between India and China and examine the role of the services–manufacturing linkage in their growth as well as their integration into the global value chains through altering the trade performance.

The organization of the chapter is as follows. In section two we discuss the significance of services as an input in a typical manufacturing production process. Next, we discuss the concept of servicification explaining the importance of nexus between manufacturing sector and service sector in section three. To exemplify this concept, we provide the existing empirical evidence. Since proper servicification of manufacturing sector enables a nation to participate in Global Value Chain

(GVC), in section four we provide empirical evidence from existing literature and OECD (Organisation for Economic Co-operation and Development) TiVA (2018) database for India and China to discuss how these countries are participating in GVC and to what extent service industries are contributing towards the participation index. Section five concludes the chapter.

## Services as an Input in Manufacturing Production

The neoclassical production process considering capital and labour as the primary input for production function has been representing the manufacturing production process over decades. Given the evolution of the service sector and the growing importance of service in today's economy, a manufacturing production function is no longer restricted to manage capital and labour as the primary input of production. As stated earlier, service has emerged as an important factor of production for a manufacturing firm. Considering the nature of service as input, it is not theoretically wise to ignore the separability issue between the factors of production capital and service or labour and service. This in turn modifies the neoclassical production function while incorporating service as a separate input for a manufacturing firm. In this section we provide a brief discussion on how service as an input has been integrated into the production process of a manufacturing firm.

A typical manufacturing production process has always used service as an important component in the manufacturing value chain. Service input embedded in production process can thus encompass a vast range of components such as transportation, information transmission, education—as on job training process or research and development—and financial and professional services. Some components of services input are required at the early stage of production, such as research and development required for process or product innovation. While some service components like maintenance and repair are essential requirements in intermediate stages of production. Further, marketing, advertising, distribution are indispensable service components required for the manufacturing firm at the final stage of operations. Furthermore, in the age of cloud-based business service components such as communication or data management are needed at every stage of production process. These serve to better manage the production process and at the same time be well connected with the clients. Thus, in order to remain competitive, a manufacturing firm cannot ignore the significance of a full spectrum of services as inputs. Hence, in the digital age of business operations, services become an integral part of the 'business ecosystem' for which the key to innovation and productivity is collaboration with multiple stakeholders such as customers, partners and contractors.

The evolution of the service sector over the last decade has altered the mode of embedding service inputs in the manufacturing production process. Further, the fast-changing nature of service sector has introduced a new type of technology-based service inputs to the manufacturing production process. To adopt these rapid changes into the nature of services, manufacturing firms are also carrying out drastic changes in the production process in order to better utilize the service inputs. Similarly, increase in the technical workforce by employing skilled and specialized employees in research and development (R&D), database management, cloud computing, etc., is now a quintessential requirement for most manufacturing firms.

Further examining the transformation, the manufacturing sector is going through, another important point should be noted here. Given the steady presence and functioning of the service sector globally and the incredible advancement in the communication technologies over the last two decades, it is now possible for a manufacturing firm to outsource in-house activities to specialist service providers. This type of integration visible in the manufacturing sector needs special mention here. As postulated by Coase (1937), a firm expands its boundary and integrates important stages of production when the cost of integration is lower than the transaction cost of procuring an essential intermediate input for production from market. Thus, to increases the scale and reap the benefit of economies of scale eventually a successful firm integrates most of the important stages of production process. However, increase in the scale of production in the service sector now allows a manufacturing firm to disintegrate the in-house service activities. The transaction cost for procuring this service from typical service firm turns out to be lower than the cost of producing it within the boundary of a manufacturing firm. This type of association with a service firm further adds value to the manufacturing firm's product and helps in reducing costs of operations and thus contributes to a considerable productivity gain. Thus, the manufacturing firms which are being involved in this type of association with service firms are becoming more business service-intensive over time. However, factors such as need for efficiency gain required, competing in the domestic as well as international market, the strength of the service sector in an economy and the relative cost of in-house provision of services as against procuring through outsourcing; ultimately are the deciding factors for this type of integration to take place (Banga and Goldar, 2004).

Nonetheless, the potential competitive gains from using service input—produced in-house or procured by outsourcing—strongly incentivize a manufacturing firm to incorporate more and more service components as inputs at all stages of production. Thus, incorporating Information and Communication Technology (ICT) and transportation services at the initial stages of production, contributes to the productivity gain and allows the firm to reap the benefit of economies of scale. At the final stages of production, integrating services with manufactured products, enables the firm to deliver a more customized product to the customer allowing stronger product differentiation desirable to survive the competition.

## Service as Beyond Input for Production: *Servicification* and Global Value Chain

In the previous section we discussed the theoretical justification for integrating service as an important input in the manufacturing production process. It should be noted that in the era of rapid globalization integration of service in the production process allows a manufacturing firm to become more cost competitive in the domestic market. At the same time efficient utilization of service input has the potential to make the firm more competitive in the global market. In this section we discuss the concept of servicification (a potential outcome of the nexus between manufacturing and service sectors) and its significance in pushing a manufacturing firm up in the Global Value Chain (GVC). The literature on servicification dates back to Levitt (1972), who questioned the distinction between manufacturing and service industry way before the global economy experienced the real expansion of the service sector. According to him, 'there are no such things as service industries. There are only industries whose service components are greater or less than those of other industries. Everybody is in services'. Following Miroudot and Cadestin (2017), servicification of manufacturing describes that increasing reliance of manufacturing sector on services, whether as in-house produced inputs or procured through outsourcing or as output sold bundled with goods (Figure 13.1).

One of the primary objectives of a firm in the borderless and globalized world is to secure a strong position in the GVC. The upward shift in productivity observed from the middle of the 20th century to the middle of the 21st century was primarily due to the GVCs. As compared to trade in final goods, trade volume of intermediate goods has increased much faster over last several decades. It was not just the ICT revolution rather trade in intermediate goods was the primary driver of the observed growth (Feenstra et al., 2013). Naturally, one of the most prominent features of the present world economy turns out to be the GVC. This phenomenon has also been termed global production sharing, trade in tasks, off-shoring, fragmented production or vertical specialization (National Trade Board, 2012). Timmer et al. (2016) argued that there is a strong correlation between change in productivity and strength of GVCs as is evident from the slowdown in trade and fragmentation of production in recent time.

Servicification in manufacturing has a strong linkage to the development of GVCs. If one examines the onset of GVC, geographical fragmentation of production is the foundation of the formation of the GVC. This fragmentation is difficult in the absence of better access to transport and logistics arrangements, advanced telecommunication and IT services. The formation of GVC therefore incentivize the manufacturing firms to use these sophisticated services in production and to take advantage of GVC. This relationship between servicification and value chains can be depicted in the shape of a 'Smiley Face' (Figure 13.2). The upstream services activities are located on either

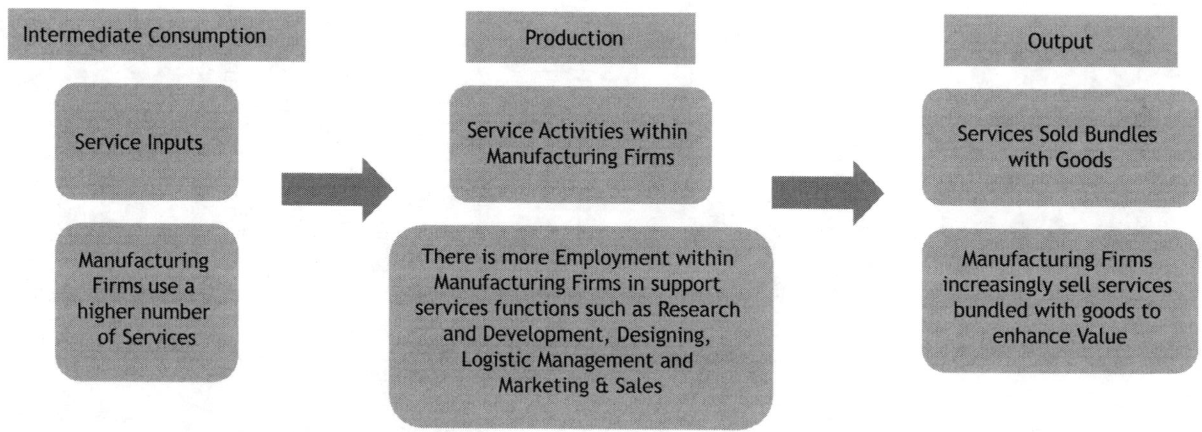


Figure 13.1 *Servicification of Manufacturing*

*Source:* Miroudot and Cadestin (2017) (Recreated by the Authors)

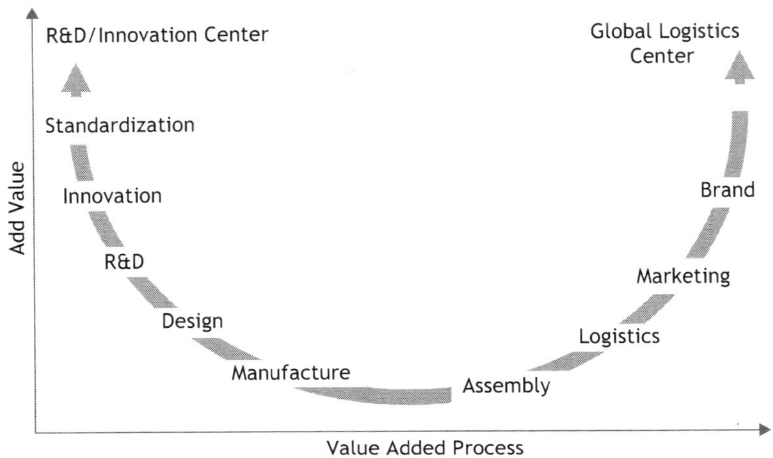


Figure 13.2 *Smiley Face: Conceptual Model of Value Chain*

*Source:* National Board of Trade, 2012/World Economic Forum 2012 (Recreated by the Authors)

side of the value chain where intellectual property is created, and services dominate the manufacturing. Also, over these areas in the value chain, maximum value is added to the core production of goods. The other downstream activities such as manufacturing, marketing, brand management fall in the middle of the value chain and add relatively less value to the production. To improve competitiveness, manufacturing firms need to move up the value chain on either side of the production node by integrating more service components in the production process.

Empirical evidences indicated that a wide range of services are used as inputs by manufacturing firms and emphasized the significance of servicification in manufacturing. Some of the services are produced internally, while some are procured from third party vendors. A study by the National Board of Trade (2010) highlights that Sandvik Tooling (Headquartered in Stockholm, Sweden), a company manufacturing tools, uses more than 40 different types of services to operate its supply chains. This set of services include delivery services, relationship management with customers, legal services (produced internally), telecommunication (acquired by existing network) and security services (procured from third party).

Another interesting example of servicification is found in the case of Aromatic (Headquartered in Stockholm, Sweden), a middle-sized company in the agri-food sector supplying ingredients to the bakery industry as it mainly specializes in ingredients for cakes, biscuits and pastry. Aromatic exports roughly 85 per cent of its production. The services needed by Aromatic can be classified into two categories; (a) services needed in producing, selling and shipping the ingredients and (b) services offered to the customers. Despite its size and the fact that the food sector is one of the industries requiring least amount of service, the company still relies on 50 different types of services to carry out its activities (National Board of Trade, 2013).

Thus, the role of services is no longer confined to serve as an input for production processes only. Manufacturing companies deliberately produce and export services either as complements or substitutes to the goods they sell in the domestic as well as global market. Production and bundling of services with goods sold is a very important strategic decision targeted at creating more value and sustaining a long-term relationship with customers.

The practice of selling the bundle of goods and service is the third component of the servicification. Vandermerwe and Rada (1988) described it as 'servitisation'. According to Baines et al. (2009) it can be described as 'innovation of an organization's capabilities and processes to shift from selling products to selling integrated products and services that deliver value in use'. It is also related to the introduction of 'service engineering' (Tomiyama, 2001) in manufacturing firms to increase value by combining services and products.

Therefore, services can create value at any stage in the value chain—both as inputs and outputs. The extra step with the service science is to understand how the whole business model and the process of value creation is transformed as services progressively redefine the firm and its operations. This evolution is also closely related to new technologies and the digital transformation of industries (Barrenechea and Jenkins, 2014).

## India, China and Global Value Chain

India and China both have undergone a thorough structural transformation over the last several decades and shifted from regulated economies to more market driven economies. Both the countries have exerted serious efforts to be integrated with the rest of the world. In the post reform years (1991–2019), India has made remarkable progress in developing a large service sector and has put a strong focus on revitalizing its manufacturing sector. This phenomenon clearly deviates from the standard practice of structural transformation and causes pre-mature de-industrialization. However, emergence of a large service sector in India has surely been conducive to the process integration with the rest of the world. On the other hand, following the traditional growth model, China has developed a robust manufacturing sector, which accounts for the largest share in the global export of manufacturing goods over the post-reform era (1978–2019). This has enabled the country to be well integrated with the global economy. Thus, countries' integration with the global economy is strongly linked with its active participation in GVC. As discussed above, a strong linkage between manufacturing and service sectors of an economy through proper servicification facilitates the nation to participate actively in the global value chain.

### Participation in Global Value Chain

The starting point to judge the extent to which a country is participating in GVC is to look at the share of value-added components of gross exports. As per the TiVA (2018) database this indicator is composed of domestic value added sent to consumer economy, domestic value added sent to third economies, domestic value added re-imported in the economy and foreign value-added content of exports.[6] Comparing these values across India and China, it can be observed that for both the countries domestic value added sent to consumer economy accounts for the largest share in total gross exports (65.9% for India and 64.3% for China; see Table 13.1). However, during the period 2005–2015, the share has been the same for India whereas it has increased by around seven percentage point for China (see Table 13.1).

Table 13.1 *Value Added Component of Gross Exports, 2005 And 2015: India and China (% Share in Total Gross Exports)*

| | *India* | | *China* | |
|---|---|---|---|---|
| *Indicators* | *2005* | *2015* | *2005* | *2015* |
| Domestic VA sent to Consumer Economy | 64.5 | 65.9 | 57.5 | 64.3 |
| Domestic VA re-imported in the Economy | 0.1 | 0.1 | 0.7 | 0.8 |
| Domestic VA sent to Third Economy (to GVCs) | 16.6 | 14.9 | 15.6 | 17.5 |
| Foreign VA content of Exports (from GVCs) | 18.8 | 19.1 | 26.3 | 17.3 |

*Source*: Authors' Calculation based on WTO 'Trade in Value-Added and Global Value Chains' profiles

Table 13.2 *Evolution of Value-Added Component of Gross Exports, 2005–2015: India and China (Annual % Change)*

| | *India* | *China* | *Developing Economies* | *Developed Economies* |
|---|---|---|---|---|
| Domestic VA sent to Consumer Economy | 10.2 | 13.4 | 7.6 | 3.2 |
| Domestic VA re-imported in the Economy | 13.2 | 15.0 | 10.1 | 3.4 |
| Domestic VA sent to Third Economy (to GVCs) | 8.7 | 13.5 | 7.1 | 3.8 |
| Foreign VA content of Exports (from GVCs) | 10.1 | 7.6 | 6.0 | 4.4 |

*Source:* Authors' Calculation based on WTO 'Trade in Value-Added and Global Value Chains' profiles

During the period of 2005–2015, volume of these components has grown at an annual average of 10.2 per cent and 13.4 per cent for India and China, respectively (see Table 13.2).

Domestic value added sent to third-world economies illustrates the multiple value-added exchanges taking place among GVCs and corresponds to the 'forward GVC participation'. Comparing the respective shares in total gross exports it can be observed that for this share has gone down from 16.6 per cent to 14.9 per cent for India but has increased from 15.6 per cent to 17.5 per cent for China over the period 2005 to 2015 (see Table 13.3). Also, for China, the volume of this component has shown higher annual growth (13.5%) relative to India (8.7%) (see Table 13.2).

Foreign value-added component of exports corresponds to 'backward GVC participation'. It is also referred to as 'vertical specialization' when expressed as a percentage of gross exports.[7] In case of vertical specialization, it is observed that in 2005 it accounted for higher share in (26.3%) China's gross export relative to that for India (18.8%) (see Table 13.3). However, India has maintained a stable share (19.1%) but in China's gross exports this component has shown a decline by around nine percentage point (17.3%) in 2015 (see Table 13.1). Although the shares of different components of value added in gross exports have shown variation across India and China and as compared to other developing and developed economies, both India and China have shown higher growth in the volume of each of these components. Thus, the GVC participation index for China in 2015 is 34.9 per cent and that for India 34 per cent (see Tables 13.3 and 13.4). Both the countries have shown annual growth in GVC participation over the period 2005–2015. India's GVC participation has grown by 9.5 per cent annually whereas China's participation rate has grown at a slightly higher rate of 10.1 per cent annually (see Table 13.3). In terms of forward participation, over this period in China, the index increased to 17.5 per cent showing two percentage points improvement whereas for India this index decreased to

Table 13.3 *The GVC Participation Index, 2005 and 2015 (% Share in Gross Exports)*

| | *India* | | *China* | |
|---|---|---|---|---|
| *GVC Participation* | *2005* | *2015* | *2005* | *2015* |
| Total GVC Participation | 35.4 | 34.0 | 31.9 | 34.9 |
| Forward Participation | 16.6 | 14.9 | 15.6 | 17.5 |
| Backward Participation | 18.8 | 19.1 | 26.3 | 17.3 |

*Source:* Authors' Calculation based on WTO 'Trade in Value-Added and Global Value Chains' profiles

Table 13.4 *Evolution of Total GVC Participation, 2005–2015 (Annual % Change)*

| | *Evolution of Total GVC Participation, 2005-2015 (Annual % Change)* |
|---|---|
| India | 9.5 |
| China | 10.1 |
| Developing Countries | 6.5 |
| Developed Countries | 4.1 |

*Source:* Authors' Calculation based on WTO 'Trade in Value-Added and Global Value Chains' profiles

14.9 per cent in 2005 from 16.6 per cent in 2005 (see Table 13.3). At the same time, backward participation index in India remained very much the same over this period but in china this index reduced drastically to 17.9 per cent in 2015 from 26.3 per cent in 2005 (see Table 13.3).

## Role of Services Value Added in Exports and GVC

As it is discussed in the previous sections that manufacturing sector today involves much more than pure production of goods and increasingly includes services, both upstream and downstream in the value chain. Thus, to increase export competitiveness manufacturing exports also require significant value added from the service sector. Intensive use of logistics, communication, business services enable the GVC to function in an efficient manner. Furthermore, services such as R&D, marketing and promotion, etc., help the manufacturing sector to customize or differentiate products for the end user and move up the global value chain. Therefore, along with studying the participation rate in GVC for India and China it is imperative to analyze the value that the respective service industry is adding to the manufacturing exports of India and China. This analysis provides a clear picture and helps to understand the extent to which India and China can exploit the potential of servicification of manufacturing sector in today's world.

In terms of participation in GVC, these two nations were not very much dissimilar. However, while looking at the services value-Added

Table 13.5 *The Services Value-Added Content of Exports, by Origin, 2015: India and China (% Shares in Manufactures and Total Exports)*

| | *Share of Domestic Services in Exports of Manufactures* | *Share of Foreign Services in Exports of Manufactures* | *Share of Domestic Services in Total Exports* | *Share of Domestic Services in Total Exports* |
|---|---|---|---|---|
| India | 8.5 | 16.6 | 6.6 | 45.0 |
| China | 6.7 | 23.0 | 6.2 | 28.6 |

*Source:* Authors' Calculation based on WTO 'Trade in Value-Added and Global Value Chains' profiles

content of exports we can observe very different scenarios across India and China. In India, value addition by services is 25 per cent for manufacturing exports and 51 per cent for the total Indian exports. Indian domestic service industry adds 45 per cent of value to total Indian export but adds only 16.6 per cent value to the manufacturing exports (see Table 13.5). On the other hand, value addition by service industry in exports by Chinese manufacturing sector is around 30 per cent and it is around 34 per cent in the case total exports by China. Domestic services produced in China add 23 per cent of value to manufacturing exports and 28.6 per cent to total export of the country (see Table 13.5).

The top service industries that add value to the Indian manufacturing exports are wholesale and retail trade, transport and storage and financial service. Together these industries add around 18.8 per cent of value to manufacturing exports. Interestingly, in terms of value addition in total, Indian IT services exports (14.2%) is the leading contributor followed by wholesale and retail trade, transport and storage industries. Together these industries add around 35 per cent of value to total Indian exports (see Tables 13.6 and 13.7).

The industry distribution in terms of value addition in the Chinese manufacturing exports include wholesale and retail trade, financial service and transport and storage, which together account for 21 per cent of value addition to Chinese manufacturing exports. Unlike India,

Table 13.6 *The Services Value-Added Contribution to Exports of Manufacture, 2015: India and China (% Shares in Gross Exports of Manufactures)*

| | *India* | *China* |
|---|---|---|
| Wholesale and Retail Trade | 10.4 | 13.5 |
| Transport and Storage | 4.9 | 6.3 |
| Financial Services | 3.5 | 5.8 |
| Total | 18.8 | 25.6 |

*Source:* Authors' Calculation based on WTO 'Trade in Value-Added and Global Value Chains' profiles

Table 13.7 *The Services Value-Added Contribution to Total Exports, 2015: India and China (% Shares in Total Gross Exports)*

| *India* | | *China* | |
|---|---|---|---|
| IT Services | 14.2 | Wholesale and Retail Trade | 13.5 |
| Wholesale and Retail Trade | 12.7 | Transport and Storage | 6.3 |
| Transport and Storage | 7.5 | Financial Services | 5.8 |

*Source:* Authors' Calculation based on WTO 'Trade in Value-Added and Global Value Chains' profiles

for total Chinese exports these three industries also contribute the most in terms of value addition. Combined contribution of these industries is around 25.6 per cent (see Tables 13.6 and 13.7).

## Conclusion

The notion of servicification very strongly pronounces the possible nexus between services and a manufacturing firm and its potential for developing a strong value chain. Considering the changes observed in cross border integration among firms, participation in the GVC has been a necessary condition for a nation to increase its production level and integrate with the rest of the world. Naturally, the emergence of service industry over the last several decades have been a common phenomenon across emerging economies. The sectoral composition of the Indian economy witnessed substantial structural shifts over the last two and half decades since the economy embarked on the path of transiting towards a more market driven economy through a set of bold reforms implemented across the sectors in the economy. With a transition from a socialist economy to a market driven economy, it can be best characterized by the changes in the contribution of agriculture (primary), manufacturing (secondary) and service (tertiary) sectors towards the Gross Domestic Product (GDP) of the economy. Developing the service sector and integrating with the global economy through exporting various kind of services has been the growth strategy deployed by India. On the other hand, after establishing a robust manufacturing sector, which can serve the rest of the world, China has also worked actively towards developing its service sector over the last decade. However, both these nations are at the cusp of another round of structural changes, which would be primarily characterized by stronger collaboration between services and manufacturing sectors with an objective to secure a higher and stable position in the GVC.

This chapter provides a comparative global value chain analysis for India and China to show the present status of these countries in the global value chain. Analysis of the data derived from OECD–TiVA database, this study finds that both the nations have been participating in a steady manner in the GVC. Relative to India, China has shown better performance in terms of forward participation in GVC. Nonetheless, both the countries have shown faster growth in forward and backward participation in GVC as compared to other developing and developed economies. To understand the importance of the service sector in placing these countries in GVC, we also analyzed the data on Services Value-Added Content of manufacturing as well as total export by these economies. The analysis shows that Indian IT services despite being a leading exporter (domestic value-added content is 92% of industry's total exports) of service to the rest of the world is not one of the leading service industries, which add maximum value to manufacturing export. However, unlike China, Indian IT services add maximum value to India's total exports. For both India and China, wholesale and retail trade, transport and storage and financial service are the leading service industries adding maximum value to the manufacturing exports.

The GVC analysis carried out in this chapter clearly depicts the significance of service–manufacturing nexus and relative positions of India and China in the GVC. However, this chapter does not shed light on explaining the differences observed across these two nations as that analysis requires a more sophisticated econometric analysis, which is beyond the scope of this chapter.

## Notes

1. https://www.indiabudget.gov.in/economicsurvey/doc/vol2chapter/echap01_vol2.pdf
2. https://www.indiabudget.gov.in/economicsurvey/doc/vol2chapter/echap09_vol2.pdf
3. https://www.indiabudget.gov.in/economicsurvey/doc/vol2chapter/echap09_vol2.pdf
4. https://www.statista.com/statistics/270325/distribution-of-gross-domestic-product-gdp-across-economic-sectors-in-china/
5. https://www.statista.com/statistics/270327/distribution-of-the-workforce-across-economic-sectors-in-china/
6. Please see https://www.wto.org/english/res_e/statis_e/miwi_e/Explanatory_Notes_e.pdf for definition of each component.
7. WTO 'Trade in Value-Added and Global Value Chains' profiles Explanatory notes.

## Reference

Allan G. B. Fisher. 1939. 'Production, Primary, Secondary and Tertiary.' *The Economic Record, The Economic Society of Australia* 15 (1), 24–38.

Baines, T., H. Lightfoot, O. Benedettini, & J. Kay. 2009. 'The Servitization of Manufacturing: A Review of Literature and Reflection on Future Challenges.' *Journal of Manufacturing Technology Management* 20 (5), 547–567.

Banga, R. and B. N. Goldar. 2004. 'Contribution of Services to Output Growth and Productivity in Indian Manufacturing: Pre and Post reforms.' Working Papers No. 139. Indian Council for Research on International Economic Relations.

Barrenechea, M., and T. Jenkins. 2014. *Digital: Disrupt or Die.* Canada: Open Text Corporation.

Chenery, Hollis B., and Syrquin, M. 1975. *Patterns of Development: 1950–1970.* New York: Oxford University Press for the World Bank.

Coase, R. H. 1937. 'The Nature of the Firm.' *Economica* 4, 386–405.

Fafchamps, Marcel, and Brigit Helms. 1996. 'Local Demand, Investment Multipliers, and Industrialization: Theory and Application to the Guatemalan Highlands.' *Journal of Development Economics* 49 (1), 61–92.

Feenstra, R., B. Mandel, M. Reinsdorf, and M. Slaughter, (2013). 'Effects of Terms of Trade Gains and Tariff Changes on the Measurement of US Productivity Growth.' *American Economic Journal: Economic Policy* 5 (1), 59–93.

Levitt, T. 1972. 'Production-line Approach to Service.' *Harvard Business Review* 50 (5), 20–31.

Kaldor, N. 1961. 'Increasing Returns and Technical Progress—A Comment On Professor Hicks' Article.' *Oxford Economic Papers, Oxford University Press* 13 (1), 1–4.

Miroudot, S., and C. Cadestin. 2017. 'Services in Global Value Chains: From Inputs to Value-Creating Activities.' OECD Trade Policy Papers No. 197. Paris: OECD Publishing.

National Board of Trade 2010. *At Your Service—The Importance of Services for Manufacturing Companies and Possible Trade Policy Implications*. Sweden: National Board of Trade.

National Board of Trade 2013. *Just Add Services. A Case Study on Servicification and the Agri-Food Sector*. Sweden: National Board of Trade.

Rodrik, D. 2015. 'Premature Deindustrialization.' NBER Working Paper No. 20935. Cambridge, MA: National Bureau of Economic Research.

Timmer, M., Los, B., R. Stehrer, and G. de Vries. 2016. 'An Anatomy of the Global Trade Slowdown Based on the WIOD 2016 Release.' Groningen Growth and Development Centre Research Memorandum No. 162, University of Groningen.

Tomiyama, T. 2001. 'Service Engineering to Intensify Service Contents in Product Life Cycles.' In Proceedings of the Second International Symposium on Environmentally Conscious Design and Inverse Manufacturing (EcoDesign 2001), IEEE Computer Society, 613–618.

Vandermerwe, S., and J. Rada. 1988. 'Servitization of Business: Adding Value by Adding Services.' *European Management Journal* 6 (4), 314–324.

CHAPTER 14

# Power Performance and Profitability Determinants in Indian and Chinese Banks

Deepak Tandon, Shubham Raghuwanshi, Kanika Jain and Neelam Tandon

## Introduction

As the banking industry is highly regulated in many countries including India, any governing policy change impacts the sector largely. For instance, any cut in the monetary policy rates affects the profitability of Indian banks significantly. Adaptability to the technological changes has upgraded the banking industry in recent days. Also, with the changing Basel norms and implementation of strict risk management policies, the buffer capital has gone up the post-financial crisis in 2008–2009 driving to the shrinking profits across the globe. The Global markets also have shown instability since 2008–2009. Whether it was spillover effects of global financial crisis or the trade war or the crashing currencies of many economies, they all resulted in turbulent returns on equity (ROE), particularly in the banks. The banking sector has also been growing in the Indian context, especially after the financial crisis of 2008. In India, RBI strictly monitors the banking industry. But the Indian banking industry has not performed very well for the investors or at the stock market in the past few years. Talking about the post-2011 scenario, Indian banks' ROE has not been as impressive as many of the performing indicators have seen on a downside movement. Due to a positive growth in specific performance parameters (Return on Equity), investors have a judicious faith in investment.

## Literature Review

There have been ample studies substantiating the profitability determinants in the banking sector. Shrivastava, Kumar, Singh, and Kumar's (2018) study finds empirical evidence that the net interest margins and advances play an important role in a bank's profitability and growth. Amongst macro-factors, high growth rate has a retarding impact on bad assets. Net interest margins and return of assets (ROA) have an indirect impact on the Non-performing Loans (NPLs). The bigger banks have high figures of NPL. Sayuri Shirai's (2002) seminal paper emphasizes that India has adopted a more comprehensive model for growth than China. She emphasized that corporate governance, removal of government intervention, rationalizing weak banks and stringent lending measures would add to risk management and profitability in declining net interest income regime. Her studies were restricted to wholly state-owned commercial banks. Among macro-factors, the high growth rate has a retarding impact on bad assets. A study conducted by Nguyen (2017) studies depict clearly that the State-owned banks generate more revenue and depict more profitability in both the Chinese and Indian banks as compared to privately owned banks.The Chinese banks are more comprehensive in cost reduction and revenue generation. The study also empirically states that Vietnam should follow the Chinese model for revenue generation. There are various studies stating the efficiency of Indian banks, viz., Das and Ghosh (2009), Ray and Das (2010), Sahoo and Mandal (2011), Das and Drine (2011) and Das and Kumbhakar (2012). Das et. al (2012) emphasized that the parameters of efficiency in the banks are depicted from the NPL figures for the corresponding period. The banks generate efficiency with lower loans to total asset ratio, lower deposits of customers with respect to total liabilities, with lower NPL to gross loans ratio; there is a higher revenue and thus depicts more efficiency. Tan Yong (2017) examined deposit, loan, net interest income and the competition in different banks for the period 2003–2013. He used the Generalized Method of Moments (GMM). Net interest margin had higher level of competition. The net interest margin of the commercial banks gets affected by the size of the bank and the macroeconomic indicators such as inflation rate, GDP and growth rate. Alicia Garcia-Herrero, Sergio Gavilá and Daniel Santabárbara (2007) substantiated that the capital-intensive banks that have good risk management techniques are more profitable. They studied 87 banks' panel data for a period of 1997 to 2004. The listed banks are more robust, resilient and have better asset quality. In the economic perspectives, NPLs are due to high volatile interest, and hamper profitability. They also concluded that less concentrated banking in China adds to more profitability. Srinivasan and Britto (2017) presented similar views for analyzing the performance of the Indian banks and summarized that the solvency, efficiency and liquidity impact the profitability of Indian scheduled banks directly. Wanniarachchige and Suzuki (2011) highlighted the parameters of ownership in bank performance in the context of Indian banks. The findings suggest that the performance of domestic banks has not yet reached the level of foreign banks in terms of both cost and revenue efficiencies. The foreign banks outperform more. They used data envelopment model (DEA). Rasidah and Mohd H.T. (2011) investigated the impact of Chinese and Malaysian bank-specific factors which include the liquidity, credit, capital, operating expenses and the size of commercial banks on their performance, which is measured by return on average assets (ROAA) and return on average equity (ROAE). Chinese banks operating ratios influence performance which is not there in Malaysian banks. Tan and Floros (2012a) in their studies of bank profitability and inflation highlighted that the effects of inflation on bank profitability are phenomenal while controlling for comprehensive bank-specific and industry-specific variables. Broadman (1999) deliberated that the Chinese state as corporate shareholder is not seen in the banks. Reforms have to be made for strengthening the overall institutional framework, especially for the property rights, corporate governance incentives and competition, thereby reducing state ownerships. Berger (1995) in his studies examined the relationship between capital and earnings in banking. He emphasized that banks capital ratios are positively related to return on equity. Capital raised higher will speak on the profitability and inversely to bankruptcy in banks. In summary, these studies show that the profitability parameters are responsible for very high content to the health, solvency, and returns of the loans given by banks. The gaps in the review of literature gives a significant difference in performance vis-à-vis the profitability of the Indian and Chinese banking industry due to various reasons. The available research on the Indian and Chinese banking industry has studied a few of the parameters. However, statistically verified comparisons based on parameters like ROA, ROE, and NPL on recent data have not been drawn.

## Objectives

Given the research gap, five objectives were defined for this research.

1. To assess the factors affecting the profitability in the Indian versus Chinese banks.
2. To make a comparative analysis of the profitability of Indian and Chinese banks included in the study.
3. To compare the non-performing asset portfolio of Indian and Chinese banks.
4. To make a comparative analysis of the types of risks faced by the Indian and Chinese banks.
5. To find out the relation between profitability and NPLs ratio in the Indian versus Chinese banks.

## Methodology and Analysis

### Data Collection

The authors have collected data for ROA, ROE and NPL for 22 Indian banks and 20 Chinese banks. The data has been used to evaluate the profitability of the banks and compare the performances of Indian versus Chinese banking sector. T-test, Chi-Square test, Regression and Levene's test have been applied and led to plausible implications. The authors tested the hypothesis with the financial statement 'data from 2011 to 2018 for banks in China and India', listed in Appendix 14C, Table 14C.1.

## Definitions and Formulae

Indicators of Profitability: The authors have selected the data of the key variables, viz., ROA, ROE and NPL on the profitability of the banks.

(i) The ability of a bank to generate the profits by using its asset is depicted by ROA. It is net profit to the average total assets.
(ii) The generation of profits through the investments is a key role by this ratio, that is, returns on equity. It is the ratio of net profits by total assets.
(iii) NPL ratio depicts the defaulted loans with respect to total loans in the stipulated period.

## Tests Applied and Rationale

(i) The test of probability distribution: The T-test is used to testify that the difference between the two groups' averages will depict real differences between the populations from which samples have been taken. The test for the mean differences indicates whether the two samples are drawn from normal distribution and variances are equal.
(ii) Chi-Square test: This test is of significance in case of nominal/ordinal variables correlation. The Chi-square test tabulations are applicable when both variables are less than the interval level. Further, the T-test is used to compare continuous dependent variable between two groups.
(iii) Regression and ANOVA analysis have been used to see the significance of the results—whether properly constructed indicator

variables are there for two or more populations. Further, F distribution, that is, F Test was conducted for testing the hypotheses of response variables with the explanatory variables.

(iv) Levene's test was conducted to see whether there is equality of variances in the said sample or not.

## Descriptive and Test Analysis

### *Comparison of Profitability and Economic Conditions between Indian and Chinese Banking Industry*

Banks' profitability is dependent on the economic conditions of the country. Banks operate in an environment of the industry in the economic conditions of the country. It is greatly impacted by the policies, regulations, and conditions prevailing in the country. They have various cost drivers, risk parameters, industry utilities to see investment returns in a competitive era. The year 2018 marked a few facts in the banking sector that highlighted the Chinese banking industry. As per, 'The Bankers 2018 Report', in terms of highest Tier I capital top four Chinese banks figure. Similarly, the world's top three most profitable banks are from China—ICBC Bank stands first with USD 56 billion in pre-tax earnings, China Construction Bank with USD 46 billion and Agricultural Bank of China with USD 37 billion. For India, it is seen that out of ten loss making banks, six are Indian banks. Punjab National Bank lost USD 3 billion (the third largest global loss), IDBI lost USD 1.9 billion (the fourth largest) and State Bank of India lost USD 1.8 billion, the fifth largest as per the report. This substantiates the fact that the pre-tax earnings of the banks both in China and India justify the profitability. Based on the theoretical background, the Chi-Square test has been conducted to find the extent of the dependence of Indian and Chinese bank's profitability on the economic conditions of India and China.

#### *Chi-square Test Analysis*

H0: ROE accounting for profitability in the banking sector is independent of the economy.

H1: ROE accounting for profitability in the banking sector is dependent on the economy.

*ROE * Economy Cross tabulation*

*Count*

| | | *Economy* | | |
|---|---|---|---|---|
| | | *China* | *India* | *Total* |
| ROE | Below average | 4 | 21 | 25 |
| | Above or equals to average | 27 | 10 | 37 |
| Total | | 31 | 31 | 62 |

*Source:* Author's own findings

*Chi-Square Tests*

| | *Value* | *Df* | *Asymp. Sig. (2-sided)* | *Exact Sig. (2-sided)* | *Exact Sig. (1-sided)* |
|---|---|---|---|---|---|
| Pearson Chi-Square | 19.371[a] | 1 | 0.000 | | |
| Continuity Correction[b] | 17.159 | 1 | 0.000 | | |
| Likelihood Ratio | 20.786 | 1 | 0.000 | | |
| Fisher's Exact Test | | | | 0.000 | 0.000 |
| N of Valid Cases | 62 | | | | |

[a] 0 cells (0.0%) have expected count less than 5. The minimum expected count is 12.50.
[b] Computed only for a 2x2 table
*Source:* Author's own findings

*Output: symmetric measures*

| | | *Value* | *Approx. Sig.* |
|---|---|---|---|
| Nominal by Nominal | Phi | -0.559 | 0.000 |
| | Cramer's V | 0.559 | 0.000 |
| | Contingency Coefficient | 0.488 | 0.000 |
| N of Valid Cases | | 62 | |

*Note:* Refer Appendix 14D for the data set.
*Source:* Author's own findings

As the P-value for the Chi-Square test is 0.000 < 0.05 (significance level), we will reject the null hypothesis (H0). This means that the profitability (ROE) of the banking sector is dependent on the economy (country). We can assess the extent of this dependency by Phi coefficient. Here the P-value for the Phi coefficient is 0.000 < 0.05, hence we can conclude that the dependency is significantly high. Also, as phi square measures the proportion of one variable that is explained by other variables, the above test shows that 31.25 per cent of the profitability of the sector is explained by the economic conditions of the country.

### *Comparison of Profitability and Bad Debts between Indian and Chinese Banking Industry*

To compare profitability and bad debts between the Chinese and Indian banking industry T-test has been conducted. The reason being that by simply scanning the data, it looks like the Chinese banks are doing better than the Indian banks with comparatively higher ROA, ROE and lower NPL ratio (Refer Appendix 14B). But to validate the observation, we have used a T-Test.

#### T-TEST ANALYSIS

*Group Statistics*

| | *Economy* | *N* | *Mean* | *Std. Deviation* | *Std. Error Mean* |
|---|---|---|---|---|---|
| ROE | India | 31 | 7.933681 | 9.5462971 | 1.7145656 |
| | China | 31 | 17.951428 | 2.9357871 | 0.5272829 |
| ROA | India | 31 | 0.610550 | 0.6534472 | 0.1173626 |
| | China | 31 | 1.100053 | 0.1341810 | 0.0240996 |
| NPL | India | 31 | 4.847709 | 3.8626742 | 0.6937568 |
| | China | 31 | 1.227824 | 0.2887223 | 0.0518560 |

*Source:* Author's own findings

*Tests performed: Independent Samples Test*

| | | *Levene's Test for Equality of Variances* | | *t-test for Equality of Means* | | | | | | |
|---|---|---|---|---|---|---|---|---|---|---|
| | | | | | | | | | *95% Confidence Interval of the Difference* | |
| | | *F Test* | *Significance.* | *T* | *df* | *Sig. (2-tailed)* | *Mean Difference* | *Std. Error Difference* | *Lower* | *Upper* |
| ROE | Assumed equal variances | 20.495 | .000 | 5.585 | 60 | 0.000 | 10.0177461 | 1.7938123 | 13.6059048 | 6.4295874 |
| | Not assumed equal variances | | | 5.585 | 35.624 | 0.000 | 10.0177461 | 1.7938123 | 13.6570989 | 6.3783933 |
| ROA | Assumed equal variances | 32.042 | 0.000 | 4.086 | 60 | 0.000 | -0.4895036 | 0.1198114 | -0.7291621 | -0.2498452 |
| | Not assumed equal variances | | | 4.086 | 32.525 | 0.000 | -0.4895036 | 0.1198114 | -0.7333969 | -0.2456103 |
| NPA | Assumed equal variances | 53.690 | 0.000 | 5.203 | 60 | 0.000 | 3.6198842 | 0.6956921 | 2.2282928 | 5.0114756 |
| | Not assumed equal variances | | | 5.203 | 30.335 | 0.000 | 3.6198842 | .6956921 | 2.1997495 | 5.0400190 |

*Note*: Refer Appendix 14D for the data set.
*Source*: Author's own findings

1. Results for ROE of the Indian and the Chinese Banks:
   H0: ROE of the Indian Banking Industry >= ROE of the Chinese Banking Industry
   H1: ROE of the Indian Banking Industry < ROE of the Chinese Banking Industry
   From the above results of the T-test we can see that the P-value is less than 0.05, hence we reject the null hypothesis and accept the alternative hypothesis, that is, return on equity of Indian banking industry is less than that of the return on equity of Chinese banking industry.
2. Results for ROA of the Indian and the Chinese Banks:
   H0: ROA of the Indian Banking Industry >= ROA of the Chinese Banking Industry
   H1: ROE of the Indian Banking Industry < ROA of the Chinese Banking Industry
   From the above results of the T-test we can see that the P-value is 0.000 < 0.05 (significance level), hence we can reject the null hypothesis or can conclude that return on assets of Indian banking industry are better than return on assets of the Chinese banking industry.
3. Results for NPL Ratio of the Indian and Chinese Banks:
   H0: NPL Ratio of Indian Banking Industry <= NPL Ratio of Chinese Banking Industry
   H1: NPL Ratio of Indian Banking Industry > NPL Ratio of Chinese Banking Industry
   From the above results of the T-test, we can see that the P-value is 0.000 < 0.05 (significance level), so the null hypothesis is rejected and the alternate hypothesis that the non-performing loans ratio of Indian banking industry is greater than the non-performing loan ratio of Chinese banking industry, is accepted.

## Comparison of Risk Associated with the Banking Industry between India and China

Risk assessment is one of the very first and most essential steps in the investing process in any business or stock. Financial institutions are not considered very safe after the Global Financial Crisis for investment and lending purposes. The banking sector specifically has also witnessed ups and downs in the past decade, but the extent varied from nation to nation. The Levene's Test has been used to compare the risk associated with the Indian and Chinese banking sector. ROE variance/standard deviation has been used as the indicator of the risk.

*Levene's Test for Equality of Variances between Indian and Chinese Banking Industry*

H0: The Indian Banking industry variances in terms of ROE <= Variances of ROE in the Chinese Banking industry
H1: The Indian Banking industry variances in terms of ROE > Variances of ROE in the Chinese Banking industry

| | *Economy* | *Std. Deviation* |
|---|---|---|
| ROE | India | 9.5462971 |
| | China | 2.9357871 |

*Source:* Author's own findings

| | | *Levene's Test for Equality of Variances* | |
|---|---|---|---|
| | | *F* | *Sig.* |
| ROE | Equal variances assumed | 20.495 | 0.000 |
| | Equal variances not assumed | | |

*Note:* Refer Appendix 14D for the data set.
*Source:* Author's own findings

From the above results we can see that the standard value of P is 0.000 < 0.05 (significance level), hence we can reject the null hypothesis and adopt the alternate hypothesis that the Indian banking industry variances in terms of ROE are more than the variances of ROE in the Chinese banking industry.

## Comparison of Profitability (ROE) and NPL between Indian and Chinese Banking Industry

The problem of non-performing assets (NPAs) has caught the eye in the past few years in the case of India, whereas in China the problem has not surfaced as critical as it has been in India. The NPAs or more specifically the NPLs impact the ROE negatively and to check the extent and to identify the mathematical relation, the authors have conducted the regression analysis.

### *Regression Model between Profitability Measure and Non-performing Loans in Banking Industry*

Conceptual model of relationship between profitability measure ROE/ROA and NPL of the banks under consideration:

#### Impact of Non-performing Loans on Return on Equity of Indian Banking Industry

*Summary of the Model*

| *Model* | *R* | *R Square* | *Adjusted R Square* | *Std. Error of the Estimate* |
|---|---|---|---|---|
| 1 | 0.899[a] | 0.809 | 0.802 | 4.2455333 |

[a] Predictors: (Constant), NPL
*Source:* Author's own findings

*ANOVA*[a]

| *Model* | | *Sum of Squares* | *Df* | *Mean Square* | *F* | *Sig.* |
|---|---|---|---|---|---|---|
| 1 | Regression | 2211.242 | 1 | 2211.242 | 122.679 | 0.000[b] |
| | Residual | 522.712 | 29 | 18.025 | | |
| | Total | 2733.954 | 30 | | | |

[a] Dependent Variable: ROE
[b] Predictors: (Constant), NPL
*Source:* Author's own findings

*Taken in study the co-efficient*

| | | *Unstandardized Coefficients* | | *Standardized Coefficients* | | |
|---|---|---|---|---|---|---|
| *Model* | | *B* | *Std. Error* | *Beta* | *t* | *Sig.* |
| 1 | (Constant) | 18.708 | 1.236 | | 15.136 | 0.000 |
| | NPL | -2.223 | 0.201 | -0.899 | -11.076 | 0.000 |

*Note:* Refer Appendix 14D for the data set.
*Source:* Author's own findings

From the above test, we can see that NPL explains 80.2 per cent of the variance in ROE of the Indian banking industry, which is surprisingly high and accounts significantly for the poor performance of the Indian banking sector. Also, the regression model is robust since the p-value for the ANOVA test is $0.000 < 0.05$.

$$ROE = 18.708 - 2.223\ NPL$$

The negative coefficient of NPL indicates the negative relationship between ROE and NPL.

### Impact of Non-performing Loans on Return on assets of Indian Banking Industry

*Model Summary*

| *Model* | *R* | *R Square* | *Adjusted R Square* | *Std. Error of the Estimate* |
|---|---|---|---|---|
| 1 | 0.902[a] | 0.813 | 0.806 | 0.2875166 |

[a] Predictors: (Constant), NPA
*Source:* Author's own findings

*Model done for analysis of variance: Table ANOVA*[a]

| *Model* | | *Sum of Squares* | *df* | *Mean Square* | *F* | *Sig.* |
|---|---|---|---|---|---|---|
| 1 | Regression | 10.412 | 1 | 10.412 | 125.959 | 0.000[b] |
| | Residual | 2.397 | 29 | 0.083 | | |
| | Total | 12.810 | 30 | | | |

[a] ROA being the dependent variable
[b] Predictors: NPL being the (Constant)
*Source:* Author's own findings

*Table for the Coefficients*

| | | *Unstandardized Coefficients* | | *Standardized Coefficients* | | |
|---|---|---|---|---|---|---|
| *Model* | | *B* | *Std. Error* | *Beta* | *T* | *Sig.* |
| 1 | (Constant) | 1.350 | 0.084 | | 16.127 | 0.000 |
| | NPA | -0.153 | 0.014 | -0.902 | -11.223 | 0.000 |

[a] ROA being the dependent variable
*Note:* Refer Appendix 14D for the data set.
*Source:* Author's own findings

Similarly, on applying the regression model for ROA (independent variable) and NPL (dependent variable), we can see that NPL explains 80.6 per cent of the variance in ROA of the Indian banking industry, which is again high and accounts significantly for the poor performance of the Indian banking sector. Also, the regression model is robust since the p-value for the ANOVA test is 0.000 < 0.05.

$$\text{ROA} = 1.35 - 0.153\ \text{NPL}$$

The negative coefficient of NPL indicates the negative relationship between ROA and NPL.

## Impact of Non-performing Loans on Return on Equity of Chinese Banking Industry

*Summary of the Model*

| *Model* | *R* | *R Square* | *Adjusted R Square* | *Std. Error of the Estimate* |
|---|---|---|---|---|
| 1 | 0.939[a] | 0.881 | 0.877 | 1.0283078 |

[a] Predictors: (Constant), NPA
*Source:* Author's own findings

*Table ANOVA*[a]

| *Model* | | *Sum of Squares* | *df* | *Mean Square* | *F* | *Sig.* |
|---|---|---|---|---|---|---|
| 1 | Regression | 227.900 | 1 | 227.900 | 215.525 | 0.000[b] |
| | Residual | 30.665 | 29 | 1.057 | | |
| | Total | 258.565 | 30 | | | |

[a] ROE being the dependent variable
[b] Predictors: (Constant), NPA
*Source:* Author's own findings

*Table for the Coefficients*[a]

| | | *Unstandardized Coefficients* | | *Standardized Coefficients* | | |
|---|---|---|---|---|---|---|
| *Model* | | *B* | *Std. Error* | *Beta* | *t* | *Sig.* |
| 1 | (Constant) | 29.673 | 0.819 | | 36.209 | 0.000 |
| | NPL | -9.546 | 0.650 | -0.939 | -14.681 | 0.000 |

[a] ROE being the dependent variable
*Note:* Refer Appendix 14D for the data set.
*Source:* Author's own findings

From this test, we can see that NPL explains 87.7 per cent of the variance in ROE of the Chinese banking industry. Also, the regression model is robust since the p-value for the ANOVA test is 0.000 < 0.05.ROE = 29.673 – 9.546 NPL

The results support the relatively better performance of Chinese banking industry as the NPL is significantly lesser in case of Chinese banking industry.

## Impact of Non-performing Loans on Return on Assets of Chinese Banking Industry

*Summary of the Model*

| *Model* | *R* | *R Square* | *Adjusted R Square* | *Std. Error of the Estimate* |
|---|---|---|---|---|
| 1 | 0.883[a] | 0.779 | 0.771 | 0.0641735 |

[a] Predictors: (Constant), NPL
*Source:* Author's own findings

*Table ANOVA*[a]

| *Model* | | *Sum of Squares* | *df* | *Mean Square* | *F* | *Sig.* |
|---|---|---|---|---|---|---|
| 1 | Regression | 0.421 | 1 | 0.421 | 102.157 | 0.000[b] |
| | Residual | 0.119 | 29 | 0.004 | | |
| | Total | 0.540 | 30 | | | |

[a] ROA being the dependent variable
[b] Predictors: (Constant), NPA
*Source:* Author's own findings

*Table for the Coefficients*

| | | *Unstandardized Coefficients* | | *Standardized Coefficients* | | |
|---|---|---|---|---|---|---|
| *Model* | | *B* | *Std. Error* | *Beta* | *T* | *Sig.* |
| 1 | (Constant) | 1.604 | 0.051 | | 31.357 | 0.000 |
| | NPL | -0.410 | 0.041 | -0.883 | -10.107 | 0.000 |

*Note:* Refer Appendix 14D for the data set.
*Source:* Author's own findings

From this test, we can see that NPL explains 77.1 per cent of the variance in ROA of the Chinese banking industry. Also, the regression model is robust since the p-value for the ANOVA test is 0.000 < 0.05.

$$ROA = 1.604 - 0.410 \text{ NPL}$$

Keeping in view of the above, the performance of the Chinese banks is better than the Indian banks as the non-performing loans are less for the Chinese banks than the Indian Banks. This can be attributed to the fact that they afford need-based credit with strict compliances and better monitoring.

## Results Summary

The authors through this empirical study conclude that the dependency of the economy is a clear highlight of ROE and thus the profitability in the banks in the country studied therein. As indicated by the results from the test, the profitability of banking is up to 31 per cent dependent on the nation's economic policies and results. We can conclude that there is an impact of the economy on the functioning and results of the banking sector. The economy, in general, does have an impact on the industry in the country.

For China, there could be multiple factors. The country has been increasing its global presence. China's top four banks have increased their foreign lending by ten folds to about USD 1 trillion. The Chinese banks have grown in asset size by 15 per cent. It has been conservative and safe for the industry. It has improved its capital position significantly. The Chinese banks have been able to achieve financial performance through growth and optimization. Though the financial performance of Chinese banks has significantly improved over the years yet the Chinese economy suffers fro high debt to GDP ratio and financial crunch in (non-banking financial companies) NBFCs.

Probably, factors that may have been impacting India's growth is predominantly the regulatory approach in India. The central bank in India has already given directions for stressed assets, income recognition, and NPL recovery stiff measures. This may have short term losses and negative impact but in the long run it does well. Looking forward, India's growth rate is expected to catch up more than China's because of the tremendous opportunities in India.

## Conclusion

The results of investigation undertaken for the study revealed the following inferences and conclusions:

First, in line with our hypothesis, results have affirmed significant dependence of profitability of banks on the nation's economic policies, economic growth and social stability. Creation of credit, capital raising, utilization of resources, monetize cash through loans substantiate this valid point. Second, the results support that banks in China have an edge in performance in terms of better ROA and ROE when compared to Indian banks due to significantly lower level of NPL in Chinese banks. Third, the result of the study by Alicia Garcia-Herrero, Sergio Gavilá, and Daniel Santa Barbara (2009) emplacing the risk management in the banking industry justified that Chinese banking is less concentrated, hence less risky. The results of the study affirm that the banks in China are more robust and less risky than the Indian banks. The returns in Chinese banks are less volatile and sound. Lastly, this also substantiates with the results of the paper by Das and Kumbhakar (2012) and states that there is high profitability with lower loan total asset ratio and lower deposits from customers to the total liabilities of the banks. The lowering of the cost of deposits will yield higher profitability. This has been affirmed by our findings of dependence of profitability on the independent factor, that is, NPL, for both the countries. The present research has been able to substantiate our hypotheses and observations. These are in consonance with the conclusions made by early researchers for the performance of Indian banks and the Chinese banks. The banking sector in both these countries have to consolidate the credit portfolios, curb non-performing assets by taking out managerial actions in consonance with regulatory reforms.

# Appendix 14A

Table 14A.1 *All Applied Test's Summary*

| *Test* | | *Standard P-Value* | *Obtained P-Value* | *Null Hypothesis (With Reference to Banking Industry)* | *Alternate Hypothesis (With Reference to Banking Industry)* | *Acceptance/ Rejection of Null Hypothesis* |
|---|---|---|---|---|---|---|
| Chi-Square | | 0.05 | 0.000 | ROE is independent of the economy | ROE is dependent of the economy | Rejected |
| T-Test | For ROE | 0.05 | 0.000 | ROEIndia>= ROEChina | ROEIndia<ROEChina | Rejected |
| | For ROA | 0.05 | 0.000 | ROAIndia>= ROAChina | ROAIndia<ROAChina | Rejected |
| | For NPL | 0.05 | 0.000 | NPLIndia<= NPLChina | NPLIndia>NPLChina | Rejected |
| Levene's Test | | 0.05 | 0.000 | VarianceIndia>= VarianceChina | VarianceIndia<VarianceChina | Rejected |
| Regression | For ROEIndia | 0.05 | 0.000 | ROEIndia = 0*NPL + C | ROEIndia ≠ 0*NPL + C | Rejected |
| | For ROAIndia | 0.05 | 0.000 | ROAIndia = 0*NPL + C | ROAIndia ≠ 0*NPL + C | Rejected |
| | For ROEChina | 0.05 | 0.000 | ROEChina= 0*NPL + C | ROEChina ≠ 0*NPL + C | Rejected |
| | For ROAChina | 0.05 | 0.000 | ROAChina= 0*NPL + C | ROAChina ≠ 0*NPL + C | Rejected |

*Source:* Authors' calculations

# Appendix 14B

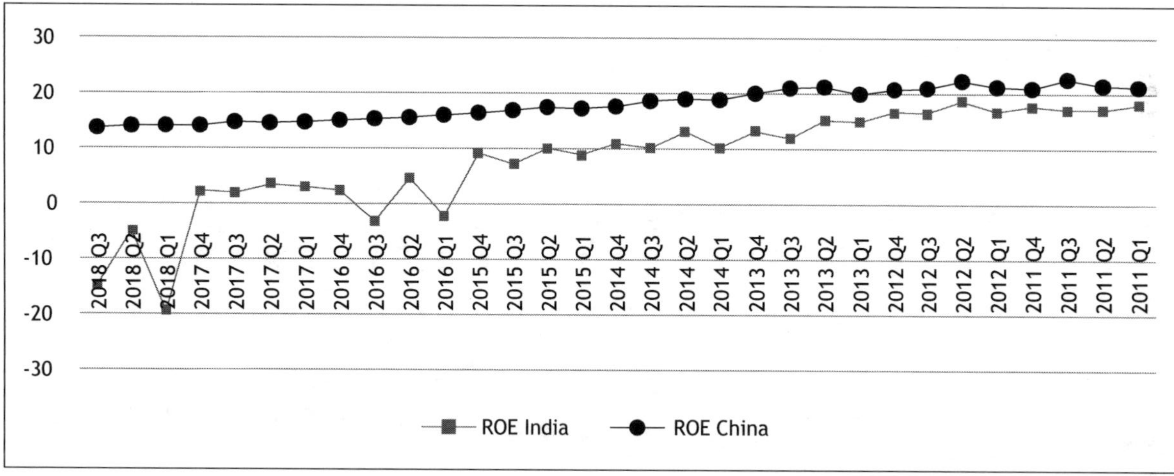


Figure 14B.1 *ROE India and China in Percentage*

*Source:* Authors' calculations

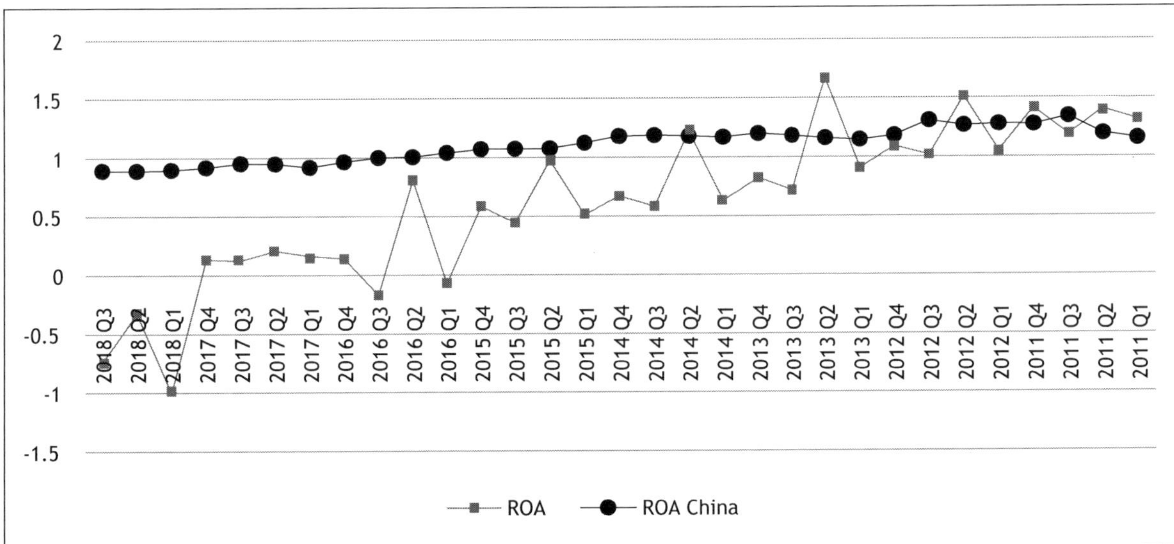


Figure 14B.2 *ROA of Indian and Chinese Banks*

*Source*: Authors' calculations

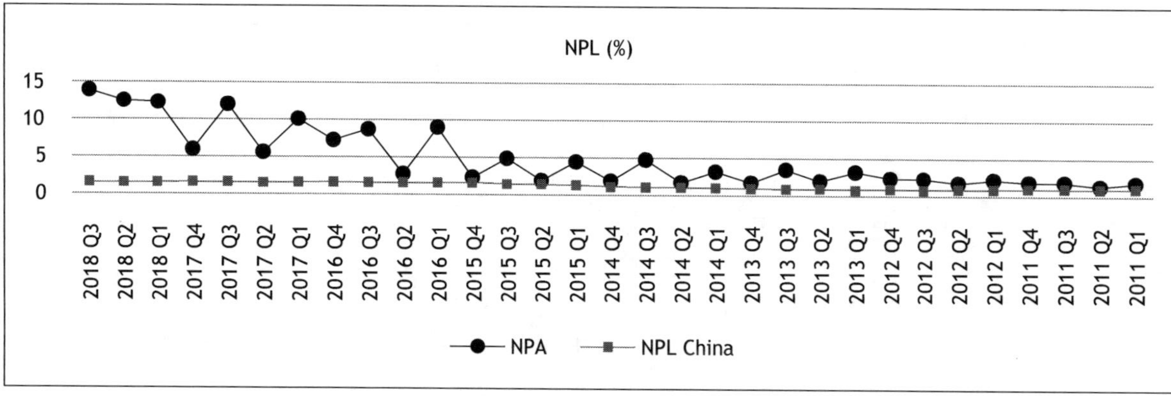


Figure 14B.3 *Comparison of NPA of Chinese and Indian Banks*

*Source:* Authors' calculations

# Appendix 14C

Table 14C.1 *List of Banks Whose Data Has Been for the Study*

| *Indian Banks* | *Chinese Banks* |
|---|---|
| Allahabad Bank | Agricultural Bank of China Ltd |
| Andhra Bank | Bank of China Ltd |
| Axis Bank Ltd | Bank of Chongqing Co Ltd |
| Bank of Baroda | Bank of Communications Co Ltd |
| Bank of India | Bank of East Asia Ltd/The |
| Canara Bank | BOC Hong Kong Holdings Ltd |
| Central Bank of India | China CITIC Bank Corp Ltd |
| Corp Bank | China Construction Bank Corp |
| HDFC Bank Ltd | China Everbright Bank Co Ltd |
| ICICI Bank Ltd | China Merchants Bank Co Ltd |
| IDBI Bank Ltd | China Minsheng Banking Corp Ltd |
| Indian Bank | Chongqing Rural Commercial Bank Co Ltd |
| Indian Overseas Bank | Dah Sing Banking Group Ltd |
| IndusInd Bank Ltd | Hang Seng Bank Ltd |
| Kotak Mahindra Bank Ltd | Harbin Bank Co Ltd |
| Oriental Bank of Commerce | HSBC Holdings PLC |
| Punjab National Bank | Huishang Bank Corp Ltd |
| State Bank of India | Industrial & Commercial Bank of China Ltd |
| Syndicate Bank | Postal Savings Bank of China Co Ltd |
| UCO Bank | Standard Chartered PLC |
| Union Bank of India | |
| Yes Bank Ltd | |

*Source:* Authors' compilation

# Appendix 14D

Table 14D.1 *Data Set Used for T-test, Chi-Square and Levene's Test*

| *Time* | *Economy* | *ROE (%)* | *ROA (%)* | *NPL (%)* | *Indicator* |
|---|---|---|---|---|---|
| 2018 Q3 | India | -14.8464 | -0.75 | 13.90062 | 0 |
| 2018 Q2 | India | -5.02653 | -0.33 | 12.47183 | 0 |
| 2018 Q1 | India | -19.5772 | -1.01 | 12.26689 | 0 |
| 2017 Q4 | India | 2.288056 | 0.13 | 5.939453 | 0 |
| 2017 Q3 | India | 1.85846 | 0.12 | 12.00038 | 0 |
| 2017 Q2 | India | 3.401828 | 0.20 | 5.573989 | 0 |
| 2017 Q1 | India | 2.969414 | 0.16 | 10.06141 | 0 |
| 2016 Q4 | India | 2.309528 | 0.14 | 7.237709 | 0 |
| 2016 Q3 | India | -3.16012 | -0.17 | 8.681881 | 0 |
| 2016 Q2 | India | 4.597896 | 0.81 | 2.725831 | 0 |
| 2016 Q1 | India | -2.25097 | -0.08 | 8.983228 | 0 |
| 2015 Q4 | India | 9.141888 | 0.58 | 2.300919 | 0 |
| 2015 Q3 | India | 7.187409 | 0.44 | 4.86001 | 0 |
| 2015 Q2 | India | 10.05678 | 0.97 | 1.893169 | 0 |
| 2015 Q1 | India | 8.87817 | 0.51 | 4.430231 | 0 |
| 2014 Q4 | India | 10.9163 | 0.67 | 1.87006 | 0 |
| 2014 Q3 | India | 10.10882 | 0.58 | 4.73447 | 0 |
| 2014 Q2 | India | 13.05148 | 1.22 | 1.682792 | 0 |
| 2014 Q1 | India | 10.24724 | 0.63 | 3.170737 | 0 |
| 2013 Q4 | India | 13.16569 | 0.82 | 1.683349 | 0 |
| 2013 Q3 | India | 11.92368 | 0.71 | 3.468423 | 0 |
| 2013 Q2 | India | 15.16382 | 1.67 | 1.950254 | 1 |
| 2013 Q1 | India | 14.92261 | 0.90 | 3.176542 | 1 |
| 2012 Q4 | India | 16.71371 | 1.09 | 2.312477 | 1 |
| 2012 Q3 | India | 16.526 | 1.01 | 2.268107 | 1 |
| 2012 Q2 | India | 18.63679 | 1.51 | 1.721837 | 1 |
| 2012 Q1 | India | 16.75803 | 1.05 | 2.164236 | 1 |
| 2011 Q4 | India | 17.70689 | 1.41 | 1.858368 | 1 |
| 2011 Q3 | India | 17.15263 | 1.19 | 1.822381 | 1 |

*(Continued)*

*(Continued)*

| *Time* | *Economy* | *ROE (%)* | *ROA (%)* | *NPL (%)* | *Indicator* |
|---|---|---|---|---|---|
| 2011 Q2 | India | 17.07864 | 1.40 | 1.320981 | 1 |
| 2011 Q1 | India | 18.04353 | 1.31 | 1.746395 | 1 |
| 2018 Q3 | China | 13.60207 | 0.888809 | 1.51149 | 0 |
| 2018 Q2 | China | 13.93768 | 0.888092 | 1.490833 | 0 |
| 2018 Q1 | China | 14.00106 | 0.894425 | 1.496853 | 0 |
| 2017 Q4 | China | 13.99894 | 0.916661 | 1.552596 | 0 |
| 2017 Q3 | China | 14.69017 | 0.949208 | 1.513949 | 1 |
| 2017 Q2 | China | 14.47323 | 0.946498 | 1.565509 | 1 |
| 2017 Q1 | China | 14.69362 | 0.915569 | 1.53955 | 1 |
| 2016 Q4 | China | 15.00642 | 0.963029 | 1.59875 | 1 |
| 2016 Q3 | China | 15.28329 | 0.997919 | 1.560754 | 1 |
| 2016 Q2 | China | 15.5432 | 1.003963 | 1.544407 | 1 |
| 2016 Q1 | China | 15.99209 | 1.038296 | 1.542833 | 1 |
| 2015 Q4 | China | 16.38145 | 1.069623 | 1.583002 | 1 |
| 2015 Q3 | China | 16.86611 | 1.070619 | 1.432324 | 1 |
| 2015 Q2 | China | 17.45195 | 1.074183 | 1.405539 | 1 |
| 2015 Q1 | China | 17.21277 | 1.120364 | 1.291453 | 1 |
| 2014 Q4 | China | 17.58158 | 1.175396 | 1.194479 | 1 |
| 2014 Q3 | China | 18.60598 | 1.183075 | 1.097416 | 1 |
| 2014 Q2 | China | 18.94453 | 1.175979 | 1.030046 | 1 |
| 2014 Q1 | China | 18.82266 | 1.167522 | 0.995254 | 1 |
| 2013 Q4 | China | 20.00996 | 1.196234 | 0.963105 | 1 |
| 2013 Q3 | China | 20.98003 | 1.178535 | 0.903736 | 1 |
| 2013 Q2 | China | 21.19284 | 1.157255 | 0.897207 | 1 |
| 2013 Q1 | China | 19.91932 | 1.144477 | 0.873013 | 1 |
| 2012 Q4 | China | 20.73636 | 1.181014 | 0.915923 | 1 |
| 2012 Q3 | China | 20.97259 | 1.30505 | 0.867093 | 1 |
| 2012 Q2 | China | 22.28675 | 1.264799 | 0.891793 | 1 |
| 2012 Q1 | China | 21.20189 | 1.276539 | 0.892599 | 1 |
| 2011 Q4 | China | 20.91757 | 1.271622 | 0.937373 | 1 |
| 2011 Q3 | China | 22.58669 | 1.340407 | 0.980096 | 1 |
| 2011 Q2 | China | 21.4282 | 1.193793 | 0.965594 | 1 |
| 2011 Q1 | China | 21.17326 | 1.152694 | 1.027984 | 1 |

*Note:* 1 indicates above adjusted average whereas 0 indicates below adjusted average where adjusted average ROE is 14.002%

Table 14D.2 *Data Set Used for regression of ROE and NPL of Chinese Banking Industry*

| *Time* | *Economy* | *ROE* | *ROA* | *NPA* |
|---|---|---|---|---|
| 2018 Q3 | China | 13.60207 | 0.888809 | 1.51149 |
| 2018 Q2 | China | 13.93768 | 0.888092 | 1.490833 |
| 2018 Q1 | China | 14.00106 | 0.894425 | 1.496853 |
| 2017 Q4 | China | 13.99894 | 0.916661 | 1.552596 |
| 2017 Q3 | China | 14.69017 | 0.949208 | 1.513949 |
| 2017 Q2 | China | 14.47323 | 0.946498 | 1.565509 |
| 2017 Q1 | China | 14.69362 | 0.915569 | 1.53955 |
| 2016 Q4 | China | 15.00642 | 0.963029 | 1.59875 |
| 2016 Q3 | China | 15.28329 | 0.997919 | 1.560754 |
| 2016 Q2 | China | 15.5432 | 1.003963 | 1.544407 |
| 2016 Q1 | China | 15.99209 | 1.038296 | 1.542833 |
| 2015 Q4 | China | 16.38145 | 1.069623 | 1.583002 |
| 2015 Q3 | China | 16.86611 | 1.070619 | 1.432324 |
| 2015 Q2 | China | 17.45195 | 1.074183 | 1.405539 |
| 2015 Q1 | China | 17.21277 | 1.120364 | 1.291453 |
| 2014 Q4 | China | 17.58158 | 1.175396 | 1.194479 |
| 2014 Q3 | China | 18.60598 | 1.183075 | 1.097416 |
| 2014 Q2 | China | 18.94453 | 1.175979 | 1.030046 |
| 2014 Q1 | China | 18.82266 | 1.167522 | 0.995254 |
| 2013 Q4 | China | 20.00996 | 1.196234 | 0.963105 |
| 2013 Q3 | China | 20.98003 | 1.178535 | 0.903736 |
| 2013 Q2 | China | 21.19284 | 1.157255 | 0.897207 |
| 2013 Q1 | China | 19.91932 | 1.144477 | 0.873013 |
| 2012 Q4 | China | 20.73636 | 1.181014 | 0.915923 |
| 2012 Q3 | China | 20.97259 | 1.30505 | 0.867093 |
| 2012 Q2 | China | 22.28675 | 1.264799 | 0.891793 |
| 2012 Q1 | China | 21.20189 | 1.276539 | 0.892599 |
| 2011 Q4 | China | 20.91757 | 1.271622 | 0.937373 |
| 2011 Q3 | China | 22.58669 | 1.340407 | 0.980096 |
| 2011 Q2 | China | 21.4282 | 1.193793 | 0.965594 |
| 2011 Q1 | China | 21.17326 | 1.152694 | 1.027984 |

Table 14D.3 *Data Set Used for Regression of ROE and NPL of Indian Banking Industry*

| *Time* | *Economy* | *ROE* | *ROA* | *NPA* |
|---|---|---|---|---|
| 2018 Q3 | India | -14.8464 | -0.7459 | 13.90062 |
| 2018 Q2 | India | -5.02653 | -0.3251 | 12.47183 |
| 2018 Q1 | India | -19.5772 | -1.00629 | 12.26689 |
| 2017 Q4 | India | 2.288056 | 0.131772 | 5.939453 |
| 2017 Q3 | India | 1.85846 | 0.122648 | 12.00038 |
| 2017 Q2 | India | 3.401828 | 0.204453 | 5.573989 |
| 2017 Q1 | India | 2.969414 | 0.160221 | 10.06141 |
| 2016 Q4 | India | 2.309528 | 0.136942 | 7.237709 |
| 2016 Q3 | India | -3.16012 | -0.17212 | 8.681881 |
| 2016 Q2 | India | 4.597896 | 0.8065 | 2.725831 |
| 2016 Q1 | India | -2.25097 | -0.07671 | 8.983228 |
| 2015 Q4 | India | 9.141888 | 0.584839 | 2.300919 |
| 2015 Q3 | India | 7.187409 | 0.441755 | 4.86001 |
| 2015 Q2 | India | 10.05678 | 0.971184 | 1.893169 |
| 2015 Q1 | India | 8.87817 | 0.507137 | 4.430231 |
| 2014 Q4 | India | 10.9163 | 0.669269 | 1.87006 |
| 2014 Q3 | India | 10.10882 | 0.580359 | 4.73447 |
| 2014 Q2 | India | 13.05148 | 1.219623 | 1.682792 |
| 2014 Q1 | India | 10.24724 | 0.63086 | 3.170737 |
| 2013 Q4 | India | 13.16569 | 0.820249 | 1.683349 |
| 2013 Q3 | India | 11.92368 | 0.714695 | 3.468423 |
| 2013 Q2 | India | 15.16382 | 1.669099 | 1.950254 |
| 2013 Q1 | India | 14.92261 | 0.90265 | 3.176542 |
| 2012 Q4 | India | 16.71371 | 1.088548 | 2.312477 |
| 2012 Q3 | India | 16.526 | 1.014309 | 2.268107 |
| 2012 Q2 | India | 18.63679 | 1.511646 | 1.721837 |
| 2012 Q1 | India | 16.75803 | 1.04901 | 2.164236 |
| 2011 Q4 | India | 17.70689 | 1.411798 | 1.858368 |
| 2011 Q3 | India | 17.15263 | 1.189075 | 1.822381 |
| 2011 Q2 | India | 17.07864 | 1.400799 | 1.320981 |
| 2011 Q1 | India | 18.04353 | 1.313711 | 1.746395 |

*Source:* Authors' calculations

## References


Alicia G. H, G. Sergio, and Daniel. 2009. What Explains the Low Profitability of Chinese Banks? *Journal of Banking and Finance* 33 (11), 2080–2092.

Berger, A. N. 1995. 'The Relationship between Capital and Earnings in Banking.' *Journal of Money, Credit and Banking* 27 (2), 432–456.

Broadman, Harry G. 1999. 'The Chinese State as Corporate Shareholder.' *Finance and Development* 36 (3). International Monetary Fund.

Das, A., and S. C. Kumbhakar. 2012. Productivity and Efficiency Dynamics in Indian Banking: An Input Distance Function Approach Incorporating Quality of Inputs and Outputs. *Journal of Applied Econometrics* 27 (2), 205–234.

Das, S. K., and I. Drine. 2011. 'Financial Liberalization and Banking Sector.' *International Business and Management* 2 (1), 42–58.

Rasidah, M. S., and Mohd H.T. 2011, Performance and Financial Ratios of Commercial Banks in Malaysia and China International Review of Business Research Papers 7(2), 157–169.

Kumar, N, A. Shrivastava, D. P Singh, P. Kumar. 2018. 'Determinants of Financial Stress of Indian Banks: Hierarchical Bayesian Panel Data Modelling.' *South Asia Economic Journal* 19(2):210–228 ©2018 Research and Information System for Developing Countries & Institute of Policy Studies of Sri Lanka. SAGE Publications. http://sagepub.in/home.nav http://doi.org/10.1177/139156141879469

Nguyen, P. 2017. Comparison of Efficiency and Technology across the Banking Systems of Vietnam, China and India: A Stochastic Cost and Revenue Meta-frontier Approach. *Benchmarking: An International Journal.* https://doi.org/10.1108/BIJ-04-2017-0078

Reserve Bank of India. 2016. 'Financial Institutions: Soundness and Resilience.' Financial Stability Report, Issue Brief No. 14. Mumbai: Reserve Bank of India.

Sayuri, S. 2002, December. Banking Sector Reforms In India And China: Does India's Experience Offer Lessons For China's Future Reform Agenda? *Asia-Pacific Development Journal* 9 (2).

Srinivasan, P, and J. Britto. 2017. 'Analysis of Financial Performance of Selected Commercial Banks in India, Scientific Research Publishing.' *Theoretical Economics Letters* 7, 2134–2151.

Tan, Y., and C. Floros. 2012a. 'Bank Profitability and Inflation: The Case of China.' *Journal of Economic Studies* 39 (6), 675–696.

Tan, Yong A. 2017. Competition and Profitability in the Chinese Banking Industry: New Evidence from Different Banking Markets. http://doi.org/10.13140/RG.2.2.15412.55689

Wanniarachchige, M. K., and Y. Suzuki. 2011. 'How Does Ownership Affect Bank Performance? The Case of Indian Commercial Banks.' *International Business & Economics Research Journal (IBER)* 10 (3), 71–82.

CHAPTER 15

# A Comparative Study of the Deposit Insurance Systems in India and China

Yun Fang

## Introduction

Deposit insurance, which provides protection to depositors, especially small ones, is a very important part of the national financial safety net. People can recover their loss of deposits under the deposit insurance scheme within a maximum limit set by the legislation, which would provide confidence in the current banking system. China issued rules on bank deposit insurance scheme in 2015 and the rules took effect on 1 May 2015. As the first developing country that introduced a bank deposit insurance scheme, India has put in place a mode of operation and management methods through more than half a century's practice. This study makes a comparative analysis of the similarities as well as the differences that the deposit insurance systems present in India and China in order to provide some useful suggestions to improve the deposit insurance scheme in China.

## The Background of the Deposit Insurance System

### *The Banking System in India and China*

The diverse structure of Indian banking system determines the complexity of the banking market. Natarajan and Parameswaran (2013) point out that the whole country's organized banking institutions are generally divided into two groups: scheduled banks and non-scheduled banks. Scheduled banks mainly consist of scheduled commercial banks and scheduled cooperative banks. Scheduled commercial banks, which constitute a major proportion of the financial business that scheduled banks engage in, are often divided into four different categories: public sector banks, private sector banks, foreign banks and regional rural banks. The classification is based on their ownership and the way of their establishment. Scheduled cooperative banks are made up of scheduled urban cooperative banks (UCBs) and rural cooperative banks based on the banks' locations. Scheduled cooperative banks are made up of scheduled urban cooperative banks (UCBs), state cooperative banks and district central cooperative banks (DCCBs) based on the banks' locations. According to the data released by the Reserve Bank of India (RBI) in December 2020, there are 53 UCBs, 33 state cooperative banks and 365 DCCBs. The latest official data shows that the banking sector accounts for 63 per cent of the market share of financial assets and public sector banks continue to dominate the banking sector with a 72.8 per cent market share of financial assets and 83 per cent of branches (Subbarao, 2013).

Before the reform and opening up which started from 1978, the banking system in China was called a mono-banking system in which the Peoples' Bank of China (PBOC) not only played a key role in the state at macro-control, but also monopolized nearly the entire commercial banking business of the country at the same time. The modern Chinese banking system started its evolution since market reforms that were implemented by Deng Xiaoping in 1978. Within 30 years of reforms, China has established a multilevel, diversified commercial banking system which is summarized in the Table 15.1. Recent figures collected from the China Banking and Insurance Regulatory Commission (CBIRC) indicates that there are 4,112 deposit-taking banking financial institutions operating within the territory of China by the end of 2018.

Table 15.1 *Deposit-taking Banking Financial Institutions in China*

| *Bank Name* | *Number of Bank Branches* |
|---|---|
| China Development Bank | 1 |
| Large Commercial Bank | 5 |
| Joint Stock Commercial Bank | 12 |
| Postal Savings Bank of China | 1 |
| Sino-German Bausparkasse | 1 |
| City Commercial Bank | 134 |
| Rural Commercial Bank | 1311 |
| Rural Cooperative Bank | 31 |
| Rural Credit Cooperatives | 907 |
| Village Bank | 1594 |
| Rural Mutual cooperatives | 47 |
| Foreign Banks | 41 |
| Private Banks | 17 |

*Source:* CBIRC (2019a).
*Note:* China Development Bank (CDB) was founded in 1994 as one of three policy-oriented banks in China. The reform of CDB in 2008 has transformed the once largest policy-oriented bank in China into a commercial bank. Sino-German Bausparkasse founded in 2004 is the first China-German mortgage savings bank in China, which is jointly hold by China Construction Bank and Bausparkasse Schwäebisch Hall hold. The bank provides housing financing solutions.

According to the data issued by the Statistics and Analysis Department of PBOC (2019), the fund balance that China's entire economy obtains from the financial system was RMB 200.75 trillion (USD 29.73 trillion) up to the end of December 2018 and bank-based financing business accounted for 76.3 per cent. Within the banking system, five large commercial banks enjoy 36.67 per cent of the market share of financial assets and the second is joint stock commercial banks which take 17.53 per cent, a relatively small share (CBIRC, 2019b).

While comparing the organizational structure of the financial market in India and China, we find that the two markets do have many similarities. First, banks definitely dominate the two countries' financial system.

Second, the majority stake on the banks are held by the government, which continue to dominate the banking system. The primary reason that makes public sector banks obtain a control status in Indian banking system could be attributed to the nationalization of major commercial banks and the expansion of bank branches during 1969–1991. In China, similar situation resulted from the centralization of allocation power of financial resources during the Forging Ahead Strategy under the joint action of planned economy, public ownership and financial sovereignty. Although in recent years, both governments have continuously engaged in the market-oriented banking reform, the structure of the financial markets in the two countries has not changed fundamentally. This special structure is one of the most important factors that should be taken into consideration while designing the deposit insurance scheme.

### *The Banking Supervision System in India and China*

In India, RBI is authorized with sweeping powers to regulate and supervise most of the banking institutions as per the Banking Companies Act of 1949. The act was later renamed as Banking Regulation Act of 1949 according to an amending Act of 1965. As a regulator and supervisor from the central government, the RBI provides guarantee for healthy development, orderly competition and continuous stability of the banking sector by carrying out preventive actions and corrective measures. However, it should be pointed out that RBI is not the only banking supervisor in India. Besides, some governmental agencies, either central or local, share the responsibilities with RBI. For example, National Bank for Agriculture and Rural Development is mainly responsible for the regulation and supervision of regional rural banks, and the urban banks departments set up by local authorities are the principal regulators and supervisors of Urban Co-operative Banks.

In China, PBOC used to be the primary regulator and supervisor of banking financial institutions during the early period of the banking sector reform that started in 1979. The powers and responsibilities were handed over to the China Banking Regulatory Commission (CBRC) since 2003 and for many years CBRC was responsible for supervising and regulating banking financial institutions. Changes happened on 13 March 2018, when the National People's Congress announced a reform plan of China's financial regulatory system according to which

CBRC was merged with China Insurance Regulatory Commission and was renamed as CBIRC. The purpose of this merger was to try to address some new problems such as cross-sector regulation and overlapping responsibilities when the mixed operation has become a mainstream in the country's financial market. It may be noted that the newly created CBIRC will transfer some authority to PBOC including the responsibility for drafting key regulations and prudential oversight rules in banking and insurance industries. The CBIRC came into effect on 2 April 2018. It may be noted that deposit insurance fund management institution is authorized to impose early intervention actions and risk disposal measures on problem banks according to the Deposit Insurance Regulation (DIR) of 2015. Meanwhile, there are some special arrangements for the supervision and regulation of rural banking financial institutions that consist of the following types: rural commercial banks, rural credit cooperatives, rural cooperative banks and village banks. Of particular note is that the provincial government is mainly responsible for the resolution of rural banking financial institutions when these institutions failed.

## An Overview of Deposit Insurance System

### *Development of the Deposit Insurance System in India*

The development of deposit insurance system in India can be divided into the following four stages.

#### Stage 1. The Establishment of Deposit Insurance Scheme

It is commonly believed that the failure of the Travancore National and Quilon Bank in 1938 caused the public in India for the first time to realize the importance of providing insurance of deposits kept in banks. Thorat (2007) studied the early history of deposit insurance in India and found that the legislation of deposit insurance was not put in place until the subsequent failures of Laxmi Bank and the Palai Central Bank happened in 1961. The Deposit Insurance Corporation (DIC) Bill was passed by the Parliament in 1961 and came into force on 1 January 1962. Initially, the deposit insurance scheme only covered commercial banks, which means that the depositors of cooperative banks such as UCBs or rural cooperative banks could not get any compensation from the deposit insurance scheme if these banks failed. In order to broaden the protection scope and make the deposit insurance scheme benefit more detail depositors, the membership of policyholders was extended to all the eligible co-operative banks as per the enactment of the DIC (Amendment) Act in 1968.

### Stage 2. The Merger of DIC and Credit Guarantee Corporation of India

The Credit Guarantee Corporation (CGCI) was set up by the RBI, the purpose of which is to encourage commercial banks to offer a variety of loans to promote the development of hitherto neglected sectors. The specific approach was that CGCI provided loan and advance guarantees that were issued to small and needy borrowers by the commercial banks within the priority sector lending. In 1978, DIC combined with CGCI to form the present the Deposit Insurance and Credit Guarantee Corporation (DICGC) and the DIC Act was then renamed DICGC Act of 1961. After the merger, DICGC switched its focus from deposit insurance to providing credit guarantees. Part of this change was due to the fact that most of the large banks that time in India were public ownership banks and all stakeholders of the society had a perceptual understanding that banks shall never fail.

### Stage 3. The Evolution of Deposit Insurance System

With the deepening of the financial sector reform that took place in India during the 1990s, commercial banks' demand for credit guarantees significantly decreased. After the1997 Asian Financial Crisis, though public sector banks still dominated the banking system, the market shares held by private banks and foreign banks gradually increased. All of these made the DICGC veered its focus back to deposit insurance that used to be its original function, the purposes of which were stated as to avert public panics, reduce financial systemic risk, and ensure the financial stability.

### Stage 4. Reforms of Deposit Insurance during the Post Financial Crisis Era

After the 2008 global financial crisis, support to reform the present deposit insurance system in India has been growing. The Union Cabinet of India approved the legislative proposal to introduce the Financial Resolution and Deposit Insurance (FRDI) Bill on 15 June 2017. The FRDI Bill proposed to establish a Resolution Corporation to take over the deposit insurance functions from the DICGC. Compared with the DICGC Act of 1961, the FRDI Bill made significant reforms in many aspects like making the deposit insurer an independent legal entity with extensive powers to deal with problematic banks. The purpose of FRDI Bill was to set up a new resolution regime of the failed financial institutions like banks and non-banking financial institutions. However, the opposition parties severely criticized that some of the FRDI Bill's provisions were anti-people, especially the poor. For example, the 'bail-in' clause is one of the most controversial issues related to the FRDI Bill, which suggests that deposit might be written-off or be subject to a cut in order to help the failing financial institutions to avoid liquidation. Depositors and bank customers are extremely worried that their money could be used to save problematic banks that get into trouble just because of their own greed. Finally, the Indian government announced that it had withdrawn the FRDI Bill from the Lok Sabha on 7th August 2018.

### *Evolution of the Deposit Insurance System in China*

China passed the DIR on 31st March 2015, nearly 22 years after the Chinese government first began to discuss the necessity of establishing a deposit insurance scheme. Table 15.2 shows the long and difficult process of the legislation.

Table 15.2 *The Legislation Process of DIR*

| *Time* | *Important Movement* |
|---|---|
| December 1993 | Deposit insurance was first mentioned in the official document in China |
| October 2004 | The proposal of establishing a deposit insurance scheme was reported to the State Council by POBC |
| January 2007 | The third National Finance Working Conference announced that the deposit insurance scheme should be extended to all functioning depository institutions |
| January 2012 | The fourth National Finance Working Conference announced that relevant departments should pay close attention to the study and formulation of deposit insurance scheme |

| *Time* | *Important Movement* |
|---|---|
| March 2014 | Building up a deposit insurance system was officially written into the Work Report of the Chinese Government in 2014 |
| November 2014 | The DIR draft was released for public comments |
| March 2015 | The DIR was officially issued |
| April 2015 | The Financial Stability Bureau of PBC has been provisionally designated as Deposit Insurance Fund Manager by the State Council in the initial stages of operation. |
| May 2015 | The DIR came into force |

Now, all the deposit-taking banking financial institutions formed within the territory of China have undergone the deposit insurance formalities. According to the latest report issued by the financial stability bureau of PBOC, the deposit insurance fund has reached a level of RMB 82.12 billion by the end of December 2018 (Financial Stability Bureau of PBOC, 2019). The National Enterprise Credit information disclosure system shows that the Deposit Insurance Fund Management Company (DIFMC) with registered capital of RMB 10 billion was established on 24th May 2019 (Wu, Zhang and Jia, 2019). As an independent deposit insurance fund manager, DIFMC shall play a much more important role in cleaning up deposit-taking banking financial institutions' risks in the foreseeable future.

## Fundamentals of the Deposit Insurance System

According to the Revised Core Principles for Effective Deposit Insurance Systems made by the International Association of Deposit Insurers (IADI), the legislation mode of deposit insurance from all countries and regions can be classified into four categories based on the differences of the powers and responsibilities that the deposit insurer assumes during the resolution of failed banks. These four modes are pay box, pay box plus, loss minimizer and risk minimizer (IADI, 2014). In a pay box mode, the deposit insurer is only responsible for making compensation to the insured depositors within a maximum limit set by the legislation when a bank goes into bankruptcy. In a pay box plus mode, the deposit insurer has assumed some additional responsibilities besides the reimbursement, like providing special financial support during the resolution of failed banks. In a loss minimizer mode, the insurer plays a very important role during the resolution of failed banks and has more powers to use multiple strategies to minimize the resolution cost. In risk minimizer mode, the deposit insurer has comprehensive risk minimization functions, which range from the early intervention to the final resolution, and in some countries like the United States, the insurer even becomes the main regulator of some certain kind of depository institution such as state banks and state savings and loan associations that participate the deposit insurance scheme but are not in the Federal Reserve System. After the 2008 financial crisis, all countries and regions are universally concerned about role of the deposit insurance system as an important resolution platform for problem financial institutions. Those countries that have not established deposit insurance scheme such as China, have prioritized the drafting of legislation. Those countries that have already put in places their deposit insurance system such

A. The Mandate of Deposit Insurer

| *India* | | *China* |
|---|---|---|
| *DICGC Act* | *FRDI Bill (Draft)* | *DIR* |
| Paybox | Risk Minimizer | Risk Minimizer |
| Deposit insurer is responsible only for payment of funds in the event of bank failure | Deposit insurer has comprehensive risk reduction and mitigation functions and commensurate powers of assessment, oversight, early intervention and final resolution | Deposit insurer has comprehensive risk reduction and mitigation functions and commensurate powers of assessment, oversight, early intervention and final resolution |

B. The Organization of the Deposit Insurance Institution

| *India* | | *China* |
|---|---|---|
| *DICGC Act* | *FRDI Bill (Draft)* | *DIR* |
| DICGC<br>a subsidiary of RBI | Resolution Corporation<br>Independent entity | DIFMC<br>Independent entity |

## C. The Covered Deposits

| *India* | | *China* |
|---|---|---|
| *DICGC Act* | *FRDI Bill (Draft)* | *DIR* |
| DICGC insures all bank deposits, such as savings, fixed, current, recurring, etc. except the following types:<br>①Deposits of foreign governments; ②Deposits of Central or State governments; ③Inter-bank deposits; ④Deposits of the State Land Development Banks with the State co-operative banks; ⑤Any amount due on account of any deposits received outside India; ⑥Any amount which has been specifically exempted by the corporation with the previous approval of the Reserve Bank. | No special regulations | China will insure deposits denominated in RMB and foreign currencies. Financial institutions' inter-bank deposits and deposits by senior managers in their own institutions are not covered. The Deposit Insurance Fund Manager may also exclude certain other deposits from the program. It's unclear if structured deposits are covered. |

## D. The Membership and Insurance Premium

| *India* | | *China* |
|---|---|---|
| *DICGC Act* | *FRDI Bill (Draft)* | *DIR* |
| All commercial banks including the branches of foreign banks functioning in India, Local Area Banks and Regional Rural Banks, and all eligible co-operative banks as defined in Section 2(gg) of the DICGC Act are covered by the Deposit Insurance Scheme.<br>The consideration for extension of insurance coverage to banks is payment of an insurance premium.<br>The premium paid by the insured banks to the corporation is required to be borne by the banks themselves so that the benefit of deposit insurance protection is made available to the depositors free of cost. | No special regulations | All deposit taking institutions are covered except foreign banks' branches, domestic banks' branches overseas and rural mutual cooperatives (RMCs).<br>The deposit insurance premium rate is made up of a basic rate (flat fee) and a risk-based differential rate determined by factors including the business management and risk conditions of the insured financial institution. |

## E. The Sources and Uses of the Deposit Insurance Funds

| | India | | China |
|---|---|---|---|
| DICGC Act | | FRDI Bill (Draft) | DIR |
| Sources | ① Deposit insurance premium; ② Recoveries from the assets of the failed banks; ③ Advance from RBI; ④ Money transferred from General Fund or Credit Guarantee Fund; ⑤ Income from investments | No special regulations | ① Deposit insurance premium; ② Recoveries from the assets of the failed banks; ③ Income from investments; ④ Others |
| Uses | ① Make payments of insured deposits; ② Meet liability of an advance from RBI; ③ Transfer money back to the General Fund or the Credit Guarantee Fund; ④ Investment; ⑤ Deposit in the RBI; ⑥ Administrative expenses | ① Make payments of insured deposits; ② Make payments to the other insured service provider that takes over the deposits and the assets of the insured service provider; ③ Make payments to the other insured service provider that takes over the insured service provider; ④ Make payments for liquidating and forming a bridge bank | ① Paying insured deposits; ② Providing guarantee, loss sharing or financial support for other qualified institutional policyholders to facilitate their acquisition or assumption of all or part of the businesses, assets, and liabilities of institutional policyholders to be taken over or cancelled or applying for bankruptcy; ③ Deposit in the PBC; ④ Investment ⑤ Others |

## F. The Coverage Level and Claims Settlement

| | *India* | | *China* |
|---|---|---|---|
| | *DICGC Act* | *FRDI Bill (Draft)* | *DIR* |
| Coverage Level | In the event of liquidation, reconstruction or amalgamation of an insured bank, every depositor of that bank in all branches is entitled to repayment of his deposits held by him in the same capacity and right in that bank up to a monetary ceiling of ₹1,00,000. | Uncertain | The maximum payout amount per depositor per institution is RMB 5,00,000 (USD 76,001), including principal and interest, with unpaid amounts in excess of the maximum payout to be claimed from the liquidation of assets of the relevant financial institution. This plan is estimated to fully cover 99.6 per cent of all Chinese depositors but constitutes only 46 per cent of all money on deposit. |
| Claims Settlement | ① Where an insured bank has been ordered to be wound up or to be taken into liquidation, the corporation shall pay the amount payable to the insured depositors directly, or through other agency, or to the liquidator within five months;<br>② Where any depositor to whom any payment is to be made cannot be found or is not readily traceable, adequate provision shall be made by the corporation for such payment and the amount of such provision shall be accounted for separately in its books. | ① The corporation shall pay the amount payable to all the depositors of the insured provider directly or to the transferee insured service provider within three months since the resolution scheme takes effect;<br>② Where an insured service provider has been ordered to be liquidated, the corporation shall pay the amount payable to all the depositors within 150 days in the same way above | ① Directly paying insured deposits within the limit set by this regulation.;<br>② Engaging other qualified institutional policyholders to pay insured deposits for it within the limit set by this regulation |

as India seek for reforms and improvement by drawing lessons from the crisis (Committee Draft of the Financial Resolution and Deposit Insurance Bill, 2017). The comparative analysis of the fundamentals in the deposit insurance system between the two countries could provide some insights when evaluating advantages and disadvantages of the DIR.

A comparison of the institutional factors in the deposit insurance schemes in India and China, reveals that 'great minds think alike'. For example, the present system in India chooses the paybox mode which has been proved incompetent during the 2008 financial crisis in dealing with moral hazard and regulatory forbearance. This is mainly because the deposit insurer does not have the power to take prompt corrective actions when the insured depository institutions could not meet the capital standards set by the authorities. This partly explains why Indian government tried to introduce the FRDI Bill that adopted a risk minimizer mode to provide the deposit insurers with extensive regulatory and resolution powers. Though it is still unclear what DIFMC's full mandate will be, the provisions in DIR of 2015 make clear from the very beginning that China chooses the risk minimizer mode. This is evident from the following:

> Article 7: The deposit insurance fund management institution shall perform the following duties: ... (6) Taking early corrective actions and risk disposal measures under this Regulation....
>
> Article 18: The deposit insurance fund management institution may use the deposit insurance fund by the following methods to protect the interests of depositors: ... (3) Providing guarantee, loss sharing or financial support for other qualified institutional policyholders to facilitate their acquisition or assumption of all or part of the businesses, assets, and liabilities of institutional policyholders to be taken over or cancelled or applying for bankruptcy. (DIR of 2015)

Another example is the insurance attendance. Considering the importance of banking sector and the differences in capital adequacy ratio, management level, quality of assets and liquidity between different deposit-taking financial institutions, both India and China choose to set up a compulsory rather than optional deposit insurance scheme to avoid adverse selection in the banking market.

However, we should realize that the Chinese deposit insurance system is still in its initial stage with inherent limitations compared with those mature deposit insurance system in countries like India. It is evident that there are three pertinent issues.

First, certain types of deposit-taking banking financial institutions are excluded from the insured depository institution list under the present deposit insurance scheme. The most controversial objects are the foreign banks' branches. Foreign banks, since 1979, have established more than 1013 operations in the Chinese mainland, increasing at an average annual growth rate of 13 per cent over the last 15 years, and their total assets grew more than tenfold from 2001 to RMB 3.2 trillion as of the end of 2017 (Jiang Xueqing, 2018). According to the draft amendment of the Detailed Rules for the Implementation of the Regulation on the Administration of Foreign-Funded Banks of 2018 (the Draft Amendment of AFFB Rules of 2018), which was published last year by CBIRC for public consultation, a foreign bank's branches are not subject to the deposit insurance scheme unless China has established a special arrangement with the parent country (the Draft Amendment of AFFB Rules of 2018). Generally speaking, there are four types of legislation to deal with the problem that whether or not to take the foreign banks' branches into the host country's deposit insurance scheme. In the first type, taking the United States for example, it is compulsory for all the foreign banks' branches to participate in the host country's deposit insurance scheme regardless whether the parent country shall provide deposit insurance or not. In the second type, the foreign banks' branches could choose to stay out of the host country's deposit insurance scheme provided the parent country has offered such kind of insurance, even if the coverage level in the parent country are lower than that in the host country. In the third type, which is adopted by the European Union, the parent country priority principle is usually set down in regional agreements, which requires the parent country to provide deposit insurance first and the host country will fill in the gap of compensation to the depositors if its coverage level of deposit insurance is higher than the parent country.

In type four, the host country shall not provide any protection of the deposits kept in the foreign banks' branches. China has taken the last approach. If the parent country adopts 'the principle of personality' and excludes the banks' branches overseas from the insured depository institution list, the depositors in the host country that chooses type four could not recover their loss from any deposit insurance scheme. With the deepening of global financial liberalization, bank's risk could easily transmit from the host country to the parent country. Besides, it is doubted that China's option, to some extent, deviates from the principles of 'national treatment' and 'same market entry and administrative standards' elaborated by the Draft Amendment of AFFB Rules, which is just announced by CBIRC last year. Most Asian economies such as India and Japan have already extended the coverage of deposit insurance to foreign banks' domestic branches. Some Asian countries like Korea and the Philippines have gone further by extending their membership of policyholders to domestic banks' branches overseas. Another controversial object is the RMC, a community-based mutual banking financial institution, which is jointly funded by the farmers of a township (town), administrative village, and rural small enterprises and provides their members with multiple financial services such as deposits, loans and settlements (Interim Provisions on the Administration of Rural Mutual Cooperatives of 2007). According to the current legal provisions, RMCs can do business of deposit taking but is restricted to their members only. In the written answers to No. 7668 and No. 9089 proposals made by the fifth session of the 12th National People's Congress, CBRC (now is CBIRC) explained that the reason why RMCs are excluded from the deposit insurance scheme is because the DIR of 2015 defines the insured institution to banking financial institutions but the Law of the People's Republic of China on Banking Supervision and Control (LBSC) of 2006 limits the banking financial institution only to those financial intermediations taking deposits from the public. If we compare RMCs with rural cooperative credit institutions in India, we can find that the two banking entities do have many similarities in the organization structure and business operation except the former are excluded from the insured depository institution list while the latter are included. One of the core purposes of the deposit insurance is to guarantee the small depositors' legitimate rights and interests, especially those who live in rural areas. That explains why the Deposit Insurance Scheme in India extends the coverage to all eligible co-operative banks as defined in the DICGC Act of 1961. RMCs exert important functions in supporting the development of rural economics, but at the same time, this new-type rural financial institution is facing great risk due to its late starting, small scale and poor governance. Apparently, shutting RMCs out of the deposit insurance scheme will increase the institution's credit risk and put the depositors in a weak position, most of whom are farmers and rural enterprises.

Second, the powers and responsibilities of DIFMC during the resolution of problem banks are ambiguous. For example, the DIFMC is authorized to take early corrective actions such as requiring the problem bank to replenish capital, control asset growth and credit granting in major transactions if the capital adequacy ratio of the bank drops sharply, which seriously endangers the safety of deposits and the deposit insurance fund (DIR of 2015). However, beyond these general descriptions, few details about DIFMC as to how to work during the early intervention stage are prescribed in the current legislation. The absence of detailed rules has caused many controversies in practice when China implemented its deposit insurance system. The biggest controversy is the regulatory overlap. CBIRC has been assuming the responsibility of using early intervention measures to help problem banks as per LBSC of 2006, but there is no consensus on how to divide the powers as well as the responsibilities appropriately between DIFMC and CBIRC. The unpredictability of the trigger mechanism of early supervisory intervention regime has not only hindered banks' operation performance but has also impaired the stability of the whole banking market. Experience from the 2008 financial crisis has proved that the vague position of financial safety net players would cause a lot of problems when dealing with problem banks. India is doing much better than China in this aspect. Though the present deposit insurance system in India chooses paybox mode, the draft of FRDI bill tried to set up a special resolution regime of problem financial institutions in which an independent entity named Resolution Corporation is mainly responsible to enable timely and orderly resolution of failed banks and subsume DICGC to provide deposit insurance to the depositors in

India. The draft bill also attempted to introduce a basket of resolution tools by learning from the United States and European Union, which include purchase and assumption, bridge bank, bail-in, merger or amalgamation, acquisition and liquidation. The draft of the FRDI bill did not make a simple list of the resolution tools but set clear principles with a large number of specific rules for the application of each resolution tool. The legislative technique displayed in the draft bill is worth learning by Chinese legislative department.

Third, regulatory provisions in China's deposit insurance scheme are insufficient and poor in operation. At present, DIR of 2015 is the single source that can provide legal norms for the implementation of the deposit insurance scheme in China, but it has only 23 articles. There are some important provisions need to be further supplemented. For example, the present legislation just generally stipulates that the insurance rates applicable to each insured depository institution shall be determined by DIFMC on the basis of factors such as the operation and management situation and risk status (DIR of 2015) without providing any instruction as how to quantify the indexes and determine the percentage of different indexes. Another example is that legislation makes a requirement that DIFMC shall establish information sharing mechanisms with other banking regulatory authorities (DIR of 2015) but does not provide any further provision for DIFMC as how to coordinate and cooperate with other banking regulatory departments such as PBOC and CBIRC during the process of information sharing. It is quite necessary to establish a formalized and permanent mechanism to make sure that the DIFMC could obtain enough information in time and increase the efficiency of information exchange between DIFMC and other related financial regulators, otherwise the functions of the deposit insurance scheme shall be affected since the DIFMC does not have a steady flow of timely, comprehensive and accurate information.

## Conclusion

Three legislative suggestions are made here to improve China's deposit insurance scheme based on the comparative analysis above. First, in order to provide a higher level of protection for depositors and demonstrate the commitments made by China's central government to further relax existing restrictions and open up the banking sector to foreign investment, it is necessary to modify the definition of banking financial institution set up in LBSC and to extend the coverage of deposit insurance scheme in DIR to all deposit-taking banking financial institutions that includes foreign banks' branches and RMCs. Second, specify the powers as well as responsibilities of the DIFMC when it serves as the receiver or liquidator of a failed bank, and refine the coordination and cooperation process between the DIFMC and other financial safety net players. Besides, the 'No Creditor Worse Off' principle should be set up to restrain DIFMC's behaviour during the resolution of failed banks, which is that no creditor shall suffer greater losses than they would have incurred had the entire deposit-taking institution been subject to liquidation if the DIFMC decides to take a resolution action. Third, detailed rules for the implementation of DIR should be introduced as soon as possible by learning the successful experience of India and other countries where the deposit insurance schemes are well established. The new legislation program will fill in the legislative gaps in DIR and provide more operational basis for DIFMC.

## References

China Banking and Insurance Regulatory Commission (CBIRC). 2019a. *List of Banking Financial Institutions (up to December 31, 2018).* http://www.cbrc.gov.cn/chinese/files/2019/88C2C82DFD34470D9B2D441D553B80C4.pdf.

China Banking and Insurance Regulatory Commission (CBIRC). 2019b. *Statistical Targets of Banking Regulation.* http://www.cbrc.gov.cn/chinese/home/docView/C990691733D644B39582DEFA3EF1EF69.html

Committee Draft of the Financial Resolution and Deposit Insurance Bill 2019. 2017, § 2, 3, 13–21, 29–32, 48–83. https://dea.gov.in/sites/default/files/PressRelease02012018.pdf.

Deposit Insurance and Credit Guarantee Corporation Act. 1961. 2015, §2, 3, 6, 13–13D, 16–21, 23, 25A, 26, 27.

Deposit Insurance Regulation. 2015. §2, 4–7, 9, 11, 14, 16, 18–19.

Draft Amendment of the Detailed Rules for the Implementation of the Regulation on the Administration of Foreign-Funded Banks (2019, September 28). 2018, § 34. http://www.cbrc.gov.cn/chinese/newShouDoc/9CDBB24B331344EE91A47154B4340B2C.html.

Financial Stability Bureau of Peoples' Bank of China. 2019. *The Income and Expenditure Situation of Deposit Insurance Fund in 2018*. http://www.pbc.gov.cn/jinrongwendingju/146766/2165207/3794891/index.html.

Interim Provisions on the Administration of Rural Mutual Cooperatives, 2007, §2.

International Association of Deposit Insurers. 2014. *IADI Core Principles for Effective Deposit Insurance Systems (November 2014)*. https://www.iadi.org/en/assets/File/Core%20Principles/cprevised2014nov.pdf.

Jiang Xueqing. 2018. *Overseas Banks Urged to Tap Bay Area Opportunities*. http://www.chinadaily.com.cn/a/201805/25/WS5b0763d0a31001b82571c37c.html.

Law of the People's Republic of China on Banking Supervision and Control 2006. §2, 37–40.

Natarajan, S., and R. Parameswaran. 2013. *Indian Banking: For Students of B.Com/B.A. & Management Courses*. New Delhi: S. Chand & Company Ltd.

Reserve Bank of India. 2020. *Banks in India*. https://m.rbi.org.in/CommonPerson/english/scripts/banksinindia.aspx#SCB

Statistics and Analysis Department of Peoples' Bank of China. 2019. *Statistical Report of the fund balance of the Social Financing Scale*. http://www.pbc.gov.cn/diaochatongjisi/116219/116225/3745275/index.html.

Subbarao, Duvvuri. 2013. *Banking Structure in India Looking Ahead by Looking Back*. https://www.bis.org/review/r130813b.pdf.

Thorat, S. U. 2007. *Deposit Insurance—The Indian System*. https://www.dicgc.org.in/PUB_Spe_DepositInsurence.html.

Wu Yujian, Zhang Yuzhe, and Jia Denise. 2019. *PBOC Sets Up Deposit Insurance Fund Management Company*. https://www.caixinglobal.com/2019-05-30/pboc-sets-up-deposit-insurance-fund-management-company-101421410.html.

CHAPTER 16

# Price Dispersion in Retail Market in India

Nidhi Yadav

## Introduction and Background

Retail sector is emerging as one of the largest sectors in Indian economy. The retail market size is expected to grow from USD 672 billion in 2016 to USD 1,200 billion in 2021,[1] making India world's fifth largest destination in retail sector.[2] Indian retail market can be broadly divided into two categories 'Organized Retail Market', which was only 7 per cent of the total sector during financial year 2016–2017 and 'Unorganized Retail Market' constitutes rest 93 per cent of the sector.[3] The organized sector penetration is forecasted to reach 10 per cent by 2020 as organized retail is growing at fast pace threating the existing 15 million pop and mom stores.[4] Unorganized retail can be further divided into *kirana* (traditional variety) stores, street markets and kiosks.[5] Organized retail can be further divided into supermarkets, hypermarkets, specialty stores, department stores and e-grocery retailers.[6] Online retail business has also started gaining momentum and has huge potential for growth. Online retail is expected to grow by USD 60 billion by 2020 (Research on global markets, online grocery market in India 2018 report). The convenient and economical access to internet has led to explosive growth of e-commerce in developing economies.[7] As per Internet World statistics, India had 560 million internet users by June 2019, which is the second largest population of internet users in the world, just behind China.[8] While the e-commerce sales as percentage of total retail sales in India is just 2.2 per cent. Hence it is forecasted that India has huge potential for online business and that is why major online players such as Amazon and Flipkart (Walmart) are investing billions of US dollars in India. Online retailing has benefits like low-entry barrier, easy access to information and low transaction cost. These features have the potential to attain economic ideals for a truly competitive frictionless market: low search cost, fierce pricing strategies, low margins and weak market power. The outcome of this can translate into customer welfare and benefits (Tang and Xing, 2001). Today's customers want best of both worlds, they want information about a product and price online but may want to make the purchase offline in store after seeing the product. This practice is called webrooming.[9] This helps customers reduce their search cost, gives an idea about competitive price and the security and reliability of an offline purchase. Some customers visit showrooms to get the touch and feel of product but may order online to get attractive offers in the form of cashbacks. This practice is called showrooming.[10] Sometimes purchasing decisions may be influenced by convenience offered and urgency of consumption. Hence, all these factors directly or indirectly affect the price and can be used by retailers while deciding the price for their products strategically.

## Literature Review

Price dispersion is defined as the distribution of prices of an item with same measured characteristics across sellers of the item at a given point in time (Pan, Ratchford, and Shankar, 2004). Most of the studies done on price dispersion can be categorized into four broad categories:

1. Comparison between online and offline price dispersion
2. Persistence of price dispersion
3. Sources of price dispersion
4. Effects of price dispersion

Study on price dispersion in online market as compared to offline market has attracted a lot of research in past including Bakos (1997), Baye et al. (2004), Brynjolfsson and Smith (2000), Baylis and Perloff (2002), Clay et al. (2002), Brown and Goolsbee (2002) and Zhuang et al. (2018). From an economic perspective, it was predicted that online markets would operate more efficiently and in a friction free manner, hence, have low-price dispersion (Baylis and Perloff, 2002). However, some studies have found that price dispersion is higher online (Ancarani and Shankar, 2004; Clay et al., 2002), while others have found offline price dispersion is higher (Brown and Goolsbee, 2002; Brynjolfsson and Smith, 2000). Few others have found that there is no significant price dispersion between online and offline retailers (Scholten and Smith, 2002). Multi-channel retailers have a lower price dispersion than pure online retailers (Pan et al., 2003), while Xing et al. (2006) and Tang and Xing (2001) find a reverse result. Since price dispersion is there and studies have found contradictory results some scholars attribute this inconsistency to immature online market. The theory of immature market suggests price dispersion may be a result of random noise of an immature market (Baylis and Perloff, 2002). While others differ suggesting that though internet is evolving, price dispersion is persistent in online market (Pan et al., 2002; Ratchford et al., 2003; Xing et al., 2006; Lach, 2002). Hence, it is necessary to study the sources for price dispersion in online markets after analysing past studies done in this area, which suggest these different results from studies may be due to different measurement of price dispersion, product categories chosen and market differences. Many studies have tried to explore sources of price dispersion, which are homogeneity in sellers and products, search cost, information asymmetry (Ghose and Yao, 2011) and retailer characteristics, market characteristics and product uniqueness (Pan et al. 2003). Apart from these, few studies suggest brand recognition and loyalty program also lead to price dispersion (Pan et al., 2004). Different studies have suggested different theoretical models to capture the sources of price dispersion. The conceptual model given by Ghose and Yao (2011) shows a relation between price dispersion and product cost, order cycle time, price elasticity and transaction quantity in electronic markets. Another detailed conceptual model representing effects of consumer information search (including cross-site and in-site search) and evaluation factors on internet retailer's pricing (Walter, Gupta, and Su, 2006; Pereira, 2005). Finally, the least researched area is effects of price dispersion. Studies on effects of price dispersion show that price dispersion may lead to uncertainty for buyers, perception of transaction risk and performance risk (Biswas and Burman, 2009), increased search effort (Biswas 2004), difficulty to perceive fair price (Chen and Bei 2005, Lai et al., 2006) and fraud (Zang et al. 2012). Lot of studies also categorize firms as good firms and bad firms based on the prices charged in lieu of services offered (Baylis and Perloff, 2002). Several studies have been done on price dispersion in late 1990s and early 1920s, when the e-commerce market was in the nascent stage and did not even exist in developing economies. There is no recent study on price dispersion among traditional and online retail firms in developing economies. While few studies have been done to see the effect of reduced search cost on price dispersion, none have been done in an Indian context.

## Research Objective

As already discussed, the Indian retail market is primarily unorganized; organized sector has penetration less than 10 per cent while the e-retail has less than 2.2 per cent penetration. But a recent surge in internet usage followed by deep discount by online giants combined with relaxation in FDI norms by government is changing the dynamics and organized retail is catching up fast. Hence, today Indian customers have the choice to pick products, be it daily needs or electronic goods from traditional variety stores or from big retail chains or they can simply buy online. Since a majority of Indian customers are price sensitive, they actually take the pain to search lowest price across all mediums before finally making a purchase, even for everyday needs (Goswami and Mishra, 2009).

As discussed in the literature review section, no study has been done in an Indian context covering all the options available to customers starting from traditional variety stores to online stores covering wide range of products available. Most of the studies were done in developed countries in early twenties using books and CDs to study price dispersion. No study has been done using standard low value as well as high value FMCG products, which are available across all the retail channels in India. This prompts us to study price dispersion across organized and unorganized retail market for standard FMCG products in India.

## Research Methodology

This study intends to compare the prices of standard (uniform quality) FMCG products like mobile, laptop, branded body lotion, washing powder, hand wash, Nescafé 100 g, Fortune 10 kg flour and Samsung S5E tab by visiting different retail stores and websites. Stores have been picked after searching on google for customer ratings. Justification for the choice of product is to cover both high-value as well as low-value FMCG products. We chose to cover a small unorganized store to a big brick and mortar store and pure play retailers to cover the whole spectrum of choice available to customers. Two nearby areas are chosen for the study as choosing stores from geographically different location may introduce more variance (Brynjolfsson and Smith, 2000).

## Research Data

Based on data collected between 9th February 2019 to 15th February 2019 on prices offered for different standard high value and low value FMCG goods by organized and unorganized retailers is shown via the following graphs. Another set of data was collected during 19th to 22nd October 2019 for few more products including Samsung Tablet, Nescafé and Fortune flour. For groceries we have considered major online retailers which includes Amazon, Flipkart, Paytm, Big basket, Gofers in addition two big retail chains in Dwarka—Modern Bazar and Reliance Smart. We also collected data from four local retail shops from Uttam Nagar and Dwarka. Similarly, for high value purchases online retailers Amazon, Flipkart and Paytm were accessed along with two organized and one unorganized retailer from Uttam Nagar and Dwarka.

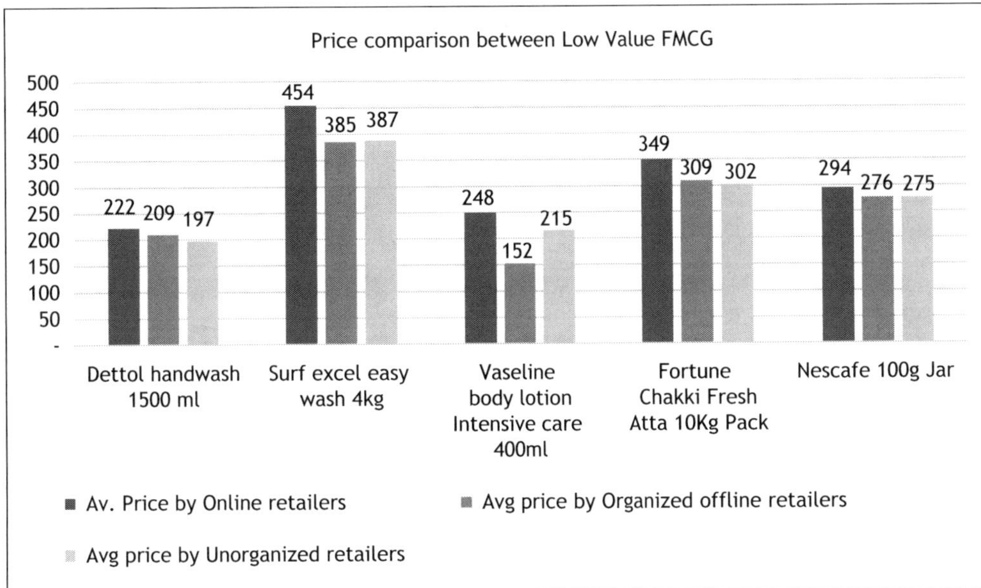

Price comparison between Low Value FMCG
500
450
400
350
300
250
200
150
100
50
-
222 209 197
454 385 387
248 152 215
349 309 302
294 276 275
Dettol handwash 1500 ml
Surf excel easy wash 4kg
Vaseline body lotion Intensive care 400ml
Fortune Chakki Fresh Atta 10Kg Pack
Nescafe 100g Jar
Av. Price by Online retailers
Avg price by Organized offline retailers
Avg price by Unorganized retailers

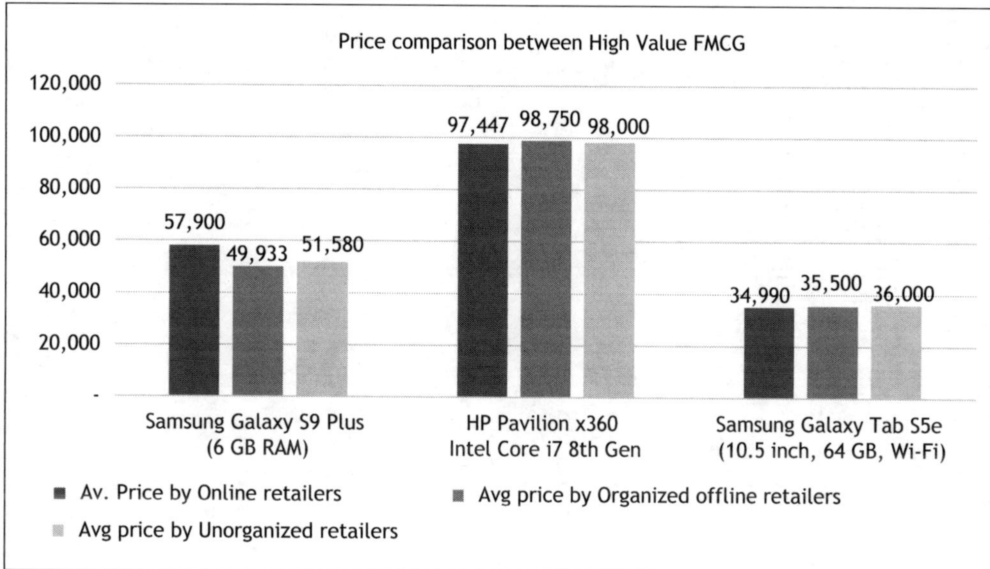
Price comparison between High Value FMCG
120,000
100,000
80,000
60,000
40,000
20,000
-
57,900
49,933
51,580
97,447
98,750
98,000
34,990
35,500
36,000
Samsung Galaxy S9 Plus (6 GB RAM)
HP Pavilion x360 Intel Core i7 8th Gen
Samsung Galaxy Tab S5e (10.5 inch, 64 GB, Wi-Fi)
Av. Price by Online retailers
Avg price by Organized offline retailers
Avg price by Unorganized retailers

## Discussion

Graphical representation of the average price of different FMCG products across different retailers shows price dispersion is there despite low search cost. For a Dettol handwash 400 ml pack average price offered by online retailers is maximum while the price offered by unorganized retailers is least. Similarly, in the case of Surf Excel 4 kg pack price offered by online retailer is maximum while that offered by organized offline retailer is least. In case of Vaseline body lotion 400 ml pack the price offered by online retailers is maximum while that offered by unorganized retailer is minimum. Similar trend continues for products like Nescafé 100 gm jar and Fortune flour unorganized offer lowest price followed by organized offline retailer and then online retailers.

For high value FMCG goods, like Samsung Galaxy S9 Plus phone, price offered by offline organized retailer is least while that offered online is maximum. Though in the case of HP Pavilion laptop price offered by online retailer is slightly lesser than that offered by organized and unorganized offline retailers. In case of Samsung's latest tablet S5E (Wi-Fi only variant) online retailer's average price is lower than the other two. It was being offered as part of a 'deal of the day' discount at Amazon. Hence, we can say despite low search cost due to internet and telecom services, price dispersion still exists in the Indian FMCG market.

Physical retail stores are offering lowest prices for various FMCG products while online stores are either matching in some cases at best but in rest their prices are on the higher side. Major cost component is delivery and returns in case of online markets, hence, customers are willing to pay extra bucks for long-tail items but not for items which are easily available at nearby grocery stores. Another value addition done by online shopping is convenience in case the purchase is a planned one. So, time to time different offers are given by online retailers to woo the customers to buy online. Warehousing of large variety of products is the biggest challenge for brick and mortar stores. While they can offer popular products at attractive prices storing specific products is a challenge, which are comparatively lower in demand. Search cost or cost of comparing prices for goods across different channels becomes cumbersome for customers after a point. All these channels try to win customers by offering discounts on few products giving customers the impression that they are the cheapest. Hence, the increased price variation across different channels has led to further increase in search cost and consequently price dispersion.

## Managerial Implications

From the study it has become apparent that trust and convenience are two driving factors when it comes to purchase decision making. The price dispersion is a tool to compensate for one or the other. Therefore, the managers will have to evaluate the short comings of their channels, so that they can realise more margins. Online retailers, while providing convenience, will also have to focus on customer perception of product quality. One way of such gaining trust in product quality could be detailed description and photographs from multiple angles showing the product in detail. Listing of open and honest reviews will also impact the trust on the product being bought. Of course, association with right brands and word of mouth reference substantiates the trust in transaction.

Offline retailers will have to make the information seeking more convenient for its customers. An effort to make the transaction convenient will go a long way in terms of retaining customers. They will have to explore the pricing discounts and convenience of free home delivery to make the purchasing decision easy for customer.

## Conclusion

The study brings attention to the fact that price dispersion has not gone down despite having access to most of the information at the fingertips of customers. Even on an online platform one can come across multiple vendors offering different prices for similar goods. Variations become wider when one compares all the options available to a modern-day consumer, starting from local *kirana* store to high end retail chains to different online retailers selling wide range of products. One of the important reasons for price dispersion is increased search cost. Majority customers today are on the lookout for discounts offered by retailers to grab the best deal. While some customers are better informed about prices, some are either less informed or do not bother to explore much. Hence, price dispersion remains in the market even in the era of internet.

## Limitations and Future Scope

The current study did not consider that online search, which normally customers do, could be curated by various platforms like Google and Amazon and hence can affect the results. Also, the time and location of the search matters significantly in the case of an online search. Future studies can consider these scenarios while comparing price dispersion between online and offline mode. Future researchers can also study price dispersion in Indian FMCG over a longer period of time say a year by taking observations every 15 to 20 days and then finding out the variance among them.

## Notes

1. https://www.ibef.org/industry/retail-india.aspx
2. https://www.ibef.org/download/Retail-Report-2018.pdf
3. Ibid
4. Ibid
5. Research on global markets -Online grocery market in India (part 1), November 2018
6. Ibid
7. https://www.internetworldstats.com/top20.htm
8. https://www.statista.com/topics/2454/e-commerce-in-india/
9. Adler, E., 2014; Reverse Showrooming: Bricks-And-Mortar Retailers Fight Back. Business Insider.
10. Ibid

## References

Ancarani, F., and V. Shankar, 2004. 'Price Levels and Price Dispersion within and across Multiple Retailer Types: Further Evidence and Extension.' *Journal of the Academy of Marketing Science*, 32 (2), 176. https://doi.org/10.1177/0092070303261464.

Bakos, J. Y. 1997. 'Reducing Buyer Search Costs: Implications for Electronic Marketplaces.' *Management Science* 43 (12), 1676–1692.

Baye, M. R., J. Morgan, and P. Scholten. 2004. 'Price Dispersion in the Small and in the Large: Evidence from an Internet Price Comparison Site.' *The Journal of Industrial Economics* 52 (4), 463–496. https://doi.org/10.1111/j.0022-1821.2004.00236.x.

Baylis, K., and J. M. Perloff. 2002. 'Price Dispersion on the Internet: Good Firms and Bad Firms.' *Review of Industrial Organization* 21 (3), 305–324. https://doi.org/10.1023/A:1020415304514.

Biswas, D. 2004. 'Economics of Information in the Web Economy: Towards a New Theory?.' *Journal of Business Research* 57 (7), 724–733.

Biswas, D., and B. Burman. 2009. 'The Effects of Product Digitalization and Price Dispersion on Search Intentions in Offline Versus Online Settings: The Mediating Effects of Perceived Risks.' *Journal of Product & Brand Management* 18 (7), 477–486. https://doi.org/10.1108/10610420910998208.

Brown, J. R., and A. Goolsbee. 2002. 'Does the Internet Make Markets More Competitive? Evidence from the Life Insurance Industry.' *Journal of Political Economy* 110 (3), 481–507.

Brynjolfsson, E., and M. D. Smith. 2000. 'Frictionless Commerce? A Comparison of Internet and Conventional Retailers.' *Management Science* 46 (4), 563–585. https://doi.org/10.1287/mnsc.46.4.563.12061.

Chen, E. Y., and L. T. Bei. 2005. 'The Effects of Price Dispersion and Suggested List Price on Consumers' Internal Reference Price.' *Consumer Interests Annual* 51, 160–170.

Clay, K., R. Krishnan, E. Wolff, and D. Fernandes. 2002. 'Retail Strategies on the Web: Price and Non–price Competition in the Online Book Industry.' *The Journal of Industrial Economics* 50 (3), 351–367.

Ghose, A., and Y. Yao. 2011. 'Using Transaction Prices to re-Examine Price Dispersion in Electronic Markets.' *Information Systems Research* 22 (2), 269–288. https://doi.org/10.1287/isre.1090.0252.

Goswami, P., and M. S. Mishra. 2009. 'Would Indian Consumers Move from Kirana Stores to Organized Retailers When Shopping For Groceries?' *Asia Pacific Journal of Marketing and Logistics* 21 (1), 127–143. https://doi.org/10.1108/13555850910926281.

Lai, H., H. S. Doong, and C. Y. Yang. 2006, January. 'The Effect of Price Dispersion in an E-market on Consumers' Intentions to Join Group Buying.' In Proceedings of the 39th Annual Hawaii International Conference on System Sciences (HICSS'06) (Vol. 6, p. 116a), IEEE.

Pan, X., B. T. Ratchford, and V. Shankar. 2002. 'Can Price Dispersion in Online Markets be Explained by Differences in E-tailer Service Quality?' *Journal of the Academy of Marketing Science* 30 (4), 433–445. https://doi.org/10.1177/009207002236915.

Pan, X., B. T. Ratchford, and V. Shankar. 2003. 'The Evolution of Price Dispersion in Internet Retail Markets.' In *Organizing the New Industrial Economy* by M. R. Baye (Ed.). Emerald Group Publishing Limited.

Pan, X., B. T. Ratchford, and V. Shankar. 2004. 'Price Dispersion on the Internet: A Review and Directions for Future Research.' *Journal of Interactive Marketing* 18 (4), 116–135. https://doi.org/10.1002/dir.20019.

Pereira, P. 2005. 'Do Lower Search Costs Reduce Prices and Price Dispersion?' *Information Economics and Policy* 17 (1), 61–72. https://doi.org/10.1016/j.infoecopol.2004.03.001.

S. Lach. 2002. 'Existence and Persistence of Price Dispersion: An Empirical Analysis.' *Review of Economics and Statistics* 84(3), 433–444. https://doi.org/10.1162/003465302320259457.

Scholten, P., and S. Adam Smith. 2002. 'Price Dispersion Then and Now: Evidence from Retail and E-tail Markets'. In *the Economics of the Internet and E-commerce.* Emerald Group Publishing Limited, 63–88.

Tang, F. F., and X. Xing. 2001. 'Will the Growth of Multi-channel Retailing Diminish the Pricing Efficiency of the Web?' *Journal of Retailing* 77 (3), 319–333. https://doi.org/10.1016/S0022-4359(01)00049-5.

Walter, Z., A. Gupta, and B. C. Su. 2006. 'The Sources of On-line Price Dispersion across Product Types: An Integrative View of On-line Search Costs and Price Premiums.' *International Journal of Electronic Commerce* 11 (1), 37–62.

Zhuang, H., P. T. P. Leszczyc, and Y. Lin. 2018. 'Why Is Price Dispersion Higher Online than Offline? The Impact of Retailer Type and Shopping Risk on Price Dispersion.' *Journal of Retailing* 94 (2): 136–153. https://doi.org/10.1016/j.jretai.2018.01.003.

CHAPTER 17

# Retailing in China and India

## *A Critical Review*

**Rituparna Basu and Sayani Mandal**

## Introduction

The term 'retail' came into existence from the French word 'tailor', which implies 'to cut off'; added by a prefix 're' meaning 'to cut off again' or 'to breakbulk'. Back in 1433, the word 'retail' was used as a noun signifying the meaning 'to sale in small quantities'. So, who is a retailer? A retailer could be any person or an agent or an agency, any organization or any company, or anyone that is instrumental in providing the final merchandise, products, or services to the customer or the buyer, the last link of the entire process. A retailer is considered to be an intermediary in the channel of marketing as she/he acts both as a marketer and a consumer or customer. She/he is a marketer to the final consumer of the product or service, and a consumer or customer to the wholesalers or manufacturers. A retailer is thus considered the important link in the complex mechanism of marketing. A retailer offers the right kind of product or service from a large assortment of merchandise or services at reasonable or discounted prices offering convenience and utility to the customers. Therefore, considering the role a retailer plays in the process of buying and selling, elaborating the process of 'retailing' stands as a pre-requisite. Now, what is retailing? The process of 'retailing' is comprehensive as it is considered to be the link, which integrates together the entire chain of production, selling and distribution. It initiates at the extractive stages of production and development and moving through the path of manufacturing, it concludes with the distribution of goods and services to the last link of the entire chain of production process, the final consumer. For a retailer, the process of retailing begins with store site selection, choice of target assortment, sourcing, vendor and channel partner selection, warehousing, distribution, inventory and replenish management. It also involves day-to-day in-store operations management alongside branding and marketing of the store and its offers. In an era where customers are considered the 'king', and satisfying them is the most important task for a marketer, the entire process of retailing could be understood as crucial and significant as it exists at the end of the chain of production and selling and it involves the most crucial aspect, the *customer contact*. This sense of customer contact gives a retailer immense power which can be used to influence the buying decisions of the customers. In this complex world of global trade today, the concept of retailing encompasses an array of activities to provide satisfaction and delight to the customers. By expanding the old boundaries, retailers over time are developing new ways of customer satisfaction by indulging in customer interaction and better relationship management with both customers and channel partners (Sorescu et al., 2011). In other words, retailing is witnessing seismic shifts on the global front. With the advent of the internet, changes are witnessed at the forefront of the retail landscape to cater to the changing tastes and preferences of customers. The changing retail scenario also got reflected in the attempts made by marketers or manufacturers to achieve superior retail advantage. The marketers or manufacturers broadened their horizon of distribution channels and took necessary measures to strengthen the relationship with their channel partners to address the seismic shifts in the retail landscape. In fact, the change in the retail landscape is also shaped by the macro-environmental changes witnessed across the world. The retail industry across countries presented a picture of increased capabilities and strong business potential as an answer to such macro-environmental changes

(Iyer and Leonard, 2007; Shabat et al., 2011). In terms of its potential to boost an economy's performance, retail plays an important role as well. The fast-growing consumer markets in China and India for instance, have been powered by the success of their respective retail development (Shabat et al., 2011). The retail markets of India and China identified the common strength of the massive population of their respective countries and took the opportunity of retail expansion across all categories of population including the class of population belonging below poverty line or 'bottom of the pyramid'. Addressing all categories of population has given birth to numerous retail innovations in India and China, which laid the path of retail expansion in these two emerging Asian economies. As per the 2006 report prepared by Economist Intelligent Unit, the market potential of India and China was found to be impressive and encouraging. Researchers emphasized on the reliable trend of business success of India and China witnessed through anticipated retail market growth of the two countries (Kim, 2007). The increased consumption pattern in India and China's markets justifies the global retail success, the countries have achieved so far. The Global Retail Development Index (GRDI) 2018 report by A. T. Kearney, puts India and China at the top two positions as the most attractive destinations for retail expansion. In a nutshell, this outlines the path of global retail success India and China are paving and thus lays the platform to critically review the past and present retail trends of India and China, the two retail leaders of recent times.

## Retailing in India and China: An Introductory Review

Indian market is still growing and thus allows space for retail growth and expansion. However, on the contrary, China's market has matured over time and allows less space for growth and expansion. China, despite being a highly saturated market, still stands dominant in its online retail business segment. Factors such as rising incomes, a young population, more women in the labour force and urbanization, have influenced the retail scenario in India in recent years, where the emergence and rapid spread of supermarkets and other modern formats of retail brought about the most dramatic change. On the other side, in China, with the digital evolution, Omni-channel[1] became a game changer. Omni-channel transformed the way of doing business, for China. Therefore, the transformation in retail has been one of the major attributes of the contemporary marketing environment of both China and India, where alongside various other factors mentioned above, the growth and development of Modern Format Stores (MFS)—supermarkets, hypermarkets and malls—has significantly contributed towards this transformation.

As per 2014 reports by Euromonitor International and Fung Business Intelligence Centre, the Chinese market is one of the largest growing markets in the world of retail. E-commerce giants like Taobao, Alibaba, and Tencent, have transformed the Chinese local market structure by extending market reach extensively all across the country. Due to this, small-and medium-sized retailers, who were earlier denied access, got the opportunity to expand and do business globally (Fung Business Intelligence Centre, 2014). Chinese retail market showcased rise in online purchase with USD 755.3 billion worth of sales in the year 2016 owing to rise in the demand for high quality products and services in the market (Yu, 2017). Despite a global economic downturn in the recent past, China's growing retail market consistently offered opportunities and investment possibilities for both local and foreign investors.

On the other hand, the retail industry is the pillar of strength for the Indian economy as it accounts for almost 10 per cent of its GDP (Gross Domestic Product) and is emerging at a fast pace showcasing retail dynamism. Till 2003, India's retail industry was mainly dominated by small shops whereas in the late 2009–2010, the country started demonstrating organized retail traits to some extent with large format stores or shopping malls or convenience stores accounting for a small four per cent of the entire retail industry (Indian Express, 2014). Post 2011, the central government of India started allowing Foreign Direct Investment (FDI) in multi-brand retail that witnessed the entry of a host of new retail market players in the economy (IBEF, 2015). As per recent reports, India permits FDI in the multi-brand retail sector with a cap of 51 per cent ownership by overseas players. Claiming the first position in the GRDI report by A. T. Kearney,

India's retail market speaks of low saturation and thus is a prospective and attractive destination for global business. Over and above these growing trends, India's position as the fifth largest global destination in terms of its retail space, adds to its attractiveness.

The rise of the BRIC nations (Brazil, Russia, India and China) during 2001–2010, marked an explosive global retail development era shaping the way of the global retail business (Shabat et al., 2011). On the strength of improved monetary and fiscal policies, India has showcased considerable competitiveness, improvement in goods market efficiency, business sophistication, and innovation, whereas, China was already leading in the forefront. The growing importance of the emerging markets like India and China caught attention of many multi-national retail firms, and thus they considered these markets for their retail expansion and globalization moves. Therefore, understanding the convergences or divergences of retail industry in these two large Asian economies becomes germane.

Hence, the present chapter attempts to compare these two important retail markets in terms of their evolutionary trends, structure and the present status.

Thus, the following section on 'Review of Literature' presents a collated note on the various research and empirical evidence around the evolution of retail in these two markets along with an understanding of their present state of affairs. The 'Discussion and Implications' section critically reviews the literature to draw some interesting insights on the synergies and divergences of retail development and practices in the two markets. The chapter ends with the 'Conclusion' section that collates the highlights of the study along with its shortcomings to give directions for future research in the domain.

## Review of Literature

### Retail Development in China and India: Past

Historically the evolution of modern retailing in China happened over the pre-reform period during 1949–1978 and the post-1978 reform period that continues till today. The retail development in the post-reform period has been characteristic of the socialist market economy prevalent in China. But in the pre-reform period, retailing was essentially viewed as an almost monopolistic government owned storage facility under the aegis of the Ministry of Commerce, where the level of individual consumer buying was also government determined. The post-reform period saw the growth of diversified retail ownership with increase in private and foreign ownerships. Decentralization of the distribution authorities, abolishment of food coupons in the early 1990s, influx of foreign competition, and importance given to the individual accountability of the state-owned wholesale channels led to widespread growth of modern retail formats in the post forbidden period till 1991. In 1992 foreign retailers were allowed to have up to 49 per cent stake in joint ventures with Chinese partners in six experimental cities including Beijing, Shanghai, Guangzhou, etc. along with five special economic zones with no more than 30 per cent imported goods in their merchandise. From 1995 onwards, foreign retailers in the chain store segment and also in the wholesale segment with 51 per cent Chinese partner stakes were given licenses up to 30 years. From 1999 onwards the scope and number of foreign retailers increased across other autonomous regions and provincial capitals, with China joining the World Trade Organization (WTO) in 2001 and lifting all restrictions on foreign retailers in 2004 (IRET, 2015). In the later years around 2007 onwards, China demonstrated a trend of online shopping as the number of Chinese online shoppers grew to 108 million in the year 2009, registering an annual growth of 45.9 per cent as per a 2010 survey report by China Internet Network Information Center (CNNIC). Furthermore, the size of online shopping transaction in China during this period reached USD 38.5 billion, doubling growth compared to 2008. Amongst all online transactions, 90 per cent of sales were consumer-to-consumer (C2C) transactions. However, a growth in the business-to-consumer (B2C) model was also witnessed in China's e-commerce market. Apparel, jewelry, audio-visual products, cosmetics, electronics, books, and toys have been among the most popular items sold online. Adding to the convenience, the online payment option also added to the ease of shopping and doing business.

The history of Indian retailing represents the gradual transformation and evolution from the primitive weekly markets or village fairs during the years of pre and post-independence to organized forms of retailing post 1991 (see Table 17.1 for a comparative timeline). The focus of retailing gradually changed from an entertainment orientation to a well structured and planned mode of delivering quality shopping experience with a fair mix of the pervasive convenience of the mom-n-pop or kirana stores and the government supported public distribution systems and the khaadi stores (Akhtar and Equbal, 2012). Modern formats of retail especially in the form of supermarkets and hypermarkers gained considerable mindshare and market share over the traditional and unorganized forms particularly in the post liberalization era of the 1990s in India. However in its true sense, the real diffusion of modern retail business models was triggered during the start of the new millennium in the third wave countries (Joseph et al., 2008). For instance, the earliest traces of modern retail format conceptualization in India were typically led by investments in the apparel sector concentrating in the top tier Indian cities. Post 2005 era saw the influx of substantial investments in the food and grocery sector characterised by commitments made by indigenous corporate giants who wanted to have a first mover advantage with their modern retail business models (IBEF, 2011). But the announcement of a progressively relaxed policy allowing 51 per cent FDI in single brand retail in early 2006 helped the propagation of modern retail trade in India. In the early phases, the small sized single category specialty stores like those for watches or mobile phones, etc., commanded the retail market followed by the multi-brand carrying departmental stores. Later on, the hypermarkets were set up to cater to the greater Indian urban communities (Joseph et al., 2008). Best recognized brands like Nike, Adidas, Gucci, Gautier, Zara, Levis, have set up their selective stores alongside the more popular multi brand stores and even indigenous brand stores like Biba, Fabindia, Gaatha, Raymond, Wills Lifestyle and so forth. This demonstrates the retail situation in India around 2008. India consistently topped the A.T. Kearney's GRDI report in the years 2008–2010. However, despite being in the top position in the A.T. Kearney's GRDI report, till 2011, India was preventing innovation in its consumer retail industry across tiers of the Indian

Table 17.1 *The Retail Evolution Graph for China and India*

| Year | India | China |
|---|---|---|
| 1947 | ***Post Independence Era*** Predominantly small scale, unorganized retail in private sector supplemented with government led PDS and Khaadi stores | ***Pre Reform Era*** Monopolistic Government owned retail and rationed consumption |
| 1978 | | ***Post Reform Phase I*** Decentralized and diversified retail ownership |
| 1991 | ***Post liberalization Phase I*** Advent of modern formats like malls, supermarkets, etc. | ***Post Reform Phase II*** Abolishment of food coupons and growth of modern retail supported by relaxed FDI to attract foreign retailers in select cities |
| 1995 | | ***Post Reform Phase III*** Progressive policy relaxations to encourage foreign retailers in chain store and wholesale segment |
| 1999 | | ***Post Reform Phase IV*** Growth of modern retail in other autonomous regions and provincial capitals |
| 2001 | | ***Post Reform Phase V*** Joining the WTO |
| 2004 | | ***Post Reform Phase VI*** Growth of modern retail in fully relaxed FDI regime |
| 2006 | ***Post liberalization Phase II*** Growth of modern retail with progressive relaxations in FDI policy saw influx of foreign retailers in single brand and cash & carry segments | |
| 2012 onwards | ***Post liberalization Phase III*** Further relaxations in FDI policy allowing 100% in single brand and 51% in multi brand retail revitalise interest of investors. | |

*Source:* Author's Own Representation on the Basis of Available Information

society. This prevention affected the food retailing business the most in the rural areas of the country. Poor retail infrastructure and poor storage facilities caused food items to get spoiled quicker, before their expiry date and also contributed to spillage and decay while in transit (from the farmer to the consumer or small retailers). This situation demanded the existence of organized retail especially in the rural sector. Post 2012, organized retail began penetrating the retail markets of India transforming lives of Indian citizens with due acceptance of the retail growth and innovation.

## Retail Development in China and India: Present

Chinese market is a collection of individual sub-markets, which represent a unified and homogeneous market defined by vastly differing demographic, economic and cultural characteristics. Chinese markets are similar to developed markets like the United States or United Kingdom as they also paint a picture of organized retail with presence of numerous shopping malls across the country. China recorded a total of 3,100 shopping malls in the year 2013 with nearly 300 malls built in the year 2012 itself (Asia Briefing, 2013). The mall culture and organized retail painted a picture of sovereignty in China. However, unlike developed markets like the United States, which is dominated by big-retail giants (e.g., Walmart and Target), the Chinese retail market is highly fragmented, dynamic and is composed of significant numbers of small and medium-sized retailers (Ye and Lau, 2018). Therefore, alongside the shopping mall culture and organized retail existence in the tier two and tier three cities, the fragmented and dynamic Chinese retail market demanded retail growth beyond these urban pockets for further retail penetration and expansion. The existence of a sizeable population belonging to the 'bottom of the pyramid' called for the existence of small and medium sized retail formats in China. The 'bottom of the pyramid' represents the price sensitive customers with low cost preferences. These customers are the ones best served by the small and medium sized retailers. Understanding the opportunity of retail growth here, many retailers started investing and expanding their businesses beyond hypermarkets formats to middle and small sized retail formats to cater to all classes of population. Such trends are witnessed prominently by many small and medium sized retailers of China. One such example would be a small Chinese grocery store chain run by the Sun Art Retail Group Ltd., who achieved a 14.3 per cent revenue increase in 2012 by just serving the price sensitive customers. Noticing similar opportunities in the Chinese retail space, a Hong Kong based retail chain group named PARKnSHOP, which entered China back in the year 1984 and started its operations post 2001, scaled up and invested in 300 mid-sized supermarkets during 2012 to take the best advantage of the retail situation of China and to not let go of the opportunity to cater to all range of customers. Even global giants like Walmart has adapted to the Chinese market by operating convenience stores instead of its signature hypermarket formats to support its long-term strategy in the country. As time passed, Chinese market grew and started to become saturated. Then came online buying and selling, which started to boost Chinese economic and retail growth in a different tangent all together. The immense growth and development in the e-commerce segment fueled the growth and development of the Chinese retail market as a whole. In 2016–2017, almost 11 per cent of retail sales of consumer goods were attributed to online sales. Chinese rural and urban households witnessed a steady growth of disposable income in the past few years and as the spending power of the Chinese population increased dramatically, so did the growth in the e-commerce segment. This matured the Chinese market into one of the largest and still growing consumer markets worldwide, a market with attention from global investors and retailers. Foreign and local retailers, eye China owing to the massive population and the spending capability of the consumers. However, the coexistence of e-commerce-based retail alongside brick and mortar physical retail are seen to be essential for retail success in a vast market like China. A fine blend of effective location driven physical retail distribution strategy with offers catering to local preferences of the Chinese consumers would be the key to long term success.

Post 2012, with liberal trade policies and identified need for organized retail, India's FDI policies in single brand retail encouraged retail establishments. International brands took advantage of the liberalized trade policies and flooded the Indian market with single brand retail stores across the country. This came with far reaching impact in transforming the lifestyle perspectives and practices of the growing urban retail consumer base in India. The Indian retail industry with 13 per cent Compound Annual Growth Rate (CAGR) reached to ₹66.39 lakh crore (USD 950 billion) in the year 2018 and economists expected it to reach to ₹76.87 lakh crore (USD 1.1 trillion) by the year 2020 (IBEF, 2019). The country is among the highest in the world in terms of per capita retail store availability. A rise in disposable income with a booming young population are the key drivers for the fast emergence of organized retail over the last 15 years in the country. Organized and unorganized store formats coexist in all sectors of the Indian market; it is often referred as the nation of '*Dukandars*' or store-keepers having a large pool of over 12 million retailers. Significant growth in the urban and semi-urban retail markets in India is giving strong indication to consider retail as the next boom industry for the country (Akhtar and Equbal, 2012). India's organized retail penetration was tracked at nine per cent back in 2017. However, this figure is expected to rise to 18 per cent by 2021. India is expected to become the world's third-largest consumer economy by 2025. Indian retail industry got a boost through increased participation from foreign and private players. The price competitiveness of India attracts large retail players for using it as a sourcing base. Global retailers such as GAP, Walmart, Tesco and JCPenney are increasing their sourcing from India and are moving from third-party buying offices to establishing their own sourcing houses and buying offices. As of now, the predominant physical store retailers include a host of shopping centers or malls, specialty stores, departmental stores, markdown stores, the manufacturing plant or factory outlets, hypermarkets, convenience stores and the category killers that are mostly categorized as multi brand stores. The most prominent of them that have been embraced well across the Indian markets are the shopping centers in the metro urban areas that range between 60,000 square feet and 7,00,000 square feet. The organized retail in India is flourishing and with revised FDI policies, the growth and development of organized retail would be even more effortless. The Government of India has allowed 51 per cent FDI in multi-brand retail and 100 per cent in single brand retail and to further give a boost to the economy and ease of doing business and make the Make-in-India project successful, the Government of India considers plans to approve 100 per cent

FDI in e-commerce by 2021. These policies would effectively strengthen the growth and development of the country's retail innovation and establishments in the years to come and would be responsible for the country's retail success.

## Discussion and Implications

The economic crisis of 2008 leading to the weakening of matured markets like the United States and Europe did have impact on the geo-political and geo-economic business environments across the world. From a retail point of view, notwithstanding the turbulences, the main five nations to develop through the trial of time were China, India, Russia, Vietnam and Chile, that were reliably included in A. T. Kearney's Global Retail Improvement list prepared for a 10 year time frame between 2002–2011 (Shabat et al., 2011). Despite the fact that the CAGR of retail has been reliably higher than the normal record of nine per cent for all these five nations, yet the business sectors vary with respect to their particular positions in the phases of the retail advancement process. Moreover, among this handful of markets, the sheer market size of India, China and Russia attracts international retailers. The power of the growing middle class along with growing disposable income and increased purchasing power adds to their potential as destinations for retail expansion.

Considering the pattern of retail development in China and India quite interestingly the two Asian neighbours forayed into the modern organized retail almost hand in hand. Yet on a comparative scale, China has been much more proactive than India in fueling retail development by progressively reforming at a faster rate. China's reform era was initiated a decade earlier as compared to the initiation of the liberalization drive in India. For China, the task seemed to be steeper in moving from an extremely controlled state to a deregulated state as compared to India. For both India and China, the retail chapters of the countries till 2012 was marked by a rigid regime of business legislation that left very limited scope for growth and development of modern retail in the countries. This restriction and rigid business regime was perhaps the reason behind the slowly eroding confidence of transnational retailers on the retail environment opportunities in India leading to a fall in its GRDI rankings around 2012 as opposed to a more stable one for China. China though was leading strong in its e-commerce business over a long period of time, India finally overtook the retail leader, China in the year 2018 as per the 2018 GRDI rankings owing to India's large, young, increasingly brand and fashion-conscious population with high disposable income. Alongside a stable growth in China's retail business through online sales, the presence of a strong distribution channel with massive existence of brick-and-mortar stores proved essential for China's retail success. The effective utilization of real estate locations and online channels simultaneously while understanding local consumer preferences is key for long-term success in the Chinese retail market.

While Table 17.2 elaborates on comparing the macro environmental factors prevalent across the two markets, it is noted that in case of India, the sizeable young population with their increasing brand and fashion consciousness will continue to support development of modern retail and encourage policy makers to progressively initiate a fully relaxed FDI regime in the sector. The rural population, which constitutes about 65 per cent of the Indian population, will also offer opportunities to enterprises to come up with the best fitting retail solutions that may even exceed the present urban share. As the country is already experiencing aggressive inroads and planned initiatives by single brand retailers like Adidas and IKEA, along with other entrants like Chanel and Louis Vuitton catering to the luxury market, the best is yet to come. Lower operating costs in tier 2 or 3 cities will also have a positive influence on the overall retail climate. Similarly, China is expected to rule the world retail market specific to grocery and luxury goods segments. The growth of the organized brick and mortar retail market is also expected to go hand in hand with the blooming e-commerce market. Times have seriously changed from the period when China was only thought of as a market for cheap labour. It is increasingly viewed as a market with growing domestic consumption power, rising income and urbanization. While, the Big 4 retailers, Walmart, Tesco, Carrefour and Metro, have heavily invested in the country, local retailers like Alibaba and the rest have enough room to make it big in a large

Table 17.2 *Retailing in China and India: A Comparison*

| *China* | *India* |
|---|---|
| **GRDI**: China is positioned 2nd in the Global Retail Development Index (GRDI) for 2018. China's retail market is expected to develop to USD 8 trillion by 2022. (A.T. Kearney) | **GRDI**: India is positioned 1st in the Global Retail Development Index (GRDI) for 2018. India's retail market is expected to develop to USD 1.3 trillion by 2020. (A.T. Kearney) |
| **Demography**: China is reaching the peak of its advantageous demographic stage. | **Demography**: India is presently in what demographers call the 'sweet spot', when the dependency ratio is low, society with a large populace of individuals in the matured age cohort of 15–65. |
| **Retail in tier cities**: Foreign retailers entered retail markets not just in first-level urban communities like Beijing and Shanghai, also in second-level and even third- and fourth-level urban areas. Presently corporates are eyeing to grow significantly further, boring down into urban areas with populaces of only 1-2 million. | **Retail in tier cities**: In India, both Indian and foreign retailers are extending outside the metros into India's developing second and third-level urban communities, and even into its rural markets. |
| **Luxury Goods Market**: Retail segment that has faced challenges in the Chinese market is the one dealing in luxury goods | **Luxury Goods Market**: India's high potential market for luxury goods, with USD 5.8 billion in its market value in 2011 is expected to reach USD 50 billion by 2020. A lot of this development has been in second and third-level urban areas. |
| **E-commerce**: The newest factor in China's retail market is the growing opportunity of the digitally driven retail business models, which presently represents up to 10 per cent of retail income in specific categories. In 2012, total online sales surpassed USD 200 billion and is still growing. | **E-commerce**: As indicated by UBS, Indian e-tail market will grow ten times to USD 50 billion by 2020. |

| *China* | *India* |
|---|---|
| **FDI**: The present guidelines on retail permit 100 per cent FDI in retail. | **FDI**: Recent reforms in the FDI policy by the Government of India mentions about 51 per cent FDI approval in multi-brand retail and 100 per cent FDI approval in single brand retail. To further give a boost to the economy and ease of doing business and make the Make-in-India project successful, government considers plans to approve 100 per cebt FDI in e-commerce. |

*Source:* Author's Own Compilation on the Basis of Available Information

market like China. Yet, it will still have its own challenges because of the sheer complexity across the provinces and the still existent scrutiny in particular pockets like those on the luxury purchases.

Given that India's favourable demographic dividend coupled with liberalized policies allowing foreign investments in the retail sector is changing, the market currently poses an additional challenge and opportunity for the global retailers to consider, especially for those who have already tasted high returns in China. The marvels of having the two markets with more than one billion shoppers that emerged in the last couple of decades in itself is a remarkable opportunity for retailers who are looking at expanding and gaining a greater foothold in the Asian markets.

## Conclusion

In an attempt to understand the synergies and divergences of retail development in two of the biggest emerging economies in Asia, the present study relied heavily on the secondary data sources to collate all relevant information that may be useful for some insightful conclusions. Hence, the secondary information based review serves as a critical step to initiate more useful research in the domain. The present study elucidates the comparitive growth trends of China and India by illustrating a brief overview of India and China's retail history and demosntrates how the present retail positions of the two Asian neighbours dominate the retail landscape in the global front. The study outlines a phase-wise comparative chart of retail development of the two retail leaders, India and China, beginning from the pre-reform era to post-reform phase I–VI and onwards. It attempts to elaborate and illustrate the present retail development of China and India as per demographics, GRDI, luxury goods market, e-commerce and retail penetration in tier two and three cities. This study showcases the development of retail in India and China and how that contributes to the literature on Asian retail management. Despite the attempts, the present study is till subject to few limitations. The historical flavour of the study does take care of the purpose for a much awaited review but lacks in terms of its specific application potential. Therefore, this lays the direction for future research in the said area. Future research in the area of understanding consumer perception towards organized retail in these two countries, a comparative study on understanding their openness to accept foreign retailers and newer formats may be useful to aid micro level decisions of retailers in these two countries. Macro environmental perspectives on their patterns of development and the sigificance of the various factors that influence the development of modern retail in these two markets will also contribute to the existing body of knowledge in a major way.

## Note

1. Omni-channel retailing is defined as an integration of cross channels business model that retailers use to improve customer experiences (Avery et al., 2013; Verhoef et al., 2015).

## References

Akhtar, S., and I. Equbal. 2012. 'Organized Retailing in India- Challenges and Opportunities.' *International Journal of Multidisciplinary Research* 2 (1), 281–291.

Asia Briefing. 2013. *India and China's Retail Industries Compared.* Accessed October 19, 2019, from https://www.gatewayhouse.in/india-and-chinas-retail-industries-compared/

Avery, J., T. Steenburgh, J. Deighton, and M. Caravella. 2013. 'Adding Bricks to Clicks: On the Role of Physical Stores in a World of Online Shopping.' *GfK Marketing Intelligence Review* 5(2), 28–33. https://doi.org/10.2478/gfkmir-2014-0015.

Euromonitor International. 2014. 'China to Overtake US as Largest Apparel Market by 2017.' http://blog.euromonitor.com/2014/04/china-to-overtake-us-as-largest-apparel-market-by-2017.html

Fung Business Intelligence Centre. 2014. *China's Apparel Market, 2014*. Accessed October 5, 2019, from www.funggroup.com/eng/knowledge/research/industry_series25.pdf

IBEF. 2011. *Retail. India Brand Equity Foundation and Aranca*. Accessed May 2012, from http://www.ibef.org

IBEF. 2015. *Retail Industry in India. India Brand Equity Foundation and Aranca*. Accessed October 5, 2015, from http://www.ibef.org

IBEF. 2019. *Retail. Indian Retail Industry Analysis*. Accessed October 2019, from http://www.ibef.org

IRET. 2015. *Development of Retail Industry in China*. Accessed October 2015, from http://www.bear.warrington.uft.edu

Iyer, R., and J. Leonard. 2007. 'Retail Evolution: Positioning for Modern Trade Growth.' *Retail Insight: Selling Global Leaders Quarter* 1, 2–6.

Joseph, N., N. Soundararajan, M. Gupta, and S. Sahu. 2008. *Impact of Organized Retailing on the Unorganized Sector*. ICRIER: New Delhi.

Kim, M. 2007. *World CEOs Prosperous Business for 3 Years*, Everyday Economy, A9.

Shabat, H. B., M. Moriarty, and D. Neary. 2011. *GRDI: A 10-Year Retrospective*. Chicago, IL: A. T Kearney Inc.

Sorescu, A., R.T. Frambach, J. Singh, A. Rangaswamy, and C. Bridges. 2011. 'Innovations in Retail Business Models.' *Journal of Retailing* 87 (S), S3–S16 https://doi.org/10.1016/j.jretai.2011.04.005.

Verhoef, P. C., P. K. Kannan, and J. J. Inman. 2015. 'From Multi-channel Retailing to Omni-channel Retailing: Introduction to the Special Issue on Multi-channel Retailing.' *Journal of Retailing* 91 (2), 174–181. https://doi.org/10.1016/j.jretai.2015.02.005.

Ye, Y., and K. H. Lau. 2018. 'Designing a Demand Chain MANAGEMENT FRAMEWork under Dynamic Uncertainty: An Exploratory Study of the Chinese Fashion Apparel Industry.' *Asia Pacific Journal of Marketing and Logistics* 30 (1), 198–234. https://doi.org/10.1108/APJML-03-2017-0042.

Yu, X. 2017. 'Alibaba Aims to Get More US Products on Taobao, Tmall via June Trade Fair in Detroit.' *South China Morning Post*, April 25, Accessed June 20, 2017, from www.scmp.com/business/companies/article/20 90496/

CHAPTER 18

# Development of Film Culture Industry in China and India

*A Comparative Study*

Fuping Yan

## Introduction

Both China and India are two large developing countries that have made remarkable economic growth in current times. Both the nations have very similar macro conditions in terms of economic development level, land area, population, market capacity and overseas nationals. Similarly, if we focus on the film industry of the two countries, they have different levels of development and different strengths, but both have great potential for future development. Both countries recognize the growing proportion and future potential of the film culture industry in the country's cultural development. Hence, this chapter compares and analyzes the development status of the film industry of both nations, and discusses the development path of mutually beneficial and win-win cultural implications.

## An Overview of the Development of China–India Film Culture Industry

### The Film Industry's Market Structure and Box Office Analysis

The Chinese film industry started at a slow growth rate and it was in 2010 that it reached 10 billion Yuan. In 2013, it reached 20 billion Yuan and in 2015, it surged to 44 billion Yuan. In 2017, the total box office of Chinese films reached 559.11 billion Yuan (about 8.99 billion US dollars), with a year-on-year growth of 13.45 per cent, much higher than the 3.73 per cent growth in 2016. Compared to a billion Yuan in 1997, the box office has increased more than 50 times. China's film box office reached nearly 32 billion Yuan in the first half of 2018 (CY329, 2018). In 2017, a total of 98 imported films were introduced to the Chinese film market, of which 64 were bought out, keeping the annual box office ratio below 50 per cent (Su Liang, 2018).

In 2017, the number of movie-goers in urban China reached 1.62 billion, with a year-on-year growth of 18.25 per cent and a record high (CY306, 2018). China's box office reached 20.218 billion Yuan in the first quarter of 2018, according to the latest data from the state film administration of China (Liu Yang, 2018). Today the Chinese film market is full of great opportunities, great development and unlimited imagination, which will surely provide unprecedented new impetus for the development of International cinema.

Similarly, if one examines the Indian sub-continent, the Indian film industry has been an important economic pillar industry of the country. The country has adopted legislation to promote the development of the film industry since the early 1990s. According to a joint report by the Federation of Indian Chambers of Commerce and Industry (FICCI) and the consulting firm Ernst & Young, the total output value of the Indian film industry grew by 27 per cent in 2017 (Song Jiaxuan, 2018). The report attributed the high growth rate to a large increase in overseas cinemas, especially in China, the growth of satellite broadcasting revenue and the increase of domestic box office revenue.

In 2017, the Chinese film 'Wolf Warrior 2' earned 5.683 billion Yuan (870.3 million US dollars) at the box office (Box Office Mojo, 2018). The Indian film 'Baahubali 2' earned 80.16 billion INR (Box Office India). However, the total box office earnings in India this year was about 2.4 billion US dollars, which is almost a one third of China's box office revenues (Song Jiaxuan, 2018).

When one looks at the global numbers, the global box office figures were USD 34.7 billion in 2012, USD 35.9 billion in 2013, USD 36.4 billion in 2014, USD 38.4 billion in 2015, USD 38.6 billion in 2016 and USD 40.6 billion in 2017. The annual growth rate of the global box office is less than 5 per cent, or even almost zero growth. This shows that the global film industry has generally entered a period of steady development, with little room for market development. According to the film industry report released by the Motion Picture Association of America, the North American box office further dropped 2 per cent to USD 11.1 billion in 2017. Ticket sales from other countries totaled USD 29.5 billion, up seven per cent from 2016. Box office sales in the Asia-Pacific region rose by six per cent in 2016 to USD 16 billion in 2017. Thus, it appears that the major film revenue growth contribution comes mainly from the Chinese market (Kuai Dao, 2018).

## Infrastructure Development: Construction of Cinemas and Movie Screens

In 2017, there were 49 cinema lines in China, and the total number of screens in urban cinemas reached 50,776, with a year-on-year growth of 23.3 per cent, ranking first in the world (CY331, 2018).

This, to a large extent, indicates that the development of China's film industry and market has acquired solid and steady internal impetus. The number of movie screens worldwide grew eight per cent to 170,000 in 2017, driven by a 16 per cent increase in the Asian region, led by China (Kuai Dao, 2018).

The Asia-Pacific region has the largest number of giant screens (1,397), followed by North America (1,115), with the United States having the largest number (Kuai Dao, 2018). With the continuous improvement of audiences' requirements for watching movies, the giant movie screen will become the major growth point of the film industry in the next decade, with tremendous growth potential.

## Comparative Analysis of the China and India's Film Industry

### Content Based Analysis: China Versus India

Since 2000, Indian films have taken on a new look as the investment environment has matured and production concepts have changed, changing the deep-rooted malpractices while maintaining the characteristics of Indian culture. New Indian films such as 'Monsoon Wedding', and 'Baahubali' have all produced extraordinary influence in the world. In recent years, they have gained a lot of fans in China. The movies '3 Idiots', 'Dangal' and 'Baahubali 2' have made spectacular box office hits. The film 'Hindi Medium' was a big hit in 2018. According to the latest Chinese film audience satisfaction survey, spring 2018, the satisfaction of the Indian film 'Hindi Medium' is higher than that of all domestic films. Indian films are more diversified than Chinese films in terms of subject matter, characters and operation mode. They pay great attention to learning from excellent Hollywood films, not only in terms of technology, but also in terms of narrative mode, type culture, dissemination of universal humanistic values and so on. While inheriting its own cultural characteristics, the themes are very close to the reality and pays attention to the needs of the public, and contains profound life themes that are thought-provoking. It often uses warmth to cure the pain of reality and reflects social and institutional problems in a light-hearted and humorous way. The content quality, ideology and dissemination of the films have been promoted to the top of the world. This reflects that after years of development, Indian filmmakers have become increasingly mature and have begun to possess the precious 'craftsman spirit' in terms of content, technology, art and narration.

However, on the other hand Chinese movies are underperforming in the domestic as well as the overseas market. On the other hand, Hollywood's 'Kung Fu Panda' and 'Mulan' have achieved good results around the world. This is a paradox of sorts, because these elements come from China. The main reason for the underperformance is that most Chinese filmmakers do not have an adequate understanding of western culture, so it is difficult for them to integrate Chinese cultural values with the international mindset. On the other hand, Indian films reflect the characteristics of local culture and deeply explore the themes with universal values that can arouse global human emotional resonance. When films carry universal values, the audiences around the world easily accepts it, and such resonance can transcend race, time and space. This can be illustrated well with the considerable success of 'Wrestling! Dad'—a Chinese film. Thus, when a film touches human emotions it can transcend boundaries and attain global appeal. Subsequently, by engaging the global movie audiences, identity movies can achieve box office success.

Another probable reason for more global perspective in Indian films is the fact a number of Indian film makers have been trained in the international arena such as Tasim Sin, Mira Nair, M. Night Shyamalan. Thus, lack of international exposure is an issue of concern for the Chinese film industry. Another area that works to the Indian film industry's advantage is that the actors and actresses are not only able to speak in English, but due to filming in foreign lands, are also able to understand what appeals to the international movie viewer. Thus, China should pay attention to cultivating international film and television talents from multiple dimensions. Besides acting skills, it should also pay attention to cultural quality, strengthen international exchanges and expand international vision.

With the increasing competition in the future, there is a dire need for the Chinese film maker and the Chinese film industry to work on contemporary topics that have global appeal. A good sign is that in 2017, which is a signal towards improving the quality of the films. In 2018, the art film 'Gangrenboqi', China began to attach importance to art-house films to cultivate audiences' appreciation. The China Art Film Screening Alliance has been joined by 579 screen rooms from 433 cinemas in 145 cities, promoting the screening of high-quality art films, and thus being able to create a world class infrastructure for the movie viewing audiences (Shi Jingnan and Duan Jingjing, 2017).

## The Role of Technology

In the 21st century, availability of internet enabled devices, big data and cloud computing, virtual reality, artificial intelligence, and high-speed development network has extended film publicity scope and also widened the movie broadcast channels. The film industry has formed a traditional film form, network, mobile phone film, micro movie formats all at the same time. Paid video on demand (VOD), streaming over the internet has become a new export and revenue contributor, upending the single model of films that used to rely entirely on box-office revenue from cinemas. Globally, the number of online video subscribers increased to 447 million in 2017, which is 33 per cent higher than the number in 2016. The number of Internet Protocol television (IPTV) and satellite subscribers has also grown over the past five years, while the number of cable subscribers fell for the second year in a row in 2017 (Kuai Dao, 2018). This is a phenomenon that deserves particular attention in India. The Indian film industry however, on the other hand is restricted by the lack of high-tech and high-quality infrastructure, relying more on traditional cinema, cable TV and home theater model. The high-technology screen facilities and technology enabled format is far behind China, so this is an area where there is a lot of opportunity for upgradation in the future.

It is also to be noted that market and consumer trends, as big data is increasingly important in film planning, production, marketing and other links. The internet is gradually and strongly being involved in the production and distribution of films, in the form of pre-paid VOD, advanced-paid VOD, synchronous paid VOD, paid premiere, etc. Thus, immense opportunities are likely to open up on the basis of technology advancement. In 2017, the online ticketing market accounted for more than 80 per cent in the whole of China's film market (Sootoo Institute, 2018).Online ticketing companies' superior resources enabled them to successfully get through the industrial chain, start to participate in the production and distribution business, and have greater bargaining power. Payment gateways have also entered an explosive growth stage as film products become the focus of video website broadcast content and purchase. In 2017, China also made a major breakthrough in the construction of high-standard and high-tech cinema facilities. In addition to IMAX screen, the configuration of China's giant screen, 120 frames/3D/4 K image cinema, RealD 6FL certified screen, LUXE cinema, Dolby cinema, Advanced Laser Phosphor Display (ALPD) projection and other high-tech screens greatly improves the user experience and movie-watching experience. After years of efforts, China has more broadcast windows and platforms, such as cinemas, television and the internet. The concept of 'big box office' has been formed through multiple efforts.

The entry of internet and capital has also impacted other aspects of the Chinese film industry. The acquisition of information, movie-watching decisions, ticket purchase, movie-watching, evaluation and sharing of films are all influenced and changed by the internet, and the ecology of the film market. This is a new economic development model with 'film and television and Internet' as the core, covering film and television, animation, video, music, literature, artist brokerage, drama, derivatives, live-action entertainment and other fields, and constant entrepreneurship, innovation and creation. Increase in number of people using mobile payment method will be an important signal to capture the future film industry, but also to bring important enlightenment to the Indian film market. By contrast, the Indian film market relies more on traditional film distribution channels and thus there is huge potential for future development.

## Policy and Regulatory Support: India versus China

In order to revitalize the Indian film industry, the Indian government has adopted many preferential policies to help realize the development of the film industry. India is one of the earliest countries in the world to legislate the sector. In 1918, the Indian Film Act was passed (Mao Baozhong, 2018). Thus, the legal system plays a decisive role in the protection of the film industry. Compared with this the Chinese movie legislation, the law of the People's Republic of China Film Industry Promotion Act was finally formally implemented only on 1 March 2017. The film industry was formally incorporated into the national economic and social development planning. It has provided a legal basis and safeguard which will boost market confidence and is an important milestone in the Chinese film industry.

After the establishment of a sound legal system and the establishment of a good film order, China should appropriately delegate its power to be a sound regulator of the industry and increase the important role of film industry associations and professionals. The two countries can take advantage of the 'One Belt And One Road' economic and cultural layout to strengthen various support efforts and practical measures, promote the construction of various 'film bridges', make film as an important carrier of culture, and help countries gain the dominant right and more say in cultural cooperation and exchange.

## Challenges: China and India

China and India have a huge domestic box office market, but there is a huge gap between the overseas box office and domestic box office of American films, and they are faced with the dilemma of overseas export of films. Overall, the Asia-Pacific accounted for only 25 per cent of the world's film market in 2017. Although the number of films produced in the United States is only 6 to 7 per cent of the world's total, it accounts for 70 per cent to 85 per cent of the world's market share. Meanwhile, the domestic box office revenue of the United States only accounts for about 30 per cent of the total film revenue (Kuai Dao, 2018).

China is the world's third largest film producer. Compared with the United States, China's export films are single in content (mainly Kung Fu films), and there are very few countries and regions to which they are exported. The overseas sales of films are extremely unstable and the box office is poor. China's film trade deficit continues to increase, and film trade competitiveness index continues to be sluggish. Compared with China, India's overseas export market is much better than that of China. The film trade has been in surplus and growing steadily. The film export ranks second only to the United States in the world, and the influence of Indian films in North America and Britain ranks first among imported films.

In addition, the export objectives of Chinese and Indian film industries are also quite different. Chinese film exports are mainly concentrated in North America, Europe, Asia Pacific and other regions, while Indian films have a strong influence in Africa in addition to North America, Europe, Asia Pacific and other regions. India has long been the most resistant country in the world to Hollywood films, with a long-term share of around 90 per cent of the country's films (Ma Haiyan, 2014). However, on the domestic front, with the growth of the young population and the influence of overseas Indian ethnic groups on the domestic market, Indian films are facing fierce competition from Hollywood blockbusters.

Besides global expansion, the two countries should still focus on Asian markets in a certain period of time, because from the experience of overseas sales of Chinese films, the proportion of overseas earnings of most films in Asia is much higher than that in Europe and America. Thus, while exporting films, Asia should be considered as the leading market and one should gradually go global.

## China–India film Cultural Industry Cooperation:

Thus, it is proposed that as two powerful and huge developing economies, the two nations will benefit a lot by mutual cooperation on this. The possibilities of mutual cooperation and growth are discussed briefly in this section.

### Development of Viewership Base: China and India

In terms of film market capacity and space, China and India have one of the largest film markets in the world. The film industry of the two countries should complement each other's advantages, enter each other's market, benefit each other and seek common development. The huge number of moviegoers is an indispensable industrial foundation for a big movie market. Both China and India are big countries with large population, and both have attracted worldwide attention. India's movie-watching market is more diverse and broader than China's. In recent years, relying on the combination of the internet and capital, China's film industry has entered a path of steady growth. The interaction between audiences and products is becoming more and more frequent, and Chinese films are entering the 'best era'. China is already the second largest film market in the world, and it is expected to surpass the United States to become the first in the world by 2020. This pivotal role of China's film market has attracted more and more Hollywood films to develop in China, and neighbouring India has more promising market space.

From the perspective of the foundation and resource background of film culture industry, China and India have abundant resources, profound historical and cultural deposits and many advantages. Rich ethnic cultural resources in the two countries, including costumes, architecture, music, dialects and folk stories, all carry unique regional culture, and the artistic value has the basis for developing high-quality films with strong ethnic lore. If China and India can conduct long-term and in-depth exchanges and cooperation, explore each other's market, draw valuable cultural connotations from each other's cultural space, and learn from each other's strengths, it will not only improve the cultural influence and innovation of their respective nations, but also tap into and extend new cultural industrial economy. The two countries should further consider how to tap the resources and advantages of both sides, cultivate high-quality enterprises and leaders, and build an industrial chain and ecological space suitable for the healthy development of the film industry of the two countries.

## Cooperation Opportunities: China and India

Indian films have been coming to China since the mid-1950s. 'Awaara' and 'Caravan' left a deep impression on the Chinese people in the 1980s. By contrast, China's influence in India is small. In recent years, cultural exchanges between China and India have been strengthened. '2015 China and India Movie Cooperation News Exchange Meetings' was held in Beijing. Chinese filmmakers started three Sino Indian co-operation film with India in 2016. In 2017, 'Kung Fu Yoga' earned more than the Indian film industry heavyweight in the Indian market. Indian movies achieved great success in Chinese market. In 2017 Indian film 'Dangal' had achieved nearly 1.3 billion Yuan at the box office in China (Shuju GongYuan, 2018). It set a box office record for a non-American film in the Chinese film market.

To achieve China's aim of box office success, the development of network technology and market of the rising and the abundant capital is needed. China and India can provide each other with stronger support in consultation, training and commercial supporting services, so as to promote in-depth and fruitful era of China–India film cooperation. Utilizing initiatives in the area like 'act east policy', both sides should further deepen the film industry cooperation.

If China and India create market for each other in their respective countries both will become main production content and consumption provider of the film industry in Asia and eventually by entering global market will become important force in films globally. This is the best way and beautiful blueprint for win-win cooperation between China and India.

### *Technology: Tool for Innovation and Development of China–India Film Industry*

The mutually beneficial development path of the film industry in China and India must make full use of the integration power of science and technology and media. Information exchange and industrial trading should be encouraged. The film industry should be vigorously promoted in the whole country where the experience of content manufacturing should be shared. New technology application, market operation, entrepreneurship and investment in the field of international new media will help in the development of the film industry. The combination of film culture industry, capital and science and technology is an inevitable trend. Therefore, it is necessary to pay close attention to and adapt to the latest comprehensive development trend of multimedia technology, continuously explore the film culture and multimedia resources of the two countries, increase the integration of science and technology and media, and take the road of innovative development.

The cooperation should start from increasing exchanges, giving free hand to cultural exchange activities such as film festivals, and deepen the understanding and identification of both countries through such activities time and again. Exhibition in the film industry acts as an extremely important platform where the film festival exhibition not only promotes the dissemination of film culture, but also drives the development of relevant industries. China and India should actively summarize and share the experience and thinking of the film festival in the promotion of brand value and regional cooperation in the film industry. In 2016, new initiative of International cooperation was started with 'BRICS Film Festival' in New Delhi, India. Quite a few measures were taken keeping in mind the cooperation between two countries which could lead to the development of their respective film industry like launching of '2017 China Chengdu BRICS Film Festival', reaching 'BRICS Movie Shooting Plan from 2017 to 2021', and introduction of 'The BRICS Cooperation Movie Chengdu Consensus'. These measures are quite significant, and China and India should take the opportunity and work together for the development of both countries.

In May 2013, China and India signed the agreement on 'promoting cooperation and contacts between Chinese and Indian provinces (states) and cities'. In October, China's city Chengdu and India's city Bengaluru established sister-city relations. Both cities are leaders in science and technology of their respective countries, and both have strong science and technology industry clusters and electronic information foundation. They should contribute to the development of film and culture industry of both countries in the new age of technology and media integration. Through these international cooperation activities, the brand influence and reputation of both sides at home and abroad will be enhanced, and the innovative development of the film and cultural industries of the two countries will be promoted.

## Conclusion

Thus, as a key industry in the tertiary sector, the film culture industry not only plays a role in promoting national economic strength, but also plays a unique and important role in cultural inheritance and social and cultural influence. Studies have shown that the most important and active factors for the development of cultural industry are culture, media, science and technology, capital and innovation, because culture is a resource, media is the support, science and technology is the productivity, capital is the blood, and innovation is the vitality. In the face of the opportunities and challenges of the future film culture industry, the overall cultural industry of the two countries should respond quickly. China and India should actively discuss ways of cooperation, jointly plan to promote film culture exchanges and discuss the blueprint for the future development of the film industry. The two parties may establish special cooperation agencies and websites to integrate the promotion efforts of both parties, provide policy support and legal advice, and advocate the establishment of cooperation and exchange fund through government-led and non-governmental cooperation. The governments of the two countries should integrate the superior resources of the industry, further improve each other's deficient industrial chain, promote the scientific and technological cooperation of the cultural industry, and build a healthy and vibrant ecological ring of the film and television cultural industry in the international region, so as to promote the sustainable development of the film and cultural industry of the two countries.

## References


Box Office India. (n. d.) 'Baahubali 2 - The Conclusion.' https://www.boxofficeindia.com/movie.php?movieid=3517

Box Office Mojo. 2018. 'Top 10 Box Offices Worldwide in 2017.' http://www.southmoney.com/paihangbang/201802/1997934.html

CY329. 2018. 'Analysis of Box Office Concentration and Box Office Revenue of Chinese Films in 2018.' *The Film and Television Animation*. http://www.chyxx.com/industry/201808/667444.html

CY306. 2018. 'Statistics on Box Office Revenue, Number of Theaters and Number of Screens in China in 2018.' *The Film and Television Animation*. http://www.chyxx.com/industry/201807/655754.html

CY331. 2018. 'Analysis on the Development Status and Prospect of China's Film Industry in 2018.' *The Film and Television Animation*. https://www.chyxx.com/industry/201803/616073.html

Liu Yang. 2018, May 20. 'The Box Office in the First Quarter Exceeded 20 Billion Yuan, Making China the World's Largest Film Market.' *People's Daily*.

Kuai Dao. 2018. 'The Motion Picture Association of America Released a Report on the Film Industry: Global Box Office Growth in 2017 was 5%.' http://www.dianyingjie.com/2018/0408/26441.shtml

Ma Haiyan. 2014. 'China-India Film Cooperation Will Change the World's Film Landscape.' http://www.cssn.cn/zx/xshshj/xsnew/201409/t20140921_1335755.shtml

Mao Baozhong. 2018. 'Film Censorship in India.' *Beijing Observation,6,* 025 *The Law of the People's Republic of China on the Promotion of the Film Industry has Been Implemented.* http://www.sapprft.gov.cn/sapprft/contents/6580/317632.shtml

Shi Jingnan and Duan Jingjing. 2017. 'A Total of 433 Cinemas and 579 Theaters Have Joined the National Art-film Projection Alliance.' http://www.xinhuanet.com/local/2017-11/27/c_1122019571.htm

Shuju GongYuan. 2018. 'From *Dangal* to *Hindi Medium,* Indian Films Are Enjoying Box Office Success in China.' http://www.eeff.net/wechatarticle-269805.html

Song Jiaxuan. 2018. 'India's Film Industry Grew 27% in 2017.' *China Culture Daily,* 4.

Sootoo Institute. 2018. '2017 Comprehensive China Online Movie Ticketing Market Analysis Report.' http://www.sohu.com/a/222454414_588947.

Su Liang. 2018. 'The Total Box Office of Chinese Films Reached 55.9 billion Yuan in 2017.' *Netease News.* http://news.163.com/18/0102/13/D75A57K000018AOP.html

CHAPTER 19

# Traditional Medical and Health Tourism in China and India

*A Comparative Study*

Weimin Huang

## Introduction

India has been well known as one of the most famous medical tourism destinations in the world and academic circles and researchers have thereby given more attention to this domain. India's experience in developing traditional medical and health tourism may be worthy for our reference but has not drawn much attention yet. India's traditional medical and health tourism is based on long history of yoga, meditation, Ayurveda and other spiritual and therapeutic practices to attract thousands of global tourists each year to travel to India for health vacation or to seek substitution therapy. Data from SRI International in the United States shows that growth in number of tourists accepting India's traditional medical treatment has been 20 per cent to 25 per cent per year since 2014. It is estimated that this number will represent 25 per cent of international market share in 2019. In terms of resource base, development pattern, strategies for developing traditional medical tourism nationally and overseas, a comparison can be easily drawn between China and India. On the basis of a comparative study on traditional medical and health tourism in China and India, this chapter attempts to summarize experiences in India to seek lessons and inspiration for the development of traditional medical and health tourism in China.

## Connotation of Traditional Medical and Health Tourism

### A Kind of 'Health Tourism'

Traditional medical and health tourism is a branch of 'health tourism', which is usually called 'wellness tourism' whose connotation is established on the basis of our understanding of the term 'health (wellness)'. In 1948, World Health Organization defined health (wellness) as 'a complete physical, psychological and social welfare more than the absence of disease or infirmity' in order to include physical dimension, psychological dimension and social dimension in determining the meaning of the term. In 1959, an American doctor named Halbert Dunn held that human body, spirit and thought are three major assets and only in harmony of all three can the joy of life on this beautiful planet be enjoyed (Wang Yan, 2008). The connotation of health lays a foundation for the exposition of 'health tourism' (Wang Yan, 2008).

Smith and Puczkó (2009) divided health wellness tourism market into hydrotherapy tourism, seawater bath tourism, holistic medical tourism, yoga and meditation tourism, and spiritual tourism. Traditional medical and health tourism here can be attributed to the category of 'holistic medical tourism'. It refers to the absorption of cultural and philosophical resources related to health and health preservation in traditional medicine. Beautiful natural resources, such as forests, oceans, hot springs, valleys and so on, are considered as the prerequisite. It is an attractive mode for recuperation, treatment or health care by means of traditional medicine and health preservation, so as to promote a room for those who seek physical, mental and spiritual harmony, for those who seek health and happiness.

## Differs from 'Medical Tourism'

Health tourism rises with increase in number of sub-healthy people and intensified awareness of pursuing happiness and quality of life when the world economy reaches a certain stage. In fact, health tourism is usually mixed up with 'medical tourism' and many countries have regarded health tourism as a subset of medical tourism to undertake merged and overlapping tourism promotion for a long time. In 2011, the Global Spa Summit 2011 differentiated 'health tourism from medical tourism on the basis of travelers' characteristics and motivation rather than characteristics of destinations where they visited for the first time (Table 19.1).

In short, medical tourism is undertaken by patients (suffering from certain disease and illness) while health tourism is undertaken by healthy or sub-healthy people. Medical tourism gives priority to 'western-style' medical treatment and surgical treatment and it is under the supervision of doctor and is passive and invasive. Health tourism on the other hand involves holistic medicine in order to achieve health and harmony among body, mind and soul. It happens on own initiative, is active and non-invasive.

### Table 19.1 *Difference Between Medical Tourism and Health Tourism*

| *Medical Tourism* | *Health Tourism* |
|---|---|
| Basic definition: It involves people who travel to different countries and places to receive treatment for any disease or illness or for cosmetic and surgical operations and are looking for lower nursing costs, higher nursing quality and better nursing opportunity or care unlike the one they can get at home. | Basic definition: It refers to the activity of people leaving for different places on their own initiative to pursue maintenance or enhancement of personal health and welfare and seek unique and real experience/treatment methods offered by different tourism locations. |
| Medical tourist: Usually sick or seek cosmetic/dental surgical procedures. | Health tourist: Seek improving their physical and mental health/quality of life by seeking integrated health and prevention methods. |

*Source:* GLOBAL SPA SUMMIT 2011, Wellness Tourism and Medical Tourism: Where Do Spas Fit?[1]

## Connotation of Traditional Medical and Health Tourism in China and India

China and India are countries with unique traditional medical systems in the world. India's traditional medical system is composed of Ayurveda, Unani, Siddha, Yoga, Naturopathy and Homeopathy, among which Ayurveda forms a major part of India's traditional medicine. Ayurveda (आयुर्वेद in Sanskrit) is derived from the combination of two words, namely Ayush and Veda, meaning 'science of life'. It is the oldest system of medicine in India, which commenced more than 5,000 years ago. China's traditional medicine is composed of traditional Chinese and Tibetan medicine, Mongolian medicine, Uighur medicine and Yi medicine of minorities, among which traditional Chinese medicine forms the major part and has a history of more than 5,000 years. Both Ayurveda and traditional Chinese medicine adhere to the notion of holistic treatment, regard 'human body, environment, and body and spirit' as a unified whole and advocate holistic therapeutics with both internal and external therapy. In contrast to western modern medicine, traditional Chinese medicine and Ayurveda pay more attention to maintenance of people's health rather than cure of a disease. Thus, they possess unique advantages from several aspects including preventive treatment of disease, health care and wellness, promotion of happiness and harmony among body, mind and soul and they are well-suited to modern people's core ideas about happiness and quality of life. Thus, they are excellent ideas that provide the basis for developing health tourism.

## Comparison of Traditional Medicine Resources and Culture in China and India

### Comparison of Traditional Medical Resources in China and India

Ayurveda and traditional Chinese medicine have striking similarities in theory and practice. From the point of view of gaining basic medical knowledge, while there is a famous medical work in traditional Chinese medicine called the *Inner Canon of Huangdi*, which is composed of two parts, namely, *Plain Questions* and *Miraculous Pivot*, the three famous texts on Ayurveda are *Charaka Samhita*, *Sushruta Samhita* and *Ashtanga Hridaya*. Again, while traditional Chinese medicine uses a set of theoretical concepts, viz., Yin-Yang and Five Elements, viscera and Qi-blood-body fluid, Ayurveda is based on the five-element (Panchamahabhutas) theory and ternary body liquid (Dosha) theory.[2] While traditional Chinese medicine nurses health, soul and spirit to bring about harmony among them by means of the *Great Ultimate*, Ayurveda tries to promote harmony among them through yoga and meditation.

Data from Ministry of AYUSH (Ayurveda, Yoga and Naturopathy, Unani, Siddha and Homeopathy) reveals that, by 2018, India had 2,946 AYUSH hospitals, among which 2,434 were Ayurveda hospitals occupying about 82.6 per cent of the total number of AYUSH hospitals; the total number of AYUSH registered medical practitioners has been 0.785 million, among which more than 0.478 million has been Ayurveda medical practitioners occupying about 60.9 per cent of the total number of AYUSH medical practitioners. It is estimated that India has more than 8,000 kinds of herbal medicines and nearly 2,000 kinds of them are recorded in *Traditional Indian Pharmacopoeia*, the country has 257 colleges having 11,887 Ayurveda undergraduate students, and there are 64 colleges having 1,109 Ayurveda postgraduate students.[3] By 2016, China had 4238 traditional Chinese medicine hospitals and 0.481 million licensed medical (assistant) practitioners in the category of traditional Chinese medicine.[4]

As recorded in the *Chinese Materia Medica 1999* there are 8,980 kinds of Chinese herbal medicines. By 2016, there are in total 294 educational institutions (i.e., colleges and universities) in China in the field of traditional Chinese medicine. At these schools, 98,169 undergraduate students and 13,636 postgraduate students are nurtured.[5] When compared from the point of view of physician resources and types of medicine, there is no such difference between China and India. However, differences mainly come from the number of traditional hospitals and the number of students nurtured in the educational institutes. China increased educational investment in Chinese medicine in recent years and the number of traditional Chinese medicine talents are around nine times the number of Ayurveda talents.

## Comparison of Resources in China and India in the Context of Traditional Medical and Health Tourism

Both China and India are among the great ancient civilizations and possess profound cultural and philosophical traditions and graceful natural scenic beauty. India's Ayurveda and yoga tourism are mainly dispersed in the Himalayas, Rishikesh, Gangtok, Kerala, Kedarnath, Goa and New Delhi. These places with beautiful landscapes and picturesque sceneries are all ideal destinations for developing high-quality health tourism. Kerala, described as the 'home of Ayurveda', is the only place where Ayurveda therapy is practiced in the purest form. The climate here is pleasant. Beaches, coconut groves, backwaters, mountains, grasslands and historic sites constitute a beautiful picture portraying a land of idyllic beauty. A travel magazine called *National Geographic* declared it as one of the top 10 travel havens in the world. Similarly, China is a vast land with abundant resources and diverse landforms. Forests, beaches, mountains, basins, hot springs, grasslands are all over the country. So, China is also very suitable for developing traditional medical and health tourism.

## Comparison in Terms of Global Influence

The Ministry of Tourism in India actively promotes Ayurveda, hydro-therapy, yoga, meditation, naturopathy and *siddha* to tourists from all over the world. India has become one of the major destinations of health tourism. Health tourists in India mainly come from North America, Europe, the Middle East and some rich Asian countries. After many years of global promotion of traditional Chinese medicine, China has made the Great Ultimate, acupuncture and Chinese herbal medicine, well known to people around the world. In 2007, Food and Drug Administration (FDA) issued *Complementary and Alternative Medicine Products and FDA Regulatory Guidelines* and included traditional Chinese medicine and Ayurvedic medicine in 'complementary and alternative medicine' category. However, in general, India's advantage with respect to the language and similar institutional and cultural background makes it easier for the western world to accept traditional Ayurvedic medicine. Moreover, celebrities have also been very important from the point of view of popularising India's Ayurveda health tourism all over the world. Many celebrities across the world including Elvis Presley, the Beatles, Prince Charles, Camilla (Duchess of Cornwall), Demi Moore, Steve Jobs, Mia Farrow and Oprah Winfrey once left for India to receive Ayurveda, yoga and meditation therapy in order to seek a healthy life and harmony among body, mind and soul, and their fame helped India's traditional medical and health tourism to spread more widely around the world.

## Comparison of Support by the Governments in China and India

To accelerate the development of traditional medical and health tourism, both the governments of China and India created a good environment in terms of the policies formulated. In 2014, Government of China introduced *Opinions of the State Council on Promoting Reform and Development of the Tourism Industry* to indicate that 'full play shall be given to the advantages of traditional Chinese medicine to form a batch of Chinese medicine health tourism service products. Service procedures and service standards shall be standardized to develop Traditional Chinese Medicine (TCM) medical tourism, sanatory rehabilitation tourism, aesthetic health care tourism and other medical tourism.' In 2015, China National Tourism Administration and State Administration of Traditional Chinese Medicine jointly issued *Guiding Opinions on Promoting Development of TCM Health Tourism* to formally put forward the concept of 'TCM health tourism' for the first time, emphasize promoting organic integration of TCM health service and tourism industry, and promote eight key tasks including development of TCM health tourism products, creation of TCM health tourism brands and expansion of TCM health tourism industry. *Outline of TCM Development Strategy Planning (2016–2030)* issued by the State Council in 2016 raised the idea to launch a batch of TCM culture communication themed TCM health tourism demonstration bases integrating TCM rehabilitation therapy, health preservation and cultural experience. In March 2018, 73 units including Beijing Changping TCM Culture Exposition Park are determined as the first batch of national TCM health tourism demonstration base creating units. These series of policies and measures will raise development of

TCM health tourism to a new height. According to the development goals set by the Government of China, the number of TCM health tourists will reach three per cent of the total number of tourists and TCM health tourism income will reach RMB 300 billion by 2020; the number of TCM health tourists will reach 5 per cent of the total number of tourists and TCM health tourism income will reach RMB 500 billion by 2025.

The fact that India's Ayurveda health tourism develops so rapidly is due to the high attention and policy support of the Government of India. In November 2014, India established the AYUSH department to ensure development and promotion of Ayurvedic medicine oriented traditional medicine. India also set up the Board of Medical and Health Tourism to promote development of traditional medical and health tourism. Subsequently, AYUSH, Ministry of Public Health, National Accreditation Board for Hospitals and Healthcare Providers (NABH) jointly held an international symposium on health tourism to define India as a 'global health tourism destination'. Government of India also implements practical and effective supportive policies in aspects including tax preference and infrastructure construction. Ministry of Tourism in India provides approved health centers with financial assistance and assists health center representatives in participating in medical/tourism fair, medical meeting, health meeting, and health fair according to the Market Development Assistance (MDA) scheme, propagandize Ayurveda health tourism through printing media, electronic media, internet and the like. Besides, Indian states introduce supportive measures and policies too. For example, the Karnataka government utilizes the strength of the IT sector of the state to develop the business of traditional medical outsourcing. Maharashtra established Infrastructure Support Development Act for convenience from the aspect of supply of land so as to encourage development of health tourism industry (Haseena V.A., 2015).

## Development Patterns of Traditional Medical and Health Tourism in China and India

Traditional medical and health tourism in China and India reflects distinctive and advantageous development patterns.

## Development of TCM Health Tourism

Under strong support and promotion of the government, provinces and cities in China regard TCM health tourism as the focus for development of a massive health industry. Various wellness mountain villas, wellness valleys, wellness manors and medicine valleys offering TCM health care services, TCM diet and TCM culture experience have been built successively. A survey on TCM health tourism service conditions of 24 provinces (cities and districts) made by National Tourism Administration and State Administration of Traditional Chinese Medicine shows that there are more than 450 scenic regions, resorts and hotels and other institutions in total; more than 90 TCM institutions take up, carry out or participate in TCM health tourism services and 15 TCM institutions are now carrying out inbound TCM health tourism projects.[6] To sum up, TCM health tourism mainly shows the following development patterns.

1. High-end medical pattern - Relies on hospitals and hotels to build modern international health service parks integrating medical treatment, preventative health care and rehabilitation, in large cities with rich TCM resources and good public infrastructure for physical examination and treatment of diseases in accordance with internationally advanced level of traditional medical services.
2. Culture popularization pattern - Considers promotion of TCM culture and popularization of TCM scientific knowledge as goals and relies on TCM planting bases, TCM museums, celebrities and TCM intangible cultural heritages to develop TCM sightseeing tourism, TCM cultural experience tourism, TCM historical inheritance tourism, TCM popularization and education tourism, other products and projects.
3. Rehabilitation and recuperation pattern - Combines TCM resources with advantages of ecological resources including sunlight, hydrotherapy, geothermy, beach, forest, hot spring and lake and integrates many wellness projects including breathing exercise, acupuncture, massage, physiotherapy, herbal remedy and herbal cuisine to create tourism products combining TCM medical treatment with wellness.
4. Research and Development (R&D) tourism pattern- Relies on one or more kinds of TCM materials to build TCM featuring towns,

establish TCM processing industry parks and TCM R&D centers. This has also led to the development of a TCM health tourism industry chain integrating film and TV series shooting, leisure tourism, TCM culture publicity and education.

## Development of Ayurveda Health Tourism

India's traditional medical and health tourism mainly relies on hotels, resorts, Ayurveda health physiotherapy centers, and holy lands of yoga, which fully reflects market-oriented features. These are discussed here. As stated by Mr Praful Patel, General Secretary of International Ayurveda Foundation (IAF), 'promotion and marketing of Ayurvedic therapy are not done by hygiene department but by the tourism development department. Ayurveda clinics gave way to the Ayurveda centers affiliated to starred hotels' (International Ayurveda Foundation).

1. **Ayurveda Spa in high-end hotels** - India's high-end hotels such as Taj Group, Leela Palace and Oberoi Group develop special spa brands for clients travelling to India. In terms of physical and mental therapy integrating India's Ayurvedic traditions, Taj has Exotica and Jiva Spa, ITC has Kaya Kalp Spa, and Oberoi has Wildflower Hall Spa. In Kerala, which is praised as the 'home of Ayurveda', all hotels and resorts include Ayurveda into the items offered by them to serve people in order to let tourists receive authentic Ayurvedic health therapy in a comfortable and quiet environment.
2. **Personalized medicine in health center** - The concept of Ayurveda stresses that medical care is a kind of high personalized treatment and as everyone has a specific constitution, therapeutic schemes offered to different persons are different. Ayurveda health centers offer each tourist customized and personalized therapeutic schemes to solve his/her health problems from the points of view of body, mind and soul.
3. **Spiritual retreat in holy land of yoga** - Relies on graceful natural environment and considers yoga culture as the basis to derive various philosophy, retreat and establish Ayurveda rehabilitation destinations. For example, Pune, Rishikesh, Dharamshala, Gokarna, Mysore and other regions with rich yoga culture are world-famous places for spiritual retreat. Personalized treatment, group curriculum,

short-term experience curriculum and long-term training classes provided at these places to tourists have become extremely popular.

## Summary

Traditional medical and health tourism regards happiness and harmony among body, mind and soul as its ultimate goal. India's traditional medicines have assisted profoundly in the development of tourism from all health dimensions, namely, body, mind and soul. Compared to India, TCM health tourism has been limited from two aspects, namely, personalized treatment and spiritual retreat. The main reasons are as follows. First, in spite of having numerous students or talents in the field of TCM, number of medical practitioners has been very less in this sector because it is difficult for physicians possessing professional qualifications to enter the TCM health tourism market due to restrictions in system, mechanism and other objective factors. Second, China has rich resources of wellness culture such as the Great Ultimate, *dhyana* and *zazen* but no spiritual retreat system is formed. The nation has not been quite able to promote TCM health tourism with high-quality and high-end tourism products.

### Suggestions for Development of TCM Health Tourism

TCM health tourism should use India's experience for reference and promote personalized treatment programs and spiritual retreats. In the future, efforts need to be made in the following aspects.

#### *Give Play to Synergy among Tourism Department, TCM Management Departments and Health Associations*

The fact that physicians are gradually getting greater freedom in China in the aspect of job selection and more professional technical talents are conveyed to health tourism market at present is good news for development of TCM health tourism. Meanwhile, there is a greater need of coordination and cooperation among the tourism department, TCM management departments and various health associations for better resource integration and market standardization. India's health tourism market is synergistically managed by the government and the private sector including National Ministry of Health and Family Welfare, Ministry of Tourism, AYUSH, NABH and various associations. Certain associations play an important role in delivering responsibilities and functions, viz., protection of India's traditional remedies (especially yoga and Ayurveda), promotion of traditional medical tourism, statistical analysis of data, establishment of industry regulations, standards and legislation.

### *Promote Standardization and Hierarchical Classification Management in the TCM Health Tourism Sector*

TCM health tourism market is huge but management issues and varying quality are witnessed due to its late start. India's experience is worth learning from the aspects like physician qualification certification, standardization of health tourism base and hierarchical classification management model. NABH is especially responsible for certification of qualification of medical practitioners in Ayurveda centers, spa centers, skincare centers, aesthetic nursing centers, gymnasiums, health centers, preventive health centers and yoga centers. Ministry of Tourism, Government of Kerala and Indian Systems of Medicine (ISM) jointly set standards for evaluating safety and service of Ayurveda centers. The Government of Kerala has commenced awarding green leaf and olive leaf certifications to Ayurveda centers. Hierarchical classification management in many aspects including physical therapy facilities and resorts has been emphasized.

### *Strengthen Brand Marketing and Expand Global Influence*

TCM health tourism falls short in developing international strategies in brand marketing. At present, only Sanya TCM Hospital is known to have expanded internationally and tourists are mainly from Russia (Zhang Guanghai and Wang Jia, 2012). Thus, it is suggested that TCM medical and health tourism should strengthen international contact, travel websites and its cooperation with domestic and foreign medical institutions. Moreover, TCM international trade should be brought into the overall strategy of national foreign trade development to promote TCM institutions. Finally, it is recommended to learn from India how to gain popularity worldwide and influence with celebrity power.

### *Explore Resources of Wellness Culture to Create Products Pertaining to Spiritual Retreat Tourism*

India's Ayurvedic medicine is combined with yoga and meditation to provide tourists with health and wellness resources from three aspects, namely, body, spirit and soul, so as to let tourists achieve harmony and unity among body, mind and soul. China should also explore rich resources of regional wellness culture and popularize the Great Ultimate, *dhyana* and *zazen* which are aimed at cultivating moral characters and promoting harmony among body, mind and soul to create products pertaining to spiritual retreat tourism with Chinese characteristics and get them integrated into TCM health tourism projects.

## Notes

1. https://www.docin.com/p-1054791297.html
2. Ternary body liquids include Vata, Pitta and Kapha (wind, bile and mucous).
3. See http://ayush.gov.in/infrastructure/state-wise-statistics
4. State Administration of Traditional Chinese Medicine. China.
5. Statistical Yearbook of Chinese Medicine 2016 [R/OL]. Retrieved from http://www.states.gov.cn/)
6. Development Status and Future Trends of Traditional Chinese Medicine Health Tourism. http://m.sohu.com/a/156407173_99915831

## References

International Ayurveda Foundation. 'Globalisation of Ayurveda: A Global Vision for the Next Decade by Mr. Praful Patel, General Secretary, IAF.' Global Scenario of Traditional System of Medicine, Ayurveda, Agriculture and Education. Smile Health Care. http://iaf-ngo.org/pdf/Globalisation%20of%20Ayurveda%20-%20a%20global%20vision%20for%20next%20decade%20(No.1).pdf

Smith, Melanie, and László Puczkó. 2009. *Health and Wellness Tourism*. London: Elsevier/Butterworth-Heinemann.

V. A. Haseena. 2015. 'The Routes of Wellness in Tourism in Kerala and Its Impacts.' *Journal of Tourism, Hospitality and Sports* 5, 21–26.

Wang Yan. 2008. 'Comparison of Basic Theories of Health Tourism at Home and Abroad [J].' *Research on Technology, Economy and Management* 3, 109–114.

Zhang Guanghai and Wang Jia. 2012. 'Research on Resources and Functional Zoning of Medical Tourism in China [J].' *Resource Science* 7, 1329.

# Part III

# Socio-cultural Insights

From the economic and sectoral insights presented in the earlier two sections, it becomes evident that for the two nations, as they move towards a fast-track growth trajectory, there are bound to be possibilities of economic rivalry and political differences when one looks at reforms and policies. However, in this section we look at India and China from a different lens and appreciate the similarities between them. Both counties are marked by a diverse and dispersed terrain as well as a large populace. Secondly, one observes a near similar regional imbalance and cultural diversity in both the countries. In terms of demographic dividend, both nations have a significant number of inhabitants who live in the rural areas and due to lack of opportunities there is a visible exodus towards urban cities that have better employment opportunities. Further, though both geographies are marked by a collectivist culture, one observes an evolution and transformation of thought towards individualism and indulgence. A large and experimental younger population that is tech savvy and more receptive to change, brings the two nations almost at a similar point of a cultural shift.

The chapters in this section on 'Socio-cultural Insights' examine an expanse of issues and perspectives ranging from historical to cultural as well as contemporary issues such as green human resource practices and health tourism. Chapter 20 traces the origin of the Indo-Chinese trade and cultural exchanges to the more-than-2000-years-old *Silk Road Economic Belt* and the modern *21st-Century Maritime Silk Road*, which are together referred to as the *Belt and Road Initiative*. It articulates at length the myriad opportunities for cultural exchange between the two nations. Chapter 21 is a detailed discussion about one of the great Chinese politicians and visionaries, Deng Xiaoping, who recognized the need for improvement in the bilateral relations of the two countries. The author examines various principles of peaceful coexistence advocated by Xiaoping and how adherence to these principles will lead to peace and development between both the great nations and contribute immensely to world peace. Chapter 22 looks at developing cultural exchanges between the Sichuan province in China and India. Sichuan is a region that has been identified after the October 2015, 'Belt-and-Road' initiative by China. The chapter examines the historical and emerging cultural exchanges between India and the Sichuan region, especially in the context of Buddhist culture. Chapter 23 looks at the tourism sector in China and India. It begins with providing a strong case for why cross border cooperation is needed to make the zone a tourist friendly and enabled region. The key enablers are identified as complementarities of tourist resources, the trend of regional economic integration, market driving force and the impetus from the two governments. Chapter 24 draws parallels between the initiatives taken by the two countries, viz., sustainability and adoption of Green Human Resource practices prevalent in organizations therein. The authors propose a conceptual framework that can be validated and tested through real time data collected from organizations operating in the two countries, which can be used to do a micro as well as comparative analysis on the sustainability focus of the two regimes. Chapter 25 looks at one of the most significant areas of Indo-Chinese synergy, that is, the amalgamation of Buddhist Cultural exchange through the east-west movement of Chinese and Indian monks. The cultural exchange is traced from the time of the first Chinese monk, Faxian, to the last Indian monk, Zhikong. Chapter 26 attempts to establish the significance of the Silk Road in establishing international peace. The short chapter traces the inception of the Southern Silk Road and its importance in encouraging the spirit of exchange and cooperation between borders and traces its importance till date in not only encouraging the transportation of goods but building synergy and harmony at international borders.

Thus, the last and the final section of the book is extremely interesting and important as it identifies not only the similarity of thought, religion and practices between India and China but also the plethora of possibilities for collaborative effort to enable cultural exchanges between the two nations and serve to contribute to the prosperity and progress of both the countries.

CHAPTER 20

# 'The Belt and Road' Initiative and Cultural Exchanges Between China and India

Huan Yang

## Introduction

'The Belt and Road' comprises 'the Silk Road Economic Belt' and '21st-Century Maritime Silk Road'. This article attempts to elaborate the significance of 'the Belt and Road' initiative in the context of cultural exchanges between China and India. As India attaches great importance to strengthening connectivity in South Asia and is ready to reinforce cooperation with China, 'the Belt and Road' initiative serves the interests of both China and India. Based on the vision of joint development, this article is of practical significance. It discusses about an outstanding envoy in the history of China–India cultural exchanges, explains how the Belt and Road construction is an opportunity to further develop the Chinese and Indian cultures and also puts forth the huge impact of the initiative on Sino-Indian cultural exchanges.

## Silk Road and the Initiation of the Dialogue Between China and India

More than 2,000 years ago, there was a trade route commencing from Chang'an on the mainland of China passing through the Hexi Corridor and Serindia leading to India, Central Asia and finally to Europe. Many of China's commodities, especially silk was sent abroad by this road. The German geographer Ferdinand Freiherr von Richthofen first named it as 'the Silk Road' in the 1870s. The 'Silk Road' was an overland trade and cultural exchange channel initiated by ancient Chinese in the Han Dynasty, starting from Luoyang and Chang 'an, connecting the eastern and the western civilizations.

In the long course of history, this road has not only played an important role in communicating the nature of the economic activities and trade of the Eurasian continent to other regions of the world, but has also had a huge impact on the exchange of Eastern and Western cultures as well as on their integration (Li Wei, 2015). The 'Silk Road Economic Belt' and '21st-Century Maritime Silk Road' is together referred to as the 'the Belt and Road' in short.

In about 164 BC, an envoy in the Western Han Dynasty, Zhang Qian started from Chang'an, to unite DaRouZhi to fight against the Huns and in this endeavour he explored the silk road for the first time. After conquering the Lucid Empire in Syria and the Ptolemaic Dynasty in Egypt, Rome obtained Chinese silk from the Silk Road through the Parthian Empire and the Kingdom of Aksum. At the end of the Western Han Dynasty, the Silk Road was cut off. In the Eastern Han Dynasty, Ban Chao set out from Luoyang to undertake another diplomatic mission to the western regions. His entourage arrived in Rome, which is said to be the 'first dialogue' between the eastern and the western civilizations. In the Eastern Han Dynasty, Indian monks arrived at Luoyang along this Silk Road and Buddhism was introduced into China leading to the popularity of the Silk Road.

## The Most Outstanding Envoy in the History of China–India Cultural Exchange

While talking about the cultural exchanges between China and India, monk Xuanzang deserves a special mention.

Xuanzang (602–664 A.D.) is a monk belonging to the Tang Dynasty. He is one of the greatest sutra translators in the history of Buddhism. It is he who widely spread the Indian culture in China. Xuanzang became a monk at the age of 13 and went west alone along the Silk Road when he was just 27 years old beginning his religious journey of 50,000 miles.

At the age of 41, he returned to Chang'an, bringing back 657 Sanskrit Buddhist scriptures. Since then, Xuanzang concentrated on translating Buddhist scriptures in Chang'an. It took 19 years to translate 1,335 volumes. The original Buddhist scriptures, however, had been lost. Thus, Xuanzang's translations became an important historical material for studying ancient Indian culture. He also translated Lao-tzu's *Tao Te Ching* into Sanskrit and introduced it to ancient India. Xuanzang also authored the 12 volumes of *Buddhist Records of the Western World*. It describes the 110 countries he experienced as he traveled to the west, as well as the mountains and rivers, land and people, products and customs. Through the journey to the west, Xuanzang could really integrate Buddhism culture into the ordinary people's life. *Buddhist Records of the Western World* recorded Xuanzang's observations and experiences about more than 100 countries on the South Asian continent and described in detail all aspects of social life in India found more than 1,300 years ago. It is thus a detailed record of Indian society and history of ancient times and is of great significance in the study of Indian culture.

Indians believe that without Xuanzang's accurate description put forth in the *Buddhist Records of the Western World*, the medieval history of India could not have been written clearly. In the eyes of Indian scholars, Xuanzang is considered to have been closely associated with the history and culture of India. It is Xuanzang who immensely helped India record its past glory. Even now, Indians still hold Xuanzang in high esteem and his name is a household name in India. Anyone who has attended a secondary school in India knows about this famous Chinese monk.

After 1300 AD, British archaeologists and Indian scholars excavated Buddhagaya, Kushinagar, Lumbini and other Buddhist holy places and countless historical sites on the ancient land of India along with the *Buddhist Records of the Western World*. The history of Medieval India has since been seen again. Indian historian M. Athar Ali once said that, without the works of Xuanzang and others, it is definitely impossible to reconstruct the history of India. British historian Vincent A. Smith also said 'Xuanzang played an utmost important role in the history of ancient India, he was the only light in the dark of medieval Indian history' (Li Wei, 2015). The *Buddhist Records of the Western World* is like a torch lighting up the history of India.

Indians believe that it was Xuanzang who initiated the first official exchange between China and India and also friendly exchanges between the two governments.

In India, the Xuanzang Memorial Museum was finally renovated in the year 2006, which became an important event in the 2006 China–India friendship year. In February 2007, the inauguration ceremony of the memorial took place. More than 300 eminent monks and government officials from China and India attended the ceremony. In the mid-1950s, Prime Ministers of India and China had proposed to cooperate to start the construction of Xuanzang Memorial near Nalanda Monastery, where Xuanzang studied and lived, to commemorate this great traveler forever. In the memorial inaugural ceremony in 2007, Li Zhaoxing, the foreign minister of China, who was visiting India at that time, said 'Xuanzang Memorial is not only a symbol of traditional friendship between the two countries, but also a witness of mutual support between the two civilizations. Memorial's restoration is perfect in bringing new motivation for cultural and religious exchanges between the two countries' (Li Wei, 2015).

More than 1,300 years have passed since master Xuanzang went west along the Silk Road to India, but his imprint on India is still clear and this has been a powerful testimony of the traditional friendship between the people of China and India. Master Xuanzang's unique experiences have written a new chapter of close contacts between countries specifically the cultural exchanges between the east and the west. Xuanzang carried out his preachings of Buddhism throughout his life and promoted Buddhism from temple to temple. He consciously undertook the historical mission of linking the concept of prosperity advocated by Buddhism with the stability of the political power and society showing an outstanding Buddhist scholar's profound understanding of social history and extraordinary insight. It is of high significance for us to deal with the development of Buddhist culture in the new period, to promote social harmony, to deepen the coordinated development of different social economies and cultures and to form a mutually beneficial and win-win relationship.

## The Construction of 'the Belt and Road' Brings Opportunities for China and India to Deepen Cultural Exchanges

### Opportunities for Deepening Cultural Exchanges Between China and India

Since its inception, 'the Belt and Road', an international cooperation initiative focusing on broad participation, sharing and win-win cooperation, has received positive response and strong support from all countries. First, people from all walks of life in India who are involved in this strategy evaluated the initiative as having high importance.

1. Tarun Vijay, member of the Indian Parliament and Chairman of the India–China friendship group, pointed out at an international seminar on 'the Belt and Road' initiative held by the Jawaharlal Nehru University that the strategy will promote political mutual trust, economic cooperation and cultural exchanges between China and India, which is of great significance to the friendly relations between the two countries.
2. Arvind Kumar, the Dean of the school of international relations at the University of Manipur in India believes that 'the Belt and Road' strategy is reasonable and easy to implement, will greatly promote the economic development of countries along the road, which will elevate the existing economic cooperation in the region to the height of economic integration.
3. Professor Chintamani of Jawaharlal Nehru University pointed out that the proposal for 'the Belt and Road' strategy and its implementation show that the current international order is undergoing tremendous changes, emerging power represented by China will gradually replace the United States and the western countries to dominate the world order, and the concepts of mutual trust, economic cooperation and cultural exchanges emphasized by the

Belt and Road will become the characteristics of a new international order, too.

4. Doctor Girijesh Pant said that India must be involved in such major projects if it wants to achieve greater success in the economic domain. India is facing an opportunity, joining the economic trend is inevitable, and it is possible to obtain a win-win result base on the initiative.

Based on the question of whether or not to participate in the Belt and Road construction, most of India's intellectual elites held a positive attitude. The Asian Century cannot be achieved without the cooperation between China and India, and the Asian civilization must be supported by two great civilizations, China and India.[1]

## Grasp the Opportunity to Promote Cultural Exchange and Cooperation

In line with the discourse held regarding the opportunities involved in the construction of 'the Belt and Road', China and India should try to reap the benefits from the cultural aspects, resource integration, etc., to further promote all-round exchanges and cooperation between them.

### *Promote Cultural Exchange and Cooperation Between Two Governments*

A long-term strategic planning in the field of cultural exchanges by the two countries' governments is sought in this respect. Proper implementation of cultural cooperation agreements, providing legal protection to cultural exchanges and cooperation, enriching cultural cooperation under the existing institutional framework are all necessary.

### *Carefully Create a New Cultural Exchange Brand*

China and India should hinge on the existing cultural achievements and brands, coordinate the existing projects while also build a new cultural exchange brand; the two countries should hold cultural forums, exhibitions and performances in various forms.

The two countries need to explore the cultural undertone and humanistic spirit of the ancient Silk Road continuously, and endow new meanings to those in the contemporary world. They should collaborate in translating and publishing books, making and screening pertinent films. The two nations should pay attention to the use of new networking platforms and new media, give full play to the role of cultural offices or groups of embassies and consulates and overseas cultural centers to further improve the layout of Chinese and Indian cultural centers.

### *Integrate Resources to Form Synergy*

China and India have special advantages in the process of building 'the Belt and Road'. They must mobilize the enthusiasm of various cultural enterprises, formulate China–India cultural exchange and trade policies, promote cooperation between their cultural industries. China and India should try to fully excavate their historical and cultural heritage to guide and to mobilize the private sector to carry out rich and diverse cultural exchange activities. In addition, they should consider the important role played by the experts and scholars in providing intellectual support for Sino-Indian cultural exchanges and cooperation from the perspective of taking the 'Land and Maritime Silk Road' initiative through regular forums, seminars and research activities.

## Cultural Inheritance and Innovation in the Context of the Construction of 'the Belt and Road'

The Silk Road had existed in ancient times reflecting the courage and perseverance of human beings to cross the barriers, to promote exchange and mutual understanding, writing an important chapter in the history of exchanges between ancient east and the west. The new 'the Belt and Road' initiative again possesses new rich connotations and far-reaching significance. The inheritance of traditional culture and the innovation of modern culture have ushered in unique opportunities for development.

## Cultural Influence Transcends Time, Space and National Borders

Cultural exchanges may be termed as a 'popularity winning' project (Beijing Research Center for Theoretical System of Socialism with Chinese Characteristics. 2015). The ancient Silk Road has been a road for cultural communication. Many scientific and cultural innovations of ancient China were transmitted to the West through the Silk Road. Through these routes, Chinese silk, porcelain, lacquer work and ironware were shipped to the West, while pepper, flax, spices, grape and pomegranate entered China. Through these routes, Buddhism, Islamic astronomy, calendar and medicine found their way to China, while China's four great inventions and silkworm breeding spread to other parts of the world. Furthermore, Buddhism originated in India, blossomed in China and was enriched in Southeast Asia. Confucianism, which was born in China, gained appreciation by European thinkers such as Leibniz and Voltaire. Herein lies the appeal of mutual learning (Economic and Commercial Office of the Chinese, 2017).

## 'The Belt and Road' is the Bond between Different Cultures in China and India

The exchanges and mutual learning between different civilizations are the main channels for cultural development and prosperity and the label of the era with increasingly diverse and mutually inclusive civilizations. The friendship between nations lies in the friendship between the people, and the friendship between the people lies in the connection between their hearts. Cultural inheritance and innovation are the core pillar for economic and trade cooperation between the two countries. Only through cultural exchanges and cooperation can two people have a common language, enhance mutual trust and deepen mutual feelings.

According to the Ministry of Culture of China, over the years, the cultural exchanges between China and countries along the road have become more creative and abundant, marking the foundation and the beginning of the future (*Economic Daily*, 2015). The people of

China need to place themselves on the existing foundation, create new models, explore new mechanisms and conduct friendlier exchanges with India in the areas of art and culture, science, education, sports, tourism. China and India should fully explore their profound cultural heritage, inherit and carry forward the cultural symbol in terms of the historical appeal of 'the Belt and Road', play an active role in cultural exchanges and cooperation and jointly promote the common development of different civilizations.

## The Significance of 'the Belt and Road' Initiative in the Cultural Exchanges Between China and India

### Importance of Culture in Strengthening Ties Between Nations

China and India are both ancient civilizations and have a history of friendly exchanges for more than 2,000 years. In the early 1950s, the two countries further advocated the Five Principles of Peaceful Coexistence, which were praised by the international community as a model for dealing with relations between nations. Mahatma Gandhi had said, 'China and India are fellow travelers in the same boat, sharing weal and woe.' The current Indian Prime Minister Narendra Modi also said that China and India are 'two bodies but sharing one spirit'. These words reveal their common intent on maintaining regional peace and the inner spiritual connection of the two civilizations.

In September 2014, President Xi Jinping officially visited India and jointly proposed a blueprint for the two countries' future relations. The most outstanding point is that both sides have emphasized that China and India should be committed to becoming 'development partners' under the new circumstances.

Regarding the traditional cultural similarities between the two countries, Xi Jinping pointed out that the relations between the countries lie in the close association between the people. He added that there are striking similarities between Chinese Tai Chi and Indian Yoga, Chinese Medicine and Ayurveda in India. The philosophy of life of the people in the two nations has been similar for thousands of years (Xi Jinping, 2014). As two ancient civilizations, China and India have the ability and wisdom to forge a path of friendly relations.

Xi Jinping further pointed out that the 'Great Harmony' advocated by the Chinese nation coincides with the 'One World' pursued by the Indian people and the 'Universal Love' advocated by the Chinese nation are in line with the notion of 'Keeping Away from Causing Harm to Others' advocated by the Indian people (Xinhuanet, 2014). He added: 'We all regard 'harmony' as the avenue taken by the world at large and we hope that all the countries will live in peace and harmony'.

About the history of cultural exchanges between the two countries, Xi Jinping pointed out that China and India have a documented history of communication of more than 2,000 years. Buddhism emerged from the west and spread to the east. There is a long account of Buddhist exchanges in the history of China and India.

In 67 AD, Indian monks Kasyapa Matanga and Dharmaraksa came to Luoyang, China. A white horse carried Buddhist scriptures for them. The *Sutra in Forty-Two Sections* translated by the masters became the earliest translation of Buddhist scriptures in the history of Chinese Buddhism. Again, monk Xuanzang traveled west to bring the Indian culture back. The great Chinese navigator, Zheng He, had also undertaken seven voyages to the Western Oceans. In this effort he arrived in India too and established friendship there.

In the process of cultural exchanges, Indian dance and music, astronomy, literature, architecture, sugar technology and so on were introduced to China. On the other hand, Chinese paper, silk, porcelain, tea, music and so on were introduced into India. All these carry an evidence of the history of mutual exchange and mutual learning between the people of the two nations since ancient times.

Culture though seems to be invisible, is the most effective way to promote mutual understanding and communication between different people and countries. Today, China and India should inherit the spirit of cultural exchanges and cooperation in history and carry it forward, so that the exchange of cultures will strengthen ties between the two countries. People-to-people ties provide an anchor for laying the foundation of the Belt and Road Initiative. To this end, extensively carrying out the idea of harmonious coexistence of mankind with nature and 'ecological civilization' can lay a solid foundation for deepening bilateral cooperation.

To realize the Belt and Road construction, China must focus on and attach importance to India, strengthen communication and understanding with India in areas including culture, spread China's peaceful development concept, carry out cultural diplomacy and actively build cooperation content and mechanism for cultural exchanges. To establish closer new diplomatic relations with South Asian countries including India, safeguarding each other's national interests in the process of peaceful development is sought.

As the importance and the benefits of cultural mutual understanding and peaceful development are accepted by all in recent times, China and India should carry out cultural diplomacy in the fields of historical culture, religious culture and ecological culture and promote peace. These endeavours will lead to conflict resolution in South Asia to quite some extent.

## Role of the Belt and Road Initiative in the Context of Cultural Exchanges Between China and India

In the process of building the Belt and Road, China must actively play the role of cultural bridge and lead the role, strengthen cultural exchanges and cooperation between the two countries. The Belt and Road initiative is significant from the following perspectives:

### *Helps to Promote the Development of Different Civilizations*

The ancient Silk Road is not only a road of mutual trust in trade, a road of economic cooperation, but also a road of cultural exchange and a road of dialogue among civilizations. The culture and inventions of ancient China which were transmitted to the west through the Silk Road played a positive role in promoting the development of civilizations in the west. At the same time, cultural achievements of the west have been introduced to China through the road which has also promoted the development of the Chinese civilization. For example, Buddhism was originated in India, blossomed in China and was enriched in Southeastern Asia. Confucianism, which was born in China, gained appreciation by European thinkers such as Leibniz and Voltaire.

China and India must fully explore their profound cultural heritage, assimilate the spirit of the 'Silk Road'—a cultural symbol and carry it forward with broad affinity and profound appeal, such that the two countries can integrate the rational contents of culture and promote common development of different civilizations.

### *Helps to Strengthen Public Opinion from the Perspective of Cultural Cooperation Between the Two Countries*

The friendship between nations lies in the friendship between the people and the friendship between the people lies in the connection between hearts. The development of relationship between China and India needs the strong support of economic and trade cooperation as well as the 'soft' power. The history, culture and religion of the two countries are different. Only through cultural exchanges and cooperation can the people of these two nations have a common language, enhance mutual trust, deepen mutual feelings, strengthen the friendship, consolidate public support and the Belt and Road project possesses the power to foster such collaborative activities.

## Conclusion

Ancient India and ancient China are listed in the four ancient civilizations of the world. It can be seen that the friendship between China and India has been established long ago and there are facts of mutual exchange and integration in all aspects.

Due to the collision and fusion of Indian ancient culture and tradition with modern culture, Indian ideas are gradually changing. India's development is bound to move towards a higher level of internationalization, which coincides with China's development. Our mutual cultural exchange will become the driving force for the development of each of us.

The Silk Road, that is, the traditional Silk Road opened during the Han Dynasty by Zhang Qian, and the 'Belt and Road' comprising the Silk Road Economic Belt and 21st-Century Maritime Silk Road, both have played an indispensable role in the cultural exchanges between China and India. In this era, when the trend is changing rapidly, Sino-Indian cultural exchanges through the new initiative can further promote each other and eventually achieve the goal of immense mutual benefit.

Regarding the exchange of Chinese and Indian cultures, Ji Xianlin, a famous Chinese scholar, once pointed out: 'In the 21st century, the key to the comprehensive rejuvenation of oriental culture is the blending of Chinese culture and Indian culture' (Qin Weixian, 2015). This is the classic saying proving that Ji has the insight of historian and the deep insight of a philosopher. This saying is of much theoretical significance from the perspective of today's Belt and Road construction.

Since China and India are both among the four ancient civilizations and are largest in the world in terms of population and as both countries have undergone reform and opening-up, the economic and cultural development of the two countries leads to the rise of Asia.

## Note

1. The Belt and Road Will become a New Opportunity further Associated with China and India. http://blog.sina.com.cn/s/blog_1613ad2b80102wc8y.html.

## References

Economic and Commercial Office of the Chinese. 2017. *Work Together to Build the Silk Road Economic Belt and the 21st Century Maritime Silk Road.* http://gn.mofcom.gov.cn/article/ddfg/201705/20170502584217.shtml

*Economic Daily.* 2015, January 29. Beijing Research Center for Theoretical System of Socialism with Chinese Characteristics. 2015. 'Cultural Heritage and Innovation under the Belt and Road Initiative.' *Economic Daily.* http://www.ce.cn/.

Li Wei. 2015, 13 May. 'The Angel of the Most Outstanding on the Sino-Indian Cultural Exchanges, Xuanzang.' *Shaanxi Daily.*

Qin Weixian. 2015. 'On Ji Xianlin's Sino-Indian Cultural Exchange Theory under the Background of 'the Belt and Road'.' *Liberation Daily.*

Xi Jinping. 2014, 19 September. 'Xi Jinping's Speech in India: Pursuing the Dream of National Renewal Together.' *People's Daily.* Retrieved from http://opinion.people.com.cn/n/2014/0919/c1003-25694074.html

Xinhuanet. 2014. *Xi Jinping Delivers an Important Speech at the Indian World Affairs Committee.* http://www.xinhuanet.com//world/2014-09/19/c_1112539531.htm

CHAPTER 21

# Deng Xiaoping's Historical Contribution to China–India Relations

Xiannong Yang

## Introduction

As the initiator of a new diplomatic route during the period of China's reform and opening up, Deng Xiaoping paid close attention to the issue of world peace and development in as early as 1988. Deng Xiaoping put forward that, to strive for a peaceful international environment for China's modernization, not only the people around the world, but China also really needs a peaceful environment. He added that China's foreign policy thereby seeks a peaceful environment to achieve the four modernizations, not only in the interests of the Chinese people, but in the interest of the people of the world at large (Deng Xiaoping, 1994). China and India are both great ancient civilizations having a long history of traditional friendship. Deng Xiaoping put forth that, to strive for a peaceful international environment, the first thing that is sought is to establish and develop good and friendly relations based on cooperation with neighbouring countries in order to achieve good and peaceful surroundings. He especially wished development of friendly relations of China with India and other Asian countries to become better friends in the context of long-term strategic directions. Deng Xiaoping played a huge role in establishing friendly relations between China and India, and is noted for his outstanding contributions in this respect.

## 'Friendship Must Be Built Between China and India' (Deng Xiaoping, 1993)

During the period of reform and opening up of China, keeping in view the experiences and lessons from the history of development of China–India relations, Deng Xiaoping pointed out that the two nations shared a long-term traditional friendship; however, for quite some time, they had been unpleasant to each other; nonetheless they now need to forget that episode to look forward to the future together (Zhang MinQiu, 2004). Deng Xiaoping laid emphasis on forgetting the unpleasant history and moving on; this notion of his has been very wise. He stressed on the fact that under the new circumstances, people need to know the development challenges, actively build a new world order to improve and develop friendly relations between China and India. In the 1960s, China and India got engaged in some conflicts. The conflicts have a special historical background pertaining to the Cold War and various other complex reasons. In the new period of reform and opening up of China, Deng Xiaoping summarized the historical experiences and lessons, wisely stressed on the choice to 'forget' the unhappy past, focusing on the development of relations between the two countries. Thus, there is a tone of clarity in terms of the importance of bilateral relations between the two countries for the development of the two nations. With the development of bilateral relations since the 1980s, though the path has been twisted, a bright future could be well expected, in general, for both the countries. As they wished for a pragmatic cooperation, the unhappy past did not affect the normal development of the relations between the two countries.

China and India are emerging countries having great influence on the world as reckoned by all. Thus, the relationship between the two countries will directly affect the construction of a new world order. Deng Xiaoping held the notion that 'both sides should do something to restore the fifties friendship' (Deng Xiaoping, 1993). He pointed out that both countries are developing countries, but both have a strong influence in Asia as well as on the economic, political and cultural development on the global front. Both China and India have large populations, which add up to more than a third of the population of the world. It has been therefore opined by Deng Xiaoping that, as these two nations are close neighbours, failure to build up mutual understanding and friendship will be disadvantageous for them (Deng Xiaoping, 1993). He added that if China and India do not develop, the Asian Century will not come. The genuine Asian Century will not arrive until China, India and other neighbouring countries are developed (Deng Xiaoping, 1993). The so-called 'Asia-Pacific Century' cannot be therefore established without the development of China and India and hence the two countries should improve their relationship and strengthen all-round cooperation between each other.

To realize national rejuvenation, India must develop their economy again and in turn, the international state-of-affairs. For this, the country also needs a peaceful development opportunity. With India and China being big emerging countries and important BRICS nations (Brazil, Russia, India, China, and South Africa), the two sides are highly complementary, their domestic reforms and development have similar goals. There is a feeling that, in the recent years, India at times has wished to learn about and use the experiences of Deng Xiaoping in reforming and opening up China, to undertake similar bold reforms to solve India's economic problems. As China and India have tried to share the achievements from the reforms and development undertaken by both sides, it became a breakthrough point to deepen the friendship between the two countries.

India should consider Deng Xiaoping's role as the chief designer of China's reform and opening up and the history as to why and how these reforms took place. First of all, as far as the Chinese Communist Party and state leaders are concerned, there is no politician in China who can replace Deng Xiaoping in the minds of the Chinese people from the point of view of the significant role played by him in strengthening the Communist Party of China and the power of the Chinese people thereby assisting the country to have profound authority in the world.

Second, as the Chinese people were looking for a new period of reforms in the 1970s, this united all powers, and Deng Xiaoping's opening-up reforms for the prosperity of Chinese people therefore received sincere support from all. This also led to a high degree of satisfaction for the Chinese people. Third, under the leadership of Deng Xiaoping, a strong team was formed, stretching from central to the local level, from the coasts to the mainland, involving a large number of people determined to direct the reform and opening up process according to Deng Xiaoping's theory and ensure that the policies are put in place successfully, breaking through the barriers. Fourth, Deng Xiaoping, who is particularly noted for his superb reform ideas and initiatives, put forward the idea of correctly handling the relationship between reform, development and stability, 'top-level design' and 'grassroots exploration', to conduct and coordinate safe, step by step, gradual in-depth reforms continuously.

As the enormous success of China's reforms got recognized in world history, the factors mentioned in this article may serve as important reference points for Indian leaders focusing on the future from the perspective of further reforms to be undertaken for the development of the nation.

Deng Xiaoping attached great importance to India's enormous strength. Thus, he knew that the two countries' hand in hand development will have a far-reaching influence on Asia as well as the world. Deng Xiaoping tried to maintain a good friendship between the two countries and actively sought to improve relations between China and India.

With the advent of the new century, China–India relations have improved and developed, the two countries' economies have developed at high speed. Therefore, the international community paid close attention to the two countries, the development of the Asia miracle and the role of the two countries in the rise of Asia. Deng Xiaoping and other leaders of China as well as the Indian leaders have shared similar strategic vision and accordingly taken practical measures for accurate strategic positioning of these two nations on the global front.

## 'Both China and India Have a Shared Responsibility to Human Beings' (Deng Xiaoping, 1993)

Deng Xiaoping felt that China and India, as big developing countries, should give first priority to economic development; the 'South-South Cooperation' between China and India can be an exemplary model for other countries and would also help to promote the establishment of a new international political and economic order. Deng Xiaoping pointed out that the two countries have a common responsibility towards human beings, which is, to make use of the improved peaceful international environment to develop themselves. With respect to the question on how to maintain the peaceful international environment, Deng Xiaoping pointed out that the two countries should aim at advocating and adhering to the five principles of peaceful coexistence. In today's world, amidst hegemony and power politics, achieving world peace and development are two pressing concerns. Though people all over the world are against hegemony and power politics, the task of maintaining world peace is still arduous. Looking at the past experiences and the international status quo, China and India's common responsibility would be to advocate and follow the principles, viz., mutual respect for one another's sovereignty and territorial integrity, non-aggression, non-interference in one another's affairs, equality and mutual benefit, and peaceful coexistence and thereby to establish peace and a stable, fair and reasonable new international political and economic order.

In the late 1980s, a variety of ideas for establishing a new international political and economic order were put forward by some powerful countries. Deng Xiaoping timely put forward his ways of dealing with the concerns in China, which called for the new international political and economic order based on the five principles of peaceful coexistence. These new principles are completely different from the old order, which had been hegemonic with power politics by handful economies.

In 1988, as Deng Xiaoping met Indian PM Rajiv Gandhi, he clearly said that the world situation had changed. All countries were considering new policies and would like to establish a new international order. As hegemony, political or treaty organizations didn't work, therefore, what principles should be followed to guide the new international relations was a major question. Deng Xiaoping mentioned that the two countries' joint proposal of the five principles of peaceful coexistence is important in this respect and can stand the test of time. He added: 'We should use the five principles of peaceful coexistence as the guiding norms of international relations' (Deng Xiaoping, 1993). In 1989, Deng Xiaoping, during his meeting with certain foreign leaders, once again stressed that in coming times all nations should try to establish a new international economic order to solve the north-south problem; they should also establish a new international political order, which matches the new international economic order. He stated that in this respect he would like to refer to the 1950s, when the Asian people put forth the five principles of peaceful coexistence as the criterion for developing a new international political order in the future (Deng Xiaoping, 1993). Deng Xiaoping promoted the five principles of peaceful coexistence, because these principles advocated by China and India, were accepted by most countries in the world because of the fact that these principles conform to the fundamental interests of the people all over the world and are conducive to world peace and development. Establishing a new international order based on the five principles of peaceful coexistence is the urgent desire of people all over the world.

The five principles of peaceful coexistence use the most scientific and concise language, consistent with the Charter of the United Nations. They reflect the essential features of the new format of international relations and also peace and development trends of the recent times. Deng Xiaoping pointed out that, the five principles of peaceful coexistence are the best way to deal with relationships between countries. On the other hand, concepts of 'political groups' or 'spheres of influence' aggravate the international situation (Deng Xiaoping, 1993). It turns out that by focusing on the five principles of peaceful coexistence of the new international political and economic order, the fundamental desires and interests of people belonging to different countries can be addressed properly. This will lead to lasting world peace through common development and prosperity, which is beneficial to people all over the world.

The five principles of peaceful coexistence originated from the diplomatic wisdom of both the Chinese and the Indian governments. Since the 1950s, these principles have played an important role in international affairs. China and India's proposal and advocacy of the five principles of peaceful coexistence has been accepted by many countries in the world. Not only in China and India, but in other countries as well, many important international conferences and documents discussed the principles, which have become a guide to different social systems, different beliefs of the nation states on the basic rules of international communication. Deng Xiaoping pointed out that China and India once had good association in the 1950s. Premier Zhou Enlai and PM Nehru jointly proposed the five principles of peaceful coexistence, which have been recognized by the whole world (Deng Xiaoping, 1993). He summarized that these five principles are very clear and should be used to guide the norms of international relations. He suggested that while China and India will definitely try to follow these principles in addressing their relationship with each other, these principles should also guide their relationship with other neighbours (Deng Xiaoping, 1993). Advocated by China and India, the five principles thus contain the basic rule of international relations. They reflect the essential features of the new international order. As the principles are based on norms pertaining to international integrity, they are more comprehensive, reasonable and moderate than other international or regional legal principles. The five principles advocated complete abolition of the old unfair and unreasonable factors inherent in the international framework and reflected common desires of emerging or developing countries, conforming to the trend of modern democracy in international relations.

Under Deng Xiaoping's proposal, the Sino-Indian Joint Press Communique in 1988 emphasized that the five principles of peaceful coexistence are the fundamental guiding principles for good relationships between countries and the key to establishing a new international political order, the new international economic order. Establishing a new international political and economic order had been a complex task for a long time. The period after the second World War made it clear that the so-called camps, groups, allies in international relations, all of which are essentially divided according to the social systems, values or ideologies, are unreliable. Only by adhering to the five principles of peaceful coexistence can we establish a just international order. China–India relations demonstrate friendly practices in the context of development, which in turn have reflected Deng Xiaoping's advocacy of the five principles of peaceful coexistence in improving friendly cooperation between these two neighbouring countries. These principles completely conform to the interests of the two countries. Deng Xiaoping said: 'If the two countries developed, we have made a contribution to human beings' (Len Rong and Wang Zuoling, 2004). Deng Xiaoping explicitly pointed out that the common responsibility of the two countries should be to practise the five principles of peaceful coexistence highlighting an era that emphasized the importance of developing an international community. He also mentioned that both these countries insist on following these rules of international relations to maintain peace and stability in Asia and also worldwide.

## China and India 'Take Reasonable Way to Mutual Concessions' (Deng Xiaoping, 1993)

The China–India boundary dispute has been an obstacle to the development of their relations, hence, solving this problem calls for serious attention as the method adopted to solve the problem will have a direct impact on the relations between the two nations. Deng Xiaoping advocated that the boundary issue between the two sides should be solved through peaceful negotiation, compromise and taking a reasonable path as soon as possible. During a meeting with the Indian foreign minister in 1979, Deng Xiaoping said: 'The two countries should seek common ground while putting aside differences, take the time to improve relations, as the boundary issue between the two countries can be solved through peaceful negotiation' (Len Rong and Wang Zuoling, 2004). Deng Xiaoping stressed several times that when it comes to the border issue, seeking a 'package settlement' as a peaceful solution, seems reasonable. The so-called 'package settlement' means that two concerned parties actively interact and move in the same direction, forming a complete plan to solve problems comprehensively. Deng Xiaoping pointed out that the factors behind China–India boundary issues have been complex and should be settled as soon as possible (Len Rong and Wang Zuoling, 2004).

Deng Xiaoping paid close attention to the fate of the developing countries. He stressed that China emphasizes peaceful socialism; it shares a common fate with all third world countries. He also mentioned: 'China will never seek hegemony, never bully others, always stand in the third world' (Deng Xiaoping, 1993). He stressed on opposing any form of hegemony and thereby safeguarding world peace. There is no conflict of fundamental interests between China and India; prospect of bilateral cooperation is huge. According to Deng Xiaoping, the problem between the two countries is not much; neither China is a threat to India, nor is India a threat to China. If the two sides address the boundary issue reasonably, there is no difficulty in solving the problem. The two nations therefore need to compromise a bit. They can definitely take up a package solution to convince their own people. Deng Xiaoping said, 'I believe that we will eventually find a good solution. Even if we cannot solve, we can put it aside, and do many things in trade, economy, culture and other fields, develop and enhance understanding and friendship. We still have broad prospects of cooperation. We want China to develop, we also hope that you [Indians] develop' (Deng Xiaoping, 1993).

Deng Xiaoping believed that, as long as peace between China and India as well as their development rests on a shared vision, they will remain partners rather than enemies, and will be able to find a common commitment towards equality, mutual benefit, mutual support and development of constructive thinking. In this context certain points need to be discussed. First, Deng Xiaoping emphasized a relationship based on equality. Thus, China and India should have a positive attitude in considering themselves to be equal in status. Both sides should respect the history and the reality, engage in peaceful talks, should not resort to any sort of quarrels or apply any force to solve problems; the two governments need to explain various steps taken by them appropriately to the respective people. Second, Deng Xiaoping emphasized that for China and India's mutually beneficial cooperation, both sides, instead of considering a 'zero-sum game' approach should look for a peaceful solution to the boundary issue, the two sides must take actions to avoid any armed conflicts. Nonetheless, if the border issue cannot be solved, the nations can put it aside in a way that does not affect the normal development of the two countries' diplomatic, economic and cultural exchange relations and promote development and prosperity on both sides. On the basis of mutual trust, honest cooperation in trade, economic, cultural and other fields, both would be able to realize a win-win situation.

In line with Deng Xiaoping's aspiration of a reasonable and effective way to solve the China–India border dispute, peace talks were held where the Chinese government put forward certain guiding principles like equality, friendly consultation and a fair, reasonable and comprehensive solution. Pursuant to the visionary thinking of Deng Xiaoping, since the 1990s, although the boundary issues between the two countries have not been solved completely, those have not affected the exchanges and cooperation between the two countries. In the new century especially, frequent exchanges between both sides have been witnessed, the relations between the two countries continuously have improved, active exchanges have increasingly taken place in the diplomatic, economic, cultural and other fields. The two sides have both displayed consensus that these developments will contribute to solving the boundary problem. Therefore, by seeking a common ground while putting aside differences, China and many countries have tried to solve border issues in a peaceful way, which proves that Deng Xiaoping's thought is very relevant even in the recent times and takes care of the interests of the people of the different nations and will continue to do so.

## Both China and India Aim at 'Peaceful Development' (Deng Xiaoping, 1993)

Both China and India shoulder the duty to strengthen their economic power; improving people's life is a great task for national rejuvenation. Since China's reform and opening up, China's economic development sped slightly faster than India. Some people with ulterior motives began advocating the 'China threat theory' and put forth the view that as both these countries are developing countries, India faces a 'potential threat' from China's rise. 'Chinese threat' has become an obstacle to the development of China–India relations. To break this barrier, a relationship based on unity and cooperation between the two countries has been sought to influence their image in the international arena.

In this backdrop, it may be mentioned here that in 1982, Deng Xiaoping had stated that China and India are not a threat to each other. He had mentioned that the problem between the two countries is not very big, neither China is a threat to India, nor is India a threat to China (Deng Xiaoping, 1993). Since the 1970s, as Deng Xiaoping led China's reform and opening-up, China has very well considered the idea of peaceful development, which takes care of its national milieu along with the demands of the contemporary period. Peaceful development has been Chinese people's sincere desire and unremitting pursuance. China unswervingly tried to follow the path of peaceful development based on its traditional culture with confidence. At the beginning of the reform and opening up, Deng Xiaoping cited the historical episode of 'Zheng He's travelling to the West' to show China's opening up to the outside world (Deng Xiaoping, 1994). More than 600 years ago, during the Chinese Ming dynasty, famous navigator Zheng He led the world's largest fleet with the largest number of people to undertake 'seven expeditions to the western seas'. He went to more than 30 countries and regions in Asia and Africa, opened the 'maritime silk road', thereby etching China's grand feat in the maritime history. The expeditions assisted in carrying out economic and trade exchanges with other countries, enhancing mutual understanding, strengthening links and promoting friendship and thereby spreading peace all around the world. 'Zheng He's travelling to the West' fully reflects that the Chinese nation is a peace-loving nation, Chinese culture longs for peace and harmony. Based on the present scenario, it may be held that China's development is not only beneficial for the 1.4 billion Chinese people, but has also been conducive to the improvement in global peace; it has led to the creation of a huge market and provided development opportunities to the world. If China does not adhere to the policy of peace, and carries on hegemonic activities itself, only focusing on its own development, it will be a disaster and will lead to a historical regression for the world. Deng Xiaoping realized that the reason for China being considered as a 'threat' to India is largely due to the existence of the differences between the two countries, and the fact that people didn't pay attention to the excavation and the development of the common interests of both. There lies a great potential in exploring and developing common interests of the two countries and greater the dependency on each-other, the noise pertaining to the potential 'threat' will be weaker.

People around the world today long for development, desire to live a decent and dignified life and this is possible if there are peaceful conditions all around. Communities across the globe need to follow a common standard to regulate the relationship between each other and it can only be achieved through peaceful coexistence. Deng Xiaoping pointed out that in today's world, a country cannot achieve prosperity with closed doors and hence cannot be successful in this endeavour if it is not a part of the wide international community or the framework (Deng Xiaoping, 1993). In order to comply with the trend of world multi-polarization, to cope with the challenges and opportunities of globalization, strengthening exchanges and cooperation with other countries, implementing comprehensive opening up to the outside world and peaceful coexistence are the correct choices. In the face of a growing number of global concerns in recent times, strengthening cooperation and coordination with other countries and promoting mutual exchanges and communication following uniform rules and common practices has been the normal trend. Peace talks, equal dialogue and consultation are the right ways to solve international conflicts and maintain national security. The mutually beneficial cooperation between countries go hand in hand with their common development; a win-win situation can be achieved through the utilization of international resources while safeguarding national interests. Deng Xiaoping advocated that if China–India boundary issues cannot be dealt with instantly, then the nations should put it aside for the time being. With the development in the field of economy, trade, culture, etc., the 'China threat theory' will also be eliminated.

From the perspective of the development of China–India relations, with the adjustment in the Indian foreign policy as well, government and people in the two countries have tried strengthening exchanges and cooperation and increasing mutual understanding and trust between the two countries, such that 'China threat' in the Indian market gets weaker. The objective has been to connect with each other, complement each other and remain interdependent while at the same time maintaining their diversities.

It is important to maintain diversities in the world and one should learn to respect people from other cultural background or countries. Countries need to emphasize the concept of mutually beneficial cooperation, complement each other and try to achieve common development to create a peaceful and stable international environment by collaboratively promoting all civilizations or different social systems in the world. The path that needs to followed for development is 'peaceful coexistence' by emphasizing the concepts of 'developing together', 'mutual respect', 'mutual consultation', 'promoting each other economically', 'common development', 'trusting each other' and 'common prosperity'. Deng Xiaoping pointed that the new international order will not emerge through fierce struggle between nations, but through consultation, gradual reform and development; the new order is not based on a 'You Lose–I Win' thinking, but on the thinking of peaceful development and a win-win coexistence, harmonious situation.

## Conclusion

The rapid development of China and India in recent times have made them two big emerging countries and this has been possible as they complemented each other and not repelled each other. This chapter has tried to specifically focus on Deng Xiaoping's significant role and contribution in promoting friendly relations and cooperation between the two nations. China–India relations are very important in the context of current global development agenda and exert a significant influence on the Asia-pacific regional integration. The combined population of the two countries being more than 2.5 billion, they are set out to build a 'new model' of international relations with the promotion of the concept of win-win cooperation forming the core of the new model.

Since the late 1990s, China and India's trade has been growing rapidly. The two countries play a dynamic role in the development of the global economy. Economic and trade cooperation lies at the center of India's China policy considerations and is considered to be most powerful in the process of reconciliation between the two countries. It is the most active force for stable relations between the two nations and for the strong development of their economies. In June 2003 the two countries, in a joint declaration, put forth that the common interests of both the nations are greater than the differences. They are not a threat to one another. Both sides should refrain from using force or threatening to use force against the other (*People's Daily*, 2003). It showed that the two countries fully agreed with Deng Xiaoping's views about China and India not being a threat to each other, about their long-term peace and development. Deng Xiaoping had pointed out a bright future in China–India relations or friendship long ago.

Chinese President Xi Jinping pointed out: 'Comrade Deng Xiaoping's contribution, not only changed the historical destiny of the Chinese people, but also changed the history of the world. Comrade Deng Xiaoping won the Chinese people's sincere love, and also won wide respect from the people of the world' (Xi Jinping, 2014b). In the context of China's reform and opening up to develop the situation at home and abroad, Deng Xiaoping timely clarified the China–India relationship status, put forward a new thinking of developing China–India friendship, and personally worked with India on a continuous basis to improve bilateral relations, melt contradictions, aiming at cooperation instead of confrontation. In order to develop China–India relations further, conflicts have to be resolved step by step, both sides need to adopt a forward-looking attitude on the basis of the five principles of peaceful coexistence to get back on the path of the good-neighbourly friendship between the two countries. China and India as emerging superpowers manifest an inexorable rising trend. The two nations need to establish a new international order not only aiming at the development of various resources, but also a more balanced distribution of such resources in order to lay the foundation for a more stable and balanced international system. Deng Xiaoping's baton has been handed over to a new generation of successors. Xi Jinping said during a visit to India, 'China and India relations have gone far beyond the bilateral scope, and have extensive regional and global impact'. He added that China–India hand in hand cooperation will not only benefit them, but also Asia and the world at large. Therefore, he suggested China and India to become closer partners for growth and development, to become strategic cooperation partners (Xi Jinping, 2014b). Chinese leaders put forward that, by following the path in accordance to Deng Xiaoping's diplomatic wisdom of peaceful development in terms of being a good partner with the neighbouring countries and adopting a series of effective actions, 'great rejuvenation' of the two nations can certainly be realized and the Asian Century, which Deng Xiaoping foresaw, will thus emerge and develop in the modern period.

## References

Deng Xiaoping. 1993. *Selected Works of Deng Xiaoping (Volume III)*. People's Publishing House, p. 18–20, 56, 78, 96, 281–283, 328.

Deng Xiaoping. 1994. *Selected Works of Deng Xiaoping*. Beijing: People's Publishing House.

Len Rong and Wang Zuoling. 2004. *Chronology of Deng Xiaoping Thought (1975–1997)*. Central Party Literature Press, 489, 659, 862–863.

*People's Daily*. 2003. 'People's Republic of China and the Declaration of Principles for Relations and Comprehensive Cooperation of the Republic of India.' *People's Daily*, June 25.

Xi Jinping. 2014a. 'Hand in Hand to Pursue the Dream of National Revival-In the Indian Council of World Affairs Speech.' *People's Daily*.

Xi Jinping. 2014b. 'To Commemorate The 110th Anniversary of the Symposium of Comrade Deng Xiaoping's Speech.' *People's Daily*.

Zhang MinQiu, ed. 2004. *The China-India Relations Research (1947–2003)*. Peking: Peking University Press, 41.

CHAPTER 22

# 'The Belt and Road' Initiative and Cultural Exchanges Between Sichuan Province and India

Bo Shen and Xiaofeng Xing

## Introduction

India and China have a long history of cultural similarity and cultural exchanges. This chapter traces the exchanges, against the backdrop of the 'Belt and Road' initiative and from the perspective of history and culture. The chapter discusses the China–India cultural exchanges. The chapter has been essentially divided into four sections.

### The Important Role Culture Plays in the 'Belt and Road' Initiative

The 'Belt and Road' refers to the 'Silk Road Economic Belt' and the '21st Century Maritime Silk Road', which are called the 'Belt and

Road' for short. In the regions along the 'Belt and Road', the population is 4.4 billion and the GDP reaches USD 21 trillion, accounting for 63 per cent and 29 per cent of the total population and GDP of the world respectively. The regions have the most active economy in the world. Most of the countries along the 'Belt and Road' are developing countries, whose markets are mostly emerging markets. Most of them enjoy strong development potentials and space and are in a rising phase. China is in close economic and trade cooperation with the regions and its foreign trade with the regions makes up a quarter of its total foreign trade. In the past ten years, the annual average trade volume has increased by 19 per cent.[1]

## The Putting Forth of the 'Belt and Road' Initiative

In September and October of 2013, during his visit to Kazakhstan and Indonesia, President Xi Jinping put forward the 'Silk Road Economic Belt' and '21st Century Maritime Silk Road' initiative for the first time. Afterwards, he delivered a series of speeches and made many expositions on the construction of 'Belt and Road' from many aspects. As a result, the 'Belt and Road' initiative received high attention from the international community and positive response from the countries and regions along its route.

In October 2015, China released the *Vision and Actions on Jointly Building Silk Road Economic Belt and 21st Century Maritime Silk Road*, which involves 18 provinces and regions of China.

## The Gratifying Achievements Made After the 'Belt and Road' Initiative Having Been Implemented for Two Years

By the end of 2015, the trade volume between China and the countries involved in the 'Belt and Road' initiative has come to make up a quarter of the total export and import volume of China and China has invested to build more than 50 economic and trade cooperation zones outside its borders while undertaking over 3,000 engineering projects.[2] In 2015, China's enterprises invested directly in 49 countries involved in the 'Belt and Road' initiative with the amount of the investment increasing by 18.2 per cent year on year. In the same year, the price of the service outsourcing contracts signed by and between China and the countries involved in the 'Belt and Road' initiative reached USD 17.83 billion and the price of the performed contracts reached USD 12.15 billion, up 42.6 per cent and 23.4 per cent respectively.[3]

## The Cultural Starting Point and Cultural Trade Achievements

In June 2014, the 'Silk Road' jointly declared by China, Kazakhstan and Kyrgyzstan was successfully included in the 'World Heritage List', which was the first success China has made in the joint application for the World Heritage with the neighboring countries, kicked off the dialogue, cooperation and exchanges between Chinese civilization and the other different civilizations in the world and facilitated the economic, cultural and trade exchanges between various regions and countries. It is a major cultural event and has become the cultural starting point for the implementation of China's 'Belt and Road' Initiative.

In November 2015, the 13 countries jointly founding the 'Silk Road' Coordination Committee, met in Kazakhstan's Almaty.[4] In the meeting, they made a proposal to connect more than 500 heritage sites along the 'Belt and Road' route to form dozens of 'Silk Road corridors'. China put forward the building of the South Asian Silk Road, that is, the 'Bangladesh - China - India - Myanmar Economic Corridor' and the 'China - Central Asia - West Asia Economic Corridor' that connects Central Asia with West Asia and other planning initiatives.

China combined the '21st Century Maritime Silk Road' program with India's 'Spice Route' and 'Seasonal and Trans-Indian Ocean Sea Route and Cultural Landscape Plan', which are two strategic initiatives of India to strengthen interactions with India and to seek common strategic interests between the two sides in South Asia (especially in the Indian Ocean region).[5]

## Rapid Growth of the Cultural Investment and Cultural Trade

Till date, Chinese enterprises have directly invested in 49 countries along the 'Belt and Road' route with the total amount of investment reaching USD 15 billion. In the first quarter of 2016, China's foreign cultural trade has achieved a good start with the favorable balance of trade at RMB 73.82 billion. The proportion of the cultural export has increased from 7 per cent to 23 per cent with the high-value-added export products keeping growing rapidly. Till now, China has become the world's biggest exporter of cultural and artistic products with a total investment of more than USD 60 billion.[6]

The total export volume of the cultural resources, performances and festivals, books and publishing products as well as visual and handicraft products, etc., has increased significantly, accounting for a substantial share in international trade. In 2015, The exports of China's film and television and related services realized a value of USD 1.43 billion, which is an increase of 19.2 per cent year on year and the films box office and other revenue reached RMB 2.77 billion in total, an increase of 48 per cent year on year.

A series of films like *Xuanzang of the Tang Dynasty*, which reflect the cultural exchanges between China and India, have been released. This expanded the influence of Chinese cultural enterprises in the world and enhanced the competitiveness of Chinese culture.

In summary, China's implementation of the 'Belt and Road' international development strategy has not only promoted international economic and trade contacts and the global economic recovery, but also enabled the world to know more about China, its long history of culture and its modernization-oriented, world-oriented and future-oriented strategic planning through cultural exchanges; more importantly, mutual assistance and interconnectivity between the countries along the 'Belt and Road' are of great significance for the construction of the new order of the world and ensuring the world advance on a track of 'peace, development, cooperation and win-win' as well as safeguarding the world peace and the interests of all peoples.

## The 'Ancient Path Culture' and Buddhism Art in the History That Connect Sichuan and India

Since Sichuan is in the inland of China, the opening of the roads leading to the outside world has been an important event for the foreign relations since the ancient times. Thus, the precious historical and cultural relics have also been accumulated along the roads, making Sichuan the transportation hub and cultural center in Southwest China since the ancient times. We can call the foreign exchange passages in the history of Sichuan 'the ancient path culture', including overland tracks and water-borne corridors.

### The Important Passage Linking the Overland 'Silk Road'—the Sichuan Road

Sichuan Road is the road stretching from the ancient Chang'an to Sichuan. It has a broad meaning and a narrow meaning. In a narrow meaning, the Sichuan Road refers to the road linking Xi'an of Shaanxi Province and Chengdu of Sichuan Province that tramps over Qinling Mountains and Bashan Mountain. This road is the main passage linking Sichuan with the overland 'Silk Road'. It is made up of the Baoxie Road, Ziwu Road, Chencang Road and Tangluo Road, which stretches from Guanzhong (the territory of Shaanxi Province) to Hanzhong (in the history, Hanzhong belongs to the Shu State) as well as the Jinniu (Gold Bull) Road, Micang Road, Litchi Road and so on. In a broad sense, the Sichuan Road includes the Xiayi (Chivalry Road), which connects Sichuan with Shaanxi Province, the Yinping Road, which connects Sichuan with Gansu Province and the outbound roads within Sichuan. For example, south of Chengdu, there is the 'Southern Silk Road' divided into three routes, which can lead to Southeast Asia, Myanmar, India and Afghanistan as well as allows people to get to Central Asia, West Asia, Europe and the Mediterranean region.

The ancient Xichuan Road has been around for more than 3,000 years. It is one of the earliest large-scale traffic remains in the world and older than the ancient Roman Road. Along it, there are extremely rich cultural relics. For example, the great ancient poet Li Bai once described it with the following verses: 'It is easy to climb to heaven than take the Sichuan Road!' (*The Steep Sichuan Road*, by Li Bai of the Tang Dynasty). Another poet of the Tang Dynasty also wrote a poem about the Sichuan Road: 'The early plum flowers decorate the precipitous road of Sichuan and the towering trees block the view of the Tomb of the beloved.' (*Twenty-two Verse Lines Composed When Passing the Huaqing Palace*, by Wen Tingyun). In addition, a poet named Chen Yi living in our times also composed a poem *Ode to the Three Gorges* to depict the roads of Sichuan: 'The roads of Sichuan leads high up to the sky and the rivers flow through ten thousand ranges of mountains.'

The cultural site Jinniu (Gold Bull) Road, also called Stone Bull Road, got its name from the historical legend that goes 'the stone bull excreted gold dung; five Hercules blaze the trail.' The legend was first seen in the *Biography of the Emperor of Shu State* written by Yang Xiong, who lived in the Western Han Dynasty. It was passed down and recorded by many generations later. There are also cultural sites such as Zhaohua Ancient City, Jianmen Pass, Bright Moon (Mingyue) Gorge and so on; the cultural relics from the Three Kingdoms Period can be seen along the way. The Litchi Road became widely known and famous under heaven because of the love story of Emperor Xuan of the Tang Dynasty and his imperial concubine Yang Yuhuan. The great poet of the Tang Dynasty Du Mu once wrote: 'Looking back, the beautiful sceneries of Lishan Mountain come into sight and on the top of the mountain, the thousands of forbidden gates are opened one after another; a horseman is riding a horse like a flash of lightning with a trail of dust left behind and seeing the rider coming, the imperial concubine smiled because her favorite litchi will be delivered.' (*A Quatrain Written when Passing the Huaqing Palace*, by Du Mu).

## The Preservation and Dissemination of Buddhism Arts in Sichuan

The building of the ancient roads of Sichuan made Chengdu the starting point of the 'silk road' Xi'an connected whereby the culture of the western regions and the Buddhism culture of India were spread to Sichuan gradually.

1. **The dissemination of the Buddhism music.** During the two Han Dynasties, Mahayana Buddhism, which had occupied an important

place in India, was spread to China and had a great impact on the Chinese Buddhism music in the Central Plains region. In the Southern Dynasty, it spread up to Chengdu. Through the appeal of the music, the Buddhism doctrines were taught to realize 'internal cultivation' and 'external improvement' and achieve the goal of 'seeking Buddhism on a higher level and convert living beings on a lower level.' Usually, there was musical accompaniment and the tune was called 'chant'. The tune of Chinese Buddhist music was called 'Fan Sheng' or 'Fan chanting'. It was composed by Cao Zhi (192–232), who lived in the Three Kingdoms Period. When he heard the Buddhism music suddenly, he imitated its sound, created the chant and passed it down.

From the Northern and Southern Dynasties to the Sui and Tang Dynasties, the Buddhist music was spread to Sichuan, leaving a lot of precious stone statues such as the four stone carvings portraying the music entertainers' performance, which is preserved in the Ten Thousand Buddhas Temple of Chengdu and the carvings of eight music entertainers on the shrine pedestals of the statue of the Bodhisattva of Great Mercy created during the Reign of Emperor Datong of the Liang Dynasty. Among the group of grotto statues of Bazhong, there were dozens of stone carvings of the songstresses and dancing girls, some of whom are playing the flute and some of whom are playing the Pipa (a traditional Chinese instrument) behind their backs. In modern times, there was Zhang Daqian, who depicted the depicts Dunhuang murals with the music entertainers clad in glorious costumes and the dancers leaping in the air gracefully.

2. **The dissemination of the talking and singing art.** The talking and singing art is also called 'Zhuan Bian' or 'Tsuan Bian', which was adapted from the sermons of the Buddhism. In the Tang Dynasty, it became the 'folk lecture' and evolved into a kind of folk art gradually. The performers sang and talked. In the script, the prose was performed in the form of talking and the verses in the form of singing. There are two kinds of scripts, that is, the monk script and the folk script. The former told and sang about the scriptures and interpreted the Buddhism stories like the Vimilakirti Sutra and the Bhaisajyaguru Sukhavati and the latter told about the historical

stories, the folk legends, the hero stories and the realistic stories like the script of Wang Zhaojun, one of the four beauties in the history of China.

3. According to records, the talking and signing art first appeared in Jiannan Prefecture. During the reign of Emperor Xuan of the Tang Dynasty (713–755), Yang Guozhong was appointed as the Conscription Officer of Jiannan Prefecture and he ordered all counties to recruit soldiers to fight in Lunan. Because Lunan is distant and remote and the roads there are steep, none of the counties followed his order. The governors came up with an idea, that is, offering food to the poor and performed the signing and talking art on the road sides. Then the poor were caught for military service. There are many Buddhist arts and full range of Buddhist art varieties remaining in Sichuan, among which there are a lot of elaborate works. There are both 'monk script' and 'folk script' in the signing and talking art, making it popular both in the monasteries and with the folks. For example, there is the Painting of Welcoming the Buddha and the Stone Carving of the Bhaisajyaguru Sukhavati.

## The Dissemination of the Buddhism Culture Promoting the Development of China's Native Culture

Since the Han and Tang Dynasties, China and India's Buddhism culture exchanges have become increasing frequent and produced a great impact in a wide scope. In literature creation, the Buddhism exchanges have expanded the imagination, strengthened the theatricality and enriched the creative themes; in art, the highlight method of India was introduced into the Cliffside statues and the paintings, which enriched the Chinese painting techniques; in language, they contributed to the birth of the method that indicates the pronunciation of a Chinese character by using two other Chinese characters and the discovery of four tones and enlarged the Chinese vocabulary. In the aspect of ethical thought and conceptual form, they had influence on both the 'refined' and the 'vulgar' cultures, for example, the emergence of the memes 'truth', 'emptiness' and 'realm'.

Why is Buddhism art still popular in China nowadays? The fundamental reason is that 'people's hearts are connected'. President Xi Jinping regards the mutual understanding of the people of the two nations as the key foundation of the Belt and Road construction. To look for the precious relics of the Buddhist culture and art in the exchanges between Sichuan and India can lay a common cultural and ideological foundation for mutual understanding.

## The Geographical Features of Sichuan in the 'Belt and Road' Initiative and Its Measures

Sichuan is in the inland of China, at the intersection of the Silk Road Economic Belt in the Northwest China and the Yangtze River Economic Belt in the Southeast China and at the junction of the Yangtze River Economic Belt and the 21st Century Maritime Silk Road. According to the network of the ancient roads recorded in the historical documents, neither Sichuan was included in the Overland Silk Road starting from Xi'an, nor was it part of the Maritime Silk Road starting from Quanzhou. However, currently it is both incorporated into the Silk Road Economic Belt and the Yangtze River Basin Economic Belt according to the Belt and Road strategic layout of the state.

Sichuan Province has formulated the 'The Implementation Plan for Sichuan Province to Participate in the Construction of the Silk Road Economic Belt and the 21st Century Maritime Silk Road' and put forward 31 key initiatives to push forward the Belt and Road, submitted the *Suggestions for Incorporating Sichuan into the Major Projects of the 'Belt and Road' Construction and the Project Library of the National 'Belt and Road' Construction* to the Fourth Session of the National People's Congress and submitted 80 major projects with the estimated total investment being RMB 997.9 billion.

Sichuan has been sticking to the interaction and interconnection between the provincial, domestic and overseas 'three markets and forms of trade' and successfully organized nearly 100 overseas promotion activities. As of November, 2015, the trade volume with the countries along the route has reached USD 12.86 billion and the number of overseas marketing outlets has reached more than 60, with 136 new overseas investment enterprises having been established, the price of the new engineering contracts having exceeded USD 3 billion, 37 new projects having been initiated in Sichuan by the countries along the Belt and Road route and the contracted foreign capital of USD 351 million having been realized.[7]

## The Sichuan-India Cultural Exchanges Entering a New Phase

Starting from the vision of the Belt and Road initiative and by considering the Sichuan-India cultural exchanges in the context of its overall foreign cultural exchanges, the following ideas are put forth in this chapter.

### *Two Approaches for Sichuan to Conduct Cultural Exchanges with Foreign Countries (India Included)*

The first approach is the connection of roads, that is, to sort out the passages connecting Sichuan and the surrounding areas in history and integrate cultural resources. Therefore, Sichuan can relate to the Silk Road in the north and the Yangtze River Economic Belt in the south to be included into the Maritime Silk Road. In the Belt and Road initiative, India occupies an important position. The road connection is conducive to Sichuan's culture and cultures of the other regions of China, to the development of 'ancient path culture' resources, and to the strengthening of the cultural and trade exchanges.

The second approach is to refine the 'theme culture' through the regional cultural characteristics, that is, to connect the same or similar theme culture zones in an inter-provincial manner to jointly participate in the Belt and Road cultural construction, for example, the full development of the Silk Road Culture, music culture and religious culture exchanges.

### *Opening Major Passages for Sichuan's Foreign Exchanges*

The implementation of the Belt and Road initiative provides a broader and more convenient transport network for Sichuan's exchanges with the foreign countries. At present, Sichuan has accelerated the construction of highways, high-speed rails, air transport, land way transport, waterway transportation and other infrastructure to form a transportation network extending in all directions; to completely change the closed state of Sichuan and provide the necessary infrastructure for Sichuan, which is located in the inland of China, to participate in the Belt and Road construction. Sichuan's 'ancient path culture' is the accumulation of the experience and wisdom of Sichuan in foreign relations in history. Sichuan's brilliant cultural and artistic heritages provide valuable cultural resources for Sichuan to partake in the Belt and Road construction. The implementation of the Belt and Road initiative provides a more extensive and convenient transportation network for Sichuan's exchanges with the foreign countries.

### *The Combined Development of the Yangtze River Economic Belt and the Yangtze River Cultural Belt*

The Yangtze River Economic Belt covers 11 provinces and regions. About 96.5 per cent territory of Sichuan Province lies in the Yangtze River Basin. It is on the upper reaches of and at the source of the Yangtze River and it is also a big province of the Yangtze River Basin.

In accordance with the deployment of the central government, Sichuan has launched a series of major cultural projects like the '1st Yangtze River Culture Belt Summit' convened in Luzhou City in April 2016. It was proposed that the Yangtze River Cultural Belt and the Yangtze River Economic Belt should be built, which are like the double helix structure of genetic DNA, is conducive to the simultaneous development of culture and economy and will help Sichuan to develop cultural industry cluster to go abroad. The Yangtze River Cultural Belt—Luzhou Consensus was issued and the Yangtze River Cultural Belt Industry Development Plan is being prepared. The Yangtze River culture and scientific survey have been started.

### *Giving Play to the Cultural Radiation Effect of the Central City to Promote the Modernization and Internationalization of the Cultural Industry*

In 2013, Sichuan Province proposed to build four major urban agglomerations and implement the multi-point and multi-polar supporting strategy. The first growth pole is the Chengdu Plain urban agglomeration; the second growth pole is the southern Sichuan urban agglomeration whose development is a priority; the third growth pole is the northeastern Sichuan urban agglomeration, whose development is being accelerated; the fourth growth pole is the Panxi urban agglomeration, whose development is push forward as a focus and which includes Liangshan Prefecture and Panzhihua City.

In 2016, the State Council approved the *Chengdu-Chongqing Urban Agglomeration Development Plan*, which clearly defined Chengdu as a national central city. Thus, Chengdu became the sixth central city after Beijing, Shanghai, Tianjin, Guangzhou and Chongqing. Chengdu City has come up with its planning for building an international metropolis.

In terms of cultural construction, Chengdu has put forward the idea of rejuvenating history and culture and reconstructing Chengdu as a center by integrating Chengdu's historical and cultural resources left in the course of Chinese civilization development and combining them with the modern culture and by giving full play to the central position and the radiation effect of Chengdu as a large modern city to drive the cultural construction of the Yangtze River Basin and Sichuan City Groups.

The year 2010 marked the 60th anniversary of the establishment of diplomatic relations between China and India. On this special occasion, China held the 'India Festival' and India held the 'China Festival' for celebration. In October, during the Western China International Fair, the closing ceremony of the India Festival was held in Chengdu. India's famous Cara Shetra Dance Academy Art Troupe presented a wonderful Bharatanatyam dance for the Chengdu people, which received a warm welcome from the audience.

In August 2016, Chengdu City formed the art group to bring Sichuan art elements to the opening ceremony of the 'Sensing China-Kazakhstan Trip' via the Silk Road. The Panda Exhibition was also held. Moreover, there was the intangible cultural heritage exhibition. On the exhibition, the paper cutting, shadow play, gourd branded painting, calligraphy, tea art and the Tibetan songs and dances were warmly welcomed, and the Sichuan Opera Face and fire breathing rocked the spectators.

In September, Chengdu and China Museum Association successfully hosted the 7th China Museum and Related Products and Technology Expo (hereinafter referred to as 'Museum Expo'), which has become the largest ever since the convening of the 2004 Museum Expo. The projects displayed and promoted at the expo preliminarily manifest an international trend. During the expo, various academic seminars were held simultaneously, which promoted the development and deepening of the international academic exchanges. The various experience, interaction and museum sales exhibition activities facilitated the development and study of the Big Data results and realized the Digitalization of the big remains, which have become a strong support for the foreign exchanges of Chengdu.

## Conclusion

In the Belt and Road initiative of China, Sichuan occupies a special geographical position in that it is connected with the Overland Silk Road starting from Xi'an and with the Maritime Silk Road via the Yangtze River Economic Belt; in history, Sichuan's exchanges with India have left the ancient path culture and the Buddhist culture authentic works. Since the reform and opening up, Sichuan has made many achievements in its cultural exchanges with India. We believe and earnestly hope that in the context of the implementation of the Belt and Road initiative, Sichuan can achieve more fruitful new results in its cultural exchanges and trade with India.

## Notes

1. Chen Fengying. 2014. 'The "Belt and Road" Initiative Put Forward by President Xi Jinping Has a Profound and Far-reaching Effect'. www.cri.cn
2. Based on the data released by the Ministry of Commerce of PRC on 20 January 2016. www.ce.cn
3. Based on the data released by the Ministry of Commerce of PRC on 20 January 2016. www.ce.cn
4. The 13 countries include China, Russia, Japan, Iran, Afghanistan, Kazakhstan, Kyrgyzstan, Nepal, Pakistan, Turkey, Tadzhikistan, Turkmenistan, and Uzbekistan.

5. 'Indian Media: China and India Seek Common Strategic Interests in South Asia', Beijing, 2015-04-07. www.cankaoxiaoxi.com
6. Based on the article 'Beijing Fair Focuses on Foreign Cultural Trade, the "Belt and Road" Becomes the New Cultural Investment Hot Spots', 2016-06-01. www.cnr.cn
7. Based on the report 'The Investigation of the Development of "the Belt and Road" Initiative in Sichuan Province by Western Department', released by National Development and Reform Commission of the PRC on 30 March 2016. www.ndrc.gov.cn

CHAPTER 23

# A Study on the Motivation Mechanism of China–India Tourism Cooperation

Jie Da and Renjie Yu

## The Chinese and Indian Tourism Industry

Tourism industry is regarded as the 'smokeless industry in the 21st century', which is an enormous driving force for the economy and employment. Statistics from World Travels Tourism Council (WTTC) show that in 2015 the production value of tourism industry reached USD 7.2 trillion (including the value created indirectly), accounting for 9.8 per cent of the global GDP. The industry also provided 284 million jobs and kept up the growth momentum.[1] Therefore, every country attaches great importance to the development of their tourism industry.

### Current Situation of the Chinese Tourism Industry

As an aftermath of the economic development and enhancement of citizens' income standards, Chinese tourism industry has entered a golden age of development. Tourism industry has been developing rapidly and is getting increasingly prominent in the national economy.

According to WTTC, in 2015 the production value of China's tourism industry was RMB 5.3664 trillion (approximately USD 794.5 billion), accounting for 7.9 per cent of the GDP, ranked 2nd in the world only after the USA. In the aspect of facilitating employment, China's tourism industry directly created 22.49 million jobs in 2015, and the indirect employment reached 6.510 million, which accounted for 8.4 per cent of the total employment in that year. Evidently Chinese tourism industry has risen to be a pillar industry in the national economy.[2]

Significant growth was also seen in the international tourism business. China received 133 million inbound tourists in 2015 (including 25.985 million foreign tourists), and generated a revenue of USD 113.65 billion, increased by 4.0 per cent and 7.8 per cent year-on-year, respectively (Table 23.1).[3]

## Current Situation of Indian Tourism Industry

India boasts abundant high-quality tourist resources and the Indian government attaches great importance to the critical role of tourism in the economic growth of the country. In the context of economic globalization, it has come up with a global strategy of 'Incredible India!' and has identified tourism as a key emerging revenue generating industry. After several years' development, the tourism industry has risen to be a very important industry for the Indian economy, which possesses a certain level of international competitiveness and is also gaining tremendous momentum.

According to WTTC, Indian tourism created a value of INR 8.3094 trillion (approximately USD 124 billion) in 2015, accounting for 6.3 per cent of the GDP and ranked 12th globally. As a driving force of employment, the Indian tourism industry created 23.45 million jobs in 2015 (first in the world), and offered 37.32 indirect jobs, which accounted for 8.7 per cent of the country's

Table 23.1 *Numbers of Inbound Foreign Tourists (from Asian Countries)*

January-December 2015

| *Nationality* | *Total (10,000 Person)* |
|---|---|
| **Total** | **2598.54** |
| **Asia** | **1662** |
| South Korea | 444.44 |
| Japan | 249.77 |
| Malaysia | 107.55 |
| Mongolia | 101.41 |
| Philippines | 100.4 |
| Singapore | 90.53 |
| India | 73.05 |
| Thailand | 64.15 |
| Indonesia | 54.48 |
| Kazakhstan | 24.15 |
| North Korea | 18.83 |
| Pakistan | 11.31 |
| Sri Lanka | 5.81 |
| Nepal | 5 |
| Kyrgyzstan | 4.37 |
| Others | 306.78 |

*Source:* Official website of China National Tourism Administration[4]

total employment.[5] Tourism industry has made considerable contribution to India's economic growth and provided abundant job opportunities to the citizens.

With 'Incredible India!' as a breakthrough point, Indian international tourism industry has seen a rapid growth and brought about substantial foreign exchange earnings. Table 23.2 shows the numbers of India's inbound tourists and its foreign exchange earnings in recent years.

Table 23.2 *Number of India's Inbound Tourists and Its Foreign Exchange Earnings*

| *Year* | *Inbound Over-night Tourists (10,000 Persons)* | *Foreign Exchange Earnings (USD 100 Million)* |
|---|---|---|
| 2010 | 576 | 141.9 |
| 2011 | 629 | 165.6 |
| 2012 | 658 | 177.4 |
| 2013 | 697 | 184.5 |
| 2014 | 768 | 202.4 |

*Source:* Statistics from the official website of Indian Ministry of Tourism[6]

## Current Situation of China–India Tourism Cooperation

China and India have been important neighbours to each other since ancient times and share strong historical and cultural linkages. With the two countries' economic growth, and ever maturing tourism industries, China–India tourism cooperation has been keeping up with the momentum. In recent years, the population of bilateral personnel exchanges between the two countries has seen a ceaseless growth. In 2015, this population reached 900 thousand, and China's Tourism Administration estimated the number would rise to 1 million in 2016, Xinhua news agency reported (2016).

However, China-India tourism cooperation is still at a relatively low level, which is not proportional to the two countries' total population, market scale and tourist resources. Given the total population of over 2.5 billion and the population of mutual exchanges between China and other neighbouring countries (e.g., more than 10 million people involved in China–South Korea mutual visits, 5 million people in China-Russia mutual visits), this population of 1 million between China and India is obviously not enough.

There is much room for growth in China–India tourism cooperation. With the global economic integration and regional economic integration, the political, economic and cultural communication between the two countries is growing more frequent and profound. China–India tourism cooperation has ushered in a significant development opportunity. Therefore, it's worth researching the problems in this cooperation, where the motivation mechanism is the key factor. This study will analyse China–India tourism cooperation from this perspective.

## The Motivation Mechanism of China–India Tourism Cooperation

The motivation mechanism to push forward regional tourism cooperation is complicated, and includes geographical resources as the motivation foundation, market competition as a driving force, as well as integration as the target. Essentially speaking, the regional tourism cooperation is a motivation game process of interests among the tourism co-operators (including governments, enterprises, non-governmental organizations and citizens). By setting up a game model, Chen Shi and Wen Xiu (2013) proposed that the motivation of regional tourism cooperation resides in the fact that the governments, enterprises and industry organizations can benefit more through cooperation, and the eventual establishment of tourism cooperation depends on the balance of the game after the strategic choices are made by the participants. Here motivation can be interpreted as the Pareto Improvement room that all the parties' interests can be reached through cooperation. The bigger the room is, the stronger the motivation becomes. This study regards the motivation mechanism as a driving element, which facilitates the cooperation by bringing about benefits and improvement room. It covers four aspects.

### Complementarities of Tourist Resources

The foremost element in the development of tourist products is the objects tourists are coming to appreciate, namely, cultural and natural landscapes, local customs and practices, etc. Quality and distinctive tourist resources found in the regional tourist cooperation constitute the fundamental motivation of cooperation.

### *China's Tourist Resources*

The latitude of China spans 50 degrees. The better part of the country is located in the Temperate Zone, while a small part belongs to the Torrid Zone. The terrain descends from west to east. Mountains, plateaus and hills account for 67 per cent of the land area, the rest of it are basins and plains. Due to the wide range of latitude, great differences of the distances from the sea, as well as the undulating terrain, there are various combinations of temperature and rainfall, which result in a wide diversity of climates. In terms of climate type, the east is dominated by subtropical monsoon climate and temperate monsoon climate; the northwest has a temperate continental climate and the Qinghai-Tibet Plateau has a high-cold climate. The combination of diverse terrains and climates presents splendid natural landscapes.

China's cultural tourist resources are likewise rich and colourful. Alongside this, China is an ancient civilization with a huge history. It has its distinctive culture and tradition, which are embodied in the unique cultural heritage ranging from architecture, painting, calligraphy, sculpture, stone inscription as well as folklore.

### *India's Tourist Resources*

The Republic of India situated between 6°44' to 35°30' north latitude, is the biggest country in the South Asian subcontinent. It spans from the south side of Himalayas to the Indian Ocean. In the east and west are magnificent coastal plains, in the north are the hills, and in the centre is located the Indo-Gangetic Plain, while in the south is the rolling Deccan Plateau. The unique geological environment gives rise to particular and enchanting natural landscapes. The Himalayas in the north are a destination for mountaineering and skiing, as well as a summer resort; the coastal holiday resorts in the south own quality golden beaches; the forest parks in the east have not only beautiful sceneries but also numerous animals that can only be found in India.

India's cultural resources are even richer. India is one of the birthplaces of ancient human civilization and the origin of Buddhism and Hinduism. The constant absorption of exotic culture and exchanges and integration of different peoples have enriched the Indian culture and with typical characteristics of multiple religions, multiple nationalities, and multiple languages, it is called the 'World Museum of Anthropology'. All the traits provide a rich material basis for tourism.

### *China and India's Quality and Distinctive Resources*

China and India both own abundant quality tourist resources. As of the 40th session of the World Heritage Committee, according to UNESCO's 'World Heritage List', China, with 50 world heritage sites, is ranked 2nd (including 25 cultural heritage sites, 11 natural heritage sites, four cultural and natural mixed sties); India, with 35 world heritage sites, is ranked 6th (including 27 cultural heritage sites, seven natural heritage sites and one cultural and natural mixed site).[7]

India has a monotonous climate, and is widely affected by tropical monsoons, while China's climate is more diverse and is dominated by temperate monsoon climate and temperate continental climate; China's terrain mainly features plateaus and mountains with considerable undulation, while the terrain of India, dominated by plains and plateaus, is relatively flat. The differences of geographical position, climate and landscape lead to the differences between China and India's natural landscapes. At the same time, the differences of historical and cultural traditions as well as religions grant distinctive features to the cultural landscapes of China and India. China and India's rich and distinctive tourist resources have ensured a considerably favourable complementarity.

Chinese and Indian citizens share a time-honoured history of exchange, which began over 2,000 years ago. Through the Silk Road, Indian music and dance, astronomy, calendar, as well as sugar-making techniques were introduced to China; meanwhile, Chinese paper-making, silk, porcelain, and tea were spread to India. Exchanges of the Buddhism religion are even more influential and Xuanzang's pilgrimage to India was known to everyone in the two countries. These connections have offered the opportunity to link the two countries' tourist resources, which will facilitate their cooperative development. For instance, in June 2014, China opened a new pilgrimage route for Indian Buddhists to worship the holy mountain Okada Rinpoche Qi and the sacred lake Manasarovar in Tibet via Nathula Pass, which has received a warm response from India.

In a nutshell, in terms of tourist destinations, China and India both have quality, rich and distinctive resources, and there are linkages between them, all of which promise a huge cooperation potential and constitute the fundamental motivation of China–India tourism cooperation.

## The Trend of Regional Economic Integration

The regional economic integration is pushing forward cooperation and exchanges in all walks of life, which include tourism industry for sure. At the same time, the internal and external accessibility has a significant impact on tourist products, while the reinforcement of cross-regional connection also facilitates the cooperation.

### *Direct Impact of Regional Economic Integration*

Regional economic integration is pushing forward cooperation and development of every kind of industry, and tourism is one of the important links. Therefore, the integration appeal directly drives tourism cooperation and development.

Regional economic integration is both a product and a manifestation of the internationalization of the world economic life and it is also an inevitable result of product socialization and technological advancement, development and upgradation with the expansion of economic globalization. From 1990s till now, regional economic integration has formed a new and strong trend. With ever-deepening cooperation, extensive content and diverse forms, it has been developing fast. In recent years, all forms of bilateral and multilateral, sub-regional, cross-regional cooperation have been flourishing, including the construction of The ASEAN Free Trade Area, as well as the '10+3' collaboration between ASEAN and China, Japan and Korea. Improvement of Asia-Pacific economic integration at a higher level and on a bigger scale, is generally in line with the members' development benefits and is also the development trend for future Asia-Pacific cooperation.

China and India are important neighbours to each other. Against this backdrop, their exchanges of economy and trade are getting increasingly close. Under the guidance of building a strategic partnership oriented towards peace and prosperity, under the frameworks of mechanisms such as 'BRICS' and G20, the two countries have been strengthening mutual cooperation and increasing mutual exchanges. As of the end of 2015, China's indirect investment in India accumulated to USD 3.55 billion, China's projects in India reached a value of USD 65.78 billion, and generated a revenue of USD 44.01 billion. China–India trade values have been rising in recent years, as it is showed in Figure 23.1.

Moreover, China–India cooperation is also developing to a higher level. Since the advent of the new century, China and India have established a strategic mechanism of dialogue and cooperation, which has boosted trade between the two countries and expanded economic cooperation. The two countries have signed many cooperation memorandums and inter-enterprise mutual investment agreements of intent. On 19 September 2014, China and India issued a 'Joint Statement between the Republic of India and the People's Republic of China on Building a Closer Developmental Partnership'. With the increase in China–India negotiations, China–India cooperation has deepened

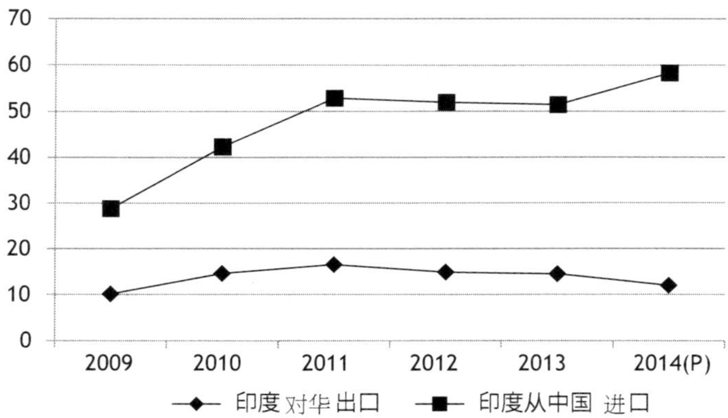


Figure 23.1 *Numbers of China–India Trade (USD 1 Billion)*

*Source:* Official website of Ministry of Commerce and Industry[8]

and the Regional Comprehensive Economic Partnership initiated by the East Asian countries, including China and India, is expected to be a breakthrough point in China–India cooperation.

### *Indirect Impact of Regional Economic Integration*

Regional economic integration has enhanced the accessibility within the region, and internally improved the cooperation room of tourism industry. According to the well-known theory of regional tourist products proposed by Bergvanden, Borgvander and Meervander (1995), the accessibility has a significant impact on the tourist products. Here the accessibility includes the internal accessibility, which covers transportation convenience and travel cost, as well as the locals' friendliness and language communication ability and external accessibility including the distance from the outside world and transportation convenience, etc. Regional economic integration has improved the accessibility of tourist products, brought convenience to tourists, provided conditions for enterprises to develop cross-border tourist products, and at the same time brought down the enterprise cooperation cost. It is a driving force of regional tourism cooperation. Frequent exchanges pushed forward China–India economic integration, which resulted in smoother transportation, more convenient personnel exchanges, better cultural communication, as well as more effective information sharing and flow. All of these increased the accessibility and rose to be a driving force for China–India tourism cooperation.

## Market Driving Force

Tourists' new demands and tourism enterprises' growing desire to expand the market are boosting the development of tourism cooperation.

### *From the Perspective of Tourists*

The total population of China and India exceeds 2.5 billion, which accounts for about one third of the world population. Outbound tourists have been growing in both countries. Both indicate a huge number of potential tourists and an enormous market.

China is now going through a consumption upgrade. With the improvement of living standards, Chinese citizens are increasingly fond of tourism. Moreover, Chinese tourists in recent years are no more satisfied with domestic tours, but more and more people are choosing to travel abroad, and the number of overseas tourists has risen dramatically. In 2015, the number of Chinese outbound tourists hit 120 million, and they have spent USD 104.5 billion, up 12.0 per cent and 16.7 per cent year-on-year.[9] The Tourism Statistical Report for the First Half of 2016 issued by China National Tourism Administration (2016) shows that in this period, China's tourism market has expanded steadily and is still leading the macro economy. The number of Chinese outbound tourists amounted to 50.03 million, representing a year-on-year increase of 4.3 per cent (Zhao Shan, 2016). China continues to top the world not only in global outbound tourist number but also the amount of consumption.

Overseas tours are also very popular in India, and these tours have risen to be the primary issue in many Indians' lives and have been keeping up good momentum. In 2015 the number of Indian outbound tourists reached 17 million, increased by 21.4 per cent compared with 14 million in 2014. Indian tourists' expenditures have also been seeing a rise. In 2014, Indian tourists' overseas expenditure per capita was USD 3.746 thousand, 15 per cent more than USD 3.264 in 2013.[10]

Given the two countries' huge population and steadily growing economy, India has become China's important emerging tourist market, and China is also one of the tourist markets with the biggest growth potential, which shows a rosy prospect of the tourism market for the two countries. Therefore, from the angle of tourists, China and India both have a large and still growing tourist population and with the consumption upgrade, their desire for outbound tourism will only strengthen. However, exchanges between the two countries remain at a low level, which leaves a great market room for the China–India tourism cooperation.

### *From the Perspective of Tourism-Related Industries*

When tourism industry reaches a certain scale, the original region can no longer meet the demand of tourism's further development, and the market will push it to expand to the surrounding areas, seek cooperation with other countries or regions in the same area, then it will drive and promote further development of tourism industry in the whole region (Zhu Yuanxiu and Wu Yanwei, 2009). Enterprises are targeted at making profit. After the industry develops to a certain level, the tourism enterprises will have more motivation to expand the market and pursue external exchanges and cooperation, including expanding the market with the purpose to increase diversity, expand scale, pursue regional economy of scale, lower trade costs, etc. The market expansion enlightens enterprises that cross-regional development and cooperation are profitable, which will promote cooperation.

After years of development, a group of excellent tourism enterprises have emerged in China and India. They have already set out to seek external cooperation and development, and they are aware that only by developing new projects, new markets, and new products as soon as possible can they attract more tourists and more markets and strengthen their global competitiveness. For China, India is an emerging market. The geological advantage enjoyed by a neighbour possesses great attractiveness for its tourism enterprises, and to develop tourist resources jointly with Indian enterprises is an inevitable development trend. This also works for India. For example, according to a report published by Huanqiu.com on 7 January 2016, Ctrip (NASDAQ: CTRP) announced it would invest USD 180 million in India's biggest online travel company MakeMyTrip (NASDAQ: MMYT) via convertible bonds. Furthermore, Ctrip was also permitted to purchase a certain number of MakeMyTrip shares on the open market. Thus, with the convertible bonds included, Ctrip can hold 26.6 per cent of MakeMyTrip's total tradable shares at the most.

## The Impetus from the Governments

In regional tourism cooperation, governments play a dominant role that cannot be overlooked. According to Chen Shi and Wen Xiu's study (2013), in regional tourism cooperation practices, the supply of public tourist products may encounter the 'prisoner's dilemma' and give rise to insufficiency, on the other hand, the 'chicken game' in the supply of private tourist products may lead to an imbalanced supply structure. Under these circumstances, it requires governments' intervention to give proper guidance on the planning and development of regional tourism resources as well as tourism enterprises' co-opetition (i.e., cooperation and competition). The study contends that governments play a critical role in regional tourism cooperation, especially in the case of cross-border tourism and cooperation between the governments is the premise to any cooperation.

The impetus from the governments is a driving force to prompt regional tourism cooperation through integrated factors including foreign policies, agreements, regulations and control of development and planning. Sometimes the force is directly imposed onto regional tourism cooperation, but most of the time governments can influence the cooperation by influencing regional society, economy and environment. The direct and indirect forces come together and rise to be a powerful driving force to achieve the cooperation. In the cross-border tourism cooperation, governments boost the cooperation mostly by all kinds of diplomatic agreements and strategic events.

### *Governments' Cooperative Willingness*

Since the impetus from the governments shall be accomplished via the governments' spontaneous actions, analysis of the governments' cooperative willingness shall precede that of the governments' impetus. Only when governments are willing to cooperate can the impetus play a positive role.

While promoting cooperation, the governments are not only concerned about economic interests but also social benefits. Exchanges and cooperation push forward the economic growth. For both China and India, tourism cooperation can not only bring about direct gains, but also promote the two countries' exchanges of commerce and trade, culture and education, as well as science and technology to develop even deeper and wider. Tourism is becoming an important window for many kinds of cooperation. As a result, it is necessary for Chinese and Indian governments to facilitate tourism cooperation.

As a matter of fact, Chinese and Indian governments have been working on China–India tourism cooperation and have put a lot of effort in promoting the cooperation. This can be seen in the series of important strategies facilitated by China and India in the following diplomatic agreements.

## Government Regulation and Important Events Let Us Examine Important Regulatory and Policy Initiatives Taken by the Two Countries Which Have Given the Sector a Boost

### China–India Tourism Cooperation Agreement

On 15 May 2015, China and India signed an 'Agreement between the National Tourism Administration of the People's Republic of China and the Ministry of Tourism of the Republic of India on Cooperation in the field of Tourism'. The Tourism Administration of China and Ministry of Tourism of India will set up a joint working mechanism in order to deepen the cooperation in the areas including tourism information sharing, hotel and travel agency business, as well as exploitation and sustainable development of tourism human resources.

### Launch of China–India Tourism Year

In the past years, a series of tourism years held in the countries all around the world proved that tourism years can help the cross-border tourism exchanges develop even deeper and wider. According to Xinhua News Agency (2016), in September 2014, during his visit to India, President Xi Jinping and Indian Prime Minister Modi jointly decided to hold an 'India Tourism Year' in China in 2015 and a 'China Tourism Year' in 2016. This is an important event, which enhanced tourism cooperation, gave play to the diplomatic functions of tourism, and helped in promoting China–India pragmatic cooperation. For now, the tourism years have been effective and have improved the tourism cooperation and development.

### 'One Belt, One Road' Initiative

In 2013, China came up with two initiatives, namely, to together build the Silk Road Economic Belt and the 21st Century Maritime Silk Road, which were together named as 'One Belt, One Road'. This initiative is China's important national strategy based on the trend of global economic integration and regional economic integration. In the process to achieve this initiative, development of tourism cooperation plays a vanguard role. Promoting the 'One Belt, One Road' initiative in South Asia would facilitate China–India tourism cooperation and development.

### 'Bangladesh-China-India-Myanmar Economic Corridor'

In May 2013, during Premier Li Keqiang's visit to India, China and India together came up with the proposal to construct the Bangladesh-China-India-Myanmar (BCIM) Economic Corridor to tighten the relationship between the markets of China and India. China and India also jointly stated that the two countries would set up a joint working group to strengthen the connections within the region. BCIM Economic Corridor will play an important role in the development of South Asian economy and will have a positive significance. The establishment and development of BCIM regional economic cooperation and development has made positive contributions to China, South Asia, South East Asia and even other areas (Chen Shuai and Tao Ying, 2013). The proposal of BCIM Economic Corridor' provided important policy support and rare chances for the tourism cooperation in that region.

### Other Cooperation

Under the framework of the tourism cooperation agreement, Chinese and Indian tourism administrations have carried out fruitful cooperation and exchanges of various forms. With a combined effort from the two countries' central governments and relevant local governments, four pairs of tourist friendly cities (provinces) were selected, namely Dunhuang and Aurangabad, Qingdao and Hyderabad, Chongqing and Chennai, as well as Sichuan and Karnataka. In 2015, China–India tourism cooperation had seen a great number of breakthrough developments. Not only the central governments but also the local governments took part in the tourism cooperation, which signified China–India tourism cooperation would develop into a more profound and at a more diverse level.

## Conclusion and Suggestions

Regional tourism cooperation is a dynamic game process of all the tourism participants, and the motivation mechanism of regional tourism cooperation lays the foundation to attract all the parties for cooperation and is also a force to coordinate the participants' interests to improve development in the cooperation process. The four motivations explained in this study facilitate regional tourism cooperation by improving each other. First, the complementarities of tourist resources is a fundamental condition and it is the natural resources that ensure room for cooperation in the first place; second, market driving force and the trend of regional economic integration is an intrinsic force, which drives the participants to cooperate out of certain motivation, which can be industrial economy of scale or saving regional trade expense, etc; finally, the impetus of the government can be regarded as an external driving force, which can directly push forward the cooperation and can also facilitate regional tourism cooperation by altering the basic conditions of internal forces.

## Increasing Publicity of Tourism Between China and India

China and India should hold tourism promotion activities of prominent characteristics, precise targets and diverse forms. First, take specific tours and featured tour as a breakthrough point to drive the tourism cooperation and development. For instance, India can try to attract tourists by emphasizing featured tour content including sea beaches, national parks, religious pilgrimages and yoga vacation; second, positioning and analysing the publicized object, then taking advantage of various new media and posting advertisements precisely according to the features of the object; third, the forms of promotion should be diverse. Apart from organizing tourism festivals, exhibitions and expedition activities, one can also organize exhibition of antiquities, culture festivals, food fairs, etc., so that the tourists from the two countries will be more interested in better knowing each other through cultural exchanges; apart from the direct ways of promotion like traditional commercials and posters, one can also conduct some soft promotions by tourism TV programs, feature stories and movies, so on and so forth; last but not least, one can also set up a mechanism to access the result of tourism promotions, so as to get feedback in time.

## Facilitating Tourist Travel

China and India can take various measures to facilitate the citizens' travelling into the countries, so as to cut down tourists' travel cost and to build a travel market between the two big countries. China and India can both simplify the customs formality, shorten the time to get the entry and exit permits and gradually simplify the customs formality for tour groups. Transportation facilitation has a direct impact on the numbers of tourists, and the two countries should strengthen the connection between roads and railways, as well as increase the numbers of airlines and flights. China and India should co-construct a tourism information website, where information of prices, weather, routes, accommodation and food are shared. It is not only easier for tourists to keep informed, but also provides valuable information for the enterprises.

## Less Restrictions, Boosting Inter-Enterprise Cooperation

China and India should be open to each other for the tourism investment and enterprise entrance, so as to boost the tourism cooperation.

First of all, simplifying the tourism cooperation procedures, eradicating or reducing the restrictions on the examination and approval of market access, providing support for tourism companies' cross-border businesses and inter-enterprise cross-border cooperation; secondly, encouraging mutual investment and cooperation in each other's tourism industry. China and India both have their own traits and edges in tourism development, for instance, India is good at hotel management, while china is good at the construction of tourism infrastructural facilities. Therefore, China and India can exchange their experiences, develop the tourist market in an all-round way, and give tourists a more comfortable environment; last, China and India can work together to develop tourist products and routes. They can also call on tourism departments and enterprises to do research and design some excellent cross-border routes with its national characteristics that are suitable for foreign tourists, so as to not only attract the tourists of the two countries, but also carry out outward joint promotions and expand foreign market.

Generally speaking, 'mutually sharing resources, mutually sending tourists, mutually promoting routes, mutually beneficial policies, mutually sharing information, mutually celebrating festivals, mutually transportation connecting, mutually negotiating over conflicts' (Nan Yu and Li Lanjun, 2010) should be an effective way to promote tourism.

## Establishing Consulting Assurance Mechanism of Regional Cooperation

The coordination of interests plays an essential role in cross-border tourism cooperation. China and India should set up an assurance mechanism for the tourism authorities' contact and conversation, to make the best use of the government's coordination and management function. At the same time, the two countries should further organize and improve unofficial exchanges including academic forums and entrepreneurs' form, to provide a communication and cooperation platform for the two countries' enterprises and scholars. Thus, a complete consulting assurance mechanism of the regional tourism cooperation can be formed.

## Giving Play to Governments' Role of Coordination and Improvement

Chinese and Indian governments should continue to promote the ongoing friendly exchange plans, for example, the construction of the BCIM Economic Corridor, initiative of 'One Belt, One Road', and 'Chinese Tourism Year' in this year, etc.; in the future newer cooperation and exchange activities can be promoted. All the activities provide strong support for China–India Tourism cooperation.

In order to make the best use of the governments' impetus, not only should the central governments collaborate with each other, but the local governments should also be proactive in promoting the cooperation and exchange activities among the provinces and cities. One shall also take note that the provinces with distinctive tourist resources and their neighbouring provinces can gain direct interests from the cooperation, so it's more possible for them to join the cooperation, and they should be thus encouraged. Cooperation among local governments is beneficial for the China–India tourist industry to achieve a richer and deeper level of cooperation.

## Notes

1. WTTC official website. (n.d.). https://www.wttc.org/
2. World Travel & Tourism Council. (2016). https://www.wttc.org/
3. China Tourism Statistics Bulletin 2015 (2016). China limits [Data file]. https://www.huduser.org/Datasets/IL/IL08/in_fy2008.pdf
4. Number of Foreign Tourists Entering China from January to December 2015 (2016). http://zwgk.mct.gov.cn/auto255/201601/t20160118_832355.html?keywords=
5. World Travel & Tourism Council. (2016). India limits [Data file]. https://www.wttc.org/
6. Statistics from the official website of Indian Ministry of Tourism. (n.d.). http://tourism.gov.in/market-research-and-statistics
7. World Heritage Conven. (n.d.). United Nations Educational, Scientific and Cultural Organization. http://whc.unesco.org/zh/list/
8. Ministry of Commerce and Industry (2016). https://commerce-app.gov.in/eidb/iecnt.asp
9. The National Tourism Administration Issued A Report on Tourism Statistics for The First Half of 2016. http://zwgk.mct.gov.cn/auto255/201608/t20160801_832360.html?keywords=
10. Economic and Commercial Counsellor's Office of the Embassy of the People's Republic of China in the Republic of India (2016). http://in.mofcom.gov.cn/

## References

Bergvanden, L., J. Borgvander, and J. Meervander. 1995. *Urban Tourism*. Aldershot: Avebury.

Chen, Shi, and Wen Xiu. 2013. *Studies on the Regional Tourism Cooperation in Western China*. Beijing: China Economy Publishing House.

Chen Shuai, and Tao Ying. 2013. *Analysis of China-India Tourism Cooperation and Development from the Perspective of China-South Asia Economic Circle*. Modern Property Management-Modern Economics 7.

Huanqiu. 2016. 'Ctrip Announced a $180 Million Investment in MakeMyTrip'. https://tech.huanqiu.com/article/9CaKrnJSZdQ

Nan, Yu, and Li Lanjun. 2010. 'Studies on the Northwest Silk Road's Tourism Mode of Cross-region, Accessibility and Integration—Analysis from the Perspective of Silk Road's Application of the World Heritage [J].' *Social Sciences in Xinjiang (Chinese version)* 4, 35–39.

*Xinhua News Agency*. 2016. 'Xi Jinping Sends Congratulations to the Opening Ceremony of '2016 China Tourism Year' in India.' *Xinhua News Agency*. http://www.xinhuanet.com/politics/2016-01/16/c_1117796285.htm

Zhao, Shan. 2016. 'Why China's Outbound Tourism Has Reached a New High [N].' *People's Daily*, overseas edition, 4.

Zhu, Yuanxiu, and Wu Yanwei. 2009. 'A Discussion on the Dynamic Mechanism of Regional Tourism Cooperation [J].' *Economic Research Guide* 19, 143–144.

CHAPTER 24

# Green HR Practices and Employee Pro-environmental Behaviour

*A Study on India and China*

Soni Agrawal and Roma Puri

## Introduction

Green management, sustainability and sustainable development have become important buzzwords in organizations. In fact, sustainability has emerged as the new megatrend (Mittelstaedt et al., 2014; Lubin and Esty, 2010) and research shows that organizations that are serious about their environmental commitment tend to focus on issues such as toxic emission, raw material and energy consumption, and waste production (Zhu and Sarkis, 2004). Sustainability is a necessary condition for most businesses today and one finds that numerous organizations have institutionalized sustainability roles and sustainability reporting in their functioning (Dyllick and Hockerts, 2002).

## What Is Being Sustainable?

One of the oft-quoted definitions of sustainable development is the one given in the Brundtland Commission's Report in which sustainable development is defined as 'the kind of development that meets the needs of the present without compromising the ability of future generations to meet their own needs'. (Robert, Parris and Leiserowitz, 2005). Later, Dyllick and Hockerts (2002) amended the definition of sustainability to make it more applicable to corporates and included the stakeholders' perspective. They defined it as 'meeting the needs of a firm's direct and indirect stakeholders (such as shareholders, employees, clients, pressure groups, communities, etc.), without compromising its ability to meet the needs of future stakeholders as well'. An analysis of the different terms associated with sustainability shows that it is a very inclusive term. It encompasses the concepts of producing in a cleaner way, minimizing the usage of resources and an eco-friendly design as far as possible thus preventing pollution as well (Glavic and Lukman, 2007). According to another broad definition of sustainability, it is an aggregation of the economic, environmental and social dimensions (Dyllick and Hockert, 2002) for a firm. This was similar to the triple P (people planet profit) concept of Elkington (2013).

Another term that is very closely associated with sustainability is the concept of 'green', as organizations are adopting green practices and green technologies (Babiak and Trendafilova, 2011; Murugesan, 2008; Vachon, 2007). In their pursuit to be more environmentally responsible, there are applications of green in marketing (Ottman and Herbert, 1993), supply chain (Green et al., 2012; Vachon and Klassen, 2006), accounting (Owen et al., 1997) and information technology (Murugesan, 2008 and Mishra et al., 2014). Darnall et al. (2008) have argued that environment management systems and green supply chain management are complementary to sustainability and green supply chain management can be utilized to make system-wide environmental changes in organizations.

Sustainability is not only a broad, societal or superordinate goal for organizations; there is confirmation that sustainability has an influence upon the overall performance of an organization (Goyal, Rahman and

Kazmi, 2013). A number of studies have corroborated that sustainable actions have favourable performance outcomes for corporations in refining financial performance and in improving investors' perception as well (Klassen and McLaughlin, 1996; Artiach et al, 2010; Eccles, Ioannou and Serafeim, 2014; Lourenco et al., 2012). Many other studies have also established a relationship between sustainability-oriented innovations and organizational performance (Maletič et al., 2014; Ngwakwe, 2008).

Lee, Kim and Kim (2018) found that social expectations, organizational support, and stakeholder pressure were the key influencers in the adoption of corporate environmental responsibility and green practices. Stakeholders can positively influence organizations to become environmentally responsible (Depoers, Jeanjean and Jérôme, 2016; Yu and Ramanathan, 2015). Further, studies have also reported a strong influence that customers exert upon organizations to adopt green practices (Le Van, Viet Nguyen and Nguyen, 2019; Yen, 2018). Investors favour firms that share environmental data (Cordeiro and Tewari, 2015). Other factors that were found to have a bearing on sustainability were environmental statutes, organization size, characteristics of the TMT (Top Management Team), organization's green shared vision and human resources in organizations (Etzion 2007; González-Benito and González-Benito 2006; Lin and Ho 2011; Chen, Chang and Lin, 2014; Luthra, Garg and Haleem, 2015). It is seen that the personality, characteristics and environmental disposition of employees can also have a very strong impact on the organization's sustainability and green initiatives (Wiernik, Dilchert and Ones, 2016).

## Studies on China and India: Need for Sustainability in These Two Countries

### Sustainability Initiatives in China

In the early 1980s when multinational corporations (MNCs) entered the Chinese territory, they had to source material from abroad or from other MNCs due to the poor quality and low environmental compliance by the local Chinese manufacturers. The Chinese firms were facing major environmental challenges in the form of pollution and resource wastage.

Till date automotive and raw material sectors are criticized and subject to intense focus as being overwhelmingly responsible for the environmental degradation in China (Geng et al., 2014; Zhao et al., 2013). The Chinese organizations began paying attention to their environmental performance in order to meet the expectations of their foreign customers (Christmann and Taylor, 2001; Zhu and Sarkis, 2016). The Chinese firms obtained environmental certifications to signal their sustainability intent to the community stakeholders and foreign customers (Qi et al., 2011). In a study of 377 Chinese firms, Zhu, Cordeiro and Sarkis (2012) found that foreign partnering was driving Chinese firms to take up proactive environmental practices. In several cases the foreign customers insisted on the implementation of Environmental Performance Systems and procurement of ISO 14001 certification by their Chinese partners (Zhu and Sarkis, 2004). Guoyou et al. (2013) also found that off-shore customers had a major role in prompting organizations to take up green product and process innovations and their influence was more than that of the local community and regulatory stakeholders.

The Chinese government at this juncture introduced some major environmental policies to counter the environmental degradation problems (Lin and Ho, 2011). Despite the governmental intervention, the environmental challenges still prevail, as China is considered to be one of the worst polluters, attracting global attention (Bai, Sarkis and Dou, 2015). In a study of 89 firms of the Jiangsu Province in China, Zhang et al. (2008) found that although environmental compliance happened initially due to the government's influence, later community participation and market demand became influential drivers for firms to take up environmental management. Researchers have a difference of opinion when it comes to the role of government as an enabler of environment management. According to Zeng (2012), China is not very strong in its environmental law enforcement (Zeng et al., 2012) and a contrary view suggests that the government has a very strong role in ensuring environmental compliance due to its overwhelming presence in the country (Shroeder, 2014). Many companies in China have adopted the practice of applying ISO standards such as ISO 14001 certification and disclosure on environment and sustainability related initiatives (Bai, Sarkis and Dou, 2015). Zhu and Sarkis (2006), who have done immense work on sustainability in Chinese enterprises, have mentioned that the Chinese corporations' sustainability practices were still at a nascent stage, lagging far behind the practices followed in developed countries. The impact of external stakeholders such as regulatory authorities, competition and non-governmental institutions is insufficient to compel firms to adopt and report their environmental performance or activities in the public domain (Weber, 2014; Liu and Anbumozhi, 2009). Studies reveal that sustainability practices are mostly adopted by environmentally sensitive sectors and large Chinese firms (Zhu and Sarkis, 2006). This could be attributed to the diligence of regulatory authorities, market demand and customer pressures making the adoption of sustainability skewed among firms, with large firms taking the lead and the medium and small firms not being very serious about the environmental consequences of their operations (Kostka, Moslener and Andreas, 2013).

However, over the years there is an increase in environmental awareness and in one of the reported studies, employees working in an energy sector company in one of the biggest coal mining regions of China had started valuing initiatives related to environment management (EM). Several research studies have explored how Chinese organizations are making big endeavours to 'green' their supply chains (Zhu, Sarkis and Geng, 2005; Zhu and Sarkis, 2006; Zhu, Sarkis and Lai, 2007 and 2008; Li, 2011).

## Sustainability Initiatives in India

A lot of parallels can be drawn while comparing India and China's sustainability journey. Indian studies show that the extent of reporting is higher for firms with larger size and for firms with membership in the manufacturing industry (Goel, 2010). In the Indian context, the regulatory framework attempts to ensure that manufacturing organizations are environmentally compliant but not with complete success (Mittal et al., 2012). Due to the weak regulatory pressures, the Indian organizations do not arduously take care of their environmental responsibilities. The recent times have seen newer regulatory norms introduced by Securities and Exchange Board of India (SEBI) mandating the top 100 companies on the bourses to include a business responsibility report covering environmental, social and economic aspects in their annual reports (Afsharipour and Rana, 2014). The latest amendments to the Companies Act, 2013 stipulates that firms that meet certain criteria in terms of profitability need to make investments in activities that are socially and environmentally responsible (Verma, 2011). Indian organizations are also voluntarily publishing their sustainability reports in conformance with the Global Reporting Initiative (GRI) framework (Yadava and Sinha, 2016).

Just like China, in India, green supply chain management is an emerging theme on the environmental front but there are limited studies to show how Indian organizations are operationalizing green supply chains (Gupta et al, 2018; Mitra and Dutta, 2014).

Although research points to the favourable impact of green supply chains on organizational financial results and market standing, green supply chain management is still not very popular in India owing to the lack of initiative from customers and less legal push to enforce environmental norms (Mitra and Dutta, 2014). Other reasons for inadequate conformance to environmental standards are lack of execution, manipulation, difficulty in adoption of environmental systems and short-term orientation of the organizations (Vijayvargy, Thakkar and Agarwal, 2017). Smaller organizations are not as aware of their environmental responsibilities as the large and medium sized organizations are (Sajan, Shalij and Ramesh, 2017), although they comprise a major chunk of the Indian manufacturing sector (Nulkar, 2014).

## Green Human Resource Management

An organization's environmental initiatives could be effective only if they spread across the organization instead of being concentrated to a few departments and roles (Wagner and Blom 2011). It is important for employees across the organization to be engaged in pro-environmental behaviours (Steg and Vlek, 2009). This would be possible only if employees understand the environmental impact of their work and are motivated to make their actions environment-friendly. This form of attitudinal and behavioural change at a systemic level would not happen in the organization without the facilitation of the Human Resource Function (Dumont, Shen and Deng, 2017). The need for the integration of environment management and human resource management has been voiced in the literature (Schuler, Jackson and Jiang, 2014; Jackson and Seo, 2010; Mandip, 2012). In the year 1996, Wehrmeyer published an amalgamation of research papers and practitioner contributions on the greening of organizations in the form of a book. He advocated the integration of environmental management and human resource management (HRM). Since then, there has been immense work in this field and many authors have attempted to define this environmental orientation of HRM and called it Green HRM or GHRM. It has been defined as the association between the human resource practices and environmental goals of the organization (Renwick, Redman and Maguire, 2008). Mampra (2013) has described GHRM in detail as 'the use of HRM policies to encourage the sustainable use of resources within business enterprises and promote the cause of environmentalism, which further boosts up employee morale and satisfaction'.

Renwick, Redman and Maguire (2008) in a review of Green HRM literature described the environmental dimensions of the different HR practices, which affect the entire life cycle of the employee using the Ability-Motivation-Opportunity Framework. It is possible for organizations to project their green employer brand image (Dögl and Holtbrügge, 2014; Mandip, 2012), define the green component of job descriptions (Opatha and Arulrajah, 2014), spell out green competencies for different roles (Renwick et al., 2016) and include green competencies in the selection criteria for recruitments (Grolleau, Mzoughi and Pekovic, 2012). Similarly, inclusion of green behaviour in performance management systems to assess the degree to which employees consciously perform their duties in environmentally responsible ways (Ahmad, 2015; Renwick et al., 2013) has also been discussed. Environmental training is another area in which there has been a lot of research to prove that environmental training promotes proactive green management (Teixeira, Jabbour and de Sousa Jabbour, 2012). Environmentally focused learning makes employees aware of the possibilities of environmental damages and encourages them to follow environmentally conducive routines and practices. It promotes knowledge sharing and learning for better green management among the employees (Teixeira et al, 2016). Enhancing employee involvement through team work and suggestion schemes can further help organizations identify the areas for environmental improvement in work processes (Mandip, 2012; Renwick et al., 2016). The offering of rewards to employees for sharing innovative ideas to cut wastes, emission and resource usage may prove useful to motivate employees to participate in process related enhancements (Dumont, et al., 2017). In fact, Guerci, Longoni, and Luzzini (2016) found that Green HRM practices which include green hiring, green training and involvement, green performance management and compensation mediated the connection between customer and regulatory stakeholder pressure and firm's environmental performance.

## Studies on Green HRM in India and China

There are few studies on Green HRM and employee pro-environmental behaviour in the context of China and India. Some of the notable studies in China on employee pro-environmental or green behaviour include the study by Dumont et al. (2017) of a Chinese subsidiary which was a part of an Australian MNC. The study found that Green HRM had an impact on in-role employee green behaviour (i.e., the behaviour employee demonstrates while performing the job) and to some extent on the extra role green behaviour (i.e., the behaviour that goes beyond the call of official duty) and this relationship was mediated by the psychological green climate. Subramanian, Abdul Rahman, Wu and Nath (2016), in a study of Chinese employees, found that acquired green competencies such as environmental knowledge, green purchase attitude and intention during employee selection had a favourable impact on the organization's green practices. In another study, Shen et al. (2016) found that Green HRM was positively related to employee task performance and organizational citizenship behaviour directed at the organization and negatively related to employee intention to quit, via the mediation of organizational identification. In a similar study, Paille et al. (2014) mentioned that there is a relationship between organizational environmental performance and organizational citizenship behavior and strategic HRM. Moreover, internal environmental concern moderated the effect of strategic human resource. Fryxell and Lo (2003) found that the managers had a 'strong disposition' towards taking environmental action, and environmental knowledge and values were predictors of personal environmental behaviours. Studies have also shown that top managers are more engaged in corporate sustainable development in comparison to the other employees (Zhang et al., 2014; Dong et al., 2014).

In the Indian context, there are conceptual studies that have tried to develop a process model of HRM linking it with Green HRM (Mukherjee and Chandra, 2018; Rani and Mishra, 2014; Mandip, 2012) and there are studies that have extolled the virtues of Green HRM (Sharma, 2016; Bangwal and Tiwari, 2015; Deshwal, 2015) without capturing the narratives. Mishra (2017) explored the application of Green HR practices in the Indian manufacturing industry and studied factors that facilitated green behaviour. The rather dismal finding revealed that the GHRM practices were neither being formally structured nor meticulously followed. Moreover, there was no proper documentation of the HRM data that supported the green initiatives. In a study of Indian public sector units, it was found that there was very low level of acceptance of the importance of Green HRM and inadequate implementation of the environmentally conducive HR practices (Mishra, Sarkar and Kiranmai, 2014). Hence the exploration of the application of Green HRM has not been conducted in-depth to unravel the nuances and complexities in the India context. Other unexplored areas are identification of the antecedents of Green HRM and understanding the reasons behind the limited implementation of Green HRM as revealed by Mishra (2017) and Mishra et al. (2014).

Hence, it is very evident that both Indian and Chinese organizations have begun to realize the importance of sustainability and the role of Green HRM due to the pressures from stakeholders. But there are no large-scale studies to show how Green HRM impacts the green competencies of individuals leading to pro-environmental behaviour. There is a need to strengthen the relationship between environmentally conscious corporate social responsibility (CSR), sustainability and employee pro-environmental behaviour. It would be useful to understand people's perspective and the linkage between organizational HR focus and green competencies of employees in fast-developing countries such as China and India. Hence, this study proposes to assess the above in the form of the following objectives.

## Study Objectives

- To assess all the factors that are important in influencing pro-environmental behaviour and perceived organization performance.
- To propose a conceptual framework that demonstrates linkages among an organization's environmentally focused initiatives and HR practices influencing pro-environmental behaviour.

## Study Methodology

In the present research, data were collected from secondary sources such as academic literature on sustainability, green management, Green HRM practices, perceived benefits to the organization, societal outcomes.

Thereafter, based on the extant literature and qualitative insights, a conceptual framework is proposed. The conceptual framework is further supported by earlier studies with respect to the factors that are included in the model.

### Theoretical Framework

In the present chapter, an attempt is made to assess all the factors that were found important for influencing pro-environmental behaviour, perceived organizational performance, the linkages among the factors, and the role of HR practices. The conceptual framework is further validated with the help of secondary data.

Greening of organizational culture was emphasized by Brio et al. (2007) in their studies. They argued that weak organizational culture leads to inefficiencies of human resources, which in turn negatively affects firm's environmental performance. Fadhilah and Ramayah (2012) in their theoretical deliberations pointed out the importance of top management's environmental orientation being a decisive factor in determining sustainability related innovations or green innovations in organizations. It was also emphasized that it is important that top management or leadership support at first shapes the HR practices, which subsequently influences employees' pro-environmental behaviour. It was also accepted that there are mainly two motivating factors that encourage organizations in enforcing green practices namely, the potential financial benefits and environmental regulations. The policy makers and intellectuals that care for environment had voiced the need for sustainable development in general, and specific sustainable standards that can be followed by organizations for reducing carbon emissions. It is accepted that the active role of government bodies plays a significant role in promoting green practices because of mandatory compliance issue.

After the assistance from United States Green Building Council (USGBC)* started a voluntary, consensus-based national rating system for developing high-performance and sustainable buildings such as Leadership in Energy and Environmental Design (LEED)** certification program to address environmental issues to some extent. After this, owners and builders are needed to secure green credentials by publishing distinct rating systems for their several different building types. These energy-efficient solutions and green building practices have proven to be cost-effective. Financial benefits are achieved because of reduced cost (emphasized by all respondents), substantial contracts with the business partners, and decreased amount of penalties accomplished because of improved environmental performance as analysed in the study by Wu et al. (2015).

Though pro-environmental behaviour is studied in both public and private organizational context, very few studies have examined this in work settings (Ones and Dilchert, 2012). The findings of the social exchange framework showed that when the employees are satisfied with their job roles and other returns received from the organization, they tend to become more devoted and subsequently, it results

* The U.S. Green Building Council, a nonprofit organization, describes itself as 'a community of more than 7,500 organizations from every sector of the building industry united by a common purpose: to transform the building marketplace to sustainability'. U.S. Green Building Council, 'Who Are We', available at www.usgbc.org/DisplayPage.aspx?CMSPageID=1498&

** For example, LEED-NC identifies 51 specific standards for awarding rating points in six major categories applicable to new commercial construction and major renovation projects: Sustainable Sites; Water Efficiency; Energy and Atmosphere; Materials and Resources; Indoor Environmental Quality; and Innovation and Design Process. U.S. Green Building Council, LEED-NC Green Building Rating System New Construction and Major Renovations for (Ver. 2.2, October 2005) [hereinafter LEED commentators offer serious criticisms of the USGBC system].

in their organization citizenship behaviour. According to the social exchange framework, perceived organizational support, job satisfaction and commitment to the organization were found feasible drivers for employee motivation in helping the organization towards preserving the environment (Lee et al., 1995; Ramus, 2001).

Brio et al. (2017) demonstrated that different green HRM practices (i.e., green hiring, green training and involvement and green performance management and compensation) mediated the relation between external environmental pressures and environmental performance. Hence, studies have established the intervening role for sure, but this is either mediating or moderating the organization performance and green workplace behaviour is not very clear in different contexts, thus there is a need for empirical evaluation with real data. The same is being done in contributing to the designing of Green HRM practices. The Green HR practices are needed to be strengthened by the existence of a green support culture. It is also noted that such measure have helped firms in gaining better social reputation and more social awards by rendering heterogeneous support to stakeholder such as employees, customers, business partners and the community at large.

The analysis of earlier literature and theoretical building leads to a conceptual framework towards environment and organizational performance as given in Figure 24.1.

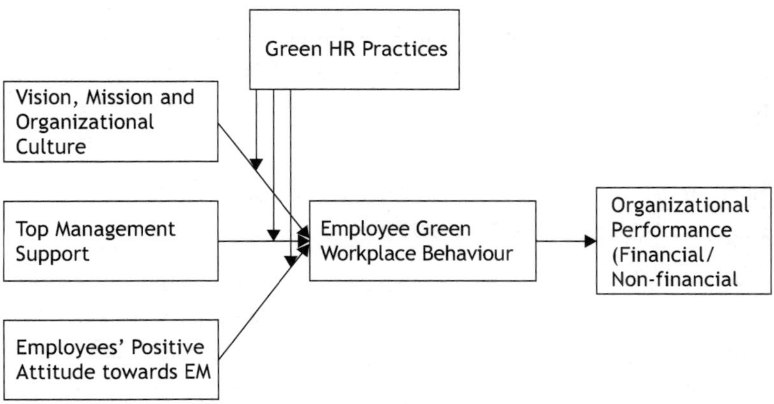


Figure 24.1 *Research Model*

*Source:* Dr Soni Agrawal and Dr Roma Puri.

**Factors Supporting Green Workplace Behaviour and Organizational Performance:** In this section we explain the factors that are considered as antecedents to organizational performance (Brio et al., 2007).

## Vision, Mission and Organizational Culture

The variable is defined as the organization that projects itself as an environmentally conscious organization. The vision and mission statements of the organization include environmental conservation initiatives in a focused manner. Also, it has a clear policy statement urging environmental awareness in every area of operation. The organization takes initiatives in environment management beyond those required in the regulations. There are several formal and informal communication channels to spread green culture in the organization. Also, the leadership of the organizational encourages employees to value environmental concerns (Brio et al., 2007).

## Top Management Support

Green initiatives and practices are actively praised and followed by top management in various forums. Senior leaders take efforts to get the support of all the stakeholders towards environmental protection for minimizing pollution and wastage. The emphasis is given on getting assurance from senior leadership that the support of all the employees towards environmental issues is ensured. This is done by factoring team level efforts in departmental budgets (Paille et al., 2014).

## Employees' Positive Attitude Towards Environment Management

Employees support is expected in taking initiatives, conserving environment and reducing waste. It is either in-role or extra- role towards pro-environmental behaviour, wherein the employee acts to enhance their surroundings or inhibit the hazards that threaten the environment, thereby mitigating environmental damage, which ultimately leads to environmental sustainability in their workplace and beyond. They volunteer for projects, endeavours or events that address environmental issues in the organization. Also, they not only encourage their colleagues to express their ideas and opinions on environmental issues, but also makes an impact outside the organization (Renwick et al., 2016).

## Green HR Practices

The message that environmentally driven HR practices have an influence on job performance is clear in these organizations. The organization uses green employer branding program actively. The recruitment messages include environmental behaviour/environmental commitment criteria. Job description includes environment sustainability related roles and responsibilities. Employees are given specific green targets, goals and responsibilities that are a part of their key result areas (KRAs). Employees receive regular feedback on achievement of environmental goals. Extensive environmental training programs to increase environmental awareness, skill and competencies are provided for individuals in the company. Formal environmental training programs are offered to employees in order to increase their promotability in the organization. Employees who receive green training have the opportunity to apply green knowledge in everyday activities. Organization offers environmental education via raising campaigns/publicity, for example, series of lectures/seminars/debates for employees. The organization involves employees in formulating environmental strategy. Suggestion schemes are linked with reward system by introducing rewards for innovative environmental initiatives and performance. Organization offers monetary and non-monetary rewards/recognition in the form of dinner and appreciation based on environmental achievement (Li et al., 2011).

## Employees' Attitude Towards Environment Management

Employees demonstrate behaviour and attitudes that validate that employees are appreciating and following green practices and behaviour in their day-to-day working. Such efforts are reflected in a way of saving energy, sacrificing little personal comforts, preference towards reusing products if possible, rather than throwing them away. Also, they prefer public transportation while coming to the office that is a contribution towards pollution reduction. Additionally, they take extra efforts to dispose biodegradable and non-biodegradable wastes separately and prefer car-pooling whenever possible (Jackson et al., 2014).

## Green Management

The organization puts investments in renewable energy assets based on techno-commercial feasibility. Also, there are mechanisms such as audits, benchmarking, target setting for progressively reducing specific energy consumption. There is a continuous monitoring and review of energy usage through organization wide data management system. Environmental impact is an important consideration while designing and developing new products. Also, special attempts are made to reduce energy consumption in transportation of raw materials, finished goods and wastes. The organization ensures maximum reuse and recycling of waste, one such example is usage of alternatives to plastic packaging (Jabbour et al., 2013).

## Organizational Performance

Organization perceives various direct and indirect outcomes by following green practices. The non-tangible outcomes are improved image of the organization globally in the eyes of regulatory bodies, customers, competitors, as well as employees and consumers. That results in recognition and respect in the community. Some financial returns include enhanced market share and growth, which results in increased profitability. Also, execution of green management strategies enables trust of enterprise (Brio et al., 2007).

## Discussion and Conclusion

The present comprehensive conceptual model shows linkages between Green HRM and organizational factors such as top management support, organizational green culture and employee pro-environmental attitude as well as impact of HR practices on green behaviour and organizational financial and non-financial benefits. Studies in the past have not integrated all these constructs in one model. But the interrelationships cannot be ignored and need to be taken into consideration in the successful implementation of Green HR practices, which would yield positive environmental outcomes for the organization later.

It was also realized that best practicing organizations with an emphasis on green vision, mission and organization culture solicit to enhance their environmental activities towards green practices. The employees of these organizations tend to become more contented towards their job and are dedicated to their organization (Wagner, 2012). The similar findings were acknowledged in a study of Paille and Boiral (2013), that perceived organizational support and job satisfaction have a consequential effect on organizational citizenship behaviour for the environment (OCBE). It was found that employees had participated in subscribing to corporate greening through mutual support among themselves by eco-helping, by detailing the environmental procedures to new employees or by supporting colleagues in enhancing their environmental knowledge and skills. Employees had started supporting the organization to the initiative through eco-civic engagement such as participation in green committees or by taking actions that help in the good image building of the organization. Employees further came forward towards attempting personal green initiatives in the workplace such as making suggestions in order to improve energy efficiency and by sharing ideas and giving feedback for enhancing energy efficiency or by putting recyclable materials in appropriate containers.

In addition, the relationship between top management support and HR has a special relation as studied by El-Kassar and Singh (2019). They highlighted the importance of management commitment and HR practices involving 215 respondents working in the Middle East and North Africa (MENA) region and Golf-Cooperation Countries (GCC). In a study conducted by Sawang and Kivits (2014) on 210 organizations, it was established that senior management's environment-related attitude, subjective norms from stakeholders and perceived green resource readiness influenced their decision to adopt Green HR initiatives. The role of a leader in influencing pro-environmental behaviour among employees was also proven in the study of Robertson and Barling (2013), where they found that leaders' environmentally descriptive norms positively influence employees' pro-environmental behaviour. Green Leadership has a special role in driving this relationship by providing support and encouragement to such endeavours and being instrumental in the infusion of Green HR practices that leads to these behaviours. According to the authors, green culture narrows the gap between green espoused values and norms and the actual norms and behaviour. So top management support, along with a green friendly organizational culture, influence HR practices.

As discussed above, many companies strongly believe in environmental protection and thus, it becomes a priority in all these organizations' major business activities. For fulfilling these commitments, lots of efforts for building the culture of care for environment and sustainable development are shaped. For creating the culture, companies take steps not only on forming and framing structures but also following these guidelines by the employees.

Employees' pro-environmental attitudes have an influence on the organization's overall HR practices and environmental performance. Findings revealed a high correlation between green practices and environmental performance (Hajmohammad et al., 2013). It was noted that few measures were taken for reducing raw material consumption, controlling emission and discharge and enhancing the recycling and waste management process. These efforts helped in decreasing raw material consumption, emission, waste-water generation and usage of energy. It must also be a viable clarification that directly and indirectly, green practices denote the improvisation of financial as well as social performance.

Regarding HR practices and their influence on green workplace behaviour and organization outcomes, Teixerira et al. (2012) focused on nine case studies of ISO 14001 certified Brazilian companies to demonstrate the role of organizational culture and teamwork, and top management support in promoting environmental training, which led to effective green management in organizations. Jabbour et al. (2013) in their study of 75 Brazilian automotive companies found a positive relationship between HR and Environment Management in organizations. In one of the studies, Guerci et al. (2016) had attempted to study the role of different HRM practices on external environmental pressure and firm's environmental performance.

There are many HR initiatives that are reflected in day-to-day working of the company. At the time of recruitment, topmost focus is to take a person that can understand the culture of the organization. The study of O'Donahue and Torgusa (2016) on a sample of 158 small manufacturing Australian organizations established the moderating role of Green HRM on proactive environment management and firm financial performance. The result of the study of Saedi et. al., (2014) showed a positive relationship between CSR activities and financial performance. According to Dües et al. (2013) and Verrier et al. (2014), lean and green practices contributed towards better competitive advantage and profitability.

The company wants a person, who is not only good on the technical side but also appreciates the culture of care towards environment and building a sustainable society. Even vendors are selected based on these aspects, who can understand and fulfil these expectations. Moreover, the important initiative towards re-usage of the resources are undertaken. Hazardous waste for environment is sorted out properly. If companies, from top level employees to the lowest level employees, follow such guidelines, the exercise will not only motivate employees but also save lots of resources in total. For better compliance, along with technical key performance indicators (KPIs), the provision of some KPIs that measure how effectively and optimally employees have utilized resource and how many resources they could save in the end, can serve the purpose of better compliance. These initiatives can be rewarded later at the end of the business cycle based on performance and can be recognized in public forums as well.

It is seen that there is a consequential positive relationship between the execution of environmental practices and environmental performance. Findings also reveal a high correlation between green practices and environmental performance (Hajmohammad et al., 2013). It was noted that few measures were taken for reducing raw material consumption, controlling emission and discharge, and enhancing the recycling and waste management process. It is a viable clarification that directly and indirectly, green practices denote the improvisation of financial as well as social performance. Environmental performance provides ways to enhance the social reputation, and the number of social awards of the firm thereby stimulating social performance. Meanwhile, improved social performance fascinates customers' positive performance and company's brand image, which translates into sales increment (Jeong et al., 2014).

The arguments made above go on to show that culture of the organization, which is supported by pro-environmental attitude of employees, support of top management and the presence of green HR provides opportunities to all the stakeholders towards a better improved green behaviour. Thus, the proposed research model, based on the discussion above seems logical and worth testing with actual data set of different types of organizations in different countries.

Moreover, a number of examples and studies are taken from India and China. Thus, the next steps seem logical to test the model with real data from both the countries. In this way, both India and China can benefit after implementing the model as proposed in the study.

## References

Afsharipour, A., and S. Rana. 2014. 'Corporate Social Responsibility in India.' In *The Conference Board Director Notes No. DN-V6N14 (August 2014)*. https://papers.ssrn.com/sol3/papers.cfm?abstract_id=2517601

Ahmad, S. 2015. 'Green Human Resource Management: Policies and Practices.' *Cogent Business & Management* 2 (1), 1030817.

Artiach, T., D. Lee, D. Nelson, and J. Walker. 2010. 'The Determinants of Corporate Sustainability Performance.' *Accounting & Finance* 50 (1), 31–51. https://doi.org/10.1111/j.1467-629X.2009.00315.x.

Babiak, K., and S. Trendafilova. 2011. 'CSR and Environmental Responsibility: Motives and Pressures to Adopt Green Management Practices.' *Corporate social responsibility and environmental management* 18 (1), 11–24. https://doi.org/10.1002/csr.229.

Bai, C., J. Sarkis, and Y. Dou. 2015. 'Corporate Sustainability Development in China: Review and Analysis.' *Industrial Management & Data Systems* 115 (1), 5–40. https://doi.org/10.1108/IMDS-09-2014-0258.

Bangwal, D., and P. Tiwari, 2015. 'Green HRM–A way to Greening the Environment.' *IOSR Journal of Business and Management* 17 (12), 45–53.

Brio, J. A., E. Fernandez, and B. Junquera, 2007. 'Management and Employee Involvement in Achieving an Environmental Action-based Competitive

Advantage: An Empirical Study.' *The International Journal of Human Resource Management* 18, 491–522. https://doi.org/10.1080/09585190601178687

Chen, Y. S., C. H. Chang, and Y. H. Lin. 2014. 'The Determinants of Green Radical and Incremental Innovation Performance: Green Shared Vision, Green Absorptive Capacity, and Green Organizational Ambidexterity.' *Sustainability* 6 (11), 7787–7806. https://doi.org/10.3390/su6117787.

Christmann, P., and G. Taylor, 2001. 'Globalization and the Environment: Determinants of Firm Self-regulation in China.' *Journal of international business studies* 32 (3), 439–458. https://doi.org/10.1057/palgrave.jibs.8490976.

Cordeiro, J. J., and M. Tewari. 2015. 'Firm Characteristics, Industry Context, and Investor Reactions to Environmental CSR: A Stakeholder Theory Approach.' *Journal of Business Ethics* 130 (4), 833–849. https://doi.org/10.1007/s10551-014-2115-x.

Darnall, N., G. J. Jolley, and R. Handfield. 2008. 'Environmental Management Systems and Green Supply Chain Management: Complements for Sustainability?' *Business strategy and the environment* 17 (1), 30–45. https://doi.org/10.1002/bse.557.

Depoers, F., T. Jeanjean, and T. Jérôme. 2016. 'Voluntary Disclosure of Greenhouse Gas Emissions: Contrasting the Carbon Disclosure Project and Corporate Reports.' *Journal of Business Ethics* 134 (3), 445–461. https://doi.org/10.1007/s10551-014-2432-0.

Deshwal, D. P. 2015. 'Green HRM: An Organizational Strategy of Greening People.' *International Journal of applied research* 1 (13), 176–181.

Dögl, C., and D. Holtbrügge. 2014. 'Corporate Environmental Responsibility, Employer Reputation and Employee Commitment: An Empirical Study in Developed and Emerging Economies.' *The International Journal of Human Resource Management* 25 (12), 1739–1762. https://doi.org/10.1080/09585192.2013.859164.

Dong, S., R. Burritt, and W. Qian. 2014. 'Salient Stakeholders in Corporate Social Responsibility Reporting by Chinese Mining and Minerals Companies.' *Journal of Cleaner Production* 84, 59–69. https://doi.org/10.1016/j.jclepro.2014.01.012.

Dües, C. M., K. H. Tan, and M. Lim. 2013. 'Green as the New Lean: How to Use Lean Practices as a Catalyst to Greening Your Supply Chain.' *J. Clean. Prod* 40, 93–100. https://doi.org/10.1016/j.jclepro.2011.12.023.

Dumont, J., J. Shen, and X. Deng. 2017. 'Effects of Green HRM Practices on Employee Workplace Green Behavior: The Role of Psychological Green Climate and employee Green Values.' *Human Resource Management* 56 (4), 613–627. https://doi.org/10.1002/hrm.21792.

Dyllick, T., and K. Hockerts. 2002. 'Beyond the Business Case for Corporate Sustainability.' *Business strategy and the environment* 11 (2), 130–141. https://doi.org/10.1002/bse.323.

Eccles, R. G., I. Ioannou, and G. Serafeim. 2014. 'The Impact of Corporate Sustainability on Organizational Processes and Performance.' *Management Science* 60 (11), 2835–2857. https://doi.org/10.1287/mnsc.2014.1984.

El-Kassar, A. N., and S. K. Singh. 2019. 'Green Innovation and Organizational Performance: The Influence of Big Data and the Moderating Role of Management Commitment and HR Practices.' *Technological Forecasting and Social Change* 144, 483–498. https://doi.org/10.1016/j.techfore.2017.12.016.

Elkington, J. 2013. 'Enter the Triple Bottom Line.' In *The triple bottom line* (23–38). London: Routledge.

Etzion, D. 2007. 'Research on Organizations and the Natural Environment, 1992–Present: A Review.' *Journal of Management* 33 (4), 637–664. https://doi.org/10.1177/0149206307302553.

Fadhilah, Z., and T. Ramayah. 2012. 'Behind the Green Doors: What Management Practices Lead to Sustainable Innovation?' *Procedia-Social and Behavioral Sciences* 65, 247–252. https://doi.org/10.1016/j.sbspro.2012.11.118.

Fryxell, G. E., and C. W. Lo. 2003. 'The Influence of Environmental Knowledge and Values on Managerial Behaviours on Behalf of the Environment: An Empirical Examination of Managers in China.' *Journal of business ethics* 46 (1), 45–69. https://doi.org/10.1023/A:1024773012398.

Geng, Y., L. Zhang, X. Chen, B. Xue, T. Fujita, and H. Dong. 2014. 'Urban ecological Footprint Analysis: A Comparative study between Shenyang in China and Kawasaki in Japan.' *Journal of Cleaner Production* 75, 130–142. https://doi.org/10.1016/j.jclepro.2014.03.082.

Glavič, P., and R. Lukman. 2007. 'Review of Sustainability Terms and their Definitions.' *Journal of Cleaner Production* 15 (18), 1875–1885. https://doi.org/10.1016/j.jclepro.2006.12.006.

Goel, P. 2010. 'Triple Bottom Line Reporting: An Analytical Approach for Corporate Sustainability.' *Journal of Finance, Accounting & Management* 1 (1), 27–42.

González-Benito, J., and Ó. González-Benito. 2006. 'The Role of Stakeholder Pressure and Managerial Values in the Implementation of Environmental Logistics Practices.' *International Journal of Production Research* 44 (7), 1353–1373. https://doi.org/10.1080/00207540500435199.

Goyal, P., Z. Rahman, and A. A. Kazmi. 2013. 'Corporate Sustainability Performance and Firm Performance Research: Literature Review and Future Research Agenda.' *Management Decision* 51 (2), 361–379. https://doi.org/10.1108/00251741311301867.

Green Jr, K. W., P. J. Zelbst, J. Meacham, and V. S. Bhadauria. 2012. 'Green Supply Chain Management Practices: Impact on Performance.' *Supply Chain Management: An International Journal* 17 (3), 290–305. https://doi.org/10.1108/13598541211227126.

Grolleau, G., N. Mzoughi, and S. Pekovic, 2012. 'Green Not (Only) for Profit: An Empirical Examination of the Effect of Environmental-related Standards on Employees' Recruitment.' *Resource and Energy Economics* 34 (1), 74–92. https://doi.org/10.1016/j.reseneeco.2011.10.002.

Guerci, M., A. Longoni, and D. Luzzini. 2016. 'Translating Stakeholder Pressures into Environmental Performance–the Mediating Role Of Green HRM

Practices.' *The International Journal of Human Resource Management* 27 (2), 262–289. https://doi.org/10.1080/09585192.2015.1065431.

Guoyou, Q., Z. Saixing, T. Chiming, Y. Haitao, and Z. Hailiang. 2013. 'Stakeholders' Influences on Corporate Green Innovation Strategy: A Case Study of Manufacturing Firms in China.' *Corporate Social Responsibility and Environmental Management* 20 (1), 1–14. https://doi.org/10.1002/csr.283.

Gupta, S., G. S. Dangayach, A. K. Singh, M. L. Meena, and P. N. Rao. 2018. 'Implementation of Sustainable Manufacturing Practices in Indian Manufacturing Companies.' *Benchmarking: An International Journal* 25 (7), 2441–2459. https://doi.org/10.1108/BIJ-12-2016-0186.

Hajmohammad, S., S. Vachon, R. D. Klassen, and I. Gavronski. 2013. 'Lean Management and Supply Management: Their Role in Green Practices and Performance.' *J. Clean. Prod.* 39, 312–320. https://doi.org/10.1016/j.jclepro.2012.07.028.

Jabbour, C. J. C., A. B. L. de Sousa Jabbour, K. Govindan, A. A. Teixeira, and W. R. de Souza Freitas. 2013. 'Environmental Management and Operational Performance in Automotive Companies in Brazil: the Role of Human Resource Management and Lean Manufacturing.' *Journal of Cleaner Production* 47, 129–140. https://doi.org/10.1016/j.jclepro.2012.07.010.

Jackson, S. E., and J. Seo. 2010. 'The Greening of Strategic HRM Scholarship.' *Organization Management Journal* 7 (4):278–290. https://doi.org/10.1057/omj.2010.37.

Jackson, S. E., R. S. Schuler, and K. Jiang. 2014. 'An Aspirational Framework for Strategic Human Resource Management.' *The Academy of Management Annals* 8 (1), 1–56. https://doi.org/10.5465/19416520.2014.872335.

Jeong, E., S. S. Jang, J. Day, and S. Ha. 2014. 'The Impact of Eco-Friendly Practices on Green Image and Customer Attitudes: An Investigation in a Café Setting.' *International Journal of Hospitality Management* 41, 10–20. https://doi.org/10.1016/j.ijhm.2014.03.002.

Klassen, R. D., and C. P. McLaughlin. 1996. 'The Impact of Environmental Management on Firm Performance.' *Management Science* 42 (8), 1199–1214. https://doi.org/10.1287/mnsc.42.8.1199.

Kostka, G., U. Moslener, and J. Andreas. 2013. 'Barriers to Increasing Energy Efficiency: Evidence from Small-and medium-sized Enterprises in China.' *Journal of Cleaner Production* 57, 59–68. https://doi.org/10.1016/j.jclepro.2013.06.025.

Le Van, Q., T. Viet Nguyen, and M. H. Nguyen 2019. 'Sustainable Development and Environmental Policy: The Engagement of Stakeholders in Green Products in Vietnam.' *Business Strategy and the Environment* 28 (5), 675–687. https://doi.org/10.1002/bse.2272.

Lee, J. W., Y. M. Kim, and Y. E. Kim. 2018. 'Antecedents of Adopting Corporate Environmental Responsibility and Green Practices.' *Journal of Business Ethics* 148 (2), 397–409. https://doi.org/10.1007/s10551-016-3024-y.

Lee, Y. J., R. DeYoung, R., and R. W. Marans 1995. 'Factors Influencing Individual Recycling Behavior in Office Settings: A Study of Office Workers in Taiwan.' *Environment and Behavior* 27, 380e403

Li, Y. 2011. 'Research on the Performance Measurement of Green Supply Chain Management in China.' *Journal of Sustainable Development* 4 (3)–101.

Lin, C. Y., and Y. H. Ho. 2011. 'Determinants of Green Practice Adoption for Logistics Companies in China.' *Journal of business ethics* 98 (1), 67–83. https://doi.org/10.1007/s10551-010-0535-9.

Liu, X., and V. Anbumozhi. 2009. 'Determinant Factors of Corporate Environmental Information Disclosure: An Empirical Study of Chinese Listed Companies.' *Journal of Cleaner Production* 17 (6), 593–600. https://doi.org/10.1016/j.jclepro.2008.10.001.

Lourenço, I. C., M. C. Branco, J. D. Curto, and T. Eugénio. 2012. 'How Does the market Value Corporate Sustainability Performance?' *Journal of business ethics* 108 (4), 417–428. https://doi.org/10.1007/s10551-011-1102-8.

Lubin, D. A., and D. C. Esty. 2010. 'The Sustainability Imperative.' *Harvard business review* 88 (5), 42–50.

Luthra, S., D. Garg, and A. Haleem 2015. 'An Analysis of Interactions among Critical Success Factors to Implement Green Supply Chain Management towards Sustainability: An Indian Perspective.' *Resources Policy* 46, 37–50. https://doi.org/10.1016/j.resourpol.2014.12.006.

Maletič, M., D. Maletič, J. J. Dahlgaard, S. M. Dahlgaard-Park, and B. Gomišček. 2014. 'The Relationship Between Sustainability–oriented Innovation Practices and Organizational Performance: Empirical Evidence from Slovenian Organizations.' *Organizacija* 47 (1):3–13. https://doi.org/10.2478/orga-2014-0001.

Mampra, M. 2013. 'Green HRM: Does it Help to Build a Competitive Service Sector? A Study', pp. 1273–1281. In Proceedings of Tenth AIMS International Conference on Management, Bengaluru, India, 6–9 January 2013.

Mandip, G. 2012. 'Green HRM: People Management Commitment to ENVIRONMENTAL SUSTAINABility.' *Research Journal of Recent Sciences, ISSN* 2277, 2502.

Mishra, D., I. Akman, and A. Mishra. 2014. 'Theory of Reasoned Action Application for Green Information Technology Acceptance.' *Computers in human behavior* 36, 29–40. https://doi.org/10.1016/j.chb.2014.03.030.

Mishra, P. 2017. 'Green Human Resource Management: A Framework for Sustainable Organizational Development in an Emerging Economy.' *International Journal of Organizational Analysis* 25 (5), 762–788. https://doi.org/10.1108/IJOA-11-2016-1079.

Mishra, R. K., S. Sarkar, and J. Kiranmai. 2014. 'Green HRM: Innovative Approach in Indian Public Enterprises.' *World Review of Science, Technology and Sustainable Development* 11 (1), 26–42. https://doi.org/10.1504/WRSTSD.2014.062374.

Mitra, S., and P. Priya Datta. 2014. 'Adoption of Green Supply Chain Management Practices and their Impact on Performance: An Exploratory Study of Indian Manufacturing Firms (2014).' *International Journal of Production Research* 52 (7), 2085–2107.

Mittal, V. K., K. S. Sangwan, C. Herrmann, P. Egede, and C. Wulbusch. 2012. 'Drivers and Barriers of Environmentally Conscious Manufacturing: A Comparative Study of Indian and German Organizations.' In *Leveraging Technology for a Sustainable World* (97–102). Berlin: Springer.

Mittelstaedt, J. D., C. J. Shultz, W. E. Kilbourne, and M. Peterson 2014. 'Sustainability as Megatrend: Two Schools of Macromarketing Thought.' *Journal of Macromarketing* 34 (3), 253–264. https://doi.org/10.1177/0276146713520551.

Mukherjee, B., and B. Chandra. 2018. 'Conceptualizing Green Human Resource Management in Predicting Employees' Green Intention and Behaviour: A Conceptual Framework.' *Prabandhan: Indian Journal of Management* 11 (7), 36–48. https://doi.org/10.17010/pijom/2018/v11i7/129940.

Murugesan, S. 2008. 'Harnessing Green IT: Principles and Practices.' *IT Professional* 10 (1), 24–33. https://doi.org/10.1109/MITP.2008.10.

Ngwakwe, Collins C. 2008. 'Environmental Responsibility and Firm Performance: Evidence from Nigeria.' *Proceeding of World Academy of Science, Engineering, and Technology* 36.

Nulkar, G. 2014. 'Does Environmental Sustainability Matter to Small and Medium Enterprises? Empirical evidence from India.' *International Journal of Environmental Studies* 71 (4), 481–489.

Ones, D. S., and S. Dilchert. 2012. 'Environmental Sustainability at Work: A Call to Action.' *Industrial and Organizational Psychology* 5 (4), 444–466. https://doi.org/10.1080/09585192.2015.1063078

Opatha, H. H. P., and A. A. Arulrajah. 2014. 'Green Human Resource Management: Simplified General Reflections.' *International Business Research* 7 (8), 101.

Ottman, J. A., and H. Herbert. 1993. *Green Marketing*. Lincolnwood, IL: NTC Business books.

Owen, D., R. Gray, and J. Bebbington. 1997. 'Green Accounting: Cosmetic Irrelevance or Radical Agenda for Change?' *Asia-Pacific Journal of Accounting* 4 (2), 175–198. https://doi.org/10.1080/10293574.1997.10510519.

Paillé P., and O. Boiral. 2013. 'Pro-environmental Behavior at Work: Construct Validity and Determinants.' *Journal of Environmental Psychology* 36, 118–128. https://doi.org/10.1016/j.jenvp.2013.07.014.

Paillé, P., and J. H. Mejía-Morelos. 2014. 'Antecedents of Pro-environmental Behaviours at Work: The Moderating Influence of Psychological Contract Breach.' *Journal of Environmental Psychology* 38, 124–131. https://doi.org/10.1016/j.jenvp.2014.01.004.

Qi, G. Y., S. X. Zeng, C. M. Tam, H. T. Yin, J. F. Wu, and Z. H. Dai. 2011. 'Diffusion of ISO 14001 environmental management systems in China:

rethinking on stakeholders' roles.' *Journal of Cleaner Production* 19 (11), 1250–1256. https://doi.org/10.1016/j.jclepro.2011.03.006.

Ramus, C. A. 2001. 'Organizing Support for Employees: Encouraging Creative Ideas for Environmental Sustainability.' *California Management Review* 43, 85e103.

Rani, S., and K. Mishra. 2014. 'Green HRM: Practices and Strategic Implementation in the Organizations.' *International Journal on Recent and Innovation Trends in Computing and Communication* 2 (11), 3633–3639.

Renwick, D. W., C. J. Jabbour, M. Muller-Camen, T. Redman, and A. Wilkinson. 2016. Contemporary Developments in Green (Environmental) HRM Scholarship. *The International Journal of Human Resource Management* 27 (2), 114–128.

Renwick, D., T. Redman, and S. Maguire. 2008. 'Green HRM: A Review, Process Model, and Research Agenda.' *University of Sheffield Management School Discussion Paper* 1, 1–46.

Renwick, D. W., T. Redman, and S. Maguire. 2013. 'Green Human Resource Management: A Review and Research Agenda.' *International Journal of Management Reviews* 15 (1), 1–14. https://doi.org/10.1111/j.1468-2370.2011.00328.x.

Robert, K. W., T. M. Parris, and A. A. Leiserowitz. 2005. 'What is Sustainable Development? Goals, Indicators, Values, and Practice.' *Environment: science and policy for sustainable development* 47 (3), 8–21.

Robertson, J. L., and J. Barling. 2013. 'Greening Organizations through Leaders' Influence on Employees' Pro-environmental Behaviors.' *Journal of organizational behavior* 34 (2), 176–194. https://doi.org/10.1002/job.1820.

Sajan, M. P., P. R. Shalij, and A. Ramesh. 2017. 'Lean Manufacturing Practices in Indian Manufacturing SMEs and their Effect on Sustainability Performance.' *Journal of Manufacturing Technology Management*. 28 (6), 772–793.

Sawang, S., and R. A. Kivits 2014. 'Greener Workplace: Understanding Senior Management's Adoption Decisions through the Theory of Planned Behaviour.' *Australasian Journal of Environmental Management* 21 (1), 22–36. https://doi.org/10.1080/14486563.2013.848418

Schroeder, P. 2014. 'Assessing Effectiveness of Governance Approaches for Sustainable Consumption and Production in China.' *Journal of Cleaner Production* 63, 64–73. https://doi.org/10.1016/j.jclepro.2013.05.039.

Schuler, R., and S. E. Jackson. 2014. 'Human Resource Management and Organizational Effectiveness: Yesterday and Today.' *Journal of Organizational Effectiveness: People and Performance* 1 (1), 35–55. https://doi.org/10.1108/JOEPP-01-2014-0003.

Sharma, K. 2016.' Conceptualization of Green HRM and Green HRM Practices: Commitment to Environment Sustainability.' *International Journal of Advanced Scientific Research and Management* 1 (8), 74–81.

Shen, J., J. Dumont, and X. Deng. 2016. 'Employees' Perceptions of Green HRM and Non-green Employee Work Outcomes: The Social Identity and

Stakeholder Perspectives.' *Group & Organization Management* 43 (4), 1–29. https://doi.org/10.1177/1059601116664610

Steg, L., and C. Vlek. 2009. 'Encouraging Pro-environmental Behaviour: An Integrative Review and Research Agenda.' *Journal of environmental psychology* 29 (3), 309–317. https://doi.org/10.1016/j.jenvp.2008.10.004.

Subramanian, N., M. D. Abdulrahman, L. Wu, and P. Nath. 2016. 'Green Competence Framework: Evidence from China.' *The International Journal of Human Resource Management* 27 (2), 151–172. https://doi.org/10.1080/09585192.2015.1047394.

Teixeira, A. A., C. J. C. Jabbour, and A. B. L. de Sousa Jabbour. 2012. 'Relationship between Green Management and Environmental Training in Companies Located in Brazil: A Theoretical Framework and Case Studies.' *International Journal of Production Economics* 140 (1), 318–329. https://doi.org/10.1016/j.ijpe.2012.01.009.

Teixeira, A. A., C. J. C. Jabbour, A. B. L. de Sousa Jabbour, H. Latan, and J. H. C. De Oliveira. 2016. 'Green Training and Green Supply Chain Management: Evidence from Brazilian Firms.' *Journal of Cleaner Production* 116, 170–176. https://doi.org/10.1016/j.jclepro.2015.12.061.

Vachon, S. 2007. 'Green Supply Chain Practices and the Selection of Environmental Technologies.' *International Journal of Production Research* 45 (18–19), 4357–4379. https://doi.org/10.1080/00207540701440303.

Vachon, S., and R. D. Klassen 2006. 'Extending Green Practices across the Supply Chain: The Impact of Upstream and Downstream Integration.' *International Journal of Operations & Production Management* 26 (7), 795–821. https://doi.org/10.1108/01443570610672248.

Verma, S. 2011. 'Why Indian Companies Indulge in CSR?' *Journal of Management & Public Policy* 2 (2).

Verrier, B., B. Rose, E. Caillaud, and H. Remita. 2014. 'Combining Organizational Performance with Sustainable Development Issues: The Lean and Green Project Benchmarking Repository.' *Journal of Cleaner Production* 85, 83–93. https://doi.org/10.1016/j.jclepro.2013.12.023.

Vijayvargy, L., J. Thakkar, and G. Agarwal. 2017. 'Green Supply Chain Management Practices and Performance: The Role of Firm-size for Emerging Economies.' *Journal of Manufacturing Technology Management* 28 (3), 299–323. https://doi.org/10.1108/JMTM-09-2016-0123.

Wagner, M. 2012. "Green' Human Resource Benefits: Do They Matter as Determinants of Environmental Management System Implementation? Online first.' *Journal of Business Ethics* 114(3), 443–456. http://dx.doi.org/10.1007/s10551-012-1356-9.

Wagner, M., and J. Blom. 2011. 'The Reciprocal and Non-Linear Relationship of Sustainability and Financial Performance.' *Business Ethics: A European Review* 20 (4), 418–432. https://doi.org/10.1111/j.1467-8608.2011.01622.x.

Weber, O. 2014. 'Environmental, Social and Governance Reporting in China.' *Business Strategy and the Environment* 23 (5), 303–317. https://doi.org/10.1002/bse.1785.

Wiernik, B. M., S. Dilchert, and D. S. Ones. 2016. 'Age and Employee Green Behaviors: A Meta-analysis.' *Frontiers in Psychology* 7, 194.

Wu, J., L. Lv, J. Sun, and X. Ji. 2015. 'A Comprehensive Analysis of China's Regional Energy Saving and Emission Reduction Efficiency: From Production and Treatment Perspectives.' *Energy Policy* 84, 166–176. https://doi.org/10.1016/j.enpol.2015.05.005.

Yadava, R. N., and B. Sinha. 2016. 'Scoring Sustainability Reports using GRI 2011 Guidelines for Assessing Environmental, Economic, and Social Dimensions of Leading Public and Private Indian Companies.' *Journal of business ethics* 138 (3), 549–558. https://doi.org/10.1007/s10551-015-2597-1.

Yen, Y. X. 2018. 'Buyer–Supplier Collaboration in Green Practices: The Driving Effects from Stakeholders.' *Business Strategy and the Environment* 27 (8), 1666–1678. https://doi.org/10.1002/bse.2231.

Yu, W., and R. Ramanathan. 2015. 'An Empirical Examination of Stakeholder Pressures, Green Operations Practices and Environmental Performance.' *International Journal of Production Research* 53 (21), 6390–6407. https://doi.org/10.1080/00207543.2014.931608.

Zeng, S. X., X. D. Xu, H. T. Yin, and C. M. Tam. 2012. 'Factors that Drive Chinese Listed Companies in Voluntary Disclosure of Environmental Information.' *Journal of Business Ethics* 109 (3):309–321. https://doi.org/10.1007/s10551-011-1129-x.

Zhang, N., F. Kong, and Y. Choi. 2014. 'Measuring Sustainability Performance for China: A Sequential Generalized Directional Distance Function Approach.' *Economic Modelling* 41, 392–397. https://doi.org/10.1016/j.econmod.2014.05.038.

Zhao, G., X. Mu, Z. Wen, F. Wang, and P. Gao. 2013. 'Soil Erosion, Conservation, and Eco-environment Changes in the Loess Plateau of China.' *Land Degradation & Development*, 24 (5), 499–510. https://doi.org/10.1002/ldr.2246.

Zhu, Q., and J. Sarkis. 2004. 'Relationships between Operational Practices and Performance among Early Adopters of Green Supply Chain Management Practices in Chinese Manufacturing Enterprises.' *Journal of Operations Management* 22 (3), 265-289. https://doi.org/10.1016/j.jom.2004.01.005.

Zhu, Q., and J. Sarkis. 2006. 'An Inter-sectoral Comparison of Green Supply Chain Management in China: Drivers and Practices.' *Journal of Cleaner Production* 14 (5), 472–486. https://doi.org/10.1016/j.jclepro.2005.01.003.

Zhu, Q., and J. Sarkis. 2016. 'Green Marketing and Consumerism as Social Change in China: Analyzing the Literature.' *International Journal of Production Economics* 181, 289–302. https://doi.org/10.1016/j.ijpe.2016.06.006.

Zhu, Q., J. Cordeiro, and J. Sarkis. 2012. 'International and Domestic Pressures and Responses of Chinese Firms to Greening.' *Ecological Economics* 83, 144–153. https://doi.org/10.1016/j.ecolecon.2012.04.007.

Zhu, Q., J. Sarkis, and Y. Geng. 2005. 'Green Supply Chain Management in China: Pressures, Practices and Performance.' *International Journal of Operations & Production Management* 25 (5), 449–468. https://doi.org/10.1108/01443570510593148.

Zhu, Q., J. Sarkis, and K. H. Lai. 2007. 'Green Supply Chain Management: Pressures, Practices and Performance within the Chinese Automobile Industry.' *Journal of Cleaner Production* 15 (11–12), 1041–1052. https://doi.org/10.1016/j.jclepro.2006.05.021.

Zhu, Q., J. Sarkis, and K. Lai. 2008. 'Confirmation of a Measurement Model for Green Supply Chain Management Practices Implementation.' *International Journal of Production Economics* 111 (2), 261–273. https://doi.org/10.1016/j.ijpe.2006.11.029.

CHAPTER 25

# The Integration of Indian Buddhist Culture into East Asian Cultures

Xiongfeng Liu

## Introduction

In the history of global cultural exchanges, no country has had such a long history of exchanges with another nation like China has had with India. The brilliant culture created by the people of India and China has immensely contributed to the progress and development of human society. In this context, the profound influence of the Buddhist culture, which is rich in wisdom and philosophy, is well-known and this culture has attracted the attention of the world at large. When it comes to Buddhist exchanges between China and India, the person who first needs a special mention is undoubtedly the Buddhist monk Faxian of the Eastern Jin Dynasty in China. Since Buddhism, which originated in India around 6th century BCE, was introduced into China, many Buddhists from South Asia (particularly India) and other places have come to China to preach the Dharma and many Chinese monks have also visited India and other countries to learn from the Dharma and then spread the Dharma to Japan and the Korean Peninsula in

East Asia. Although Faxian did not initiate the west-bound search in China, he was the 'first monk' who actually arrived in Tianzhu and obtained scriptures to return to China. Among the Indian monks who came to China to preach Buddhism, Zhikong in the Yuan Dynasty was considered to be 'the last Indian monk to come to China' (Duan Yuming, 2007). The westward movement of Faxian not only brought back the 'Sutra Theory' of Indian Buddhism, but also recorded the religion, history and geography of the ancient Western regions and South Asia including India. On the other hand, Zhikong undertook an eastward journey to China and proceeded further east to South Korea while merging Indian Buddhism with Chinese Buddhism. Thus, from Faxian to Zhikong, efforts have been witnessed to promote the integration of Indian Buddhist culture into East Asian (Chinese and South Korean) cultures and the development of the culture in those regions. A historical chapter of cultural exchanges between India and East Asia as well as India and other nations in Asia has therefore been created.

## Faxian's Search for Sutra and the Sinicization of Indian Buddhism

Faxian (367–442) was a monk of the Eastern Jin Dynasty in China. He was born in Wuyang, Pingyang County (now Xiangyuan, Shanxi Province). According to the biography of Faxian presented in the collection of monk's stories, Faxian was the fourth boy in the family. As his three elder brothers died young, his parents were very worried about whether he would also face the same fate. Therefore, they sent him to a temple as a junior monk at the age of three according to the customs during that time. Later, when he was 20 years old, he formally became a *Samana*.

It is known to all that Buddhism was introduced to China during the Han Dynasty. However, during the two Jin Dynasties, Indian Buddhism, which had already been in China for hundreds of years, gradually adapted to China's social and historical milieu and began to develop roots and flourish. Seventeen years of religious life, commencing from the age of three till the age of twenty, enabled Faxian to have a deeper feeling and understanding of Buddhism and its spread and progress in Chinese society. It can be felt that although Buddhism was introduced to China in the Han Dynasty, it became very prominent during the Jin Dynasty when Faxian lived and it was popularized among ordinary people in the society in contrast to its popularity in the beginning being limited to the upper class and some intellectuals. This implied that Indian Buddhism had begun to socialize and become popular in China, thereby leading to the process of continuous 'sinicization'. In this process of sinicization, the translation of Buddhist scriptures had become a very important link. However, before Faxian went west to seek the law, a considerable number of Buddhist scriptures were translated from both the southern and northern China (Yang Cengwen, 2005). However, none of those translated scriptures were complete and systematic, let alone the classic sutra representing new theory of Mahayana Buddhism. According to incomplete statistics, 862 Buddhist scriptures and 1,420 volumes were translated before the Eastern Jin Dynasty (Ren Jiyu, 1985).

Faxian set out from Chang'an with a number of colleagues in the first year of Yao Qinhong's reign (399), went west along the 'Silk Road', already opened in the Han Dynasty, to Tianzhu to seek Buddhist scriptures and returned to Qingzhou by sea alone in the eighth year (412) of East Jin Yixi. It took nearly 14 years and hundreds of thousands of miles to complete an unprecedented feat in the history of Buddhist culture in China and even in the world. On this westward journey to seek the Buddhist law, Faxian brought back a total of ten Sanskrit classics (manuscripts).

Faxian often felt that there was a dearth of reliable texts in China pertaining to discipline for the monks and took his vow to seek for it someday. Thus, eventually he became the first person in the history of Chinese Buddhism to seek Buddhist laws by moving westward and returning from there as well. In the history of Chinese Buddhism, there are three 'westward seekers'. The first among them is Faxian. It was Faxian's westward journey that brought back to China the Dharma of Maha Monks and other Dharma books, which were translated subsequently and had a significant and far-reaching impact on the formation and development of Chinese Buddhism.

Therefore, Faxian's great deed in seeking Buddhist scriptures from the west objectively conforms to the trend of this historical development. It provides a theoretical basis for the ideological and institutional construction of Chinese Buddhism, therefore making a pioneering contribution to the localization of Indian Buddhism in a broader cultural sense.

## Zhikong's Eastward Movement to China (Sichuan-Yunnan) and the Spread of Buddhism in East Asia (China and South Korea)

Zhikong was an Indian monk living in China in the Song and Yuan Dynasties. His Sanskrit name is *Dhyāna-bhadra*. 'Zhikong' is the name by which he is popular in China as a monk. According to historical records, Zhikong was born in northern India. When he was five years old, his father became ill and he left home to become a monk. When he was eight years old, he went to the Nalanda to study *Prajna* and other literature. Subsequently he visited many neighbouring countries to study Buddhism until the Zhiyuan 25th year of Yuan Dynasty (1288), before entering China from today's Xinjiang area in China (Duan Yuming, 2007).

After entering China, Zhikong tried to preach Dharma in places such as Yanjing and Xi 'an, but failed to do so repeatedly. After going south to Sichuan, he spent three years meditating on the Emei Mountain. In the year 1295 of Yuan Dynasty, he left the Emei Mountain, crossed the Jinsha River to reach Yunnan, to travel to Kunming, Dali and other places. He had stayed at the Zhengxu Temple in Wuding County, Yunnan from 1315 to 1320 (YuanYou of Yuan Dynasty) to spread Buddhism. In 1326 (Taiding of Yuan Dynasty), Zhikong was asked by the Yuan Dynasty court to visit Mount Kumgang in Koryo to bring incense. He started his travels from South Korea. He was summoned by the Yuan dynasty court to return to Yanjing, the capital of Yuan Dynasty in 1329 (the second year of Tianli in Yuan Dynasty). During his stay in Korea, he visited several monasteries (such as Kaijing Kanroji, Qingyuan Gandong Zen Temple, etc.) and taught monks precepts. At the same time, he also actively carried out the translation of Buddhist scriptures. For example, in the three years of the Yuantian calendar, six kinds of Buddhist books translated by Zhikong were published in Baocheng Temple in Tianmo Mountain, Koryo.

It can be noted from certain records that Zhikong lived for 108 years and that he spent 75 years in China and South Korea, out of the 100 years of his monk career. Zhikong learned lessons from the repeated rebuttals when he first arrived in these places. In order to adapt to the Chinese Buddhism at that time, he began the practice of Zen Buddhism; after three years of practice on the Emei Mountain, Sichuan, he moved to Shishan Mountain, Wuding, Yunnan, where he began preaching Buddhism in China until he advanced further to Korea. The Dharma he spread was undoubtedly the Chinese Zen. There is no denying the fact that Zhikong's Zen is really like a replica of Chinese Zen, however, it cannot also completely deny the Indian Zen thought contained in it, which can be seen from some of his quotations and related materials. At the same time, as mentioned above, Zhikong was also a tantric monk. During his Buddhist mission in China, apart from translating a lot of tantric mantras, he also went through some religious practices pertaining to tantric magic rituals (such as praying for sunshine and rain). Since judgmental theory of dichotomy and esoteric religion has been handed down since the Tang Dynasty, the Buddhism in the Yuan Dynasty has also inherited this tradition. Indian esoteric religion continues to spread to the east and Zhikong is just one of the monks who spread Indian Esoteric Buddhism eastward (Lv Jianfu, 2011).

It may be mentioned here that even though the Indian Buddhist culture represented by Zhikong has not been as significant and far-reaching as the culture represented by the early Indian monks coming to China like Dharmaratna or Kaiyuan's three Scholars, still it is of much practical importance. Additionally, his efforts in promoting Buddhism further east on the Korean Peninsula is undoubtedly noteworthy.

## Integration of Indian Buddhist Culture into East Asian Cultures and the Development of the Culture in East Asia

In the history of mankind, during 800–200 BC, the formation of culture and mutual cultural exchanges had begun and become more frequent and Buddhism, which was born in the South Asian subcontinent, became an important bridge and link. With the introduction of Buddhism to China from ancient India in the Han Dynasty, the carriers of this religious culture have been a large number of monks from South Asia, Southeast Asia and even Central Asia, as well as a large number of classics and legal objects brought by them. Due to the geographical location, this cultural migration can be termed as 'eastward advancement' for them, so they referred to the Chinese territory as the 'eastern land'. It started with the earliest and documented invitation of She Moteng and Zhu Falan to the east and ended up with Zhikong. Similarly, quite a number of monks from China like Faxian, Xuanzang, Yi Jing have travelled westward to the western regions (Central Asia) and India (South Asia) to learn the scriptures. Such a move may be called 'westward advancement' and the destination is called the 'western paradise'. These 'Eastward' and 'Westward' movements, the long-term mutual exchanges, communication and integration between different civilizations, have not only promoted mutual learning among different cultures, but also exerted a significant influence on the formation of a nation's own cultural characteristics.

Along with the westward journey of the Chinese monks seeking the scriptures, the eastward move of the Indian monks to China for preaching has also been witnessed since the ancient times. With this, Indian Buddhist culture and other cultural elements were continuously introduced into China and integrated with Chinese traditional culture, thus creating the product of the sinicization of Indian Buddhism, which is the Chinese Buddhism, which, together with the other two traditional cultures—Confucianism and Taoism, form the 'three pillars' of Chinese culture. This kind of 'westward' and 'eastward' movement has been seen in case of cultural exchanges between China and India and even between China and the West.

Looking at the history of this 'Going East', it seems that it can be divided into two phases. In the first phase, Indian monks 'marched eastward' to China to preach Indian Buddhism. In the second, Chinese monks 'marched eastward' to the Korean peninsula, Japan and other places to spread Chinese Buddhism (the 'sinicized' Indian Buddhism). The former representatives include She Moteng and Zhu Falan in East Han Dynasty as well as Zhikong. The latter, that is, Chinese monks' 'eastward movement' began in the Eastern Jin Dynasty and Zhikong has been undoubtedly one of such monks who traveled eastward. Therefore, it can be seen that in this mighty tide of the 'Going East' movement, Zhikong has played an unusual and very important role. His 'Going East' move not only played a role in the development of Chinese Buddhism, but also 'directly affected the development of Korean Zen Buddhism'. Therefore,

> we should put Zhikong's Buddhist preaching in China and South Korea into more than 3,000 years of the history of cultural exchanges between China and South Korea.... His preaching practices were based on cultural exchanges between China and South Korea for more than thousands of years, so he succeeded in preaching Buddhism in South Korea. (Ho Yiu-hua, 1996)

Therefore, not only in the history of Buddhist cultural exchange, but also in the global history of cultural exchange, it is through the eastward and westward moves of the monks from India and China that Indian Buddhist culture along with the entire Indian culture got integrated into the culture in China, South Korea and even the entire East Asian region and developed in these regions on the basis of thousands of years of cultural exchange between these regions.

## Conclusion

To sum up, in the long history of India–China cultural exchange, the exchange of Buddhist culture has always played a major role. In this context, the westward journey of Chinese monks and the eastward move of Indian monks and the Chinese monks have played a vital and an incomparable role.

The westbound Chinese monks brought back the true meaning and essence of Indian Buddhism and promoted the integration of Indian Buddhist culture with the Chinese culture (the 'sinicization' of Indian Buddhism—the emergence of Chinese Buddhism).

The eastward movement of Indian and Chinese monks led to the introduction of Indian Buddhism and the fresh nutrients of Chinese Buddhism into China and East Asia, which has promoted the fusion and spread of Indian Buddhist culture.

The eastward movement of the Indian monks and the eastward movement of the Chinese monks seem to be two unrelated events, but a man named Zhikong, the so-called 'last eminent Indian monk that came to China' carried those out in a perfect combination.

It can be said that 'in the history of cultural exchanges between South Asia and East Asia in the 14th century, Zhikong is one of the important personalities. In this context, the activities of Zhikong in China are of special importance' (He Shengda, 1998).

Obviously, it is also in this connection that Indian Buddhist culture and even Indian culture got integrated and developed in East Asia.

## References

Duan, Yuming. 2007. *Zhikong-Last Indian Eminent Monk in China.* Chengdou: Sichuan Publishing Group Bashu Publishing House.

He, Shengda. 1998. 'Indian Eminent Monks in China: Their Paths, Thoughts and Influences.' *World History* 2, 2–11.

Ho, Yiu-hua. 1996. 'Achievements in Spreading Buddhist Culture in China and South Korea by Zhikong.' *Social Sciences in Yunnan* 6, 55–62.

Lv, Jianfu. 2011. *History of Chinese Secret Religion,* revised edition. Beijing: China Social Sciences Press.

Ren, Jiyu. 1985. *History of Chinese Buddhism Volume II.* Beijing: China Social Sciences Press.

Yang, Cengwen. 2005. 'Fa Xian, Translator of Buddhist Scripture in Eastern Jin Dynasty and His Contribution to Chinese Cultural History.' In *Jie Chuang Buddhism Volume III.* Changsha: Yuelu Publishing House.

CHAPTER 26

# The Role of Southern Silk Road in Promoting International Peace

Huajun Yang

## Introduction

Current as well as past research on the Southern Silk Road have mostly focused on its economic and cultural roles. The findings of such research on the economic and cultural development in Asia are undoubtedly desirable from the point of view of both theoretical and practical significance. However, this chapter looks at the functions of this road from a perspective that is different from the earlier studies. The Southern Silk Road has existed for more than two thousand years. Spanning across a wide region, it communicates several cultures. It may be held that these long, broad international trade routes could only exist for so long due to the fact that the people whose lives were influenced by the routes shared a common vision. What is that common vision? We think it is *peace*.

In 2006, some Chinese researchers, prompted by the documentary 'Qin Straight Road', began to focus on the role of the Southern Silk Road as inter-regional routes in establishing and ensuring a culture of peace. They believed business contacts between different regions play a role in promoting peace (Hao, 2006). On one hand, a peaceful environment is needed as the premise and foundation for the continued normal trade routes; on the other hand, the smooth trade routes also promote peace in the areas along the routes. This has been especially true for the Southern Silk Road.

With modernization, the role of the Southern Silk Road in fostering peace became even more important. Chinese academia during the 1940s became increasingly inclined to study about the Southern Silk Road. During that time, many scholars such as Yan Deyi, Fang Guoyu, Yao, Xia Guangnan gathered in places such as Kunming and Chengdu to conduct research related to the Southern Silk Road in terms of the benefits accrued from allied transportation of military supplies, environmental factors or development of infrastructure. It is worth mentioning that the Chinese government sent ten experts to America to join a study group on post-war problems there in 1943, and their aircraft started from Chongqing, passing through Kunming, exactly flying along the Hump Air Route[1] (Wu, 2001). Hump Air Route together with Yunnan–Myanmar highway being a new component of ancient Southern Silk Road in wartime, played a positive role in building peace at that time. During 1944–1945, Chen Hansheng, a famous Chinese economist, conducted a research on the Southern Silk Road, and had some important research outputs on 'Xishuangbanna's land use system', economic regions of India and Pakistan, and so on. After the founding of new China, Tong Enzheng, Professor of the Department of History, Sichuan University, also conducted a comprehensive study on the 'Southwest Silk Road'. This research is worthy of attention. With the reform and opening up, many inland provinces of Southwest China proposed 'restoration of the Southern Silk Road' (Wang, 1992). It would help inland southwestern provinces to quickly embark on the international economic track (Cao, 1992). This would also help China's opening-up extend from coastal areas to inland regions and would promote regional as well as comprehensive development.

In the twenty-first century, especially after the 18th Congress of the Communist Party of China, General Secretary Xi Jinping presented the 'Four Comprehensives' as the strategic thinking for China's development. In this context, this chapter attempts to find out how the Southern Silk Road will play an important role in China's peaceful rise. It will discuss the functions of the Southern Silk Road from the point of view of creating and promoting a peaceful environment.

## Purpose for Opening the Southern Silk Road

In the early days of Emperor Wu's reign, people began to explore and open up the Silk Road in the south. The leader of the Western Han Dynasty took the Taoism way of governing the country. The methods helped to stabilize the political situation and develop the economy. At that time, Western Han Dynasty became strong and Emperor Wu attempted to expand his territory westward, but his westward conception was temporarily hindered by Huns ethnic groups living in the west of his imperial territory. In order to open up a wider space for the economic development of the Han Dynasty, based on the information provided by the imperial envoy Zhang Qian, Emperor Wu felt that opening a trade route to the south of China is possible. He ordered Sima Xiangru to develop southwestern China, in order to establish a channel for economic and cultural exchanges between China and South Asia. Three routes, viz., Ling Guan Road, Five Feet Road and Yongchang Road came to be called by the people as the 'Southern Silk Road'. Today, the Southern Silk Road stretches through Sichuan and Yunnan provinces, connecting Burma and India, leading to Southeast Asia and West Asia and European countries thereby forming an international trade channel. It is thus quite clear that though traditionally these trade routes had existed, the idea and efforts of Emperor Wu of Han actually led to the opening up of these trade routes formally. Since then, rulers have attached great importance to peace on this route. In the context of the several geopolitical factors affecting the regions connected by these routes, prevalence of peace has been of utmost importance. Especially at the end of the Tang Dynasty and the Northern Song Dynasty, the unrest in the north highlighted the need for promotion of peace and prosperity in southwest of China.

In fact, silk is not the only factor that keeps the Southern Silk Road open. Since the Tang and Song Dynasties, silk has no longer been a symbol of wealth and authority. Today, silk is available to the rich as well as the poor. Essentially, the Southern Silk Road has existed due to the fact that it helped in establishing and promoting economic symbiotic relationship between nations and thereby consolidation of international peace.

In the modern history, the Southern Silk Road has made great contribution in maintaining peace of the Far East. Traditional and modern vehicles, airplanes, trains, cars and horses have been busy on this line, contributing a lot to the peace of the entire Far East and the world and also playing an important role in the victory of the world anti-fascist war. Yunnan province had become a hub for strategic material transfer in the 1930s and 1940s. As witnessed in history, the Southern Silk Road has been a kind of a gateway to contemporary economic, social and cultural life and for multi-dimensional peacekeeping activities.

## Role of Trade on the Route in Fostering Peace

Beyond silk, Southwest China engaged in trade in tea, horses, salt, ceramics, canes and medicinal items of daily life through the Southern Silk Road. Different from the Silk Road, the Southern Silk Road, in fact, has not been dominated by silk trade. The name 'Southern Silk Road' was possibly used by people to refer to its relation with the famous Silk Road. In terms of linguistics and semiotics, names do not always need to match the reality. However, if one wants to state the reality, s/he may also call it the Southwest Trade Channel. Through this channel several goods and cultures were exchanged between different regions on a mutual consensus, thereby fostering peace.

### Transfer of Various Commodities

In the *Historical Records—Dawan Biography*, Zhang Qian (1982) mentioned that he saw cloth made in Shu in the Xia Kingdom. Xia Kingdom was the name used for Bactria. It is said that Afghanistan's Balkh area had been Xia Kingdom's capital. However, there are different views on the connotation of Shu cloth as discussed here.

1. Shu cloth refers to silk. A lot of researchers believe so. Indeed, although there is a dispute over where and when silk was invented, Sichuan is undoubtedly considered as one of the earliest silk producing areas. Legends, archaeology, the origin of the name and

several other evidences prove this point. Thus, it may be said that there is a long association between Sichuan and silk.

2. Shu cloth includes silk, but is not limited to silk alone. Thus, some people also hold the view that besides silk, Shu cloth also meant ramie cloth. Indeed, it is quite normal that this kind of cloth due to its texture would be popular in a hot tropical country like India. Indian scholars have pointed out that ancient Sanskrit literature put forth that Hindu Gods love to wear Chinese silk; Lord Shiva especially loves yellow silk. However, it should be noted here that the Shu cloth may not be necessarily silk and this so-called 'yellow silk' is very likely to be a ramie fabric. Yang Xiong's 'Shu Fu' mentioned that 'yellow and very soft linen, the price is very high'. Therefore, keeping in view the temperature and humidity of India, this fine linen may be very suitable for India and other South Asian countries in terms of their clothing habits.

With the development of textile technology and the silk being no longer regarded as a symbol of wealth, the silk was no longer one of the main trading products transported along the Southern Silk Road. Different from the Qin and the Han Dynasties, tea and horses became the two most important commodities on the Southern Silk Road in the Tang and Song Dynasties. Thus, instead of silk, tea and horses gradually emerged as important commodities which helped in promoting peace. Therefore, the Sichuan–Yunnan section of the Southern Silk Road later came to be called as the 'Ancient Tea Horse Road'. During the Ming and Qing Dynasties, China, India, Burma, Thailand and other South Asian countries have established close trade relations through the Tea Horse Road. During the Qing Dynasty, the main function of the Southern Silk Road had been to transport tea from Sichuan and Yunnan to Tibet, and in turn let the horses, medicinal herbs and other items from Tibet come to the mainland of China or to the central plains. In short, through silk, tea and horses, the closed trade ties via Southern Silk Road maintained the internal stability of the Chinese Empire and kept peace within external cultural groups.

## Significance of the Qiong Bamboo Stick

In the context of trade, the Qiong bamboo stick is worth mentioning in this chapter. After Sima Qian, one of the great historians, mentioned about the Qiong bamboo stick in his 'historical records', it became a focus of research on the history of Chinese foreign trade. However, Yan Shigu pointed out that 'everyone knows the Qiong bamboo stick, do not need to explain' (Ban & Yan, 1962). Thus, history did not appropriately mention the Qiong bamboo stick in terms of its meaning, place of origin, functions or its cultural significance. These are undoubtedly worthy of studying.

First, the name only suggests that the stick is made of bamboo canes from Qiong (in Sichuan). Studies have mentioned that the Qiong bamboo stick is likely to be first produced in Sichuan and that Qiong bamboo sticks were transported to India and beyond along the Southwestern Silk Routes. This bamboo is found extensively in the southwestern region of China especially in Yunnan and Sichuan provinces. These plants are usually 3–6 meters in height. These characteristics are consistent with the ancient records.

Second, the Qiong bamboo stick not only possesses practical value, but also cultural value. Many Chinese researchers have pointed out the cultural significance of the Qiong bamboo stick. Ren Naiqiang (1987) pointed out that from the practical point of view, such stick being light and strong, the wandering monks and merchants liked to carry it. Some research further pointed out the adaptability of the Qiong bamboo stick carried by travelers on the Ancient Tea Horse Road. But if one traces back to the original physical form of the stick, 'it is just a common walking stick used in people's daily life' (He, 2012). Again, from another perspective, some people find the Qiong bamboo stick to be a cultural symbol. Scholar Xiao Bing believes that the Qiongzhu stick rod transported by Shu to India, or to Afghanistan and other places, is a big event in western transportation history and in cultural history. He infers that the western people paid much attention to this commodity as there is a layer of mystery around it and it has been symbolic from the cultural perspective. He concluded: 'The so-called Qiong bamboo stick is actually the 'Shoumu' or 'Lingshou's wood" as mentioned in the book *Shan Hai Jing* (Xiao, 1995). Furthermore, these sticks when transported to other regions not only implied trade of goods, but emphasized exchange of culture, consensus among people.

The ancient Indians loved the Qiong canes, probably because it not only suited the Indian way of life, but also the philosophy of India.

Thus, while on one hand anyone can find the pictures of Mahatma Gandhi in which he is seen using his bamboo stick, on the other hand, in terms of the philosophy of India, a similarity is found with the Chinese concept of nature. Indian scholar Rajendra K. Patil has cited Swami Bhajanananda's comment on the Veda. He said that 'In the universe, there is a rule in operation. In the 'Veda' it is called Ritam, in ancient China, Lao Tzu called it Tao, the ancient Greek philosophers called it the logos.... In harmony with the law, it is in harmony with the Tao, the so-called natural state, a state of peace.' (Patil, 2013). It can be said that the agreement between China and India on the philosophical level is likely to be the deep-seated reason behind the bamboo stick coming to India and being popular.

The Qiong bamboo stick has played an important role in Buddhism. According to the Indian Buddhist doctrine one should refrain from killing living beings. At the same time, the practice of wandering and begging is very common in Buddhism. It may be inferred here that the Buddhist wandering monks have been mostly seen to carry a stick possibly to drive away insects and snakes. The Qiong bamboo stick is well-associated with such behaviour of the monks. Therefore, the amalgamation of the role of Qiong bamboo stick and the Buddhist teachings became an important aspect in the communication between China and India.

Delving into research, we may arrive at the following consensus: (1) Though Qiong bamboo grew in both Sichuan and Yunnan, the Qiong bamboo stick is mainly produced in Sichuan. This shows the significance of Sichuan on the Southern Silk Road. (2) The communication between the people of China and India and other countries in the context of their daily cultural life persisted through the exchange of products, which may be also viewed as the carriers of consensus among people belonging from different regions.

With the interdisciplinary and more comprehensive research in the 1990s, the academic community affirmed the existence and the value of the Southern Silk Road. In 1991, after Qian Weichang and Fei Xiaotong visited the Panxi area, they also proposed the 'Reconstruction of the Southern Silk Road' from the height of the national strategy, and it would also lay the foundation for the industrialization and modernization of the southwest of China. It was proposed to rebuild the Southern Silk Road starting from Chengdu passing through Panzhihua, Xichang, Baoshan of the Sichuan Province and the Yunnan Province (Fei, 1999). As an international channel for trade, this proposed road would emphasize exchanges with countries, viz., India, Bangladesh and Myanmar, thus promoting international peace in the exchange of goods, purchase and sale of goods.

## Qiongzhu Temple (Bamboo Temple)—A Case of Peaceful Cultural Exchange

In the context of the spread of Buddhism to China, the Qiongzhu temple in Kunming, Yunnan, China deserves a special mention. It has played a vital role in a peaceful cultural exchange between nations. With the amalgamation of the function of the Qiong bamboo stick with the spirit of Buddhism, Chinese monks naturally used these sticks. Today, if one travels to the holy Buddhist Mount Emei, buying a Qiong bamboo stick is actually a good choice. The role of Qiongzhu temple situated on the Southern Silk Road in the interaction between China and India has been important from the point of view that the temple symbolized commercial culture with respect to exchange of necessary goods and friendly exchanges. In this manner different countries have accepted foreign objects or cultural values with open arms.

## Conclusion

The Qiong bamboo stick may not be an important commodity in international trade today, but we still can find the spirit it possesses, which benefits peaceful international trade, for instance, a peaceful impact caused by product exchange. It is easier to achieve a peaceful international environment when different economies trade in goods that are complementary and there is division of labour. Studies show that China's 'One Belt and One Road' strategy should be linked up with India's Spice Road and Monsoon Project, which will mark a new beginning of Sino-Indian cooperation (Mao, 2015). Obviously, spices were once an important popular complementary commodity on the Southern Silk Road, which is called the Spice Road in India. Whereas in China these routes are called the Silk Road, Shu Cloth Road or the Ancient Tea and Horse Road. Today, while on one hand the Chinese businessmen continue to sell sandalwood, bodhi seeds and other products imported from India and Nepal, on the other hand, India, Nepal, Laos, Myanmar and other countries import a variety of made-in-China products. A peaceful Sino-Indian trade is advantageous to the peaceful development of the neighbouring countries as well and the interregional trade routes like the Southern Silk Road possess the power to successfully foster peace through trade in complementary goods as well as cultural exchanges and dissemination.

With the passage of time, complementarity in international commercial trade is integrated into a peaceful culture, which also enhances international trade in turn. Therefore, the Southern Silk Road is not only a complementary channel for commodities, but also a link for the spread of peaceful culture.

## Note

1. The 'Hump Route' starts from Assam, India, eastward across the Himalayas, entering China's Yunnan Plateau and Sichuan Province. The flight route has been a major air passage between China and the Allied forces during World War II. The terrain is at an altitude of 4,500 to 5,500 meters. The highest altitude is 7,000 meters. The peaks are undulating, like the back of a camel, hence it is named as 'Hump Route'.

## References

Ban, Gu and Shigu Yan. 1962. *The History of the Han Dynasty* [M]. Beijing: Zhong Hua Book Company, 2690.

Cao, Lisheng. 1992. 'On the Reconstruction of the Southern Silk Road [J].' *The Journal of the Exploration on Economic Issues* 1, 42.

Fei, Xiaotong. 1999. *Collected Works of Fei Xiaotong (twelfth volumes) [M]*. Beijing: Qunyan Press, 174–175.

(Han) Sima Qian. 1982. *Historical Records Dawan Biography [M]*. Beijing: Zhong Hua Book Company, 165–166.

Hao, Chengzhi. 2006. 'The Peace Function of the Qin Dynasty Straight Road and the Tourism Value of the Lady Zhaojun [J].' *Yinshan Academic Journal* 1, 59–64.

He, Da. 2012. 'On the Origin of Qiong Canes [J].' *The Journal of Literature and History* 4, 29.

Mao, Siwei. 2015. 'Why Don't India Join the 'Belt and Road Initiative'? [N].' *Phoenix blog* 6–17. http://maosiwei.blog.caixin.

Patil, Rajendra K. 2013. 'India and India Philosophy of Non-Violence and Peace [J].' *Journal of Historical Science* 12, 14.

Ren, Naiqiang. 1987. 'Textual research on Sichuan's Betel Jam, Shu Cloth, Qiong Bamboo Stick [M].' In *Sichuan Historical Research Collection [M]*. Chengdu: Sichuan Academy of Social Sciences Press, p. 16.

Wang, Ji. 1992. 'Open the South Gate, Restart the Southern Silk Road [J].' *The Journal of International Economic Cooperation* 5, 41.

Wu, Xiangxiang. 2001. *The Biography of James Yen Y. C.* [M]. Changsha: Yuelu Publishing House, 339.

Xiao, Bing. 1995. 'Textual Research on the Qiong Canes Which Zhang Qian saw in Daxia is Lingshou Wood _ a Mystery in the History of Chinese and Western Traffic [J].' *Chinese Journal of Culture* 2, 28.

# About the Editors and Contributors

## Editors

**Neena Sondhi** is the Shashi Budhiraja Chair Professor for Management Research at International Management Institute (IMI) New Delhi. Sondhi also currently holds the portfolio of Dean Research, Accreditation and Regulatory Affairs at IMI New Delhi. An alumnus and a merit holder from the Faculty of Arts, University of Delhi, her areas of expertise are consumer psychology, behaviour, marketing research and luxury marketing. An avid researcher, with a diverse experience of over 25 years in teaching, research and consultancy, she has to her credit more than 50 publications: peer-reviewed international and national journals of repute and case studies with teaching notes with international case clearing houses. Her co-authored book titled *Research Methodology: Concepts and Cases* has been widely adopted in prestigious business schools across the country and is rated as one of the top 25 books in management education. She has been felicitated for her academic and professional work by various national and international bodies.

**Ramakrushna Panigrahi** is a Professor in the area of Economics at IMI Bhubaneswar. His PhD is in the area of environmental economics and green national income accounting from Institute for Social and Economic Change (ISEC), Bengaluru, a premier social science ICSSR research institute in India. His MPhil in Applied Economics is in the area of agricultural economics from Jawaharlal Nehru University (JNU, 1995). He has completed his Master's in Economics from the University of Hyderabad (UoH, 1993). He graduated from Utkal University with a distinction in Economics

(Honours) in the year 1991. His teaching interests include managerial economics, macroeconomic theory and policies, international business and geopolitics. In addition to teaching, he is an active researcher in the area of economics, particularly development economics. He has published a number of research papers in refereed journals of high repute such as *Journal of International Development* and *Journal of Human Development*. He has written bestselling case studies that are published by IVEY. He has over 20 years of teaching, research and consulting experience in the area of economics.

**Miao Pang** is a Senior Research Fellow at Sichuan Academy of Social Sciences (SASS). She currently works in the Institute of Rural Economy of SASS with her major in forest resource management and has 25 years of expertise in rural policy, resource management and ecological construction. She has completed two National-sponsored projects on ecological compensation and community adaptation on climate change in ecologically-vulnerable regions. She has also completed over 20 provincial and international research projects with governments and many NGOs. She has published over 6 monographs and more than 40 papers in relevant research fields.

**Rajashri Chatterjee** is Assistant Professor (Finance and Accounting) at IMI Kolkata. She holds a doctorate from the University of Burdwan, West Bengal, India. She completed her MCom from the University of Calcutta and MBA from Maulana Abul Kalam Azad University of Technology, West Bengal. Prior to joining IMI Kolkata, she worked as Finance Executive at Rabindranath Tagore International Institute of Cardiac Sciences and AMRI Hospitals Ltd in Kolkata. She has contributed articles for journals of eminence, viz. *Global Business Review* and *The Chartered Accountant*, and also written for a Bengali daily, *Sangbad Pratidin*. She has co-authored book chapters and has papers to her credit that have been presented in conferences in India and abroad. She has organized a few conferences at IMI Kolkata and has also acted as a moderator for a webinar on the COVID-19 crisis. She is the Editorial Manager of *IMI Konnect*, the scholarly management publication of IMI Kolkata and has also contributed articles for the same.

## Contributors

**Soni Agrawal** is an Associate Professor of Human Resource Management and Organization Behaviour (HRM and OB) at International Management Institute Kolkata. Agrawal holds a doctorate in management from Indian Institute of Technology Kharagpur. She specializes in HRM and OB. She has over 16 years of industry–academia experience. She has conducted training sessions to train senior and mid-level executives—national (public and private enterprises) as well as international executives in the area of HRM, HR analytics and measurement and performance management. Some of the companies where she has conducted these trainings are CESC, PCBL, Oxford University Press, India Post, LIC, etc. Her areas of academic interests are employee engagement, green HRM, performance management, training, industrial relations, HR for new age organizations, and career and succession planning. She had served as Chair Admissions, Chair Anti-ragging and headed various other committees. She is also mentor of HR club at IMI Kolkata. Prior to joining academics, she worked in the industry in the area of strategy and human resource development. As a researcher she has published research papers in reputed national and international journals. As a reviewer she has reviewed a number of books and manuscripts. She has also chaired sessions in various seminars and conferences.

**Devesh Baid** is an Associate Professor in the area of Accounting and Finance at IMI Bhubaneshwar. He is a graduate from Shri Ram College of Commerce (University of Delhi), Associate Member of Institute of Cost Accountants of India and a PhD from School of Management, IIT Bombay. He builds on four pillars of management education, that is, teaching, consulting, research and training. He has been into management education and consulting for small and medium-sized enterprises (SMEs) for more than a decade. He writes and uses management cases for teaching. His expertise is in the areas of costing, corporate financing, fund raising, and management controls and performance management. Baid has conducted management development programmes for both private and public sector companies. He has also organized many workshops for faculties, research scholars and students.

**Arindam Banik** is an Indian economist. He earned his PhD at Delhi School of Economics, University of Delhi in 1994. He holds the position of Distinguished Professor and Associated Cement Companies Chair Professor in International Finance and Business at IMI New Delhi. He pursued his post-doctoral research at Manchester Business School and Department of Economics, University of Cambridge during the period 1994–1995. Banik has taught at Department of Economics at the University of West Indies, Cave Hill Campus, Barbados (West Indies, period 2000–2005). He has been a recipient of numerous awards and positions including the prestigious SANEI Research Award (South Asia Network of Economic Institutions by World Bank and Global Development Network), Campus Research Award in two consecutive years (May 2002 and 2003), University of the West Indies, Cave Hill Campus, Barbados and so on. He has worked as a consultant for various government and multilateral agencies including World Bank, FICCI-New Delhi, International Development Research Centre (IDRC), ACC Mumbai, UNIDO, ILO, Indo-Canadian Cooperation Unit, GTZ and Government of India (Ministry of Rural Development), Caribbean Development Bank and Government of Barbados. He has authored more than a hundred scientific articles on international economics, macroeconomics, corporate governance and economic development and several books as well. He has also authored articles for various magazines and newspapers. Editor of a reputed management journal entitled, *Global Business Review*, published by SAGE, Banik is currently the Director at IMI Kolkata deputed from IMI New Delhi.

**Rituparna Basu** is an internationally acclaimed academician and researcher in the domain of management. She won the first prize in the Global ISB-Ivey Case Competition 2017 and thereafter has a dual win to her credit with two teaching cases in the next edition of the global case competition with her India-centric case against some of the best management case writers from across the world. She received the prestigious AIMS Outstanding Woman Management Researcher Award 2017 and AIMS-IRMA Outstanding Young Woman Management Teacher Award 2016 among many other awards for her contribution to management teaching and research in the country. Basu is an economics honours graduate from St. Xavier's College, Kolkata, a gold medallist MBA from Viswa-Bharti University, West Bengal and has a Doctorate from IIT Kharagpur. She has more than 15 years of industry–academia experience and is an Erasmus+ grant awardee. Her teaching cases are indexed in Harvard Business Publishing and are taught across best B-schools across the world. She writes for top marketing journals and is cited across the world for her contemporary research in the domain of marketing and retail. She is currently an Associate Professor at IMI Kolkata and chairs the marketing area. She has been an adjunct faculty to IIT Kharagpur.

**Ying Cao** holds a PhD and is an Associate Research Fellow at SASS. His research field orientates towards regional economics. His paper and research topics cover development of regional economy, post-earthquake reconstruction, third party logistics, poverty alleviation, evaluation of infrastructure projects, etc. Other research projects include compilation of regional economic and social development plans and analysis of industrial development. His papers include 'Sustainable development of energy science and technology in Sichuan', 'Analysis on the economic growth in Sichuan from the perspective of convergence', etc.

**Jixiang Chen** holds a Master's degree in Law and a Doctorate in Economics. He is an Associate Research Fellow at SASS. His research interests include company law, securities law, international economy (South Asia Economic Research), regional economy, law and economics and the like.

**Rahul Gupta Choudhury** has done his schooling from St. Xaviers School and College, in Durgapur and Kolkata. He has subsequently done his Chemical Engineering from NIT, Durgapur in 1987 and his MBA from Indian Institute of Management (IIM) Lucknow in 1989. He was also a Fulbright scholar from Carnegie Mellon University in Pittsburgh, USA (2001). Choudhury also completed his PhD in Marketing and Management Science from Alliance University, Bangalore (2016). He has 30 years of work experience—initial 14 years in the industry and the subsequent 16 years in academics. He has worked in sales and marketing and also in supply chain management in some of the largest and most reputed companies in India and the world. In the industry he quickly rose through the hierarchy to be given the responsibility of independently handling a particular unit of the group. He also led the unit to conceptualize and implement a supply chain reengineering project of the unit which was cutting-edge and absolutely new to the world. The company/group has benefitted immensely from this path-breaking reengineering exercise and was well recognized across the world for this pioneering activity. In academics, Choudhury has so far worked with some of the most reputed private business schools, as well as universities, in India. He enjoys teaching and the feedback score he gets from the students is of the top order. He currently teaches courses including marketing management, marketing strategy, sales and distribution and consumer behaviour. In the research area, he has published more than 30 papers in peer-reviewed Indian and international journals. He has presented papers in reputed conferences across the world. Some of the papers among them were very well received at domestic and international conferences. In 2019, IGI Global, USA published his book on sales and distribution. The book is currently classified as a reference book and has been accepted well in the international market. Choudhury also has administrative responsibilities. Currently in IMI Bhubaneswar, he is the chairperson for placements.

**Jie Da** holds a Doctorate in Economics. He is the Director of the Institute of Industrial Economics, SASS. He is also the President of Sichuan Association of Stock Economy and Securities, Executive Vice President and Secretary General of Sichuan Association of Urban Economy and Director of the Research Center of High-tech Industry and Park. His main research interests include industrial economy, investment and capital market. In recent years, he has published 3 monographs and more than 20 papers, edited 8 blue books and led research on dozens of national and provincial projects.

**Arnab K. Deb** is presently working as an Associate Professor in Economics at IMI New Delhi. He holds a doctorate from University of Connecticut, Storrs in the area of Economics. He earned his BSc (Honours) and MSc degrees from University of Calcutta. His research interest includes applied microeconomics, production economics, data envelopment analysis, mathematical economics and applied econometrics. Deb has more than 10 years of experience in teaching and research. He has worked on an NSF (National Science Foundation) funded project 'Economic and Social Rights: Obstacle or Handmaiden to Growth'. Before joining the PhD programme he had served as a Research Associate in AC Nielsen ORG Marg, Kolkata and worked on two projects 'District Level Monitoring of all Programs of Ministry of Rural Development, India' and 'Moving out of Poverty: Growth and Democracy'. He has attended and presented research paper at international conferences. Deb has received multiple fellowships and awards in his career. He has been awarded the Pre-doctoral Fellowships by the Department of Economics for the period 2007–2011 and Doctoral Dissertation Fellowship by the Graduate School in the year 2012. He was also recognized with the Abraham Ribicoff Graduate Fellowship by the Department of Economics, University of Connecticut in 2011. Along with various publications in peer-reviewed journals, such as *Empirical Economics, Indian Economic Review, Management Research Review* and *Global Business Review*, Deb has presented his research work in several prestigious national and international conferences such as NAPW VII, 2012 Houston, Texas, USA, 2012, 50th Annual Golden Jubilee Conference of The Indian Econometric Society (TIES), IGIDR, Mumbai, 2013, 17th International Conference on Data Envelopment Analysis, University of Calgary, Canada, 2019 and IMI-SASS Conference, Chengdu, 2019.

**Yun Fang** is Assistant Research Fellow at SASS and the Deputy Secretary General of Sichuan Commercial Law Society. Her research interests predominately cover civil and commercial law. She has published 2 monographs and more than 10 academic papers. In recent years, she has led and completed two provincial philosophy and social sciences projects.

**Mudit Gera** is currently an FPM scholar of IMI, New Delhi in the area of marketing with focus on digital marketing and mobile marketing. An engineer from Kurukshetra University and an MBA from

ICFAI Business School (IBS), Hyderabad, he has been an active blogger for almost a decade in the technology niche with hands-on experience in WordPress CMS, SEO, web analytics, content marketing, social media marketing and affiliate marketing. He is certified by Google in Analytics, AdWords Display, AdWords Mobile, AdWords Search, AdWords Shopping and AdWords Video in the area of digital marketing. He has also been awarded the title of 'Digital Marketing Certified Associate' by Simplilearn. Before joining IMI as a research scholar, he gained vast experience as an IT Consultant with top multinational IT companies, including Tata Consultancy Services (TCS) and Cognizant Technology Solutions (CTS) as well as India's premier R&D organization, Defence Research and Development Organisation (DRDO) as a Management Consultant.

**Weimin Huang** is Senior Researcher, Institute of Literature and Art at SASS. Her research interests include Chinese literature, cultural sociology, cultural industry and tourism, comparative study of Sino-Indian cultures, etc. Weimin has more than 20 academic publications to her credit, including two books. She was also awarded the third prize for scientific research by the Sichuan government in 2019.

**Xiwei Huang** is a Research Associate, Institute of Sociology, SASS. She joined the Academy in 2017. Prior to joining SASS, she studied and practised social work in New York City, USA and Chengdu, China. Her major research interests cover social work practice and indigenization, social policy and community development. She is engaged in collaborative research projects with a range of government and non-governmental organizations. She works closely with local social work organizations to generate new knowledge to improve policies, services and practices in serving migrant workers and other marginalized populations in China. She co-edited the Annual Report on Social Development of Sichuan (2018) and published Case Management in Family Social Work in Cross-Cultural Environment in a national journal *China Social Work*. She also took an active role in third-party evaluation on poverty-stricken counties during Targeted Poverty Alleviation.

**Kanika Jain** is PGDM final year student at IMI New Delhi.

**Rohit Vishal Kumar** is an Economic Honours graduate of St. Xavier's College Kolkata. After completing his graduation, he did his Master's in Economics from Centre for Economic Studies and Planning (CESP), Jawaharlal Nehru University (JNU), New Delhi. Subsequently, he joined Indian Institute of Social Welfare and Business Management (IISWBM), Kolkata and completed his MBA in the area of marketing. He was picked up from campus by Indica Research Private Limited and for three years he worked in the marketing research sector with various clients and organizations. He has worked in ORG-MARG Research Limited, New Delhi and TNS-MODE, Kolkata and handled clients including ITC, TATA Steel, Bengal Ambuja, ABP Group, Eveready Industries, Smithkline Beecham and Maruti Udyog Limited. Given his economics, marketing and research combination, he entered academics in 2001 at the behest of his alma mater IISWBM Kolkata. He joined IISWBM, Kolkata as a research associate and within one year he was promoted to lecturer. In 2003, he registered for his Doctorate with the University of Calcutta and the degree was granted in 2007. His topic of doctoral research work was 'Lifestyle and Psychographic Segmentation and Classification of Metropolitan Consumers in India for Effective Marketing'. In 2006, he joined Xavier Institute of Social Service (XISS), Ranchi as Reader. He joined IMI Bhubaneswar as Associate Professor in July 2016. As on date, he has a total of 16 journal publications, out of which 8 are in international journals of repute. He is well versed in marketing, marketing and social research, and statistical software (R, SPSS, Systat and Statistica).

**Zujun Liao** is the Director, Senior Research Fellow and Master Tutor of the Institute of Regional Economics and Urbanization at SASS. His research interests predominantly cover rural economy, regional economy, organization and institutional innovation. He has presided over three National Social Science Fund youth projects, participated in dozens of national and provincial ministerial projects. He has published more than 80 papers and more than 10 monographs. In recent years, he has submitted dozens of research reports to the State Council, Sichuan Provincial Party Committee and Provincial Government.

**Xiongfeng Liu** holds a Doctorate in History and is currently working at SASS, China. His main research interests lie in religion and philosophy He has published more than 200 articles in domestic and foreign publications and presided over and participated in many national projects.

**Sayani Mandal** is pursuing Fellow Programme in Management from IMI Kolkata. Her doctoral specialization lies in the areas of retail marketing and private label brand management practices. Prior to this, she has worked with IMI Kolkata as a Research Officer for two years. Mandal holds a Master's degree in Commerce with specialization in marketing from the prestigious St. Xavier's College, Kolkata. She has authored a book chapter, published research papers in journals and presented papers at conferences across the country.

**Roma Puri** is an Associate Professor of HRM and OB at IMI Kolkata. Puri is a Fellow from IIM Calcutta. She has more than 15 years of experience in teaching and academics. Her domain has been HRM and OB. She has taught courses at graduate and post-graduate level. She has participated in several national and international conferences and has published book chapters and papers. Her research interests include gender studies, diversity management, green HRM, and sustainability in the manufacturing industry and management of paradoxes in social enterprises.

**Shubham Raghuwanshi** is PGDM final year student at IMI New Delhi.

**Bo Shen** is a Research Assistant at SASS. He is a PhD candidate at the Sichuan University. His main research fields include history of Ancient China: from the origins of civilization to 221 BC (pre-qin history), history of Chinese art, music and archaeology. He has published two monographs and five papers and has participated in three national fund projects. He has won the third prize at the 18th Outstanding Achievement Award of Social Science of Sichuan Province in 2019.

**Delang Song** is a teacher at Sichuan University of Light and Chemical Technology. He has published five papers and three monographs.

**Deepak Tandon** is a Professor in Finance at IMI New Delhi and has 37 years of work experience. He has a PhD, MBA, LLB and MSc. He has worked in various banks including PNB, PNB Capital Services, Vysya, J&K, Indus Ind and Oriental Bank Of Commerce at the level of Vice President/Senior Faculty—Forex and Risk Management (Scale I to Scale VI). He is an approved ISO Lead Auditor from Nigel Bauer & Associates (Germany), IRCA certified (London) Auditor. He has authored well over 124 research papers, duly published in international and national journals of repute. He has also authored eight books in the area of finance. Tandon has been awarded a Gold Medal termed 'Jewel of India Award' and 'Vidya Gaurav Gold Medal Award' from Indian Solidarity Council, New Delhi and International Institute of Education and Management, Mumbai, respectively. He is also a recipient of Lifetime Achievement Awards from UGC Sponsored RIMT Mandi Gobindgarh and from D.A.V. Institution Board, Punjab. He is a Life member of the Professional Risk Managers' International Association (PRMIA), Wilmington DC, USA: Kolkata Chapter and an affiliate member of Global Association of Risk Professionals (GARP), New Jersey, USA. He received 'Best Professor in Financial Management' Award at 22nd Dewang Mehta Business School Award on 15 November 2014 in Mumbai. He has received a Lifetime Award from AICTE sponsored by the Indian Chamber of Commerce in 2018. He is also on academic boards of various universities and has been an examiner for various research scholars for award of Doctoral degrees.

**Neelam Tandon** is a Professor in the area of Economics and Finance at Jagannath International Management School (JIMS), New Delhi. She has a rich experience of over 18 years as an academician. She has also worked in an MNC in Singapore. She is PhD, MPhil, MA (Economics) and MBA. She also holds a Post Graduate Diploma in Export Management. She has an accredited recognition of teaching in leading business schools in Delhi/NCR on regular as well as visiting assignments. She has also been a visiting faculty for well over 10 years in leading business schools in Delhi/NCR, namely, IIFT, IMT Ghaziabad, National Institute of Advertising, etc. She is an approved PhD University Guide at JIMS University, Jaipur and specializes in the area of banking and economics and a PhD examiner at Faculty of Management Studies: Women Institute for Studies in Development Oriented Management Banasthali Vidyapith, Jaipur. Her books titled *Risk Management in Indian Banks in BASEL* and *Management of Banks: Text and Cases* have been acclaimed by bankers, researchers, and professionals. She has been instrumental in conducting national seminars and international conferences in the areas of finance, risk management and international business. She has been an instrumental key resource personnel for sessions conducted by PHD Chamber of Commerce, New Delhi and National Institute of Banking Studies and Corporate Management (NIBSCOM) on 'Foreign Exchange Exposure and Risk Mitigation Challenges for SMEs in India' and 'Foreign Exchange Business: Profitability and Growth Potential of Banking Industry in India'. She has contributed to the research assignments of PHD Chamber of Commerce Research division as a Senior Research Fellow. She is one of the 100 shortlisted candidates selected by All India Council of Technical Education and United Kingdom–India Education and Research Initiative for the leadership programme from all over India.

**Kalpana Tokas** is currently working as an Assistant Professor of Economics at IMI New Delhi. She received a doctorate from IIM Bangalore in the Economics and Social Sciences area. Prior to this, she pursued her Master's degree in Economics from Gokhale Institute of Politics and Economics, Pune and her Bachelor's degree in Economics from the University of Delhi. She has qualified the UGC-NET Exam in Economics and was also awarded JRF by UGC. Her primary research interests lie in the fields of international trade, regional integration, global value chains, international production networks, trade in services and international business. Along with publications in peer-reviewed journals, she has also presented her work in many national and international conferences such as ACEGD at ISI Delhi, Singapore Economic Review Conference, EIBA (University of Leeds), IMI-SASS Conference (Chengdu). She has received best paper awards at several of them including COSMAR at IISc Bangalore, the PhD Consortium at SJMSOM, IIT Bombay, the 15th AIMS International Conference at IMT Ghaziabad and the Young Scholar's Conference at Centre for East Asian Studies, JNU.

**Yufei Wei** works as an Assistant Research Fellow at the Institute of Economic Studies, SASS. She holds a Bachelor's degree from Inner Mongolia University and a Master's degree from SASS. Her main research areas include population ageing, ageing industry, population and economic development. She has participated in 3 national and provincial projects and more than 10 other projects as a key member. She has published 7 articles (including co-authors) such as Tianfu New Theory and Sichuan Provincial Affairs.

**Xiaofeng Xing** is a Professor at SASS. Her main research interests lie in history of Chinese culture and art, music archaeology and history of Sichuan art. She has published more than 10 monographs and more than 80 papers. She has won the National Book Award and the first prize of Art Research of the Ministry of Culture of China. In recent years, she led and completed three projects subsidized by the National Social Science Fund of China.

**Nidhi Yadav** is a research scholar at IMI New Delhi. She is currently doing research in the area of platform governance strategies. Her other research interests include platform architecture and design, driver of network effects, Omnichannel retail and joint ventures. Recently, she has presented a paper at the conference held at IIT Delhi in July 2019. Before turning to academics, she worked for 10 years in the technology industry, with roles ranging from software development to project management at Aricent Technologies, a product engineering company now a part of Altran, French consulting firm.

**Fuping Yan** holds a Master's degree in Literature and Art. She is an Associate Research Fellow at the Institute of Literature and Art, SASS. She is engaged in the study of Chinese and foreign literary and art criticism and Sichuan literature research. She has published more than 20 papers in domestic core publications. She is a regular movie literary criticism writer for Sichuan Literature Almanac. She has participated in writing a book series on Sichuan Literature History of the Late Qing Dynasty. She has co-authored books such as *Dynasties Poetry Intone Sichuan* and has worked on several research subjects on provincial and other major issues.

**Huajun Yang** is an Associate Research Fellow at the Sociology Institute, SASS. He is mainly engaged in historical and cultural sociology research. His main academic achievements include *Biography of Yan Yangchu's Paintings* (2012) and *A Study of Yan Yangchu as an Educator* (2015). He has also published many papers in reputed journals.

**Huan Yang** is Associate Research Fellow and Deputy Director at SASS. She is mainly engaged in the study of national history and culture. She has published more than 40 papers and received National Book Awards. Up till now, she has presided over and completed various projects of the National Social Science Foundation and various other general projects. She also presided over and participated in a number of horizontal projects in the Tibetan region and won many awards at the provincial and ministerial levels.

**Xiannong Yang** is a Professor at SASS and the doctoral supervisor of Marxism theory major at the Southwest Jiaotong University. He mainly focuses on the theory and practice of Sinicization of Marxism and construction of socialist culture with Chinese characteristics. He has published five monographs, including History of Deng Xiaoping Theory, Sinicization of Marxism and Sublimation of National Spirit.

**Renjie Yu** is a PhD candidate at the Southwestern University of Finance and Economics, Sichuan province. He graduated from SASS with a Master's degree in Industrial Economics. He has published papers such as 'Study on Sustainable Development of Resource-Based Cities in Sichuan Province', 'Study on the Incentive Effect of Employee Stock Ownership Plan' and 'Study on the Issue of Implementing Employee Stock Ownership in Mixed Ownership Enterprises in Sichuan Province'.

**Xiaojuan Zhou** is an Assistant Researcher at SASS. In October 2014, she started her career at SASS and engaged in the research of agricultural economic theory and policy and rural poverty control. She has published more than ten academic papers, presided over one National Social Science Fund Project and participated in eight national and provincial level projects. She has won several prizes for excellent achievements in philosophy and social sciences.

# Index